AWAY FROM THE FOLD

An Encyclopedia of Utah Performers
Stage Through Early Silents
1850-1920
Volume 1

By
Linda Dunning

Away From the Fold
An Encyclopedia of Utah Performers
Stage Through Early Silents
1850-1920
Volume 1

By Linda Dunning

ISBN13: 978-0-9884254-2-2

Published by the author in Salt Lake City, Utah.

Dunning, Linda, 1949-
AWAY FROM THE FOLD
An Encyclopedia of Utah Performers
Stage Through Early Silents, 1850-1920
Volume 1
Includes bibliographical references.
ISBN 978-0-9884254-2-2

Cover design and book layout by Brett Jensen, Luminosity Web Solutions, LLC.

Printed in the United States of America

10 9 8 7 6 5 4 3 2 1

Cover photos courtesy of the Utah State Historical Society and The University of Utah Special Collections.

"I love my little dressing room.
It smells of greasepaint and perfume.

It gives me three full hours reprieve,
From my real self with make-believe.

It knows my joys. It knows my tears.
It knows how brief are actor's years."

-Ruby D'Imperio
"Ruby Ring" Contortionist

CONTENTS

INTRODUCTION

A 1923 movie entitled "Souls for Sale" starring Richard Dix and Eleanor Boardman, explores how people felt in those days about a son and especially a daughter running off to be on the stage or in the silent movies. At that time the stage was a little bit more acceptable than "posing." Since actors and actresses did not speak any lines in these films, silent movie work was considered a low-class form of simply "posing" or mime. On the other hand, most actors performed their own stunts and so quite often were literally risking their life or at least running the risk of serious injury on the set. In "Souls for Sale" Boardman escapes a serial murderer whom she has just married, when she finds out that he weds women for their money and then murders them. She cannot go home because of her "disgrace," and penniless, she becomes stranded out in the California desert after jumping off a train. She wanders about near death, and then is suddenly rescued by an Arabian sheik on a camel, who looks a lot like Valentino.

Having wandered onto a movie set she is soon dressed as an extra, pursued by both the sheik playboy leading actor and the director, who is the more upstanding character in the film. She begins to get small parts in movies and her very mid-western religious parents come to rescue her from the evils of Hollywood about the time that she has become a rising star in the movies. Her husband, in the meantime, has murdered one more wife and is out of money when he sees Boardman in a film and heads for Hollywood presumably to blackmail her. Turns out things are worse than this because the husband thinks he really loves her and wants to stay with her in Hollywood and live off of her. When she rejects him, both the hero director and the rakish leading man have to rescue her from her husband's attempts to murder her, while at the same time everyone is trying to fight a huge fire started on the set. It is quite an exciting ending, her husband is killed in the fire, the director survives and the leading man rescues her, but she chooses the director over him, choosing to live happily and quite well off in Hollywood, while buying her parents a new home.

The moral of the story was that if the young actress or actor made it through all the difficulties and evils of Hollywood to become a star, even her parents would forgive her and happily accept a portion of the "spoils." While a great comment on Hollywood "magic," the truth was that not many made it to stardom and not many got forgiveness from their parents or the judgments of the times. The "casting couch" or at least financial corruption and control, didn't make many directors, producers or actors look that good, and many young women especially, ended up falling prey to a myriad of so called "evils." So that many young men and women who left for the stage in Brigham Young's day, could easily believe what he consistently counseled them about, against not only leaving the territory but also their faith. He would always admonish them that as long as they remained as actors for his theater in Utah, they would not fall prey to the evils of the outside world and of course this was an easy thing to do, because making it on the stage was extremely difficult and could bring down certain wraths, often with nothing to fall back on. Especially during the LDS Reformation period in the late 1850s to the early 1870s, leaving the Territory of Utah was a quite difficult and often life threatening thing to do for any reason at all, let along to act on the stage.

An example of the fear of this desertion from either the territory or even Mormonism would be that which I read over and over again in similar scenarios between a young woman and Brigham Young as he counseled Sarah Elizabeth Carmichael when she was beginning to reach national fame as a poet. "Use your gifts to help build up truth and righteousness in the earth and your gift will be preserved as long as you shall live. If you prostitute your powers to gain fame and gold, your light will go out in darkness." And of course in Sarah's case, supposedly God did strike her down either to genetics or a fall or both, because she suffered from brain damage and mental illness for the rest of her life after writing a nationally popular poem about the death of Abraham Lincoln. So while for many young women and some men, it was easy for this type of prophecy to come true, there were many others who did succeed on the stage or in Hollywood, both Mormon and non, even during Brigham Young's time. Eventually, as time went by and the world changed, actors and actresses from Utah became lauded and praised for their work and the state was proud of having produced them. ("Sarah Elizabeth Carmichael (1838-1901) Poetic Genius of Pioneer Utah" by Miriam B. Murphy in Worth Their Salt edited by Colleen Whitley, Utah State University: Logan, Utah, 1996, p. 64).

Away From the Fold from the stage through the silents tells the stories of the people who left Utah seeking fame and fortune on the stage or in Hollywood. These stories tell it all: the tragedies, the painful childhoods, the shunning, the shame of being an actress or even an actor in that day, and even the "curses" that were put upon them if they did not stay home. These are the trials and tribulations of those who left home never to return, and those who returned to their hometown triumphant. From the early heritage of drama in Utah, to the stage and on through the early silent's, book readers will find stories of a famous neighborhood theatre and the playwrights who wrote and performed there as children, a lesbian writer and actress, a world famous magician, ethereal Broadway stars, world famous opera stars, a jazz great, and anti-Mormon and Mormon made films from the silent's. Then there were the photographers and filmmakers and actors and polygamists who chased actresses fairly equally, senators and mining millionaires and their mistresses, and even a few prophets who had crushes on actresses. There are also stories of "miracle" conversions and odd friendships or relationships. Readers will also meet producers, directors, stage and film house managers, cinematographers, set decorators, composers, a war hero, singers and dancers, and those performers I could find little about.

Readers will also learn why Utah really did supply Broadway and Hollywood with many more stars than any other state. The earliest stars came from somewhere in the British Isles, somewhere from the Scandinavian countries, somewhere from Canada and even as far as India, as settlers to the new Utah Territory. The later entertainers came from the larger cities of Utah: Ogden, Salt Lake City, Provo, Logan, and Brigham City. The old mining and smelting towns of Utah: Park City, Enterprise, Mammoth, Mercur, Magna, Lark, Bingham City and Garland. They came from some of the medium sized towns in Utah: Richfield, Roosevelt, Price, Moab, St. George, Payson, Salina and Parowan. They also came from really small towns like Prattsville or Glenwood, Marysvale, Circleville, Willard, Lake Point, Pleasant View, Bountiful and even small towns that in their day were not considered part of Salt Lake City, but small towns of their own: West Jordan, Granger, and Magna. Some even came from farms somewhere out in a particular county like Millard where no town existed or were even born on their family's kitchen table. And some of them came from early Mormon settlements in the old Utah Territory and eventually found each other in New York or Hollywood. These people came from such places as Snowflake, Arizona, Rock Springs and Afton, Wyoming, Pocatello Falls, Cardiff, Caldwell, Weiser and Annis, Idaho, or Denver and Manassa, Colorado. Other actors came from some other part of the country and joined the Mormons in Utah; most of these people came from California and New York.

I was amazed at the numbers I found too, in all three volumes. There were approximately 50 major stars, directors, cinematographers, composers, screenwriters, film editors and playwrights, stage actresses and actors, film actors and actresses and radio and television performers. And then there were the minor actors, actresses and stage support staff just at the old Salt Lake Theatre alone, over 200 people over the years and that is a conservative estimate just for the Utah born or Utah connected. Several dozen of these performers from the old Salt Lake Theatre went on to bigger, better careers in stock companies or even on the stage in New York, California or overseas. And in the lesser known category were others connected with the film industry. Approximately 420 people from Utah were either on the stage or tried their luck in Hollywood from the mid-1800s to the end of the 1920s when the silent era was ending. The closest state in the west to this count would be Colorado with around 100 performers from 1850 to 1960, while all other western and Midwestern states only had from 10 to 20 such famous people. There are those who say that Utah led the entire nation during this time, second only to California in the later eras of Hollywood.

So many of the life stories are more entertaining than any fiction story would be, there are great love stories, grand adventures, unbelievable tragedies, much mayhem, assorted mysteries and murders, unusual suicides and other quite strange demises. There are exotic and intriguing paths taken in life, lots of graft and corruption, and amazing "stranger than fiction" encounters and much more in these many and varied biographies of those who left "the fold" for Hollywood and Broadway. It is amazing to think that all of these many celebrities came from Utah or were closely connected to Utah. We sent more people from our state than from the entire nation to perform on stage or screen and only California and New York even come close to us because these people came from one of these states. Have fun reading them all, or just those that sound interesting to you! For some, their adventures took them around the world and they brought back other cultural perspectives and experiences, helping us to ponder world events and even perhaps to experience just a little more from several places all over the world.

I - FROM STAGE TO SILENT SCREEN

Brigham Young in "Pizarro"
Utah State Historical Society

The Big Ten – Brigham Young's Daughters

A BRIEF HISTORY OF DRAMA & THEATRE IN THE UTAH TERRITORY

"Even before the Latter-Day-Saints migrated to Utah, they staged plays and elaborate pageants in Nauvoo, Illinois, in the early 1840s. Brigham Young himself played a Peruvian high priest in the play 'Pizarro'." Joseph Smith thought so highly of drama that he had formed a dramatic Company in Nauvoo with Brigham Young, Erastus Snow and George A. Smith, who had roles in the plays performed there. Thomas A. Lyne was a prominent eastern dramatic actor who came to Nauvoo on the advice of an actor friend to perform in the company. He eventually joined the Mormon faith but when called to a foreign mission some years later, he disappeared for some twenty years and then showed up in Salt Lake City to perform once more at the old Salt Lake Theatre and died in Salt Lake City as an old man.

The Mormons, once settled in Utah, established their first community gathering place at the Warm Springs Hot Springs where the newer and now abandoned Warms Springs building is next to the little park that was also built soon after the first pioneers arrived. This present building was built in the late twenties, but before this, the pioneers had erected a large adobe building to be used for social meetings in conjunction with bathing in the hot springs nearby. The Amusement Hall was used chiefly for dances for only two years from 1850 to 1852 but it was soon apparent that the bad roads and dark nights made this hall difficult to get too, so no stage was ever built there.

Later they established the Deseret Musical and Dramatic Association by the fall of 1850. They also established the Nauvoo Brass Band and performances were held at the Bowery on Temple block. "The first bill included the drama, 'Robert Macaire, or The Murders,' dancing, and a farce entitled 'Dead Shot'." In 1852, the Social Hall was just down the street from the Prophet's residences. ("History of Theatre in Utah" by Ann W. Engar, Utah History Encyclopedia, edited by Allan Kent Powell, 1994)

By 1852, the Deseret Dramatic Association had reorganized and expanded and the Social Hall had been erected and music was provided by the first string band in the city consisting of Hopkins C. "Hop" Fender, Jesse Earl and Jake Hutchinson. It was built of adobe and had a shingled roof with a stage that measured twenty by forty feet and had several dressing rooms off stage and also under the stage. Tallow candles were used for footlights and the orchestra director was the former bandmaster at West Point. The Social Hall gained a new name for its fame entitled "First Little Theatre in America," because it was. Brigham Young was considered by many at the time as the father of little theaters in America, and it was true that many of the smaller towns across the state began to erect their own opera houses and social halls so they could present local theatre to their communities. And this was with a little prodding from Philip Margetts and many others.

When Johnston's Army arrived in 1857, locals were too busy to continue their plays at the Social Hall. The soldiers, however, created their own Camp Floyd Theatre, which was essentially constructed of canvas and pine boards. By 1859, a second company, called the Mechanics Dramatic Association was formed. A man named Harry Bowring let them use the first floor of his new home for the Bowring Theatre which held 150 seats. This was located at 100 South between 300 and 400 East. Brigham Young decided that he needed to then build a "real" theater for his people. (Ibid, 551)

In 1991, workers dug an underground walkway from the Z.C.M.I. center that housed the Zion Mercantile for many years. It later became the Meier & Frank store on the other side of State Street. They broke through into the foundations of a rather old but famous pioneer building. All work stopped on the project and archeaologists and city planners were called in to investigate. Salt Lake City's very first theater had been unearthed; the old original Social Hall for which there is a replica built in "This Is the Place" Heritage State Park up Emigration Canyon. An extensive excavation, or "dig," took place right in the middle of State Street. When the archeaologists were done, it was decided to create a small Heritage Social Hall Museum just inside the east doors of the Z.C.M.I. Center. There, one could go down the stairs into a small alcove and read the historical information placed there, as well as see

Old Social Hall
Utah State Historical Society

artifacts from the dig: old photographs and a glassed in room where a section of the old Social Hall could still be seen. Presently, however, this entire area is now open for the new upscale City Creek Center and next door at 51 South State is the small Social Hall Museum.

The Social Hall opened on New Year's Day in 1853 with a dance social and the first theater performance was on January 17, 1853. Plays, bands, orchestras, dances and various other functions took place there for the entire city, including concerts by the Nauvoo Legion Military Band, which was part of the militia created by Joseph Smith to protect his people. Mary and Ida Cook, considered the founders of education in Utah, ran the first school there in the 1850s. The Social Hall had the first movable dance floor in the valley, and many other such halls were then built around the state in imitation of this first one. The dance floor allowed for dance socials and could then be rolled out of the way for other types of functions in the Social Hall. When the old Salt Lake Theatre opened in 1862, the two existing theater troupes, once performing both at the Social Hall and around the state, merged together and began preparing their plays in the green room of this brand new theater. The old hall was taken over by the LDS Church and became a ward social hall. One can still see what it was like however by visiting the Heritage State Park across from Hogle Zoo. This was evident during special event times such as the one I attended some years ago in the replica Social Hall. There was a Civil War re-enactor's grand ball and dinner at Christmas time, where visitors lined up along the hall's walls and watched another era being re-enacted for them.

The Social Hall did have one more era of revival, though, when Maud May Babcock, considered an important founder of theater in Utah, opened its doors once again in 1893 to run the Utah School of Physical Culture until 1898, on the second floor. She created a special exercise costume for her ladies consisting of navy blue bloomers, sailor blouses, and matching ruffled hats. For the next few years, the hall was rented out upon occasion. It then began to deteriorate. Maud May really loved the Social Hall because in 1918 she had it renovated and brought her college students in to perform as the Varsity Theater Troupe until 1922. For ten years before the theater was built, the old Social Hall was the center of social, musical and theatrical life for the pioneers.

A huge undertaking, the old Salt Lake Theatre had been a work of great love for those in the community, like a cathedral would have been for a small town. Built near a steam bed, special excavation and placement of the foundations had to be considered. Sandstone slabs from Red Butte Canyon were put in place first, and giant red pines from Big Cottonwood Canyon supported the parquet and stage. Four-foot thick stonewalls were plastered and covered with adobe bricking. Almost everyone in the community, at that time, 12,000 people, had a hand in the building or managing of this theater. Eighty-foot spans of stringers were tiered together by handcrafted wooden pegs. These thousands of pegs were hand whittled by the women of the city in their evening hours after their chores were done and former sailors who were used to heights in the ship's yardarms, volunteered to work on the upper floors. It took $100,000 in funds and less than a year to complete the building.

On March 6th, 1862, the old Salt Lake Theatre was dedicated. William H. Folsom was the main architect for the building, but it was E.L.T. Harrison, newly arrived from London, who did most of the ornate decorations in the interior. George Martin Ottinger painted the beautifully detailed stage scenery for four years and then Alfred Lambourne painted for the plays after that for many years. One of his elaborate backdrops can be seen in the Daughters of the Pioneers Museum building, which is an exact, though smaller, replica of the original theater. After losing their fight with the LDS Church and the city to preserve the old theater in 1928 and 1929, the Daughters of the Utah Pioneers organization built a smaller but exact replica of the Salt Lake Theatre for their museum as a reminder of this fight. While the inside of the museum is different from the old theater, they do have one large room devoted to the old theater and even have Brigham Young's old theater box seats on display as well as the painted backdrop and curtains. They may have also wanted to give the city planners a constant reminder of their lack of preservation interests by having the museum built right next to the state Capitol building. The LDS Church sold the theater building for the money and a telephone company building went up in its place. While the support of the arts has always been great in the state of Utah and was really fostered by the LDS Church, especially with the many ward plays and later "road shows" that became quite extravagant affairs, it seems that even back then, money and politics always had the upper hand.

Another more recent example is the two old Orpheum theaters. One of these theaters has won its battle and has become the home for both the opera company and the ballet, the Capitol Theatre. The other old Orpheum, the former Promised Valley Playhouse's façade, was kept to satisfy the preservationists. The entire inside of the building was demolished for a new office building and behind this is a parking lot. Those in the arts who tried to save it as a second facility for the ballet, probably know what I as a simple private citizen know already; it came down because of the need for money and space. This time it was a feud between the city council and the LDS Church who owned the theater. The LDS Church needed to use the money they were losing on the empty theater for more current affairs. They also needed more parking slots for their members to get to Temple Square and for other church offices. The City Council tried various ideas out trying to raise the funds to purchase the old theater but to no avail. I doubt the beautiful Venus, which sits on top of the building, will ever smile again. While she still sits atop the building's façade, the old theater and many of those people tied through their memories to this old theater, mourn the loss of another beautiful old building in downtown Salt Lake City.

The first plays performed at the Salt Lake Theatre had a small cast of actors, many of whom performed at the theater for many years to come. The company played 15 times that month and then the theater closed to get its interior work finished and opened again at Christmas and the Tabernacle choir sang before the opening performance. Those who could not afford to pay for a 37 cent to $1.25 cent ticket brought other things to exchange. Most often these items included fruits, vegetables and poultry. Some people even got "change" back for their bartering, such as two spring chickens for one large turkey. For the first

Old Salt Lake Theatre
Utah State Historical Society

Interior of the Theatre
Utah State Historical Society

ten years, oil lamps were used and then later, gaslights were installed. When electricity came in, the railroad company furnished the lighting. A floor made in sections which covered the entire parquet and was built on trestles, was used for many dances and cotillions during the winter months. The green room was a huge planning room where those who managed the theater and those who performed, met together for various functions. It was a huge sitting room and every bit of cloth and carpeting in it was decorated in various shades and hues of green. A smaller green room was where the actors changed for the various scenes in a production. The larger room was eventually not in use and the Deseret Dramatic Association took it over for a while. The Home Dramatic Club used it after this. These were both community theater groups whose actors, actresses and crews worked day jobs and performed in the evenings and on weekends.

The old Salt Lake Theatre was not a very large building being 80 by 144 feet and holding only about 1,500 people, but audiences packed the theater for every performance. At first, hometown companies performed in the theater with perhaps one touring star among them. Later, whole touring companies came to Utah to perform. A vast array of famous actors, actresses and singers passed through the doors at one time or another. Such famous names as P. T. Barnum, Maude Adams, Sarah Bernhardt, Billie Burke, Edwin Booth, Eddie Foy, Buffalo Bill Cody, Al Jolson, John Drew, Fanny Davenport, Lillian Russell, Dewitt Talmage, Charles and Daniel Frohman and all of the Barrymores graced its stage at one time or another. All sorts of vaudeville acts also passed through as well as various famous speakers such as Oscar Wilde, Sir Richard Francis Burton, and Horace Greeley. Some of the Republican and Democratic conventions were held there. In addition to this, they continued to have grand balls on the movable floor with over 200 at a time in attendance.

In 1873, massive renovations were done on the interiors to make it much more elegant. Fashioned in the style of a European opera house, it had four ascending circles and two boxes that overlooked the gently sloping stage. The new renovations received much praise in the national newspapers. It was said that no eastern theater of such a large population could boast of a finer structure. It ranked with those found in America's largest cities, the local papers exclaimed. However, the Mormons also wanted their theater to rise above a mere mirror of humanity and only present what was exalting and uplifting. The irony of this in a theater would haunt it through all its days. While Brigham Young wanted his theater to always be "proper," he could not always stop the moments in a play when that mirror reflected what was not considered "proper." Young was so involved in the building and maintaining of this theater that its nickname was "Brigham's Playhouse." Brigham Young was so powerful a presence almost every night, that whenever the audience made too much noise or applauded too loudly, he merely had to stick his head out from the curtain where he was shielded from them and a quiet hush would follow immediately.

The theater not only housed productions but also children's parties and extravagant cotillions. As President Young grew older, he attended the theater less and less, and the theater became much broader based in its presentations and philosophies. Guest speakers such as Oscar Wilde and political gatherings took the place of dances and parties, while the plays became much more eclectic. With the coming of the railroad, Utah was placed on the national theater circuit, and the Salt Lake Theatre became increasingly secularized as New York booking agencies virtually controlled its attractions. By 1872, the 385 oil lamps had been replaced by gas. The Railway Company also placed six street lamps on either side of the building.

Another building, the Walker Opera House on the south side of 200 East between Main and West Temple, gave the Salt Lake Theatre a run for its money. Dr. D. Banks McKinzie was a temperance lecturer and reformer, who had organized a Temperance Club in Salt Lake City and through this organization, had succeeded in raising over $30,000 in contributions to build a first-class lecture hall, with a library, and even accommodations for overnight guest speakers. The Walker Brothers had contributed a building site where the Atlas block stood, it was a piece of land 50 x 100 feet. The Walker Brothers contributed $13,000 to the project and several of those involved, spearheaded by the writer of this theater history, John S. Lindsay, suggested that if they were going to spend that sort of money, why not make the building a little larger than this and build a theater in it as well. This way they could pay for the building by renting it out to stock companies when the building was not being used for lectures.

The Walker Grand Opera House was a result of this movement, but it only stood for one year. It opened on June 5, 1882, with a vocal and instrument concert, and then a stock company did three nights of a play called "My Partner." In the spring of 1882, Dr. McKenzie went to New York to secure attractions for the new theater. The theater ended up being worth $100,000 before it was completed. Lindsay was the manager. In 11 months, with a single booking agency dividing up bookings evenly between the old Salt Lake Theatre and the new Walker Opera House, Dr. McKenzie had secured so many acts and quality stock companies that he had literally run the old Salt Lake Theatre out of business. Naturally, the opening night audience was sparse, because the Mormons were strongly prejudiced against any "gentile" theater in town. Rumors spread that the new theater wasn't safe, but soon subsided as the Mormons too, came to the brand-new theater. "Brigham's Playhouse" was meeting its end, anyway. Jack Haverly, soon became the manager of both theaters and it was he who came up with the idea of alternating bookings to help keep the Salt Lake Theatre alive, but also allow the Walker to prosper.

Walker Grand Opera House
Utah State Historical Society

Because a gentile, Haverly, ended up running both theaters and once again the Mormons were not very happy about this. It was a blow to them, that the once grand Salt

Lake Theatre, which had been President Young's pride and joy, and had always offered wholesome entertainment, was now not only being run by gentiles, but taking on all forms of entertainment that weren't necessarily "wholesome." Once the Mormons were cognizant that they no longer owned their own theater, they quit going to the Walker and won an audience back to the old Salt Lake Theatre, giving the Walker a run for its money. Haverly, once the king of theater in Utah, began to run into financial problems. He had his hands in too many fires, including his mining interests, and with all these lieutenants running things for him; he was unable to keep track of just exactly what they were all doing. Several of them began to get what they could out of his interests and behind his back. In only a few years, he was bankrupt and by 1898 he was in poor health and died in a Salt Lake hospital in 1901.

Destroyed by fire on July 4, 1891, the Walker Grand Opera House was the unlucky participant in either an accident or even a clandestine deal among some of Walker's enemies, lieutenants or even Haverly himself. How the fire started is somewhat suspicious. After a performance of "Held by the Enemy," another ironic touch to this story, the audience was home by then; the company had left the theater. Stagehands were lowering the drop, when a gust of wind blew open the front door and sent the drop sailing against a gas jet; in a moment, it was all ablaze. The stagehands lost their heads and made for the exit, when a little presence of mind would have saved the building. The house, especially the stage, was well provided with water plugs and hoses, and it seems incredible that no effort was made to extinguish the fire. Perhaps no effort was made on purpose, but we will never know.

Mr. Will Burgess could have also been the culprit as manager of the theater at the time, because two other theaters that he managed had also burned down. A wealthy manager of theaters, it was after this quite suspicious fire that he lost one in Omaha and another in Kansas, soon after the second one. Perhaps he was paid off, but whatever happened, the Walker was no more and was never rebuilt. Instead, a large barn was converted into a small theater on the property called "The Wonderland," the only barn theater larger than the Thomas's child-run theater "The

Barnacle." Wonderland had been Conroy's Livery Stable and was directly across from where the Walker had been. The upper story was a curiosity shop and in the Main level had a stage for vaudeville acts. Later, Wonderland was remodeled and converted into a theater that would seat 600 people. It was then called The Lyceum.

For one year a stock company ran the Lyceum, fairly successfully, then the theater went into its decline for two years and finally the building was converted into a saloon and wholesale liquor house. But before its demise, one more stage theater was built called "The Grand." Two men, Frank Maltese and Brig Pyper entered into this venture on a bet, when they won $12.50 between them in a contest. Jokingly, they were touring around with some ideas in how to invest their big winnings, perhaps investing it or entering another contest. While venturing various ideas with each other, finally one of them said, "Let's build an Opera House with it!" At first it was a joke and then they sort of got to planning it to see what it would take to do such a thing. They then decided to do it. They took some property they owned, got some walls up and a roof on it and then ran out of money. Mr. Alec Rogers suddenly appeared and came up with the remaining $16,000 they needed to complete the building. They got a manager and opened the season on Christmas Eve 1894. But it didn't take long for business to drop off and the plainness of the building might have been one reason that their Opera House wasn't very successful. The most important reason, however, was that they didn't have enough capital to run it. However, it does show the ardor with which Utahns loved the theater in those days!

An interesting intrigue to early theater "wars" in Utah, would be the question, was this fire at the Walker Opera House accidental or made to look accidental? When Julia Dean Hayne's manager decided to open his Academy of Music, he also had plans to build an even bigger and better theater than the Salt Lake Theatre, but ended up bankrupt instead, probably due to lack of local support for his project. Theaters often burned down due to the dangerous lighting techniques. On the other hand, most cities rebuilt their theaters several times because the city wanted them and would help the owners to come up with the funding to rebuild them. Since the gentile shops were in a constant battle with the ZCMI Mercantile stores, it would be quite possible that a successful gentile theater's presence in Salt Lake City at this time would be unwanted, especially since drama was Brigham Young's passion and he wanted to keep the entertainment in them clean and moral. The "wicked" gentile city of Corinne across the Great Salt Lake from the Mormon city of Salt Lake City was always a dangerous rival to the growth of the main city in Utah. This city was effectively cut off and died because Brigham Young had the new railroad re-routed. When he discovered that the railroad would not be able to route the trains through Salt Lake City at the time, and the choices were Ogden and Corinne; Ogden became the railroad junction in the intermountain west.

Amateur theater groups began to blossom all over the state in the 1860s and 1870s. The best Opera Houses were in St. George, Provo, Springville, Ogden, Brigham City and Logan. By the 1890s, theater was so popular that all the local newspapers devoted an entire section to this topic, and yet there was still no major dramatic company permanently housed in Salt Lake City until Maud May began her University theater club. By then there were many other theaters established in downtown Salt Lake City: the Garrick, the Colonial, the Grand, the Orpheum, the Empress, and the Princess. The Orpheum II was built in 1905. Maud Babcock eventually formed the community theater group, the Utah Players Stock Company in 1915, making her the "mother" of Utah theater and Brigham Young the "father." Moroni Olsen formed his Moroni Olsen Players in 1923. A former student of Babcock, his repertory company toured the west and became the only successful company in the 1920s. After seven years and the Great Depression, the company disbanded and Olsen went to Hollywood to become a famous actor. It is interesting to note, however, that in the early days of stage theaters in Utah, not many of the locally grown stage actors or actresses had gone on to New York City to try and make it on Broadway. But this changed rather quickly as time went on.

The old Salt Lake Theatre became host to traveling productions from out of town and actors and plays from the east were more readily accepted. The local newspapers complained about a "Lower style of entertainment, melodrama, juggling and tumbling, now serve to fill the house." Nearly all the stars of the American stage appeared on its stage in the golden age of drama. Other church leaders refused to attend the theater as well. Heber J. Grant, who had loved this theater, watched the changing times and when he became the prophet of the LDS Church complained about the lack of plays with "...clean, sweet, morals." The theater had never been a big money maker and towards the end of its run, it was making less and less. By 1921, Grant had closed the theater, as the LDS Church owned the property and the building. ("Shattering the Vase: The Razing of the Old Salt Lake Theatre," by Ronald W. Walker and Alexander M. Starr, the Utah Historical Quarterly, Winter 1989, Volume 57, Number 1, pp. 64-88).

For the next few years, the heated and very emotional debates on what to do with this theater continued. Even theater actress Ethel Barrymore got in on the fight when she was quoted in several newspapers as loving the charming old theater and hating the thought that she would have to go to Salt Lake City and perform in some brand new building without any of the charm or atmosphere of its predecessor. Grant first tried minor renovations, trying to keep his people happy and retain the building as a "monument." The strongest protesting group was the Daughters of Utah Pioneers. Grant then tried to get the city to take out a twenty-year lease on the building. When this failed, he tried to get a foundation started that would control the theater and absorb its losses. Between the lack of morally upstanding theater and the disgrace it would bring to the Mormon Church owning it, and the financial difficulties the theater was having, Grant finally gave into the final plan. He sold it to the highest bidder. There had even been talk of moving the entire structure from State Street to another location much further away from church headquarters, and just selling the land. The plan was to literally heft it up on vehicles of some kind and roll it down State Street.

In the end, after a final idea of turning the place into a picture show house, the building was sold. It was, however, a shining moment for the Daughters of the Utah Pioneers, who loudly and thunderously opposed the selling and razing of this theater. They even tried to get other groups to join them in raising the money to purchase the old theater so they could turn it into a museum. And it was they, when the next move was to condemn the building that proposed the idea of moving the building from its present location. A string of women, 'heartbroken' by the sale, confronted him (Grant) in his office. President Grant took a lot of criticism, name-calling and read a lot of nasty letters because of his decision, which he was very sensitive about. That is why today when one visits the Daughters of the Utah Pioneers Museum, built in 1962, next to the state capitol building; it is housed in a smaller replica building of the old Salt Lake Theatre. This museum houses a lot of memorabilia which they salvaged from the old theater including one of the original painted backdrops.

When the old theater's fate was sealed, people came from all over the state to bid it farewell. They were also caught taking pieces of the building with them as memorabilia. The theater's final production consisted of speeches, a standing ovation for the theater orchestra, a dedication by an old-time favorite actress of the stage, Sallie Fisher, a scene from "Robin Hood" performed by old-time favorite actors and actresses and lastly a scene from "La Traviata" with Brigham Young's granddaughter, Emma Lucy Gates, singing the lead. A film taken of theater employees coming in and out of the building, as well as panning shots of the interior and exterior was shown at the theater in its last moments, but unfortunately, this film was destroyed in a fire. Furniture and chandeliers, etc. were taken out and sold all over the intermountain area and when the last wall of the theater came down, a large crowd stood in front of it crying. Some of them held up signs that read: "Built by a Prophet and Torn Down for Profit!"

At first the telephone company planned to build a park there. Then they changed their minds and said they were going to build a parking lot. Finally, they said that they would build a gas station shaped like an airplane, which they did. It was not until a decade later that they built the art deco office building that stands there today. At the time it was considered a "handsome" building, but by today's standards, even the airplane gas station would be an improvement over this rather plain edifice. In 1940, a commemorative plaque was placed on the building following a small ceremony dedicated to the old theater. In 1964, "Marking their own 100th anniversary, a Utah-German theater group decorated the plaque with flowers. 'It's a pity the old theater isn't there,' one member was heard to say, "We in Germany can never understand how you can do away with such things in America." (Ibid. p. 88)

After World War I, theaters began to falter all across the nation; some burned down as did the Colonial in Salt Lake City. Many of them had folded by the Second World War. Others were built with the advent of motion pictures, especially as movie theaters rather than stage theaters. The silent westerns came to southern Utah and in the meantime, the LDS Church continued to sponsor amateur dramas in their Mormon ward and stake houses, called "The Road Shows." For many years, these "Stake Road Shows" were well attended and quite the extravaganzas, until the LDS Church decided within the last twenty years that this time, energy, and money could be put to better use elsewhere. In the meantime, new theaters were being built on University campuses across the state, as well as many local committees who were renovating old theaters in major cities and towns.

The ancestral interest in drama and theater can be seen everywhere in the state, from producing an abundance of many fine actors and actresses for the stage and screen to the many early film companies that flooded the state in the twenties, thirties and forties. However, in the last few years' film companies have gone elsewhere to film, finding cheaper places to do this. But while LDS filmmaking was beginning to flourish outside the state with better quality films and a broader appeal to a national if not international audience, Utah had always had top quality entertainers early on. Recently, the state film commission asked the state government to stop having such high taxing laws which is what stopped the outside movie companies from coming to Utah, and they did. They have finally realized that the revenue from these companies coming to Utah is well worth the risk.

There are several interesting stories about the old Salt Lake Theatre, when it was in operation. A very early story in the first days of the theater and with the first troupe of actors to perform on its stage, involved a wig. "One circumstance shows how the early pioneers were ready to sacrifice anything for the public good. The President (Brigham Young) demanded correct costuming for the plays put on at his theater, and he called an actress to task for wearing what he considered her improper make up. The part was that of a brunette and as the actress was a blonde he thought she should have worn a dark wig. Well, she cried as only an actress can cry and told the president that if she could have the hair worn by a man pointed out to her, named John McDonald, the character could be dressed perfectly."

"John McDonald was the father of our fellow townsman John G. McDonald, the nationally known chocolate man, and he had a glossy, curling black mane that reached below his shoulders. He prized his wonderful hair, too, almost as he did his life. All the same, when the president learned that John's hair was necessary for the play he said to the actress, 'You shall have it!' So John was summoned. The president explained the situation, saying, 'John, we must have your hair.' With a gulp, John said, 'All right, Brother Brigham, you shall have it.' And in a few minutes, with the help of John Squires, the theater barber, the hair was figuratively speaking, laid at the president's feet. The next night John McDonald went to the theatre sheared and shorn, while his gorgeous raven locks adorned the head of the leading lady." Perhaps this was a sillier reason than when the famous lawman, bodyguard and occasional outlaw, Orrin Porter Rockwell, who believed his long locks protected him from harm and Brigham Young had told him so, cut off his long hair for an elderly lady who he knew who had lost her hair to an illness, so that a wig could be made from it for her to wear." (The Romance of an Old Playhouse by George Dollinger Pyper, The Seagull Press: Salt Lake City, Utah, 1928, p. 230).

One of the most interesting stories about the famous theater concerned something actor George Pauncefort staged for the play "Macbeth." "Macbeth" is a play that has a long history of hauntings and bad luck for those who stage it or especially perform in it because it is thought that when the original play was put on, Shakespeare engaged real witches to perform in it. These witches took it upon themselves to curse the play for time and all eternity, or so the main story about this play goes. Pauncefort brought in 100 voices from the Tabernacle choir to really give the "Witches Chorus" a powerful presence in the play. At the dress rehearsal, a quartet of voices were hidden from the audience and echoed what the larger chorus said on stage. The echoes carried across the whole theater from the back of the auditorium to the front, and the effect was downright frightening for the audience when the actual play was presented. The audience was quite terrified.

Sometimes tempers flared, for example, when the cue was given to the orchestra to play a plaintiff, mournful song as the corpse in the play was carried off stage on a stretcher, the conductor played a jig instead. The old man delivering his lines above the jig, actor W.C. Spence, waited until the curtain came down and then, not being able to contain himself, pushed aside the curtain, stuck his head out and shouted to the conductor of the orchestra right in front of the audience, "Blast your eyes, professor, if I had a brick bat, I'd let you have it on the head!" (The Drama of Utah: the story of the Salt Lake Theatre, by Horace G. Whitney, The Deseret News: SLC, Utah, 1915, p.32)

The most famous incident of the theater involved a cannon. In "The Lonely Man of the Ocean," during the shipwreck scene, all the crew had been stricken with yellow fever and the hero and heroine were about to give up on the deck, when they saw a distant ship on the horizon. The hero went to light the cannon onstage to signal the ship for help. The cannon did not fire but instead sizzled and sputtered. The property man who had loaded the cannon whispered offstage to the hero, David McKenzie, to touch the cannon again, at which point, Charles Miller, the property man, fired a pistol off in the wings in place of the cannon. McKenzie was able to shout the last lines of the play "Our signal is heard. We are saved!" The curtain fell, and just barely out of sight of the audience, as the actors got up from all over the stage, the cannon fired. Phil Margetts was right in front of the cannon and it struck him in the back, the "wad" rebounded onto actor Bert Merrill's hand and severely wounded it. The audience heard the explosion and sent a small committee back behind the curtain to see what was going on.

Another interesting bit of trivia about the theater was the play that no one in Utah ever saw. In 1870, the Rankin Stock Company came to Salt Lake and they had a repertoire of plays which they ran through for their regular season engagement. One of their plays was quietly left out of the repertoire when they played at the Salt Lake Theatre. McKee Rankin and Kate Blanchard were the stars of the company and everywhere else they went, this play was a great success, owing to how the Mormons were viewed at the time. "...owing to the odious light in which that play presented the Mormon leaders, they did not dare produce it at the Salt Lake Theatre. Of course, the managers would not consent, and the great wonder is that Rankin could secure dates at all at Brigham Young's theater. While he was starring across the country in a play so well calculated to stir prejudice against the Mormons... it may be of interest to note the fact here that 'The Danites' was never played in Salt Lake or anywhere in Utah." (Ibid, p. 38)

In the winter of 1878, another incident happened when Mr. and Mrs. Frank Fraye were starring in a play at the old Salt Lake Theatre. They also performed a rifle shooting stunt in front of a live audience. Mr. Fraye had reached national renown for shooting an apple from his wife's head, splitting the apple with a rifle bullet instead of an arrow. Right after appearing in the play together in Salt Lake City, at their very next performance in a new city, Mr. Fraye shot his wife dead on stage in front of a live audience. He had performed this trick hundreds of times without incident but this time he missed. Only Mr. Fraye and their pet performing bulldog remained. No one ever heard if he ever tried this again, as the act seemed to have stopped altogether.

In the later years of the theater Mr. Glen Miller was a U.S. Marshall for Utah and was also the dramatic critic for The Salt Lake Tribune. One time during his term in office he was required to bring twenty Sioux Indians to Salt Lake City as witnesses in a case that was to be tried there. Trying to be a good host, he arranged for the twenty men to attend a performance at the Salt Lake Theatre free of charge. They were going to see the play, "The Eleventh Hour." The twenty men sat in the first two rows from the stage as an added bonus. The first two acts were tame and the men seemed to be enjoying the play.

When the third act came on everything changed. A great fight had to be staged each evening for the third act. Chairs and tables were smashed, lights were broken and the battle went on and on. Even when the act began the Sioux seemed uneasy and as the fight progressed, the line between reality and theater grew thinner. All of a sudden one of the Sioux men jumped up, gave a wild war hoop and jumped over the footlights onto the stage. Pandemonium broke loose and the only thing that would stop a real fight was to lower the curtain and turn the lights on. The U.S. Marshall Mr. Miller said afterwards that he would rather write a hundred critiques of a play than chaperone twenty Sioux to a play ever again.

In George D. Pyper's book, The Romance of an Old Playhouse, published in 1928 by Seagull Press, the author has a whole chapter on the "Spooks" of the old theater. One wonders if the old telephone building that stands there now has experienced any of these phenomena or if all these ghostly stories went down with the original building. On the other hand, the Daughters of the Utah Pioneers Museum have a huge room devoted to the old theater and its memorabilia, and the whole building is a slightly smaller replica of the original theater as well. The question is, do spirits follow objects to a new location or do they stay in the original location and continue to haunt? Perhaps both types of phenomena take place? Since the DUP Museum recently had a very spectacular "haunting" experience which was even videotaped over several days by the security cameras, perhaps it is the theater's memorabilia that is attracting these spirits, or even keeping them trapped there? Of course the place is huge and one could probably never decipher which objects among so many might be haunted!

Most theaters claim to be haunted and so it was a treat to learn that even the old Salt Lake Theatre was. Some of the old superstitions that I had not heard before, the obvious ones being the need for a ghost light on stage or putting on the play "Macbeth" as bad luck, etc., involved actors believing that they should always take the same path to the theater to avoid bad luck, no player could carry a round top trunk because this was also bad luck and other actors had actually smashed such trunks to smithereens on stage if one appeared among the traveling trunks in the stock company. No peacock feathers were allowed in the theater, no yellow clarinets were allowed in the orchestra, no cast member or stage crew member could whistle anywhere in the theater and yellow advertising paper on the walls meant poor business. This particular superstition seemed to have been true on many an occasion according to the box office managers. And last, never sell or give away old ticket boxes, they were to just be repaired and soldered as needed if a theater wanted to have financial success.

Spiritualism at the time was quite prevalent even in Salt Lake City and many a Salt Lake home would have a séance or spirit communications of one kind or another. There was a whole family of actors who arrived in Salt Lake City ready to join the Mormon Church because they had had "spirit communication" telling them to come to Utah. Actors and stage crews tended to be more superstitious than the general population then, and this is probably still true today. The theater itself had a few creakings and things that go bump in the night, even without the actual ghost stories connected to real incidents in the theater. For example, rappings, thuds and footsteps on stage sometimes became so violent that the terrified caretaker refused to stay alone there at night. The leading LDS Church officials had to make a prayer circle in the theater and exorcise the evil to make the noises on stage and in the galley cease.

A great story about Brigham Young, as a miracle worker, also illustrates the mystical qualities of the times. "Another tale is that on one occasion President Young gave explicit instructions that the curtain should not go up on the play until certain requirements were obeyed. The stage manager, with willful intent to disobey, rang the curtain. Brigham Young, the modern Joshua, so the story goes, commanded the curtain to stand still, and she stood still. The flyman pulled and struggled. He called others to his assistance, but the stubborn curtain didn't budge until the President's instructions have been fulfilled – then it glided up as softly and quietly as a piece of silk." (Ibid, p.194).

There were three deaths that happened at the theater over the many years it was in operation. Many of the stories about the hauntings at the theater were based around these three deaths. All three of the deaths happened on the premises, and all three men, died inside the theater walls.

John Tullidge was the father of Edwin W. Tullidge who was the historian for the theater, as well as for many other sites around the city. John Tullidge was one of the composers for the early theater productions. His office was one flight up in the front part of the theater, but you had to go up some circles stairs to get there. Tullidge went one evening to visit Alfred Lambourne, who was one of the young scenic artists working on a backdrop. Tullidge often did this because he was interested in watching the scenery come to life. That particular evening, Tullidge accidentally lost his footing and fell down the circle steps and died on the spot. Lambourne who eventually succeeded Ottinger as the set designer, remembered the ghost this way: "...at the moment of tragedy, with the sighing of the wind, the east door at the paint gallery silently opened, a freezing presence seemed to stock across the room, the west door, silently opened and shut, then all was silence." (Ibid, p.195).

The next death involved a flyman at the theater named Jim Livingston. Jim was a big man who drank too much and gambled too much. He was extremely strong and equal to the task of raising and lowering the various backdrops at the theater. But Jim began to become angry and sullen and quarrelsome. After giving him several chances to improve his manner on the job, Jim came at his boss in a threatening manner and was close to being fired. At the time, J.H. Stoddard, the famous actor, was in town, starring in the play "Beside the Bonnie Brier Bush." It was the second night of the new play, and it was just before the many actors were arriving for the evening's performance, that the manager received a phone call from the treasurer, telling him to go downstairs immediately.

There in the basement of the theater was a very gruesome sight and not one that the manager had expected. With the way that Jim had been behaving, he expected damage to the theater or some kind of a threat to the theater or even a threat to another person. Instead, when the manager arrived in the basement, he discovered that Jim had climbed up on the rail of the flight gallery, tied one of the lines he had been manipulating for some years around his neck and had made a "fearful leap into eternity." Jim was still swinging from the gridiron when everyone arrived at the theater. Knowing how superstitious performers are, the manager and the treasurer managed to temporarily convince everyone that the body that was swinging there was only a straw effigy. Jim's body was then taken to the green room, while they waited for an ambulance to arrive, thus averting, at least for the evening, panic among the actors and actresses, superstitious about going on to perform, when there had been a death in the theater.

Both Tullidge's accidental death, and Jim's suicide, accounted for footsteps heard on the stairs, noises and knockings in the theater, and even voices calling out to members of the stage crew, when no one else was there. On more than one occasion, Jim was sighted in dim light near the place where Jim had jumped over the pin rail, not jumping, but calmly pulling on the ropes for the backdrops in the "fly galley." Various stage crew members continued to see Jim's ghost in this area over the next few years.

The last death involved two young stagehands who got in a fight where their tempers had gotten out of control. One of them yelled, "I'll get you!" Then he ran to the box office where a revolver was always kept by the treasurer in a holster on the wall. The one young man got the pistol and the other man jumped him and a struggle ensued for possession of the pistol. In this struggle, one of the boys was shot and killed. And although the other boy was prosecuted, he was let go on the grounds of self-defense. The theater was haunted by this murder for quite some time. People would hear the racing of footsteps to the theater, a struggle in the box office, and the echo of a gunshot reverberating through the hallways of the old theater.

Then there were the incidences that people reported happening to them, always when they were alone in the theater, or the last one to lock up. For example, the wind would moan piteously, a door would be seen to be open when it had been locked and shut, or the pilot light on the stage would go out (the ghost light) and the last person to leave the theater would have to grope their way through the darkness to find the exit. Or, on one occasion, a janitor, who was changing a pistol from the drawer opposite the manager to his hip pocket, accidentally discharged a bullet from the chamber. That would have gone straight to the head of the manager had he not just stood up and turned in a different direction and avoided the bullet altogether. Sometimes the piano in the orchestra pit could be heard playing all by itself. And unfortunately, sometimes the house cat was seen crossing the stage while a play was in progress, which is extremely bad luck for everyone involved. Sometimes in the darkened stage, a tremendous and bloodcurdling scream could be heard, sometimes explained by the house cat, and sometimes there was no explanation.

All the actors and actresses that graced the stage of the Old Salt Lake Theatre probably left their own form of atmosphere as well. The drama of this old theatre even continued in the books written about it. The conflict between the drama on and off the stage and the many performers and behind the scenes contributing to these biographical stories will intrigue you!

MOST FAMOUS ACTORS & ACTRESSES OF THE SALT LAKE THEATRE

The Drama Lovers Who Started It All

Brigham Young and Philip Margetts are usually credited with the founding of drama in Utah. But there were a few others who also promoted drama in Utah and those men were: William C. Dunbar, John S. Lindsay, John T. Caine, David McKenzie and John C. Graham. Margetts on the other hand, is the only actor to have acted on the stage in Utah for all of his life, dying just two years after his last performance on the old Salt Lake Theatre stage. Some of these men were managers, some were financial backers, and others were just plain theater lovers who did whatever was needed to bring theater to Utah. All of these men acted on the Salt Lake Theatre stage at one time or another. John S. Lindsay, a manager of the old theater, wrote the most interesting book about the Salt Lake Theatre itself and went into much detail about the many people who either acted on stage or provided other services for the old theater. His book came out in 1905 and was 122 pages. In 1915, another man involved with this theater, Horace G. Whitney, came out with his much shorter (33 pages) and much more general version. And then George Dollinger Pyper, who was the theater manager from 1898 to 1929 put a much bigger book out, and pretty much the definitive version of the entire history of the old Salt Lake Theatre (342 pages) entitled Romance of an Old Playhouse in 1928. Pyper also wrote a revised edition of his book which was published in 1937. It was updated and he altered some information, although he also added a lot of new and interesting material. He later got involved in the LDS silent film industry in Utah, before he retired.

However, it is Lindsay's book that is packed with stories about theater people, and they are the kind of stories by today's standards that would enthrall even modern day audiences. He lets us see what these people were really like through the incidents and relationships that we get to read in the most telling of details throughout the many years of the theater's existence. Pyper's book is interesting and entertaining but little is said about the seamy side of some of these people, and that side is the most interesting. So now, for a "History's Mystery!" After having written all of these tales down, I was checking in special collections for the many photos that I would need to go with all of these short biographies. I ran across a single copy of Lindsay's little book hidden among the playbills, posters, photos and other memorabilia. As I opened the first page I was met with an unsigned note, written in pencil and one would have to say, standing in testament to something that had happened long ago. And something that today would be impossible to do without repercussions, a book burning.

Upon reading these two lines, I suddenly knew that something had happened long ago, to once again change history. Something that happens with most historical events, the twisting of such tales to fit how people and even buildings, want to be remembered, or how people think they want to be remembered, or even how the powers that be want us to remember something . None of us were there when all of these events took place and only the dead could really tell us, how, why and exactly where their history took place. And even then, it is really only that one person's perceptions of any given life or event. The lines read: "All gathered up from Mrs. Lindsay and burned by the Church when Pyper's book came out."

Was it simply because Pyper's was the bigger, better version? Or that he had been the theater manager much longer than any of the other writer's? Or maybe that he had held quite a few very important positions both in the arts and in the LDS Church? Or was it simpler than that? Perhaps that "the powers that be" really just wanted people to only read certain facts and not others? Was this incident done to just paint a pretty picture to a mighty edifice, now long forgotten and not really controversial for anyone anymore? Whatever the reason, I tend to believe what I read from individuals rather than institutions. So I also believe that "revisionist history" is still alive and well in America, and having read all three of these books, I still like John Lindsay's the best.

The irony is, that now Whitney's, which is also quite interesting, and Lindsay's books can be downloaded by anyone online and George Pyper's book is either impossible to find or a very expensive antique book for purchase. Not many are now the least bit concerned about preserving the history of an old theater which once represented the people in the old Utah Territory. A theater long since demolished and its inhabitants long since passed away. However, there are still people who do like to read about other people and their lives, especially celebrities, even if they are long dead! The computer world has all kinds of information available about these performers, but it has also increased the misinformation as well.

Philip Margetts

Phil Margetts was a comedian and character actor in the early days of theater in Utah. When he later played "Othello," and "Beverly" in "The Gamester" and "Duke Aranza" in "The Honeymoon," he surprised all of his theatrical friends who thought of him as a brilliant comedian. He is the one who went to Brigham Young, also a lover of great theater, to form the first theatrical company in Utah, and from which all the other theatrical companies sprang.

Michelle Margetts, the great granddaughter of Phil Margetts, was looking for a trick wig that her father had used in his stage performances in the basement of his father's home. Ralph Margetts was a professor of theater at the University of Utah who Michelle knew had some of her great grandfather's costumes in the basement of his home. What she found was a treasure trove of papers, letters, costumes, photos and 117 handwritten playbills as well. The handwritten plays she found had been almost entirely written in England and Philip Margetts had a resurgence of posthumous fame just recently when "Antiques Roadshow," shown on PBS, aired its three episodes from Salt Lake City.

Michelle Margetts brought in only a small sampling of the huge collection of memorabilia that had been passed down through the family to Mr. Margetts's descendants. In this collection were photos, old playbills, ticket stubs, handwritten scripts, and correspondence – including many letters back and forth between Brigham Young and Phil Margetts. This collection made national news because it was one of the largest amounts ever assessed on the show, with a conservative value of $150,000. But it also brought to the attention of many Utahns, who the real founder of theater in Utah had been. Most people assume that this had been Brigham Young. While he helped finance the theater and encouraged its development all over the state, it was really Phil Margetts who did all the work involved. ("Pioneering Escape Act" by Celia R. Baker, The Salt Lake Tribune, Sunday, May 23, 2004, The Arts section).

Phil Margetts was born in 1829, five miles from Stratford-Upon-Avon in England. Besides having an avid interest in theater and in acting, he also belonged to the Deseret Brass Band and after forming several acting companies in the state; he eventually formed the Phil Margetts Salt Lake Star Combination troupe and toured the entire Utah Territory. By trade Margetts was a wine merchant and owned the Margett's California Wine Depot just a few blocks from the old Salt Lake Theatre where patrons would stop to refresh themselves after the performances. While Margetts was somewhat handsome, he preferred to play character parts and was Utah's favorite comedian.

Philip Margetts – Founder of Utah Theater

"When Margetts signed on to drive oxen for Thomas Bateman in St. Louis in April of 1850, Bateman had 'new wagons, wild cattle, and a lot of green English boys to hand them' – and a 16-year-old daughter. Margetts remembered first seeing Elizabeth in a large room sewing wagon covers. As he left, Margetts told his brother Henry she would one day be his wife." Near Casper, Wyoming, the Margetts brothers left the starving wagon train and set out on their own with only a knife and a derringer. Having no food, they ended up helping a few Lakota warriors get back their stolen ponies and these Indians paid them back with some buffalo meat. It took them 19 days to cross 300 miles of dangerous territory to reach Salt Lake City. They even inadvertently slept over fifty shallow graves and found themselves surrounded by a pack of snarling wolves in the middle of the night, but they had all the buffalo meat that they could carry. ("Early Utah's most famous actor adored his leading lady" by Pat Bagley, History Matters, The Salt Lake Tribune, Sunday, July 11, 2004).

By September of that year, Margetts had arrived in Salt Lake City and had a job as a blacksmith. Elizabeth had also arrived in Salt Lake City and six weeks later they were married. They had a very long and happy marriage with 14 children to take care of. They really loved each other, even though they had to overcome a few hardships of one kind or another. Margetts served in the militia during the Utah War, he helped arrest Jim Bridger and went on a mission to England while his wife waited for him with many of their children on a farm near Mountain Meadows. A misfiring cannon almost killed Margetts on stage but the handsome character actor performed with all of the greats of the day on stage. Brigham Young also put pressure on Philip Margetts to enter polygamy but his response was always the same: "Well, I could do that, but I wouldn't gain anything – because my first wife would leave me!" (Ibid, B2).

GROUP OF PIONEER PLAYERS
Standing, left to right: James A. Thompson, Phil Margetts, Henry Maiben. Seated: David McKenzie, Annie (Asenath) Adams, Nellie Colebrook, John S. Lindsay.

LEADING FIGURES OF THE EARLY DRAMA IN UTAH IN THE AUTUMN OF THEIR LIVES
Standing, left to right: David McKenzie, John T. Caine, Hiram B. Clawson. Seated: Phil Margetts, Mrs. Margaret G. Clawson.

Managers and Founders of the Salt Lake Theatre

The Margetts entertained many of the famous actors and actresses of the day who came through Utah to perform at the Salt Lake Theatre and also named several of their own children after these thespians. Margetts never left Salt Lake to take the many acting offers that he received from other companies around the west; he preferred to be true to his religion instead. He called his wife "My Lizzie" and always said that she was the object of all of his affections and on their seventh anniversary together he wrote that Lizzie had always brought him "joy unspeakable – happiness beyond measure – love without bounds!" He was known to say that Lizzie was the ideal of his soul, the wife of his youth, and his partner in all of his joys and sorrows. In 1892 they were able to afford a big mansion house on West Temple and in that home they entertained both Mormon and theater royalty. Elizabeth died four years later and Margetts left the house that he had built for her. He did his last performance in 1912 from his wheelchair, Macbeth's soliloquy, for the Salt Lake Theatre's 50th anniversary celebration and died two years later, joining the love of his life, "my dear girl" Lizzie, in the Salt Lake Cemetery in 1914. (Ibid, B2).

T.A. Lyne & Brigham Young

However, long before coming to Utah, it was Brigham Young who had played a high priest in a play in Nauvoo, and who had "discovered" a young Hiram Clawson, who became a premiere actor in Utah for many years. It was also Brigham Young who maintained an active, personal and affectionate interest in the theater throughout his lifetime. Joseph Smith had formed a dramatic group in Nauvoo and also had an active interest in theater. One interesting character was T. A. Lyne, who came from the east to join the company in Nauvoo and performed in quite a few plays there, being an excellent dramatic actor from Philadelphia. While he was in Nauvoo he joined the faith, but when asked to go on a foreign mission he left. He was quite a skeptic before joining, not believing in any organized religion at all. George J. Adams, another actor, had already joined the Mormon Church and had talked Lyne into going with him to Nauvoo. Being one of Philadelphia's most popular actors, Lyne was enticed to go to Nauvoo, because the elders had raised the money to rent a theater, formed a company, and asked Lyne to play the lead in "Richard III." Lyne donated his salary to the cause of the theater company, was enamored of the young prophet, but still decided to return to Philadelphia, even though he had had the lead in several plays in Nauvoo.

Lyne was quoted as jokingly saying that by casting Brigham Young as a high priest in one of the plays, he had encouraged Young to play this part for the rest of his life. Smith wanted Lyne to go on a mission thinking Tom Lyne's great elocutionary powers would make him a great preacher for the faith. But Lyne could demand a large salary being a popular actor and the idea of preaching, "without script or purse," did not appeal to him. Tom Lyne, once a popular convert drifted away, but not forever. Twenty years later, he came out west to the new Salt Lake Theatre and performed there from 1862 to 1870. He stayed in Salt Lake after he retired from the theater, living with his French wife, Madeline and lived in a little cottage in the city until he passed away at the age of 84. While he did believe in an afterlife, he never joined any church again and never believed in the doctrines of the Mormon Church. Yet he was always a friend to the Mormons throughout his life.

Another interesting incident about Tom Lyne happened in 1871, when a small stock company, starring Mr. and Mrs. Carter played for only one week at the Salt Lake Theatre. T.A. Lyne was back in Salt Lake performing at the theater and Mrs. Carter happened to be his ex-wife, Carrie Cogswell. He felt she'd come there expressly to annoy him and absolutely no one could convince him otherwise. His concerns were very real however, as the courts had given him custody of their two children and he was afraid that the Carter's were there to kidnap his children. But the Carters had one more child of their own, and came and went without incident, except for Mrs. Carter being able to visit her children, who Lyne had attending school in town. The story behind their marriage and divorce, was another "acting soap opera" all its own. Lyne was a two-time widower when he met Carrie Cogswell, he was 50 and she was 16. Carrie was soon the leading lady with Mr. Lyne and the only Mrs. Lyne to act on stage. Tom Lyne was still very handsome with dark raven hair and a commanding presence, even in his 50s.

They were married several years and had two children, but a young man whose father was Jared Carter, one of the founders of the Mormon Church in Nauvoo, came into the company as an actor. He was handsome and young and dynamic. While nothing is mentioned about there being anything clandestine when the Lynes parted company, Carter was a definite factor in their divorce. After the divorce, on the grounds of "disparity of ages and temperaments," both parties quickly married someone else. Mrs. Lyne was now Mrs. Carter and Mr. Lyne had married a French widow named Madeline. Lyne was mainly in mortal fear that the Carters were planning on settling down in Salt Lake City so that Mrs. Carter could see her other children more often. This never happened, sadly for all parties involved. (The Mormons and the Theater, or, the History of Theatricals in Utah, by John Shanks Lindsay, Century Publishing: Salt Lake City, Utah, 1905, p. 67)

In his younger years, Young attended the theater as much as he possibly could and took as many of his wives and relations as he could with him. He personally corresponded with Margetts many times and in one of these letters he states that Salt Lake City needed a theater of its own, personally promising Margetts the funding for such an enterprise. In his later years, he sent agents who kept him informed as to the plays performed and entertained him with the stories of the various plays. He was always quoted as saying that there was enough tragedy in everyday life and that a little amusement could make up for this. He also felt that all such entertainment should be morally uplifting and monitored his theater to this end. His private carriage often carried the women actresses to and from the Social Hall and did the same when the Salt Lake Theatre began operating. Brigham Young also had a love of the art of dancing and singing. While he could not monitor everything in these troupes and early theaters, he did have a hand in the immediate dismissal of actors or actresses whom he thought had improper conduct while working.

Deseret Musical & Dramatic Association & Others Before The Theatre

The first theatrical company was entitled the Deseret Musical and Dramatic Association and they performed plays in the Old Bowery for about two years. The actors in this company were: Hiram B. Clawson,

Philip Margetts, James Ferguson, Robert Campbell, Edmund Ellsworth, Edward Martin, William Glover, William H. Kimball, William Clayton, John Kay, R.T. Burton, Horace K. Whitney, Henry Margetts, George D. Grant, and A.M. Musser. The actresses were: Miss Minnie Margetts (Phil Margetts's daughter), Miss Margaret Judd, Miss Mary Badlam, and Miss Mary Orum, Hiram B. Clawson was a character actor and John Kay was a baritone singer as well as an actor. "Horace K. Whitney filled in so well that without him it would have been like a song without a beautiful obbligato on the flute or violin. Robert Campbell played old man character parts, and the rest of the men filled in very well. Miss Orum was leading lady, Miss Margaret Judd (Mrs. H.B. Clawson) soubrette, and Miss Mary Badlam, dancer and fill in parts." When the old Social Hall was completed two years later, this theater company performed the first play there. Even then, Margetts was planning to present his idea for a grand theater to Brigham Young. (Carter, Kate B., editor, "History of Drama In The West", Historical Pamphlet, November 1941, Daughters of the Utah Pioneers, State Central Company, Copyright 1941, p.82)

The new acting troupe at the Social Hall was named the Deseret Dramatic Association. No one got any salaries and Alonzo H. Raleigh was the president of the company. The first play was on January 19, 1853 and there is some disagreement as to which play it was. It was "The Lady of Lions" or "Pizarro." The following actors and actresses were added to those who already had been performing in the original company: James W. Cummings, James Smithies, Mrs. M.G. Clawson, and a Mrs. Coray. Like his predecessor, Brigham Young, who had performed small parts in some plays before the Mormons came out to settle the Salt Lake Valley and establish the Utah Territory; the infamous Porter Rockwell played the Spanish soldier in the play "Pizarro." Still making plans for his grand theater, Phil Margetts organized a new company in the fall of 1859.

This theatrical troupe was christened the Mechanic's Dramatic Association. This company presented plays in the old Bowring Theatre in Salt Lake City. All of the members of this troupe were brand-new actors and actresses. The men still outnumbered the women however, starting with Harry Bowing, Henry McEwan, James A. Thompson, Joseph Barker,

William Wright, William Price, John B. Kelley, John Chambers, Joseph Bull, Pat Lynch, and William Poulten. There were three women in the company: Mrs. Marion Bowring, Ellen Bowring, and Elizabeth Tullidge. It appears that Margetts was seeking a little bit of creative freedom when he started this company. Brigham Young immediately made a personal request that another company be formed, which would absorb the Mechanic's Dramatic Association, and made himself president of the company.

Brigham Young was once again in control. It was a positive move. The Deseret Dramatic Association, which absorbed many of the best actors and actresses from all of the other existing companies at the times, became a premier stock company in the west. The company rapidly rose to a first class performing troupe and was a well-recognized stock company that eventually performed in the newly built Salt Lake Theatre. There were also many new actors in the casts and several more women were included. Among the new men members were: Dominico Ballo, Myron Brewer, William Broomhead, David Candland, Claude Clive, J. Grimshaw, Leo Hawkins, Thomas Higgs, J.F. Hutchinson, John N. Jones, Jessie M. Little, Edward Martin, Joshua Midgely, William Pitt, Joseph M. Simmons, James Smithies, William C. Staines, John Squires, Robert C. Taylor and William Willis. The new female members were: Mrs. Careless, Nellie Colebrook, Mrs. Sarah Sutton Cooke, Miss Kate Denim, Mrs. Leo Hawkins, Mrs. John Hyde, Sarah H. Kimball, Mrs. E. Lawrence, Mary Cyrus Wheelock, Miss E. Wood and Mrs. Woodmansee.

The story of how Margetts got Brigham Young to build his theater is interesting. The old Bowery and the old Social Hall had been built by and controlled by the LDS Church, and therefore, many other functions filled these buildings so that the theater troupe could not perform regularly. Both places had become too small to accommodate the increasing interest in the theater and the crowds that wanted to come and see the various plays. Margetts invited Brigham Young to a performance at the theater in the old Social Hall. "The President was so well pleased that he accepted an invitation for himself and his counselor, Heber C. Kimball, and their families for the following evening. "The

Honeymoon" was the play presented. After seeing these plays, Brigham Young was so impressed that he thought the time was right to build a large theater. After the performance, Phil Margetts made a curtain speech, to which Brigham Young responded complimentarily. In his speech, he said, 'The people must have amusement as well as religion,' a saying which has become almost proverbial with the Latter-Day Saints. Immediately after this incident, Brigham Young instructed Hiram B. Clawson to negotiate for a suitable site upon which to build a great playhouse. Credit must be given to Philip Margetts, then, as being largely responsible for bringing the decision to build a great theater – the renowned and much-loved Salt Lake Theatre, which was dedicated in 1862." (Ibid, Eva J. Olson, Lindsay, p.81)

First Salt Lake Theatre Actors & Actresses

The new company performed in the Salt Lake Theatre and the first performance to charge an entrance fee was presented on March 8, 1862. The Salt Lake Theatre continued to be the home for this acting company as well as many traveling acting troupes, and the Salt Lake troupes very often outdid the more professional troupes that came through town because of their many years of experience and community effort. One of the actors worth mentioning is Bernard Snow; he was easily the lead actor for the troupe. He had been a Mormon actor in California and was known for his striking performance of "Othello." Snow's "Damon" in "Damon and Pythias" was, according to the other actors, brilliant. Snow performed in the theater 10 years before T.A. Lyne arrived in Salt Lake, and each man's performances were considered equal in their stature. Before Snow retired, the two actors performed in several plays together.

In 1880, another acting troupe was organized, The Home Dramatic Club. It was organized with the idea that there needed to be a return to more wholesome entertainment. All of these actors and actresses were "Utah Grown," and they included the following performers: J. M. Barlow, Lottie Claridge, Birdie Clawson Cummings,

Dellie Clawson Cummings, Mrs. L.A. Cummings, Larson Cummings, Lavon Cummings, A. Culmer, H.L.A. Culmer, H.M. Dinwoodey, Ivy Clawson Green, R. Grundhand, Kitty Heywood, Mamie Honies, A.A. Hovey, Hazel Taylor Peery, George Drollinger Pyper, Joseph Simmons, Robert G. Taylor, Miss Lyde Wells, Orson F. Whitney, Mrs. E. Wood, Luna Young, and "Bid" Young, who later married Lottie Claridge. By the 1890s, the old Salt Lake Theatre was very popular. Other main theaters had been constructed; Maud May Babcock had entered the scene and formed the last stock company from her university players, Utah Players Stock Company, to perform at the theater in 1912. Moroni Olsen brought his troupe to Salt Lake City and Babcock went on to be instrumental in the building of Kingsbury Hall on the University of Utah campus. However, the national theater circuit began changing the face of uplifting moralistic theatre forever in Utah.

At the same time, the many Ward Dramatic Associations began forming when the world of drama and theater took the entire state by storm. A lot of local talents from these "Mormon Roadshow" productions were drafted into the bigger companies in Salt Lake City. A feature of these many productions was the "Juvenile Show," and many a child actor or actress got their start there and then went on to perform in the bigger companies in Salt Lake City as well. Annie Adams Kiskadden, who was later a principle actress in the old theater, and her daughter, Maude Adams, got their start in the 10th Ward Roadshows. Baby Maude was on the stage as an infant in these ward productions. The famous story of her first production as a little toddler is actually not quite true, as little Maudie had already performed before. It is plain to see that acting was in the blood of many a Utahn, long before any national troupes arrived.

One other acting troupe that I need to mention at this time was the Camp Floyd Theatre, which was established in 1858 when Johnson's Army was stationed south of Salt Lake City for three years. Sergeant R.C.White formed his troupe as the only successful gentile theater in early Utah. His troupe was entitled The Military Dramatic Association. They presented their first play on November 15th of that same year. Most of the actors and actresses were, of course, husbands and wives stationed at the camp. And while they were amateur actors, they did maintain a large audience throughout their existence. The first cities to form their own dramatic associations were Farmington, Centerville, Monroe, Ogden, Provo, Springville, and Spanish Fork. Following their lead, the cities of Gunnison, Beaver, Fillmore, Manti, and even the whole of Uintah County formed their own dramatic associations. Outside of Utah, there were also some other Mormon acting associations that performed. These were in Mesa, Arizona, Los Angeles, California, and in the states and settlements of Wyoming and Nevada. These many associations were above and beyond the various "Ward" Dramatic Associations.

Mercy Tuckett & R.C.White

Another interesting story in the Daughters of the Utah Pioneers pamphlet comes from the gentile side of acting, concerning the Camp Floyd Military Dramatic Company and two people: Dick White and Mercy Tuckett. It is the stuff of which many of the plays of that period were made, both romantic and tragic. The narration to this story comes from Mrs. Lillie Tuckett Freeze who was a daughter of Mercy Tuckett. The story had always been that the Mormon actress, Mercy Tuckett had abandoned her husband and children to run away with a gentile soldier actor named Dick White. Her daughter wanted to set the record straight as presented in the various early books written about theater in Utah.

"In 1848, Jane Tuckett's four sons, Charles, Henry, John Joseph, and one daughter, Jane Tuckett, and Richard and Ann Webley Westwood, with eight children, four sons and four daughters – Phillip, David, Richard, Joseph, Hannah, Mercy, Temperance, and Patience – all came across the Atlantic in a sailing vessel from London England. Forty-six people died of cholera on the ship, but all of the two families named escaped – till they reached St. Louis, when Richard, Ann, Patience, a baby, and Philip's wife died of the plague inside of one week."

"Mercy, a beautiful girl of 16, and Temperance, 13, found employment in the home of Roswell Field, of St. Louis, one to help with the housework, the other as a nursemaid to little Eugene – a baby in arms. The girls remained there until one, Mercy, married Henry Tuckett. Temperance lived with the Fields for years. She describes the home as large and beautiful – with a splendid library where she spent much of her time amusing Eugene with fairy stories, which he loved the best of all. She put him in his first pants, and describes him as a very bright and lovable child."

"Philip Westwood, of marked dramatic tendencies, organized a company in St. Louis to give performances for the benefit of the cholera stricken families. Mercy Tuckett was among the members. She displayed considerable inherent dramatic talent, without education or training. She has been described as tall and beautiful, with an abundance of dark brown hair – responsive, magnetic, and cheerful – and with a sweet voice. Here, the first child of Henry and Mercy, Henry A., was born. He became a noted composer and musician, and a man of business in Salt Lake City.

"When President Brigham Young was asking for talent to amuse and instruct the pioneer people, he called in Mrs. Tuckett to accept a mission for two years to perform in the Bowery, and later in the Social Hall. She played leading roles in many plays, until the coming of Johnston's Army, when the family joined in the 'move' and went to Spanish Fork. Here, Philip Westwood went with the company to play in Camp Floyd for the entertainment of Johnston's Army. Mrs. Tuckett, who was among the players, was an instantaneous success, and became a general favorite, her two children occasionally taking parts. The little girl Lillie (Mrs. Freese) was taught fancy dancing by Richard White and appeared between the acts – and all were reaping a financial harvest, so much needed. But jealousy, and envy, and intolerant misrepresentation wrought their destructive influence, till the company was disbanded. Some of the members remained with Philip; among them Mrs. Tuckett, who, when the army was called east to engage in the Civil War, left Camp Floyd with her brothers Philip and David, their families, and went to Nevada, taking the youngest child, Philip, with her, and leaving the two older children, who had been spirited away and secreted by the father, with his relatives – because the mother had no intention of deserting her children, and arranged to have them taken with her later. Mr. Tuckett obtained a divorce from Mercy on the grounds of desertion."

"When the last company of soldiers left Camp Floyd, Richard White, several months later, left for California, but joined the Dramatic Company in Nevada. Two years later he married Mercy Tuckett. They had one child – who died with its mother in Fulsom, California, and both lie in an unmarked grave, leaving two children, Philip and Evaline, a child of Henry Tuckett, born four months after the separation. Philip Westwood had charge of the children till Mr. Tuckett had them brought back to Utah, where the four children, after many years, were reunited. They all married and became useful members of the community." (The Mormons and the Theatre by John Shanks Lindsay, Century Printing: SLC, Utah, 1905. Pp. 13-15)

In George Pyper's 1937 revised edition of The Romance of the Old Playhouse he set the record straight about the Mercy Tuckett incident through her descendants who stated that Lindsay's version of things were a bit off. In their version of the incident, Mercy Tuckett was merely accused of spending too much time with the camp players, including Dick White who was tutoring her children to learn to dance and act as they sometimes had already played bit parts in the camp plays. The troupe discontinued due to "jealousy, envy, and intolerant misrepresentation wrought their destructive influences, till the company was disbanded." Her brothers David and Philip had also acted in the troupe and when the plays were no more, Mercy went with her brothers and their families to Nevada, taking only her youngest child with her. She had made arrangements for her other children to join her but was obviously leaving her husband. Mr. Tuckett in the meantime obtained a divorce on the grounds of desertion and spirited Mercy's two older children away from her.

When the last of the soldiers left Camp Floyd, Richard White went to California. However he soon joined the Dramatic Company in Nevada which Mercy and her brothers had joined earlier. Two years after this she and Dick White were married and had one child together but she died with the child. Her children Evaline and Leila stayed with their father while Mercy had a younger child with her, her son Philip. Four months after she left Henry Tuckett she gave birth to their last child together, Henry Tuckett Jr. Richard White obviously didn't want these two children because he was not their father. Henry Tuckett Sr. came and got the other two children and reunited all four of them many years later. The two younger children were raised by Mercy Tuckett's brother Philip and his family, probably per the wishes of Mercy before her death. So while the circumstances are all the same, this definitely puts Mercy Tuckett in a better light as a mother. (The Romance of the Old Playhouse by George D. Pyper, The Deseret News Press, 1937, pp.27-73)

"Temperance, the nurse of the afterwards celebrated Eugene Field, came to Utah and married Henry Moon of Salt Lake City, and became the mother of thirteen children. When Eugene Field became a famous writer, he wrote to Mrs. Moon and an interesting correspondence followed. Photos were exchanged and these are in the cherished possession of her family." (Taken from The Romance of the Old Playhouse, by George D. Pyper, Seagull Press, 1928, pp.61-67, as quoted in the "History of Drama in The West" pamphlet, edited by Kate B. Carter, pp. 101-103)

Another version of this affair was that Sgt. Richard or "Dick" White opened up correspondence with Mrs. Tuckett to get her to perform at the Camp Floyd Theatre. He was an excellent writer and poet and accomplished his objective quite quickly, against Tuckett's husband, friends and even the Church authority's wishes. She was looked upon from that moment as a lost sheep from the fold. Mrs. Tuckett never came back to Salt Lake and was eventually the wife of the actor, poet, artist, White. They moved to Folsom, California and just a few years later she died in childbirth in 1863. She had been a polygamist wife in Salt Lake and all of her extended family were actors. Her husband kept their four children Mercy had had with him in Salt Lake. Four years later, White visited Salt Lake City traveling with the John S. Langrishe Company. Apprehensive about performing there, White stayed secluded during the day and only appeared in costume to perform each evening. He was still discovered and in fear for his life, quietly dropped out of the company for the remainder of their tour in Salt Lake.

However, he stayed in Salt Lake two more weeks, just long enough to romance another local single actress who married him and the two of them rejoined the troupe. They eventually settled in Portland, Oregon with four children to raise and worked in Maguire's Stock Company. All of their children eventually became interested in acting. They then moved to San Francisco where White became stage manager of the Tivoli Theatre.

Mrs. Mary Cyrus Wheelock - Lydia Gibson Maggie Romaine Browning

Another Salt Lake actress, Mrs. Wheelock, also left the stage and the Mormon Church. She traveled to California in 1857, going under the protection of Colonel Steptoe's command. She never explained why she left the territory, the Mormon Church and her husband, but settled in Sacramento and married another man a while later, named Rattenbury. Losing these two actresses definitely affected interest in going to the Salt Lake Theatre, as Mercy Tuckett and Wheelock had been the two leading actresses of the theater's troupe.

One of the actresses to eventually fill this void was Lydia Gibson, a very talented and promising young actress. Wife of William Gibson, she had only recently been converted to the Mormon faith and Gibson had made her his second wife. She was quickly a most popular actress, although many a young man who was struck by her beauty and talent, were saddened to see that her husband was so many years older than she. She had two seasons of fame, and then was stricken with illness and died. According to the records, she was buried in Brigham Young's private cemetery near where the prophet was eventually buried, having had a brief but brilliant career in the theater. However nearly all of the markers were moved long ago from this cemetery. I don't know if this means that the people were also moved or if the LDS Church had some reason for doing this, but it looks more like a little park with only a few graves with

ACTRESSES WHO APPEARED IN THE SIXTIES
Madam Scheller, Mrs. Selden Irwin, Zina Young, Nellie Colebrook, Emily, Fanny and Marinda Young, in "The Marble Heart"; Mrs. Lydia Gibson, Mrs. Marian Bowring, Mrs. T. B. H. Stenhouse, Lizzie Platt.

Lydia Gibson and Early Stage Actresses

gravestones, although Brigham Young's grave is still well marked and covered in a huge block of cement. I am assuming that Lydia Gibson is still there somewhere, as many others were buried there.

Maggie Romaine Browning was on Broadway the same time as other Utahns: Maude Adams, Blanche Thomas, Ada Dwyer, Hazel Dawn, Sallie Fisher, and Viola Gillette. Maggie Browning was a Mormon from

Utah who was not often recognized as being Margaret Browning but instead went by the name Margaret Romaine; she was one of the sisters of Hazel (Tout) Dawn. Margaret (Tout) Romaine Browning was only on Broadway in the mid-teens and then she signed with the Metropolitan Opera Company where she had a long and illustrious career. She was Margaret Romaine on Broadway but re-married later and became Margaret or Maggie Browning when singing with the opera company. Sallie Fisher was an opera singer with ties to Utah even though she was born in Wyoming. All the rest of these women on Broadway were from Salt Lake City, Utah.

Hiram B. Clawson & Margaret Judd Clawson

It was Joseph Smith who introduced a young boy to Lyne as having great mimicry talent and asked Lyne to give him a part in the play that was being performed at the moment. The only opening was a stagehand position where his only duty was to throw fire from the Heavens at the proper cue. It happened that Brigham Young was playing a High Priest in the same production, and in the end, this established a lifelong friendship between Hiram B. Clawson, and Brigham Young, and eventually T.A. Lyne, when he returned to Utah to be the manager of the old Salt Lake Theatre. Clawson was the first manager of the theater until Brigham Young engaged Lyne to bring in a more national awareness of his theater. Hiram B. Clawson's family included many actors and actresses including Margaret Gay Judd. Judd was eighteen when she arrived in the Salt Lake Valley in 1849. She married Hiram B. Clawson three years later, became an actress in the original company, helped form the first acting association, and managed to give birth to eleven children along the way. She was in the 1851 spring play "Robert Maciare" at the old Bowery Theatre and continued to perform at the old Social Hall. When the old Salt Lake City Theatre opened with her husband as manager, she and her husband performed minor parts in the productions. She eventually retired from the stage to help raise her various talented children and lived well past eighty.

Margaret Judd Clawson
University of Utah Special Collections

Hiram B. Clawson
University of Utah Special Collections

Most famous of the Clawson children was Edith Helen Clawson Knowlton. A brilliant actress with a beautiful soprano voice, she played leading roles for twenty-five years with the historic Home Dramatic Club and sang leading parts for the Salt Lake Opera Company. She began acting when she was only twelve years old and the leading performer of the play she was in was a famous national actor named Junius Brutus Booth, brother of Edwin Booth. He was so pleased with her performance that he invited her to travel with his company but her father refused his permission. "Many years later, when she sang 'Comin' Through the Rye' in the Tabernacle for the renowned Edwin Booth, he insisted that she sign a Tabernacle guest book as a member of his company because she had once played with his brother." (Ibid, Ivy C. Towler, Pyper, p.91)

Edith appeared in her first leading lady role in a play in 1880. In the spring of 1895, she was asked to play the lead part in an opera to open in the Salt Lake Theatre within two weeks. Like a story from an early Hollywood movie, the original leading lady of this opera had resigned, only giving those producing the opera two weeks to try and make it work. "They found Edith in bed, with her infant son, Hooper, not two weeks old and the crib nearby. She agreed to do the part. In the short time allowed, she learned the score, prepared her costumes, wore a dainty pink China silk with organdie collar and cuffs, another canary yellow; and the curtain rose on schedule. This was her final appearance on stage. She died December 31, 1940." (Ibid, Ivy C. Towler, Pyper, p.91)

T.A. Lyne left the stage where he was performing in Denver to coach the young actors in the troupe performing at the Salt Lake Theatre. At the urging of both Brigham Young and Hiram B. Clawson, Lyne came back to Salt Lake City but was not content with just a coaching job. By 1863, he was playing many lead roles in the plays performed there. Young did not like all the tragedy that Lyne tended to choose for his performances, but eventually he was won over and even let one of his daughters, Alice, play a tragic performance where she was killed by her own father. Alice married into the Clawson clan and gave birth to the noted local artist, J.W. Clawson. A few of the other leading actors and actresses who performed at the theater at this time were: Bernard Snow,

George M. Ottinger, James Ferguson, John C. Graham, John R. Clawson, C.R. Savage, D.J. McIntosh, Sara Alexander, Annie Asenath Adams, and David McKenzie.

The Smiths, the Youngs & the Clawsons

Jeanette Young Easton, who became a principal lead on the Salt Lake Theatre stage, was one of the famous "Ten" or main daughters of Brigham Young who performed in a play together at the theater. An interesting story about this is that the girls wanted their costumes a fashionable length and Brigham Young had given strict orders to have their skirts reach the ground. The girls were so upset about this that the costumer mistress kept the girls happy by raising their dresses a little before each performance. These girls were named Caroline or "Carlie," Ella, Emily, Eveline or "Eva," Fanny, Jeanette, Maria, Marinda, Mary and Zina.

While Susa Young Gates had performed at the theater and did enjoy and support it, she had many other interests and pursuits. It was Jeanette Young who carried out a lifelong interest and passion for the theater in Utah. She later became the New York correspondent from The Deseret News for many years after her youthful days performing in comedy roles at the theatre. She reviewed all of the plays performed and eventually became an "encyclopedia" of information concerning all of the plays and all of the performers both local and those who passed through. Emily Young, Zina Young, and Louisa Young were the ones to continue to perform in other plays. "Bid" Young, John W. Young and Levi Edgar Young were the only sons listed as performers at the theater. Levi Edgar Young continued in the early silent films made in Utah as a producer and director. When the girls married they became Mrs. Zina Card, Mrs. Caroline Cannon, Mrs. Emily Clawson, Mrs. Marinda Conrad, Mrs. Mary Croxall, Mrs. Eveline Davis, Mrs. Maria Dougall, Mrs. Jeanette Easton, Mrs. Ella Empey and Mrs. Fanny Thatcher.

Ivy Clawson, from another very famous drama family in Utah performed at the same time in ingénue and boy's parts at the theater until she married and then retired from the stage. Edith Clawson, Birdie Clawson, Alice Clawson, Leoni Clawson, Dellie Clawson, Edna Clawson, Georgie Clawson, and the in-laws Mrs. Stanley H. Clawson and Margaret Judd Clawson also performed there. John R. Clawson, Bradley Clawson, Leo Clawson and Willie Clawson also performed in the early days of the theater. The early Smith performers were John L. Smith, George Smith, Emily Smith, and Annie Smith.

John D. T. McAllister
George & Mary Jane Abbott McAllister

My great grandfather, William James Frazier McAllister helped herd cattle alongside George Ottinger when Will was just 16 years old and George was 28. Ottinger married Will's sister but they were only married a little over a year. Later the famous painter married someone else, but not until after he painted his mother-in-law, my great great great grandmother. Her sad and sour-faced portrait hangs in the Springville Museum of Art today. Will was a bee keeper, a forty year choir director, musician and singer, who took two wives, the last one when he was an old man and the young woman was just sixteen. My great grandmother lived with him for many years before he took this second wife. Waiting until Will and the girl he was courting left for the evening, she went into the main room and took the rocker, which she had given him and he had been using to rock his new girlfriend on his knees, outside and chopped it up for fire wood. Eleanor Jackson Adams McAllister was a business woman who was on the town council, ran a millinery shop, an ice cream shop and a boardinghouse in Kanab. Both of them started a drama troupe and performed in all the local plays together when they were younger in Kanab, Utah.

It was said of W. J. F. McAllister that he played a significant role in the dances and performing arts of both Kanab and in his later days, American Fork. "In addition to having a good singing voice, he could dance and play nearly every musical instrument. He brought with him a small portable organ, which he carried from place to place wherever the dance happened to be...He was a popular figure on the dance floor even in his eighties." He had an ice house, a beekeeper's house, and a carpenter's shop on the second floor of this house just outside of Kanab, and could strap his baby organ over his shoulders with a special harness he designed to carry it anywhere. ("Dancing – A Pioneer Recreation," Treasures of Pioneer History by Kate B. Carter, editor, et. al. Daughters of the Utah Pioneers, Volume Two, SLC, Utah, 1953, p. 377).

"In about the year 1880 a dramatic troupe was organized with W. J. F. McAllister as coach and manager... They put on plays at first for funds with which to obtain stage equipment and costumes...In the early years the leading parts were usually played by Sarah Mariger and W. J. F. McAllister, although Eleanor McAllister sometimes played the leading lady." A play was put on every week and rehearsals were held in the tithing office and the plays were presented in the school room, so the stage had to be dismantled every Sunday night and put up again every Friday afternoon. A permanent stage was built in the new school house and by 1890, the drama association was reorganized and many of both my great grandmother's and great grandfather's relations were still performing in the plays. John Daniel Thompson McAllister, Will's older brother, sang at The Salt Lake Theatre, a favorite vocalist for Brigham Young. Mary McAllister, their sister, was a leading lady at the theater. (History of Kane County by Kane County Daughters of the Utah Pioneers & Kane County Commissioners, The Utah Printing Company: Salt Lake City, Utah, 1970, p.281-182)

John T. Caine

John T. Caine was another important name in the first years of drama in Utah. Caine immigrated to Utah in 1852 and was present at the opening of the Social Hall in 1853. He became a member of the Deseret Dramatic Association and was in charge of the events at the Social Hall with living quarters in the basement of the Hall. His first-born son was born in that basement shortly before he went on a mission for the LDS Church to the Hawaiian Islands. When he returned from his mission, he became stage manager for the Social Hall. When the Salt Lake Theatre was built, he often played the leading male roles in the plays. It was at this time that John T. Caine and Hiram C. Clawson formed a sort of business and stage manager relationship. In 1865, Caine played with Julia D. Hayne and Mr. George B. Waldron in "East Lynne" at the benefit performance that Julie Dean Hayne gave to her Salt Lake City patrons. This happened shortly before John T. Caine left on his trip to the east to study theater management in the larger cities.

Caine gave a speech on this occasion and offered some insights for his devotion to the theater. "Isolated as we are in this country – as we used to say 1000 miles from everywhere – it is pardonable to be proud of so noble a structure at best. Conceived, designed, and executed by a mastermind, it stands today as noble tribute to the refining and elevating influence of the drama. To carry out the design of its founder; it is the name of my worthy colleague – Mr. H.B. Clawson – and myself, never to present anything on the stage that was debasing, or demoralizing and its tendency, or that would cause the blush of shame to crimson the cheek of purity and innocence... So they had ever be' and made the drama, occupying its legitimate sphere, go hand-in-hand with his sister arts – music, sculpture, and painting – on its mission of exultation to man." (Ibid, Pyper, p.89)

Caine named his second daughter after Julia Dean Hayne and both Sara Alexander and Asenath Adams were good friends of the Caines. Maude Adams made her first appearances at the theater due to Caine's influence. But while Clawson remained a theater manager, Caine was elected to the position of City Recorder and eventually to the Utah Congress. The entire Caine family had free reserved seats at the Salt Lake Theatre for years. When Caine retired from managing the theatre, a large reception and party was held at the theater. During the same year, he also became managing editor of the newly founded newspaper, The Salt Lake Herald. Caine's wife, Margaret Nightingale, gave birth to thirteen children and never tried acting. And besides a silver pitcher inscribed with several of the actors and actresses names, the family owned a yellow brocade dress with an interesting story behind it. Read about the dress in the Annie Lockhart section of this article. Both of these items ended up at the Utah Daughters of the Pioneers Museum next to the Capitol Building in Salt Lake City. (Ibid, Margaret Caine Patrick, Pyper, pp.88-89)

David McKenzie

A few other lesser known actors and actresses are mentioned in Kate B. Carter's pamphlet such as David McKenzie, George Pauncefort, Mr. And Mrs. Shelden Irwin, Emma Green Bull, and Nellie Colebrook Taylor. David McKenzie tells of his many roles from his scrapbooks and the green room stories in the theater where people spent time between performances. And although I found a great photo of David McKenzie and I know he was greatly involved in the development of the theater over many years, holding important positions for the old Salt Lake Theatre as well as acting there, I could not find any biographical information. It does appear from a photo I found that he did live a very long life and continued to be involved in theater life as an actor until he was much older. But, he had been arrested at one time for counterfeiting.

Mr. & Mrs. Shelden Irwin

Mr. and Mrs. Shelden Irwin arrived in Utah in 1863 and they produced a series of plays while there. They remained in Utah for six months and then returned two years later for another engagement at the theater. Knowing good public relations when they saw it, the Irwins' first play was full of fairies and was entitled "The Mountain Sylph." They presented the idea of allowing several of Brigham Young's daughters the opportunity to appear briefly in the play. Young agreed to this proposal but insisted on the girls having dancing dresses that were ankle length. It was during this time that Sara Alexander was Young's dance and acting teacher for his many daughters. The dresses were made longer and ten of his daughters performed in the play. However, the daughters were upset about this compromise and voiced their concerns to the Irwins. Mr. Irwin did the only thing he could do and before every succeeding performance, he had a couple inches cut off the bottom of the dresses so the girls would be happy, the dresses would grow a bit shorter each night and their father would never notice the difference. By the last performance, the dresses were mid-calf.

Emma Green Bull – Charles Ellis Johnson – Charles Roscoe Savage & Daughters

Emma Green Bull started out as a dressmaker and never did get paid for any of her performances on stage. She performed in the Bowring Theatre and the Social Hall, as well as the Salt Lake Theatre. She arrived in the valley from England in 1853 and later married Joseph Bull in Salt Lake City. She died in 1895. C.R. Savage, the famous Utah photographer acted on the Salt Lake Theatre from time to time, as did another famous photographer Charles Ellis Johnson and a famous Utah painter George Ottinger. Savage had four wives and produced at least three or four actresses for the Salt Lake Theatre: Ida May Savage, Lennie Louise Savage Riter, Marianne Sharpe and possibly Nan Savage, although Louise Savage was the most famous of the four, having a beautiful face and figure, with a beautiful voice to match. She sang in the chorus until she was discovered then began to get leading parts in operettas and operas on the Salt Lake Theatre stage. More about the Charles Roscoe Savages appears in the last story in this section.

C.W. Couldock & Eliza Couldock

Another quite poignant story is about the actor C. W. Couldock who was a foreign star and was often dubbed "the grand old man of the stage." He performed at the Salt Lake Theatre on many an occasion and it was one of his favorite places to perform. Considered a sterling actor, he was not known to have a mild manner when directing a play on stage. When he "coached" a play his language was pretty foul and he had a temper to match this. "There was a heat in it that fairly scorched... He shocked the erstwhile modest and mild-mannered ensemble beyond

Marianne Sharpe

Ida May Savage
Utah State Historical Society

Lennie Louise Savage Riter
University of Utah Special Collections

Charles Roscoe Savage

expression, but he got results." But Couldock had long been enshrined in the hearts of Salt Lake Theatre-goers and came out from New York one year to perform several plays with the Salt Lake troupe accompanied by his daughter Eliza. (Ibid, Romance of the Old Theatre, p. 237-238).

Couldock and his daughter Eliza Couldock appeared together on this stage several times. C.W. Couldock was best remembered for his performances in the plays "The Willow Corpse" and "Hazel Kirke." He was best at character parts, such as a gypsy in the play "Rosedale." When he gave his farewell performance in New York City, he was given red carpet treatment and actually ended up getting two farewell ceremonies because he was so popular.

In the middle of the 1860s quite early in his career, because he did not retire until the 1890s, he and his daughter were performing together at the Salt Lake Theatre when his daughter suddenly died under mysterious circumstances. In George Pyper's book he makes mention of this in the following quote: "Miss Couldlock was cast for the character of Eliza. The actor who was playing George Harris and Legree well remembered how nervous and poorly the lady was during the week's engagement. She was over ambitious and worked beyond her strength and it was evident she was in a decline. This was her last appearance, poor girl, and it was not long before we were paying our last respects and with loving hands laying her gently in the earth alongside dear Annie Lockhart, for whom we had performed the same service only a short time before." (Ibid, Romance of Old Theatre, p.200).

Since they traveled constantly, Couldock thought it best to bury her where they were, so that Liza Couldock is buried in the Mt. Olivet Cemetery apparently either next to Annie Lockhart or very near her. Every time the actor came to town to perform or on any other business, "the grand old man of the theatre" visited her grave and spent time there with her. Those who lived around this cemetery at the time, always recognized Couldock as he trudged toward his daughter's grave no matter the weather and stood there for quite some time gazing "...mournfully upon the little mound in the city cemetery under which were placed many years before the mortal remains of a loved daughter. 'Ah me, the grasses o'er her grave had twenty years been growing.'" (Ibid, p.237).

George Pauncefort & Mrs. Bell

Among the actors and actresses who passed through Utah, it was George Pauncefort, who left the strongest and not necessarily positive impression on Brigham Young or the people of Utah. He was from England and did have a fine reputation on the stage before coming to Utah. He arrived in 1864, via the New York stage and then the Denver stage accompanied by his co-star, Mrs. Florence Bell. Mrs. Bell was a pretty woman, but a mediocre actress, they wanted to retire her almost immediately after she had also signed a contract. They had to let her perform in several plays at the theater until her contract ran out. George Pauncefort was a married man with a wife and several daughters. An excellent actor, he had a new style of acting never seen before out west, and fared well in Salt Lake City, but was upset about how poorly his costar was doing. However, his intimate relations with Mrs. Bell were pretty obvious on stage and on the streets. The Mormon authorities,

GEORGE PAUNCEFORT
From an old engraving in possession of the author

George Pouncefort

while open to polygamy, were not open to promiscuity and Pauncefort was advised to cease and desist or lose his position at the theater. George immediately stopped the affair and none too soon, as Mr. Bell soon showed up in Salt Lake City and took a position as a cornet player in the theater's orchestra until Pauncefort's run was over at the theater. Mr. Bell then went west to Montana with his wife in tow.

Brigham Young, hearing of the affair, refused to attend the theater until Pauncefort had ended his performances at his "Playhouse," and immediately returned after this to his special box seats with some of his wives. In the very next season, Julia Dean Hayne performed, whose story you will soon read concerning the courting she received from both an officer at Camp Douglas and the Prophet Brigham Young. It was Annie Kiskadden's first year at the theater, and she idolized Hayne, emulating her acting style throughout her own career, while producing an extraordinary daughter, Maude Adams. At the time she was acting with Hayne, however, her name was Annie Asenath Adams and she had also been courted by Brigham Young, but chose a bit later to marry a gentile, consequently leaving her church.

Nellie Colebrook Taylor & George Pauncefort

Nellie Colebrook Taylor was from England and was only two years old when she arrived in Utah. She began her career when she was 16 years old, while her mother managed a little millinery store and she worked there as a saleslady. Her career lasted from 1863 to 1871, and she left the stage when she married Bishop George H. Taylor and devoted the rest of her life to her husband and children. She died in April of 1910.

Nellie Colebrook made her debut in 1867 on the stage of the Salt Lake Theatre and was soon the leading lady of the theater's troupe. She appeared in "Dominic, the Deserter" and the first time she spoke about her predicament she was perfectly clear: "Oh, I'm half dead with fear." She could visibly be seen shaking, and quite often could be seen shaking throughout her career, but on this occasion it fit her character well, and most people thought she was just acting. Tall and stately, she had a winning face and a musical voice and was well suited to many roles. Colebrook took Lydia Gibson's place as the leading lady of the troupe. But throughout her career she always dealt with stage fright, a little more than most actresses and actors do.

Once again, George Pauncefort was also performing in Salt Lake, after his 1864 fiasco with Mrs. Bell. George took an interest in Miss Nellie Colebrook, being surprised and delighted to not only be starring opposite such a pretty woman, but an excellent actress as well. With her nervousness, she needed his help and support as she rose through the ranks. She needed to overcome her stage fright. George was quoted as using a line from the play to describe Nellie, "The fair Elizabeth has caught my eye, and like a new star, lights onward to my wishes." A favorite with all who met her, she had many admirers both in the theater and without it, but George's growing attentions to her echoed of a few years before, even though both Nellie and George were single at the time. Close to 50, George entered the race, very handsome and experienced; he was soon ahead of the pack. Nellie was strongly attracted to him, and even though George was now divorced and available, this time it was Nellie's mother who interceded in their romance.

Her mother went straight to President Young, who had the final say in anything going on in the Utah Territory and unfortunately for George, remembered his flaunting of his affair with Mrs. Bell. And even though this time George's intentions were more honorable, Young immediately stopped any chance George had to wed his young costar, on the spot. Nellie would not be allowed to marry George for many reasons: he was not a Mormon, he was too old, his intentions might still be dishonorable, and mostly Young and Nellie's mother did not like him. The romance was ended. Nothing was said about how Nellie herself felt about all this, perhaps it broke her heart, but we will never know. If George and Nellie had really loved each other, and it wasn't just another passing affair for George, perhaps Pauncefort wasn't so much the rake and womanizer as he had been depicted. Perhaps, this all had more to do with there not being enough room for two powerful men in one place.

George Pauncefort's story would not only make a great book, but a great movie. Pauncefort finished his performances there, bought a horse and chaise, a hunting gun and fishing gear and headed for Portland, Oregon. He earned his living by giving dramatic readings in the evenings in the towns which he passed through. During the day he would hunt and fish. He reached the Utah border, sold his chaise and hopped a stage for Virginia City, Nevada. He performed there for a while and then disappeared entirely, very cognizant of the fact that he really did have to leave the entire Utah Territory, for his own safety. "A dozen years later he was discovered by some American actors in Japan, keeping a roadside teahouse for travelers with a set of pretty Japanese girls for waiters. He married a Japanese girl and latest reports credited him with a fine young Japanese colony of his own." The picture, carried back to Utah, of him with his wife and four children verified that it was indeed him. This was in 1880, and he now had a long beard and plenty of "spiritual wives," the irony being, he would have made a great polygamist patriarch had he stayed in Utah and followed the rules as they were laid down by Young. (Ibid, Lindsay, p. 50)

Annie Lockhart

Annie Lockhart came along in the 1868 – 1869 season, as it became more acceptable for more and more young single women to join the young male actors onstage. She was from England, refined and cultured. She had already had varied experiences as an actress, having performed in stock companies in England and Australia, in Melbourne and Sydney. She had met her actor husband, Harry Jackson in Australia, but had soon grown tired of his indiscretions and indulgences, and divorced him. She had left him in San Francisco and was now a single young actress again, newly arrived in Salt Lake City. She was a stock star until her illness the following November. She was just 32 years old. While not a great actress, she did perform well, was a tasteful dresser and popular with audiences, probably because of her looks.

During the season Annie Lockhart was performing on the Salt Lake Theatre stage, Niel Warner was by her side. Warner was a copyist having apprenticed under a famous actor named Brooke. With a splendid physique and a magnificent voice, he was a very magnetic presence on the stage. He could carry off serious drama very effectively, and Warner's first performance in Salt Lake was in "Richard III." All in all, he gave 24 performances in Salt Lake, starring in most of the Shakespearean tragedies. "Macbeth" was considered his best performance of these plays, a role that many actors still desire to play and play well, to this day, even though a lot of superstitions surround the role. Supposedly, an actor or actress even in this play might have bad luck, but the lead is supposed to be the most cursed of all.

Warner went to New York City after this to make it big, but never did and ended up playing second leads on Broadway. Eventually he went to Montreal, Canada and then onto California where he toured with a stock company that Annie Lockhart was in. They had performed together in Australia after this and seemed to have a very warm friendship. Annie ardently admired Warner. Everyone thought that she would go with him when he went to New York City for a second time to try his luck again. But an incident occurred that kept her from doing this. At a rehearsal, Warner humiliated her in front of the whole cast and crew "with insulting words and a heartless tone." She ran from the stage to her dressing room, sobbing. People agreed that another man was courting her affections and Warner had become jealous. Warner left without her and she stayed to perform in the last play "Waiting for the Verdict" alone.

She had had a few weeks break after Warner left while another stock company put on a play in between. But on the opening night of the play in which she was the lead, she became very ill. She did finish the play but went home that night and took to her bed. Annie Lockhart was severely wounded in the heart and had received a wound from which she could not recover. "She only lived 5 weeks after this and the cause of her sudden decline and death was more or less a mystery, for up to this time she was a hale, hearty woman, in the very prime of life. She was laid tenderly by loving hands and hearts, whom she had never known until eight months before, but whom she had endeared to her by her sweet, womanly ways. Many a tear was shed and genuine sorrow felt when Annie Lockhart was laid away in Mt. Olivet." She died on November 18, 1869, just a few weeks after the love of her life had left her, among strangers who had taken her in, and had been buried in a town that was not her home and in a resting place paid for by those who bought her costumes and other possessions. Annie Lockhart literally died of a broken heart. (Ibid, p.61)

One of the dresses belonging to Annie Lockhart was sold to the John T. Caine family. It seems that stage actress Annie Lockhart, wore this yellow brocade silk dress as her favorite. She had come to Salt Lake City from England to perform in a play at the Salt Lake Theatre. And when she died so suddenly and so young, she had not left any money for a funeral and all her costumes were sold in Salt Lake City to pay for it. Caine bought the dress for his daughters and the gown was worn on various occasions by his different daughters and then passed down through the family line. The gown ended up in the Daughters of the Utah Pioneers Museum rather than having been destroyed. John T. Caine and his wife Margaret are buried side-by-side in the Salt Lake City Cemetery. I did eventually find the dress on display at the DUP Museum right in plain sight, probably because I was thinking I would have trouble finding it! It is a very tiny dress and has faded to a light tan color over the years. Perhaps it was Annie Lockhart's ghost that the security cameras caught on tape for more than 5 minutes one recent Halloween week. The face of a young woman floats about in the darkness. Or perhaps that of another young actress, since the main floor is mostly devoted to memorabilia from the old Salt Lake Theatre close to where the face has been seen many times and many Halloweens, recorded by the night cameras. But, the woman's face looked the most like Lydia Gibson's.

Lucille Western

The next female star to stand out was Lucille Western who drew large audiences. However by this time, Young was wanting to maintain wholesome entertainment in his theater, and it was becoming more and more difficult to control what plays were performed and what special effects the traveling troupes brought with them to his theater. Miss Western was the first to challenge this code of ethics, wanting to bring in more excitement and life into her own performances. The play was called "Oliver Twist." In the scene, Bill Sykes kills Nancy (Lucille Western). But in Western's version, the murder was done offstage as Sykes beats her to death with his "ugly stick." A number of wet towels were used to imitate the blows of this stick and a thudding board completed the effect. Lucille also added some bloodcurdling screams, then a loud and very long groan as Bill Sykes stole across the stage, and Western dragged herself after him in slow motion and with her face hidden in her long dark hair. Then Herne, the actor playing "Bill," grabbed her by her hair and dragged her across most of the stage. She then turned towards the audience and threw back her hair to reveal a gory made-up face that made several women in the audience faint, because they were so shocked by it. Western had glued a large but very thin slice of beef onto the side of her face. President Young was extremely angered by this performance, and "It was even rumored afterward that a number of children were birthmarked as the result of," their pregnant mothers witnessing such a thing. Young sent messages all over the city not to attend the play and the managers could not put on the play again in deference to Young.

Lucille Western, however, continued to be daring and innovative. In her next play, she dressed as a male, a ragged cavalier. In this play, however, it was apparent to her audience she was quite drunk when she and the hero got stranded on a deserted island. The play was ironically called "Foul Play." At one point, they both had to climb a high cliff to look for a rescue ship. The poor male actor by now had realized that Western wasn't in any condition to climb the stage cliff, which were often pretty shaky affairs in those days. Lucille was also slurring her lines. On the very first step she took with the hero trying to steady her, she tumbled down and landed on her knees on the stage. She staggered to her feet and spoke her next lines but the audience couldn't understand anything she said. Realizing how bad the situation was, the stage manager just sent the rescue ship on stage early and ended the scene. Unfortunately, the play had one more scene after this in a courtroom and the audience probably stayed just to see what would happen next. The play only had to be performed one more night.

The star, James Herne, suddenly got ill and could not go on for the last night, even though Western's part was being played by someone else. A lot of people thought that perhaps Mr. Herne was just too embarrassed to go on with a novice actress and had already been embarrassed enough by last night's events on stage. He was also stressed out enough to be both physically and mentally exhausted. Herne was rushed to a doctor close to the theater, seeming to be very ill for real. The doctor proceeded with bleeding him of a quart of blood, bandaged his wound, fed him a stimulant and then told the men who had taken him there to get him to his hotel and then to bed. Lucille Western, still not recovered from her performance the night before, ran out hysterical when she saw her "Jimmie" and exclaimed, "Oh, Jimmie, I wish we were home with mother!" She moaned and prayed for Herne, who did recover. Lucille Western never came back to Salt Lake City, but James Herne did in 1874, performing in Salt Lake and in Ogden, before moving on to San Francisco where he became a stage manager.

One of the early performers at the Salt Lake Theatre was George D. Chaplin. He mainly did children's parts and then young adult parts before he went to New York to try his luck on the big stage there. He had always been a chubby boy and as a young man had weighed about 215 pounds. George Pyper, on a trip to New York many years later had learned that Chaplin was now 76 years old and retired from the stage. Pyper looked him up and discovered that now he weighed about 295 pounds, but he did not mention just how tall the actor was. They sat about all afternoon reminiscing about the various memories they both had about the old theatre. Then Chaplin mentioned the great stage actress Lucille Western. "He remembered the time when Lucille Western was prevented from continuing the play of 'Oliver Twist.' Chaplin met her (in New York) sometime after. She was excited over the 'Oliver Twist' incident, and told Chaplin about the withdrawal of the play, and how she was much incensed against Brigham Young for his action." (Ibid, Romance of the Old Theatre, p. 211).

Annie Ward – Stanley Livingston – Jimmy Harris

The romance of the theater brought about yet another poignant story some years later when Jimmy Harris arrived in town. Accompanying him was his wife or fiancée, Annie Ward. Annie had once been beautiful, but smallpox had ravaged her face, leaving deep pit marks all over it. On stage, she covered her face with lots of grease paint and presented herself as beautiful whenever she performed, wearing veils otherwise in public. Rumor had it that Annie had been the fiancée of the great African explorer, Henry Stanley of "Stanley and Livingston" fame. But he had caught, what in those days was simply called, "the African fever," and had died just before they could be married. But checking the facts, this story was probably pure fabrication. She had sought solace in her close friendship with Jimmy Harris and they were so close, in fact, that when they traveled they roomed together. When they got to Salt Lake City and secured a room together, the landlord soon discovered that they were not married. This rooming house was across the street from the St. Marks Church, which still stands today.

Jimmy and Annie were run out of two more boarding houses in town, even though they were "...in a community where many of the men were living with a plurality of wives and they had the idea it was a sort of Oneida community here; free love, etc...' Jimmy Harris' got a 'hunch' from someone that he would have to marry Annie or sever the alliance altogether, as the Mormons would not stand for anything else. It was even intimated that he might be indicted for 'lascivious cohab,' which so terrified him that he suddenly ceased his relationship with Annie altogether." And in those days this sort of threat wasn't to be taken lightly, as the 'hunch' was probably much more of a threat than this and might possibly have been a threat to his very life. (Ibid, p.72).

While Jimmy Harris gradually ingratiated himself with the Mormons, eventually having his run of the ladies who attended the theater for "courting" purposes, Annie was shunned by everyone, on and off the stage. But there were many who also thought he should have married Annie and made an honest woman of her. Annie Ward's stay in Salt Lake was made so unpleasant for her, that she left alone as soon as her engagement at the theater was finished. A year later, she was in St. Louis, her heart broken by both her close friend Jimmy and the people who had shunned her. She died there, several months later, alone and wretched. Jimmy married one of Brigham Young's pretty daughters and was given the job of managing the Salt Lake Theatre. Harris and his wife eventually moved to New York were Jimmy Harris had wealthy relatives. They had five children to whom he gave his real name of Ferguson. Harris had taken a stage name only to hide his shameful profession of acting from his wealthy relations. The Fergusons lived there among his wealthy family members for the rest of their lives.

After the Pauncefort – Bell fiasco and the Annie Ward- Jimmy Harris incident, a new rule must have been added to the theatre rules because these were the rules that had stood for a long time: no gentleman's hats in the green room, punctuality at rehearsals, ten minutes for costume changes, no drinking, a fine of one dollar for making the stage wait, a week's salary for leaving a performance early, improper language was a fine of one dollar, refusing to play a part given was also a fine of one dollar, no payment was given for sick leave, one could not address the audience directly, no noise was allowed backstage during a performance, mutilated scripts or books were a fine of fifty cents, no copying of manuscripts was allowed, actors had to provide part of their costumes, actors not engaged in the night's performance had to be on call anyway in the green room all evening, no smoking allowed in the theater, and any new rule found necessary could be added immediately once it had been posted in the green room. The new rules added shortly after the Harris/Ward affair included such things as no lady's servants could be seen behind the scenes, no children were allowed in the theater except on required business and "It is particularly requested that every lady and gentleman will report to the prompter their respective places of residence." Thereby taking care of the cohabitation between performers in local lodgings with those couples not married. (Ibid, Lindsay, p.121-122).

Susie Spencer & Ed Marden

In the 1880 to 1882 seasons, another young and tiny but beautiful actress, named Susie Spencer, joined the local stock company and got her big break as the star in "The Little Rebel." Her petite stature made it easy for her to play children, so that made her quite a versatile character actor as well as a leading lady. If one recalls, Shirley Temple played the part in the movie version of the littlest rebel. Miss Spencer was very talented and was moving up the stock company ladder with more and more leading parts. Then she met Ed Marden. "Marden was one of the Cogswell party who came from California by way of southern Utah, and waiting on Brigham Young, informed him that they had received a revelation (via the Planchette route) instructing them to come to Salt Lake and join the Mormon Church, as it was the only true and authorized Church." (Ibid, Lindsay, p.109).

All the family members were actors and were immediately installed in the Salt Lake Theatre stock company after they joined. Ed Marden immediately became infatuated with Susie Spencer. He romanced her with his much more sophisticated background, and eventually married her. Jimmy Harris was managing the theater at the time and he and Ed became fast friends, having both come to Utah gentiles and having joined the Mormon Church. They both married Mormon girls, but Ed drifted away right after Harris quit managing the theater. While Jimmy Ferguson took his wife and family with him, Ed moved back to his east coast family alone. He left the Mormon Church and his actress wife behind him. No one ever heard from Ed again, but in this instance, Susie recovered from the desertion and two years later married a wealthy banker, Mr. Rice, from the mining town of Frisco, Utah. According to all reports, she lived with Mr. Rice for several years, quite happily until she died "still quite young in years."

Sarah Ann Sutton Cooke

Sarah Ann Sutton Cooke rounds out the best stories of the actors and actresses of the old Salt Lake Theatre because she was a Mormon convert who became a gentile in her later life. She also became one of the oldest well-known actresses in the city. Sutton lived in Salt Lake City for 34 years. She taught music, acting, performed on the stage in many plays and became widowed when her husband became the first policeman to be killed in the line of duty in the city. The wagon train she was traveling with made a temporary stop in Salt Lake City on their way to the gold fields of California but Sarah never left. She converted to Mormonism while staying in the city and ended up teaching at Brigham Young's school and performing in both the Social Hall and later in the Salt Lake Theatre. Born in 1808, she had married William Cooke when she was just eighteen in England. The Cookes immigrated to America in 1828 and during this time Sarah Ann lost two of her sons who were both quite young. They then moved to North Carolina where Sarah lost her first little girl as well.

After two years there they spent the next five years in Iowa and then in 1852 the family set out for California. They eventually ended up in Council Bluffs where they met their first Mormons. Arriving in Salt Lake City in 1852, they were weary of traveling and decided to stay until spring. Finding the Mormons very hospitable and kind, by September of 1852, Sarah had been baptized into the Mormon Church. By October of that year she was also performing in plays with the Deseret Dramatic Association. This association had over one hundred local members, although only ten were actually actors and actresses who performed on the stage, while the rest of them formed the production staff. In 1852, the Social Hall was built and Sarah even had her own room in it to teach music. Brigham Young bought her a "superior English piano and melodeon for her use in the hall." ("Sarah Ann Sutton Cooke" by Patricia Lyn Scott, Worth Their Salt, Too: More Notable But Often Unnoted Women of Utah, Utah State University Press: Logan, Utah, 2000, p.8-9).

Sarah Sutton Cooke
Utah State Historical Society

Many who were lucky enough to take music lessons from her were quoted as saying that she had left her stamp or imprint of strength and versatile gifts on young and old alike. Sarah was one of the few women to be voted into various plays by committee. "The actors had little experience none had education for the stage or came from theatrical families. Few continued as professional actors anywhere. Forty-seven percent played no more than ten performances, and 22 percent played no more than one season. Fifty percent were between the ages of twenty-six and forty; Sarah was forty-four. The first season ran from the opening on 17 January to 23 February 1853, playing every night for the first week, and then on Wednesdays and Saturdays. Sarah performed in three plays that season and in all subsequent seasons through 1856. She acted character roles 'exceptionally well,' but it was in the music that she made her chief contribution. For example, not only did Sarah play the role of Widow Melonette in "Lady of Lyons" she 'rendered her services on the piano' after the performance."(Ibid, Scott, p.9).

Her husband William was soon able to travel again at this point and her grown children and their families left Salt Lake City and headed for California, where they settled, spending the rest of their lives in that state and also in Nevada. Sarah waited for William to return and stayed in Salt Lake City with her chosen people for the rest of her life. Her children always spoke kindly of their stay with the Mormons in those brief few years. Her husband William tried to get Sarah to join them but she never did. William did go on to the gold fields in Australia and was even baptized a Mormon after his wife urged him in letters to investigate the faith there. He proselytized in both Australia and New Zealand and even opened a new mission in New Zealand in 1854. William, at the age of fifty-three returned to Salt Lake City with a seven-stop organ in tow. It had been dismantled and placed in six large tins cases to protect it from the ocean voyage. The organ then came by mule teams from California and was installed in the old adobe tabernacle on Temple Square. Sarah was its organist for the early choir for the next ten years.

Finally, William and Sarah were re-married for "time and all eternity" in the Endowment House in 1857. Sarah also became Brigham Young's private music instructor for his many children and wives in the Lion House. She presented some very popular plays of the day and had to present extra performances because they were so popular. By 1858, William was working as a policeman and city jailer. In October of that year, a recently arrived teamster trying to help some of the prisoners in the jail to escape shot William in the thigh. William lingered for six days and then passed away on October 18th, having had his femur bone severely fractured. Sarah, at the age of fifty, after thirty-two years of marriage, was now a widow. She then opened a school for girls where she lived in the Fourteenth Ward building. Brigham Young then found a small home for her and bought it as well, so that she could live separate from where her school was located. She soon closed this school and opened a music school instead. Another musician had arrived from England and opened two singing classes, taking all of Sarah's business away from her and forcing her to close both her schools, even though she had been teaching music for many years in the city.

In 1862, the Salt Lake Theatre opened its doors and Sarah Cooke played the part of Gavotte in "Pride of the Market" on opening night. She continued to perform in seventeen more plays until 1863. She did some innovative musical staging during this time for the theater performers. But in 1864, she decided that this was too much for her and asked to retire from the stage. The average age of the theater performers was from seventeen to twenty-three and Sarah was now fifty-six. However, in 1865 she was asked to perform one last time in a play called "The Porter's Knot," with her and Hiram Clawson in the leads. As Sarah was leaving her dressing room, she tripped and fell down the stairs breaking her arm and dislocating her hip. The play was cancelled and Brigham Young himself offered to place his hands on her arm to heal it before the doctor arrived. Sarah, by this time, was questioning her faith and refused Brigham Young's healing hands. Her arm never fully healed and Young always admonished her that she had not had the faith that she needed to be healed by him.

The public so loved Sarah that they raised the money on their own for her to have a piano to teach music in her home rather than using the one Brigham Young had bought for her in his private school. She never performed publicly again but continued to teach music lessons in her own home until she passed away. Sarah might have lived quietly and unobtrusively after this, but instead, a great deal of conflict developed between her and Brigham Young. It was started by an ownership dispute regarding the home provided for Sarah after her husband's death. Another man came by and told her that he intended to purchase her home from Brigham Young and had been given permission to do so. Sarah wrote to Young reminding him that he had guaranteed her ownership of this home for her old age and that she had even offered to purchase the home but Young had declined to take her money. Instead of agreeing with her view of things, that she had been given ownership of this land and home, Brigham Young offered to sell her the land and home for a price that she could not afford. She was then contacted by the city to pay $2,000 to them out of the $4,000 that Young had requested. Sarah made one payment and then decided to fight both the city and the Mormon Church for the next five years.

Sarah got involved with the Godbeites, a group of intellectual Mormons questioning Brigham Young and his ideal community. She then began lecturing and giving speeches at the Liberal Institute in town and spoke against polygamy, women's lack of freedom within the church, and also spoke about the "vindictiveness" of the Mormon leader's "bitter denunciation of their enemies and prayers for their destruction." The court case to regain her property had also begun. Young never attended any of the court cases. Sarah testified that she had never rented the place but had been given it as a gift for her years as both a music teacher in Brigham's household and as an actress in his theater. The first court case was decided in favor of Sarah but Brigham Young appealed to the Supreme Court after several other legal maneuvers did not work. The Supreme Court dismissed Young's appeal and eventually he had to pay the court costs in a judgment by the court of $2,986. It was then that Sarah apostatized from her Mormon faith. She still had one more court case to go, however, to acquire the deed to her property. On August 17, 1878, after another seven-year battle, Sarah finally won her home free and clear and had become the first person to win a civil judgment against Brigham Young. The home stayed in her family for another half century.

Sarah spent her final years working to establish a good library in town and became a leader in the anti-polygamy movement as well. She personally aided Ann Eliza Young to escape from the city, who was in great fear for her life at the time, being one of two wives to divorce the prophet. After this dangerous escape, Sarah told Eliza to "Keep up a brave heart and think of the work before you." Sarah also accompanied Ann Eliza for the first two months of her lecture tour and then returned to Salt Lake City. She joined the Library club, the Lady's Literary Club and the exclusive "Blue Tea" women's society, which was, organized for intellectual culture and broad charity concerns. Sarah was also a founding member of the Anti-Polygamy Society in Salt Lake City. This society was composed of one-third Gentiles, one-third women who had been "driven out of the Mormon Church" and one-third Mormon women. "Sarah devoted the rest of her life to the anti-polygamy crusade." (Ibid, Scott, p.24-25).

She divided her time between her family, her political actions and her church, because her children were still members of it. She never lost her faith in God or in the essential truths of her religion. She worked as a dressmaker in her final years to support herself along with financial help from her children. She joined the Congregational Church in 1880. In 1885 she died at the age of seventy-seven, still being a woman of deep religious nature, the best of mothers and being revered both by her family and many others as having fought for what she believed in. She left her mark on Utah in many ways, only one of them as an actress.

Where Did Some of Them Go?

Some of the actors and actresses at the old Salt Lake Theatre did end up going onstage in New York City, some even on Broadway: Sara Alexander, Lisle Leigh, Blanche Kendall, and Maude Adams. Channing Pollock, a Salt Lake City resident for a while, who did become famous as a Broadway playwright. Most of the local actors and actresses, and only a few are mentioned in Whitney's text, retired to some other sort of life off the stage in Utah. John C. Graham went into the newspaper business in Provo, Utah. Nellie Colebrook appeared at rare intervals on stage over the years in Salt Lake City. John S. Lindsay traveled throughout the west with his daughters, acting and wrote his memories of the old Salt Lake Theatre in a book before he died. Comedian W.C. Dunbar founded The Salt Lake Herald with two partners and quit acting altogether. Margaret Clawson stayed home to care for her brood and H.E. Bowring settled in Brigham City, Utah. Henry Maiben retired, but occasionally came out of retirement to do a role or two with the Home Dramatic Club in the 1880s. The only actor who stayed in the theater, his entire life in Utah, was Phil Margetts. Margetts continued acting, mainly in Salt Lake City, until he was just too old or too ill to do it anymore. . (The Drama In Utah: the story of the Salt Lake Theatre by Horace G. Whitney, Deseret News: Salt Lake City, Utah, 1915)

Additional Salt Lake Theatre Performers From Utah Not Already Mentioned:

Before 1863: Sarah Badlam, Edgar Blodgett, William Glover, Joseph L. Heywood, Mrs. J.L. Heywood, William Hyde, Sarah Lawrence Kimball, George Nebeker, John Pyper, Ensign Rich, Henry P. Richards, John L. Smith, and W.D. Young.

The Men from 1863 to 1890: C.F. Atwood, C. Banks, E. Bowen, Joseph Bull, David Candland, R.C. Camp, George C. Chaplin, J. Conrad, J. Curtis, Theo. Curtis, S.W. Darke, E. Debenham, James L. Derr, C.M. Donelson, William C. Dunbar, J.E. Evans, W. Ford, M. Forster, Joseph Fretwell, George D. Grant, H. Green, TC. Griggs, J.M. Hardie, H. Haines, Harry Horsely, J.E. Hyde, H.W. Issacson, Zebulon Jacobs, John B, Kelly, S. A. Kenner, A. Martin. N.V. Martin, Martin Lenzi, Richard Matthews, A, Merrill, Henry McEwan, D. J. McIntosh, Mr. McIntyre, W. H. Miles, W. Moffat, A.E. Moore, R. F. Neslen, Allan Page, R.H. Parker, Logan Paul, W. Paul, J. Priestly, Harry Rainforth, Ensign Rich, G. Henry Snell, E.L. Sloan, George Spencer, John D. Spencer, S.D. Sirrine, James Smithies, James W. Spiring, T.J. Stevens, W.H. Stevens, Harry Taylor, George Teasdale, J.A. Thompson, Orson F. Whitney, C. Wilkinson, E.G. Woolley Jr., William Wright, and Young, John W.

The Women from 1863-1890: Mrs. Childs, Lottie Claridge, Miss Croxall, Maggie Curtis, Maria Davis, Miss Elredge, Miss Evans, Miss Foreman, Mrs. Grist, Keetie Heywood, Minnie Le Compte, Mrs. E. Lindsay, Mrs. Agnes Lynch, Mrs. Henry Maiben, Mrs. Mason, Mrs. Mattson, Miss Rebecca Neibaur, Miss Lizzie Nunn, Miss. I. Park, Miss C. Perkes, Miss Lizzie Platt, Mrs. R. Platt, Mrs. Roberts, Maggie Thomas Romney, Mrs. Shoufeld, Miss E. Snow, Miss Clara Stenhouse, Mrs. T.B. H. Stenhouse, Mrs. E. Thompson, Mrs. Tyler, Jean Clara Walters, Mrs. DeWitt Waugh, Miss Webb, Miss Whitehead, Ella Wheeler Wilcox, and Mrs.Woodmansee.

<u>Zion's Musical Society 1880-1882</u>: David O. Calder, Lizzie Edmonds, Henry Gardner, Duncan McAllister, Annie Midgely, J.R. Morgan, W.D. Owen, Libbie Sheets, and John D. Spencer.

<u>Evans-Stephens Grand Opera Company 1888-1889</u>: Bessie Dean Allison, Robert C. Easton, Heber C. Goddard, Nellie Druce Pugsley, Evan Stephens, Lizzie Thomas Edward.

<u>Salt Lake Opera Company 1897</u>: Lucy Gates Bowen, Margaret Romaine Browning, Hazel Dawn, Bessie Dean, Ada Dwyer, Lizzie Thomas Edward, Sallie Fisher, Viola Pratt Gillette, Heber C. Goddard, Nellie Druce Pugsley, Willard E. Weihe, Horace G. Whitney.

<u>Popular singers from the 1800s to 1930s</u>: Nellie Thatcher-Andersen, Lucy Emma Gates Bowen, Mabel Cooper, Hugh W. Dougall, Ada Dwyer, Edna Evans, Horace S. Evans, Alfred L. Farrell, Sallie Fisher, Fred C. Graham, Wanda Lyon, Emma Ramsey-Morris, Sigrid Pedersen, George D. Pyper, Hazel Taylor-Peery, "Lennie" Louise Savage Riter, Leuella Ferrin-Sharp, John D. Spencer, the Tout sisters, Irene Kelly-Williams.

ANNIE KISKADDEN & MAUDE ADAMS
BRIGHAM'S PROTÉGÉ & MAUDE'S PETER PAN

Julia Ann Banker came from New York. A Mormon missionary came through the town of Chateau, which is seven miles from the Canadian border, and fell in love with one of Julia Ann's daughters, Asenath. In 1841, Elder Duncan, blessed with the second sight, saw a tragedy in a vision, where one of Asenath's brothers would be kicked in the head by a horse and killed. When the event took place later, the Banker family accepted Duncan as one of their own. Duncan married Asenath when she was old enough and took her to Nauvoo as his newly baptized Mormon wife. Twenty-year old, Asenath brought along her sister Julia Ann, Julia Ann Banker's daughter and namesake, who was only fourteen years old. Their parents did not join the Mormon Church, being strong Baptists, but the younger daughter, Julia Ann, was baptized into the Mormon Church while living in Iowa.

Annie "Senath" Adams

Maude with Jim Kiskadden, her father

In 1846, Asenath's younger sister, Julia Anna Banker married Barnabas L. Adams. Barnabas had come from a famous family with two presidents, John Adams and John Quincy Adams. Julia Ann had an ancestor, John Howland, who came to America on the Mayflower. Julia Ann became one of the only three women who came to Utah in the first pioneer train with Brigham Young, carrying her second child. They settled in the Cottonwood area near present day Holladay. Eventually, they built a small adobe home at Seventh East and Eighth South. Julia Ann eventually had seven children, six of whom survived to adulthood. Barnabas married two other wives, which made Julia Ann the one responsible as head wife, for all the wives and children if something happened to Barnabas. They lived on a twenty acre farm, called "The Big Field" and Julia Ann worked hard all the daylight hours of every day. In 1865, Barnabas died. The three wives were very close to each other but survival became even harder as time went by. Julia Ann asked her parents to come out and assist them, which they did. However, while staying with her, they induced several family members to leave the Mormon Church and return east with them.

"Little Maudie"

Maude as a Sausy Wench!

Teen Actress

Lobby Card of Maude Adams

Julia Ann's daughter, Annie Asenath Adams, was born in Little Cottonwood Canyon on November 8th, 1848. Her sister Julia Thankful Adams had been born not long before this in August of 1847. She married a Young, making her part of the Brigham Young royalty and the oldest child of Julia Ann Adams. Joseph Watson Young was a nephew of Brigham Young who married two women. He died young of sunstroke at age 44. Julia Thankful, lived in Southern Utah in Kane County for several years, and then moved back to Salt Lake City. She also never remarried.

Julia Ann Adams and Julia Thankful Young lived as widows for the rest of their lives, near each other in Salt Lake City by where Liberty Park is today. They raised all their children on their own and Julia Ann had only one embitterment. While Brigham Young owed a great deal of finances to her departed husband, Barnabas, and did help her build a new two story brick home on the same property, Young still owed quite a bit to her family. She penned a letter to the new church president John Taylor who apparently did offer some sort of compensation that required her to sell her farm. As a result of these actions, Julie Ann's attitude toward her church changed.

She moved to Rigby, Idaho with her three remaining sons, some of whom became Methodists. When they all left home, Julia Ann returned to Salt Lake City and moved in with her sister Asenath. In the meantime, Annie Asenath Adams grew up with an avid interest in the theater. It had been the practice, even in Nauvoo, to have a theatrical entertainment every Friday night.

Annie Adams began her acting career at the age of eight when she got to read a part for a Friday night entertainment in the Salt Lake Valley. Eventually, with the help of Brigham Young, she was acting on the stage of the old Salt Lake Theatre. She made her debut performance there as Grace Otis in "The People's Lawyer" in 1864. The leading lady was none other than Julia Dean Hayne, who had just arrived for her season of performances at the theater. Annie Adams always spoke of how much she admired Hayne and how much she learned about acting that year from Mrs. Hayne. Annie continued to perform at the old Salt Lake Theatre regularly in various roles until she married.

"One important accession there was to the company just before this engagement, was that of Miss Annie Asenath Adams. Miss Adams made her debut on the 25th of July, 1865, (the same night Julia Dean Hayne and the Potter Company arrived in Salt Lake), in the character of Grace Otis Shingle in the 'People's Lawyer,' W.C. Dunbar being the 'Solon Shingle' on the occasion. Her maiden effort proved very successful and satisfactory to the management, and during Julia Dean's long engagement she proved to be a valuable acquisition to the stock company. Adams made rapid progress in the dramatic art, and before the close of the season had obtained a prominent position in the company which she held with credit to herself and satisfaction to the public until 1874, when the stock company was virtually retired to give place to the 'combination' system which then came into vogue." (The Mormons and the Theater, or, the History of Theatricals in Utah, by John Shanks Lindsay, Century Printing: Salt Lake City, Utah, 1905, p.90)

In Utah, "it was always rumored that Brigham Young was so smitten with Maude's mother that he wanted her as one of his wives... Maude's mother, Annie Adams was a long time member of the troupe. Presumably having fended off Young's importunities, she fell for an itinerant actor, James Kiskadden. They married.... The young family took to the road." "(Maude Adams: Utah's Most Illustrious daughter" by Pat Bagley, The Salt Lake Tribune Sunday, July 2, 2006)

Annie Adams said of her acting years at the old Salt Lake Theatre that those years occupied a most affectionate place "in her recollections." "As a girl, I watched its walls grow up from the ground. I saw its doors open to the public on that memorable night in March 1862, and with delight beheld the actors and actresses appear in their parts from time to time after the formal opening took place. My father hauled timber from the canyons to go into the great building and with him I frequently visited it and became acquainted with the workmen employed on the structure."

"My sister and I went to school in the first and tenth wards, and it was after a school exhibition at the latter place where with Logan Paul we played a burlesque entitled "The Lady of the Lions" that I received an invitation to come up to the Salt Lake Theatre and give a reading to the managers of the house, John T. Caine and H. B. Clawson (Brigham Young's son-in-law). No one can picture my agitation. I was hardly seventeen and I remember urging my mother to let me wear my longest dress in order that I might not be thought too girlish. My father took me on the stage where I was introduced to John T. Caine, David McKenzie, and W. C. Dunbar. They gave the play of "Ernest Maltravers" to read, and some of them went into the front of the house, while I stood on the stage reading lines of the lady's part, while Mr. McKenzie took the book and read those of the leading man. Mr. Dunbar and Mr. Caine would frequently call out their comments; and I judge the trial was satisfactory, for three days afterwards; I was notified that I was expected to play the part of Grace Otis in 'The People's Lawyer,' later known as 'Salon Shingle.'"

"What a wonderful night that was I made my first acquaintance with the interior of the old theatre, its costuming rooms, its barbershop, and all the paraphernalia of its interior, the most complete, I believe, of any in those days. Mrs. Bowring had charge of the ladies' costuming room, and Robert Nelson the gentlemen's. George Ottinger made me up; Mr. Squires, the barber, curled my hair; and Mr. Nelson assisted in touching up my general appearance. Everything was furnished for the actors; from the supplies in the house, from jewels down to shoes. Just before the curtain went up, we would all assemble in the Green Room and pass under the stage manager's eye to see if we fulfilled all the requirements of our parts."

"When the traveling stars came along, we were especially busy. One of my earliest experiences was with T. A. Lyne with whom I played Lady Macbeth just after I was seventeen. I recall well the bashfulness with which I approached certain lines in the Tragedy, and Mr. Lyne stared when I declined to repeat them. Sometime later, John McCullough came along and also played Mac Beth. I again resolutely declined to speak the lines written by Shakespeare, and while he tried to urge me at rehearsals, he very kindly said nothing when the night came and I left them out. He had a wonderful memory that man McCullough. Years later, after I was a married woman and had much more experience, he came to Salt Lake and again Mac Beth was put up as the bill. Almost the first thing he said at rehearsal was, 'Well, are you going to speak those lines tonight?' and I laughingly answered that time had changed my views and I thought I would." (Newspaper Article, Annie Adams, "Green Room Memories," Family History Book, Kenneth L. Rasmussen, Editor, p.137)

"I'll never forget my first experience as a boy. John T. Caine found me crying in the wings and tried to console me by saying, "Why, what are you crying for? You're the best looking boy I've got."

"My first long part was that of Geraldine in 'Green Bushes' with Julia Dean Hayne. I had been seven months on the stage when I played Lady Mac Beth with David McKenzie in the role of Mac Duff. How frightened I was that night, and how the parchment shook in my hands! The house was crowded and they gave me a royal reception. After the sleepwalking scene, David McKenzie said, 'Well I can't read with you.'"

"We never used to know how we were going to be cast for the various plays until our parts were given us, which was sometimes done by the call boy going around, and at other times the parts were left on the table in the Green Room. You can depend upon it—there were many disappointed faces when they discovered their lots." (The Romance of the Old Playhouse by George Pyper, The Seagull Press: Salt Lake City, Utah, 1928, p. 138)

"I remember that during one of those early sessions there was quite an excitement in the city over spiritualism. Rapping's were frequently heard, and it was said even in the new theatre unusual sounds were heard. Some of the people who were interested tried to deceive me and make me believe that my husband had written a certain letter of a compromising nature, but when the 'spirits' wrote a message they spelled Kiskadden with a "C" and the fraud was exposed."

"I was very much impressed with the manner in which every detail connected with the theatre was carried out. We had the customers to dress us; the artist to make us up, the hairdressers, and everything that we do not have now in any theatre. This has been especially called to my mind in traveling around and observing how indifferently they are in looking after the comfort of the people who do the work. The Salt Lake Theatre always gave us fine dressing rooms, which cannot be said of many theaters now, though they are generally improving throughout the country."

"In the old days, by order of President Young, a carriage always called for the ladies of the company, taking them to and from their homes free of charge. This was done even for rehearsals." (Ibid, Pyper, p. 139)

Four years after her debut at the Salt Lake Theatre, Miss. Adams was married to Mr. James H. Kiskadden on August 15, in 1869. But this marriage had not taken place without a great deal of rivalry and consternation on the part of everyone involved. "Senath" as her family called her, was not only a favorite with the public but she had a number of ardent admirers. Besides a rivalry for her affections between several members of the company, some of whom were already married and therefore out of the running, at least as much as she was concerned, there were two standouts among the eligible bachelors in town. Neither of these men were actors, both were tall, dark, handsome and while charming, they were both gentiles. Annie new one thing for sure, she was not going to marry an already married man. She had seen enough of that to make her dread it.

Jack O'Neil was beyond question the handsomer of the two men. He was a great dresser and was one of the most attractive looking men in Salt Lake City. He was very much infatuated with Annie, as was Jim Kiskadden. Jim was dashing, big, manly, and had a determined air about things. He had a good salary; he dressed well and always had a large diamond on the front of his linen shirts. He was a champion billiard player and seemed to be a good bet when it came to being a good provider. O'Neil, on the other hand, was what they called in those days a "professional sport" or gambler and had no profession to speak of. The rivalry between these two men for the affections of Annie got so heated that at one point people in town thought there would be a duel between these two men over Annie's hand in marriage. The worst part for Annie's family was that neither man was a Mormon. Annie came from a very staunch Mormon family that would consider her marriage to either man akin to apostasy. And of the two men, it was Jim who was extremely outspoken about his distaste for the Mormon faith, or any organized religion at all.

James Kiskadden (Kis-kay-den) was a gentile from back east who had come out to work in the Alta mines; however he had performed in vaudeville at one time. Going to see Annie Adams perform almost every night, he asked his brother, a Salt Lake banker, to give him a permanent position as a bank clerk so he would have something to offer Annie when he asked her to marry him. James was dark, handsome, charming, and could hold an entire room of women enthralled with his poetic eyes and handsome looks. Annie married him in 1869 and James would always boast that "She had the prettiest legs this side of the Mississippi." (Family History Book, edited by Kenneth L. Rasmussen)

Annie was not the least bit appalled by the gloomy and hopeless pictures that some of her friends were kind enough to paint for her. She went ahead and married the man that she had set her heart on and stayed with him. Annie Adams was disfellowshipped from her church for marrying a gentile, and took a great fall from grace, having been one of Brigham Young's favorite actresses. She had actually been courted by Brigham Young at one point, with his hoping that she would become one of his wives. This set her against ever being a Mormon again, but did not prevent her from continuing to perform at the Salt Lake Theatre.

Two years later, Annie had still-born twin boys. One year after this, she gave birth to Maude in her mother's adobe house and "Little Maudie" turned out to be the only child she would ever have. The Kiskaddens' moved to the then called Stephenson's cottage on State Street. Annie was traveling throughout the west at this time and Maude was with her father, of whom she was very fond. Maude was born in a narrow, two-story adobe with a kitchen and laundry lean to, on the side. The house was near Liberty Park at 7th East and 8th South. Her grandmother, Julia Adams, nicknamed her "Maudie" right after she was born and helped to raise her when her mother was acting. At eight months, when asked to put alphabet blocks together, Maudie spelled her name and taught herself to read by the time she was a year old. Maudie, it was discovered, was not only beautiful but a child prodigy as well. At nine months of age, Maudie made her first appearance on stage at the Salt Lake Theatre, carried in on an old-fashioned china meat platter. Legend has it that this was her first appearance on the stage, but actually she had appeared before this as an even younger infant.

The unofficial story about Maude's first appearance on the stage and the real one is that Phil Margetts had a grotesque looking rag baby provided to him by the property man after he had asked the man to provide a real baby. The property man replied that he had been unable to procure a live baby because nobody was willing to lend a baby for a stage production. Margetts exclaimed that he couldn't believe that in the whole Territory of Utah, where babies were their best crop, Millard, the property man, had been unable to procure one for his favorite farce. Margetts and the stage manager, Mr. Caine were in a heated discussion over this issue, when Mrs. Kiskadden walked into the center of the stage with her baby in her arms and in a good natured tone said, "Here's Maude, use her!" It was plain luck that Maude was in the theater that night as normally her mother had someone at home to take care of her but this particular evening was the "nurse's" night out and Annie had had to bring her. Maude had been carefully rocked to sleep before her mother could put her make-up on and "Here she was safely stowed away in a safe and quiet corner of the green room, where she [had] been blissfully reposing all through the first play, and was now rather rudely awakened to fill the distressing emergency." (Ibid, Lindsay, p.91).

The official story told in most of Maude Adams biographies goes like this: Annie Adams sometimes carried her baby to the theater dressing room where other company members helped care for her. Maudie lay in a stage cradle watching her mother transform herself into all sorts of character roles. Plays at that time always ended with some sort of short comedy or farce. The night that Maudie made her debut; the play she was in was entitled "The Lost Child." The baby performing in the piece did really well in the first act but when the second act rolled around, the baby began wailing and would not stop. The mother informed them that when her child got it in her head to do this it could last for 2 hours. At which point Mrs. Adams volunteered her baby for the second act. "Miss Maudie" was an immediate hit with the audience, because she had suddenly grown seven months and twenty pounds, making the play even funnier. But she was mainly a hit because the audience roared at this sudden change in age and weight. Maudie crawled forward, rose up on her hands and cooed loudly at the audience. She won the part and the other baby was dismissed.

Maudie became the pet of the green room after this, long before she could walk or talk, often coming with her mother to rehearsals or performances as needed. At the age of two, Maudie retired from the stage for the next three years while she traveled with her mother. When she turned five, she got another part and Annie asked her husband if Maudie could take it. Her father said absolutely not, his daughter was not to go on the stage and make a fool of herself. The precocious little girl overheard their conversation and stood up and replied, "Father, I would like to go on the stage, and Maudie will not make a fool of herself." Finally, her father gave his consent unable to resist this "little apple of his eye." When he was a little boy, Mr. Kiskadden had been fond of a story about a little girl by the name of Maude who was put in a basket and thrown in the Ohio River. He had always wondered what had become of this little girl, and said if he ever married and had a girl she should be named Maude. He was deeply fond of his beautiful little girl.

Maude continued to act in Salt Lake and one story relates her genius as a child prodigy. In a couple of days, Maude had memorized hundreds of lines perfectly to play a little boy named "Little Schneider." Once again, Maudie was a hit and began to be billed as "Little Maudie," and she went on tour with the company to the western states. She was always helping other actors and actresses remember their lines, which became quite irritating to them at times. Her first speaking role appearance was at five years of age in the play "Fritz" starring Joe Emmett at the Bush Street Theatre. Her second was in the play "Hearts and Oak" although the play was called "Chums" instead. When she was six years old she played little "Adriene" in "A Celebrated Case" at the Baldwin Theater. This was her first hit play, and after it ran at the Baldwin, it was taken to Portland, Oregon and performed at the New Market Theatre. It was the first play where Annie Adams and her daughter performed together in speaking parts.

"In the fall of 1874, after connection of nine years with the Salt Lake Theatre, Mrs. Kiskadden and her husband, no longer a cashier, the bank having become a thing of the past, removed to Virginia City, where Miss. Adams was engaged with a number of others from Salt Lake Theatre Company, including a writer, to form a stock company for Mr. John Piper, the Virginia City manager. 'Maudie,' now nearly two years old, formed one of the party. After playing a season with Mr. Piper, Miss. Adams went to San Francisco, where her husband had preceded her some months previous and secured a good position as bookkeeper for the firm of Park and Lacey. Here they made their home for about eight years, and she playing at the San Francisco theaters whenever she could get an engagement, and making occasional excursions with dramatic companies into the neighboring cities." (Ibid, Lindsay, p.91).

What had occurred to cause this mass exodus from the Salt Lake Stock Company was that the new "combination system" had come into vogue. This meant that companies throughout the United States were suffering correspondingly, as "home" companies lost their actors and actresses to more and better paying traveling companies which had become so popular. The Salt Lake Company lost their lead writer, leading man, leading juvenile lady, Miss Adams, the leading lady, Miss Cogswell, and the leading 'heavy.' By 1875, the Salt Lake Company had been almost completely depleted and the local engagements were becoming very intermittent indeed. While only a few intermittent plays could be offered in Salt Lake, the Comstock was in full swing and plays were being presented every night of the week in Nevada and California.

At seven, Maudie was the "reigning child actress of the Pacific Slope." David Belascoe became her manager and recalled her as a "spindle-legged little girl, unusually thin and tall for her age, with a funny little pig tail and one of the quaintest little faces you ever saw.... There was a magnetism about the child, - some traces even then of that wonderfully sweet and charming personality which was to prove such a tremendous advantage to her in the later years." "Never in all my experience have I seen an instance of such unselfish, idolizing devotion as Mrs. Adams displayed for her little girl... Mrs. Adams' love was something quite out of the common... No sacrifice was too great for her to make. Many and many a night, after the long performances and perhaps a whole morning's rehearsals, I have seen Mrs. Adams sitting up till daylight working over some new little gown for Maudie. I mean it in all seriousness when I say that whatever Maude Adams has become today she owes entirely to her mother." (Maude Adams by Action Davies, 1901, p.5)

While the whole family went to live together in San Francisco, to be together while Annie was on tour, James died suddenly. Jim had gone to San Francisco ahead of the family to get a job and a place for them to live. A friend of his talked about the fact that he was not surprised when Jim got sick because of the way he was walking around in the cold damp weather with no hat on, being dead broke, being a stranger in a strange city, and wearing a summer suit, with nothing else warm to wear. San Francisco was cold and foggy and Jim's clothes were decidedly unseasonable. When they reached their destination Jim had to actually ask for a loan from his friend, so that he could find a job and also obtain some warmer clothes. He had some warmer things in his trunk, but had not been prepared for the cold weather in San Francisco. Apparently Jim had a tendency to do this, not paying attention to dressing warmer in the cold weather. His friends felt that this may have contributed to his death several years later, Kiskadden going from a terrible cold to something far worse.

Annie returned to Salt Lake City with Maude. She buried her husband in 1883 in Salt Lake City, and shortly after this, the local dramatic company dissolved. To continue her professional career and support her daughter, Annie went on tour again. She left Maude with her mother and grandmother and sister although when appearing in Salt Lake while on brief visits, her daughter and she appeared on the stage together. Annie Adams returned to Salt Lake City many times in the 1870's and 1880's to perform on stage with those left from the stock company and with the newly formed Home Dramatic Club. She appeared in one play called "Divorce" in which her daughter Maude, then eight, sang between acts. Maude had a beautiful singing voice as well. While living with her grandmother, she used to make up whole plays and used her dolls to perform the parts on her homemade or put together stages.

Maude Adams quit acting in San Francisco at the age of ten when her father died and returned home to stay with her grandmother in Salt Lake City. For four years, she studied at the Presbyterian Collegiate Institute. At fourteen, she was only one year away from graduating with the equivalent of a high school diploma. She was the brightest pupil in the school and the favorite one as well. But Maude wanted to return to the stage and begged her mother to let her. The principal of the school wanted to make her a teacher of elocution at the school, but Annie Adams came and withdrew her from the school to begin guiding her stage career. Within a year, the two of them were in New York City and for a while Annie Adams continued to perform on the stage, with or without her daughter. Shortly after they signed Maude with Charles Frohman, a famous theatrical manager, Annie decided to quit acting, traveled with Maude until she was an established star and then returned to Salt Lake City to take care of her mother, still living with her sister, Asenath Thankful. At the age of 16, Maude joined Ectto Souther's Company in New York. She played many minor parts with some success. Frohman saw her and he was a star maker, he knew genius when he saw it. He spoke with Annie Adams and signed Maude.

After a successful run in her first play, Maude had to choose between two starring roles. The first offer had more money attached to it but it was farce comedy and Maude wanted to be a serious actress. She took the more modest role on the advice of her mother and her manager, Charles Frohman, who was the head of the stock company which had offered her a dramatic role. Neither person realized the amount of fame and fortune this contract would bring to them both. Frohman was an astute manager and eventually Maude Adams's popularity became almost a mania among her fans. Frohman knew he had a gifted, intelligent and imaginative actress on his hands and decided to sign her to star with John Drew, a leading stage star of the day, after only a brief period of working her way up in larger and larger roles in the Stock Company. She acted with John Drew for the next 5 years.

John Drew deserted his company and signed with Frohman, and then Maude Adams was signed to be his leading lady. Drew had played twelve seasons with Ada Rehan as his leading lady and there was at first a public outcry from his fans that he would star opposite "that little thing!" October 3, 1892, was opening night at the Palmer Theatre in New York. The play was entitled "The Masked Ball." Critics praised the play, John Drew, but especially newcomer Maude Adams. Only seen in minor roles before, Maude was now a "star." One critic wrote: "There is one scene in the second act where in order to punish her husband for some anti-nuptial remarks of his, she has to pretend she is drunk.... in order to carry off this scene successfully it was necessary for the wife to appear to be drunk and yet a gentlewoman at the same time."

"Miss Adams achieved the feat, achieved it so successfully that the applause lasted for a full two minutes after she made her exit. If Miss Adams had done nothing else throughout the entire play than that one scene it would have stamped her as a comedienne of the first order. But her scenes of tenderness were equally good, and her alternate rallying and contrition for her artifice in the final scene were rendered with a delightfully delicate touch. The youngest leading lady on the boards, Maude Adams had begun her amazing career." (Ibid, Davies, p.10)

She was described as delicate, slight of physique with a small, spiritual face framed in fair hair, a low sweet voice, a pretty English accent, and a very intuitive way of performing before her audiences. Her next highly successful play was "The Little Minister" which Katherine Hepburn brought so successfully to the screen. She then performed a role which Sara Bernhardt had been identified with. Critics railed on Frohman for attempting this with such a young actress. Bernhardt was performing the role in Paris and Adams performed the same role in New York. While Bernhardt literally "owned" this role, Maude Adams engagement in this play was a longer one. For what she lacked in experience and dramatic force, she made up for in depicting pathos and emotional intuition.

After a run in the play "Quality Street," Maude took a break. Rumors spread that her health was impaired, that she had tuberculosis and that she was dying. None of this was true. She had spent her vacation abroad in 1901. She spent it touring villages and lived in a convent in Paris. She brought back all sorts of sentimental memorabilia from the children of Paris and from her time by the sea; coral, seaweed, drawings, feathers and rocks, hats, scarves and frocks from local pheasants. She had had a vacation before the play but after it she took an entire year off after 17 years of acting, this fueled the rumors even more. The doctor had simply ordered her to rest. She rested at her mountain home at Oneteola Park, near Tannersville, New York, in the Catskills, at Sandy Garth, and at her town house, no. 11 East 4th street, New York. She also went abroad and took a trip up the Nile, a tented journey through the Lybian Desert, ending with a 5-week stint in Jerusalem.

These two separate years off intrigued the author Richard Matheson, and he used these two mysteries to write his fantasy novel Bid Time Return, modeling his main female character after Maude Adams. This novel then became the film "Somewhere in Time." It was soon after Maude's return to the stage that she began her real love affair with her most famous role as Peter Pan. She was the first and only actress ever to claim this role and keep that association throughout all time. Her greatest Shakespearean role was that of Juliet, but her triumph was playing a young man in "L'Aiglou" by Edmond Rostand. The play is about Napoleon's illegitimate son and his sad short life, his railings against both his fate and his caged life.

"James M. Barrie, the distinguished Scottish author, came to New York that winter to discuss play adaptations with Frohman. Frohman had urged Barrie to dramatize his successful novel, "The Little Minister." Barrie had declined because he knew no actress capable of playing Lady Babbie."

"One day Barrie called on Frohman at the Empire Theater. Frohman was out. "Why don't you go downstairs and see "Rosemary" while you're waiting?" Frohman's secretary suggested to the visitor."

"An hour later, Barrie was back in Frohman's office. 'I've found the woman to play Lady Babbie!' He exclaimed. 'Who is that?' asked Frohman, as if he hadn't known all along."

"For her role in "The Little Minister," Maude Adams steeped herself in Scottish backgrounds. She was even accused of subsisting solely on Scotch broth. The play opened in Washington on a wiltingly hot September day. Washington audiences were apathetic."

"The week's gross was disappointing. The play moved to New York under a cloud of failure. On Broadway it was an instantaneous smash. The critics described Miss Adams as "irresistible." "The Little Minister" ran for 300 consecutive performances, 289 of them to standing room only, and grossed $370,000, a record high in that time." (Ibid, <u>Family History Book</u>, Rasmussen)

Frohman knew Maude wanted to try Shakespeare again but he thought she was perfect for Barrie's "Peter Pan." So one day, he simply produced the manuscript and said, "Here's a play for children, by your beloved Barrie," said Mr. Frohman. "I do not think that I will produce it, but you may be interested in reading it." Miss Adams said: "I had not finished the first act before the quaint character of Peter Pan had charmed me. I could feel the presence of the Fairies, and the Indians and the Pirates and the Lost Boys of Never-Never-land, and in the midst of dashing, winsome 'Peter Pan.' When I had reached the last line of the play I had made my decision. I would play the character. When I saw Mr. Frohman again I said, 'You may shelve your Shakespearian plans for the present. I am going to play Peter Pan."

"It was not until then that I recalled a remark which Mr. Barrie had made to me a year before. 'A character is in my mind that has come to me through you and I am going to make a play of it.' When he learned that we were going to produce his play he wrote, 'I want you to know that it was you that inspired the title of the play.' So it was kind of a mental telepathy between Mr. Barrie and Peter Pan and me all the while." (Ibid, Davies, p.14)

"...In 1905 Barrie delivered to Frohman the manuscript of his latest play. "This script is a dream child of mine," he explained to the impresario. "If you don't think it fulfills the terms of our contract, I am giving you an extra play which will be more to your liking."

"Like many an author, Barrie was a poor judge of his own work. The dream child was "Peter Pan," which made a fortune and became an American institution."

"Peter Pan" made Maude Adams a byword in millions of homes. The country took to its heart both the elfin sprite and the actress who endowed the part with such a sense of impish wonder. No matter what other triumphs she was to enjoy, Maude Adams and Peter Pan were to remain inseparably linked in the minds of the country's theater-goers both young and old." (Ibid, Davies, pp.15-16)

Maude Adams became world renown for her role of Peter Pan, and to this day "owns" the role. It was not just her superb intellectual gifts, her intuitive timing, voice and beauty that made her a great actress on the stage. Nor was the longevity of her years performing, it was more than anything her tireless hours and hours of hard work that brought her worldwide recognition. Hours after everyone was gone, Maude Adams could be seen on stage, going over and over her lines and scenes. She never complained of "weariness" and helped her fellow actors get their lines perfect as well. She wore a long brown coat to rehearsal for years. This old worn out coat was her mascot she said. She also became the richest woman on stage at the time. During her first season as a star, she made forty thousand dollars, an amazing sum in those days.

She also made very wise choices with her money. For example, she continued to buy acreage on her farm when she could until she had two hundred acres which included walnut groves, whose profits alone would take care of her in her old age. She bought a 30,000 dollar theater train car to carry the Peter Pan Company on its travels. The car contained a stage they could practice on as they traveled. She owned several properties filled with souvenirs of her travels and a huge library of books.

Maude as "Peter Pan"

Peter Pan Plays his Flute

Maude on Stage as "Peter"

Rare books, first editions, even papyruses from Egypt filled the rooms that were otherwise plain and sparse. Her mother and grandmother lived with her in what many called "the house of silence" in New York City.

On the other hand, her farm was full of what she loved in nature, all kinds of animals, gardens to putter around in, huge fire places, touches of her Scottish ancestry about, and a half a dozen large dogs. There was a large man-made lake on the property, the walnut grove, and flower beds everywhere. This place in the Catskills was her real retreat even if she could only enjoy a single day on the weekend there. She was an excellent horse woman and also enjoyed riding. And she gave many gifts to friends, supporting dozen of charities whose bequests were kept secret. She was also very loyal to her friends in the west and especially in Utah, where she grew up. She kept her old friends and made few new ones. She also had a resort house in Anteora where during the holidays she spent time in a little literary colony there.

It was believed that she had very little of a private life. People said she had two distinct personalities, the person she was on the stage and the person she was in her private life. The only story told of any loves or relationships is the one where a young actor was interested in her and began escorting her and her mother back and forth to the theater. After a while, "Maude's mother said to him, 'I may as well tell you, that you are only wasting your time by these attentions. My daughter has no thought of young men and has no intention of marrying.' This may totally summarize Miss Adams attitude toward marriage. Her thoughts of romance, her close friends say, have always taken the direction of effective stage scenes." Although it was rumored that she was at one time in her career courted for a year by a handsome young fellow actor. (Ibid, Davies, p.15)

Critics described her as elfish, diaphanous, analysis-defying, mysterious, and almost weirdly winsome. "Elusiveness is, perhaps, her dominant note as an actress. Away from the footlights the woman is a recluse. Asceticism is the key note of her life." Maude Adams was as reclusive as a nun, seeking seclusion at all times in her private life. In the shadows of her cloistered life, was a pensive thoughtful repose as though she were haunted by some secret sorrow even when she had a radiant smile on her face. And this was how both her public and private friends saw her, as do the half dozen or so who wrote her many biographies. (Ibid, Davies, p.17)

In her townhouse, there was an oasis of scholastic peace about the place. Dark green was the prevailing color and her favorite author was Herbert Spencer. Green plants were everywhere and her small stark bedroom was like a replica of her convent home at Tours. She always said that self-study was one of the best means of development. "Genius is the talent for seeing things in a straight line without any bend or break or aberration of sight, seeing them as they are, without any warping of vision. Flawless mental sight! That is genius!" (Ibid, Davies, p.18)

Maude Adams had only one religion, although she was raised in one and that was the religion of altruism towards others. There were many stories of her individual acts of kindness towards strangers, besides her many charities and donations to the towns where she had visited or had a home. She took a present to a little girl staying upstairs from where she was while traveling, hearing that the girl was ill. She also performed for the injured soldiers coming home from the front, as well as in Paris, where her traveling company actresses knitted socks for the French soldiers between shows. New York Times critic, Alexander Woolcott, a good friend of Maude's, wrote to her from war torn France in October of 1918, speaking not only of his awe in seeing her perform "Peter Pan" long ago, but also of the hope this fantasy play had brought to a world ravaged by a world war:

"When, as all of us do sometimes, I get very tired of shells and shell-holes, tired of an endless wilderness of crumbled homes, tired of mud, I like to shut my eyes and listen to the music that was used to usher Peter in through the high nursery window, to see Nibs dancing the pillow-dance in the firelight, to wait while Miss Thing comes down the silver stairway to that absurdly perky strain. All that dear music has been with me through more than a year of exile.... I need scarcely have

Maude Adams in "Quality Street"
From Author's Collection

reported all this to, had it not occurred to me insistently the other day that you ought to know the war chroniclers are omitting something salient, when they merely tell you how brave our soldiers have been. Indeed they are brave..." "But what I want you to know is that the fiercest of them is a good deal like Michael slaying a pirate or two. I knew that, the other day, as I stumbled at dawn over an exhausted doughboy that had come out of the line and gone to sleep in his tracks with his face that has yet to meet a razor, pillowed on his gasmask. I wished, then, that you were here and I could introduce you to him. I know him so well. I know that his first-aid kit is gone because he has used it to staunch some other fellow's "wounds in the rain"- a rain, lady, of shrapnel. I know that for his buddy, as he calls his pal, he would gladly lay down his life. I know that the last time he fought for three days and nights with nothing to eat, he didn't complain. You, yourself, at first glance, would see he can't be much more than seventeen. And you would see for yourself, what I am rambling along in an effort to tell you, that the American soldier- I mean the plain, unadorned infantryman- would make his strongest appeal of all to Wendy." (Women Worth Their Salt, "Maude Adams," by Rachelle Pace Castor, edited by Colleen Whitley. Utah State University Press, p.199)

Other altruistic things she did included donating to many charities, founding schools, and during the run of "Peter Pan" in 1913; she donated a huge sum of money to the city of Dayton, Ohio. There had been a terrible flood where over 400 people had died. She donated the money by sending one night's receipts to the city, under the instruction that no one was to find out about it. However, the story leaked out and an open letter to Miss Adams was on the front page of the Dayton Daily News. In the film "Neverland," James Barrie, the author of Peter Pan, reserved a whole section in the opening night of his play for local orphans. Actually, even if Barrie ever did this, he got the idea from Maude Adams, who did this regularly for her "Peter Pan" performances for poor children of the city. Barrie's own life was full of strange and unusual tragedies, but he did pursue several petite actresses in England, as he was a mere five feet tall. Maude, according to family sources was four feet eleven inches and not the five feet that is often reported. And Barrie definitely wrote his "Peter Pan" with her in mind for the stage. There were several other tiny actresses that portrayed her role in other countries, especially in England. But in America, Maude Adams "owned" the role of "Peter Pan."

Maude Adams had many little superstitions and weird quirks for as intelligent as she was. She had her worn brown coat that she had to wear for good luck. She would not stand by a landing with others, and she had to always wear a curious blue, heart shaped stone around her neck. She had an aversion to or fear of beggars and was very austere in her dress and abodes. She had no use for society friends and had a singular focus on her career. She so valued her privacy that when she traveled, her trunks bore no labels, just red stickers for the theater and yellow stickers for her hotel. The labels had a dolphin twined around an anchor. She could not swim and had the pools she was entering measured for their depth.

Talk of Maude Adams being frail and prone to illness or chronic ailments came about because of several incidents in her life. There were two separate times that she took a year off from the stage to rest and recuperate. She did travel upon occasion as a form of recuperation and in 1918; she did almost die in the influenza epidemic. She did have a delicate constitution but always defended herself by presenting a picture of how athletic she was in terms of walking and riding horses. She even drove her own carriage through the city streets.

However the family history does give a suggestion as to what might have been a real inherited ailment in the Adams line that would explain some of her supposed weird quirks such as wearing a heavy coat outdoors, in every season of the year. It seems that several of the Adams suffered from overactive thyroid and a blood chemistry that tends to prevent the accumulation of fat and muscle on the frame, resulting in a general feeling for some, of 'freezing' even on a hot summer day. Maude always wore her fur coat, winter or summer, because she was always cold.

There was no actress on the stage whose personality appealed more directly to her audience, and, no actress about whom less was known, thus promoting the mysteriousness that surrounded her personal life and still does to this day. None of her biographers could say much about her personal life. Knowing her descendants personally, I have come to understand much about her through family stories. When Maude Adams was asked about her elusive answers and her reclusive behavior her stock answer was that she was very much interested in her work. That acting was a good profession for a woman and there was no limit to what she could do with her talents if she was willing to work hard and wait. "And as for temptations well are they not everywhere outside the protection of the home circle?" (Ibid, Davies, p.21)

"I haven't much experience. I have no theories and systems of exercise and dressing and bathing to interest people with, or rather I have beautiful theories, but I don't live up to them. I ride horse back and walk, and am ever so much stronger than I look. I don't see, anyway, why an actress must give her personality to the world, though it seems to be expected and those who curiously investigate her private life are not always careful how they use their information. I haven't very decided opinions on the great questions of the day, but there's one thing I don't believe in, and that is woman's rights. I think the men have taken pretty good care of us all in these years, and I don't see what is the matter with letting them keep it up. Any woman halfway clever can make the men do just what she wants to have them do, and at the same time keep them thinking they are having their own way - and what more would she want?" (Ibid, Davies, p.21-22)

In 1910, she made a triumphant return to Utah. The Salt Lake Council made a resolution that praised her as the "state's most illustrious daughter" and "the highest type of modest woman; idol of the American Stage." She performed the play "What Every Woman Knows" and donated the proceeds to the Salt Lake Orphans Home. An embossed copy of the city's resolution was presented to her as guest of honor. "Her welcome to her city of her birth eclipses everything witnessed her from enthusiasm." She was always quoted as saying this about her city of birth, even though she had chosen a different path in life: "Apart from the life in the theater, there are two cities that hold very dear memories. One is a lovely valley protected by friendly mountains as always." (<u>Women Worth Their Salt</u>, Maude Adams, p.191)

In 1915 when Frohmen died, Maude was 43. Her costume designer also died that year and her stage manager as well. Then her mother became ill and she closed the theater where she was performing and returned to Salt Lake City with her mother who died in March of 1916. There is an interesting ghost story connected to Charles Frohman's death with the sinking of the Lusitania. The Arch Building, now the Cobb Library, was the city's Town Hall when the Lusitania sank. The building was used as a temporary morgue in New York City. Frohman was a workaholic; he suffered from rheumatism and had to use a walking cane. He always carried a briefcase of theatrical scripts. Frohman's arthritic leg made it impossible for him to try for a lifeboat as he talked to others on the starboard deck as the ship sank. To the other actors and actresses he was traveling with, he is legendarily supposed to have said, "Why fear death? It is the most beautiful adventure in life." The others stood arm-

Maude and her Mother, Annie Adams
Utah State Historical Society

in-arm with him awaiting the on rush of water when he spoke his famous last lines.

His body was identified and shipped to Queenstown and then to New York where his remains were housed in his own building (the Arch Building) Town Hall. Buried in the Old Church Cemetery in Queenstown, his wife Inez H. Vernon committed suicide the following year and her ashes were interred with her husband's body.

The ghost story is that one of Frohman's office staff had seen him off on the Lusitania and then returned to the Empire Theatre in New York. He was to close up the building that evening when he checked Frohman's office. He found Frohman sitting at his desk, illuminated by one desk lamp. The desk was covered with a lifetime of memorabilia. Frohman spoke to him and asked him to leave him alone in his office because he could not be helped. When the man returned with a group of theater workers, the office was dark and empty and the desk was clear of papers.

In 1917, Maude Adams donated her estate at Lake RonKonKorna in New York to the Sisters of St. Regis. This Cenacle is one of many throughout the world. These communities began in 1826 at LaLouvese, France where Maude Adams had spent one of her several vacations. “Cenacle” means the room of the Last Supper where Mary and the apostles waited for the coming of the Holy Spirit. A Cenacle is a retreat center, a place for prayer and spiritual renewal for people of all faiths and religions. It was in such a place that Maude Adams found rest and peace for herself. When she died, she was buried at this center on Long Island in the Cenacle’s private cemetery there.

In 1918, Maude was dangerously ill from the influenza and decided to retire from the theater for good when she recovered. At age 46, she turned to other interests and kept her farm to live on. She received an honorary degree from Union College in Schenectady in 1921. She also received a second honorary degree from the University of Wisconsin, a “Doctor of Letters” it was called.

At age 50, she moved to Schenectady, New York to work in the labs at General Electric. Her ideas provided the special and safer stage and set lighting, which enabled the production of movies in color. Her ideas in theater lighting helped revolutionize the industry and several of her developments are still mainstays in the movie industry today. Maude never liked the poor stage lighting and after her long illness she wanted to try making a motion picture. Her friends suggested that she try creating a new kind of lighting first. She worked two years at the General Electric Laboratory and invented a high-powered incandescent lamp that later made colored movies possible. She was never given credit for her contribution to this. Her lawyer advised her to sue, deeply upset about the slight she had received, because he thought she could have easily settled out of court for a half million dollars. She decided to do nothing and wrote in her journals about the fact that she thought herself an idiot for never following this advice. While she did not sue, she often publicly claimed her invention whenever she saw the lamps being used.

In 1930 at 59, Maude decided to stage a "come-back," acting the part of Portia in "The Merchant of Venice." But times and audiences had changed. Although she was welcomed back to the stage, her acting did not "catch on." She made her final appearance in Salt Lake City before the production folded, having never made it back to Broadway in New York." (Ibid, Family History Book, p.164)

In 1937, President Wood of Stephens College, a Junior College for girls in Columbia, Missouri, asked Maude Adams to join her faculty as head of the Drama department and Maude accepted. She founded the school of acting there. There were 1,700 women enrolled that year. She taught courses in voice training and established a repertoire of plays for the students to perform. Within six weeks, she had galvanized the whole college, setting an example of hard work, no play and single-minded devotion to theater projects.

Maude's French students translated, music students wrote accompaniments, and dance teachers trained actors in movements and pantomimes. Friendly with pupils in class and on campus, the girls were entranced with her lectures. Yet, she retained her remote aloofness as well. She believed that teaching theater to young Americans was a civilizing force promoting humanity and universal appeal.

A quote taken from a speech she made at the college shows her passion for drama: "Today, we are appalled at the power of emotions by which the dictators of the world sway huge masses of people who have never learned that while emotions are the great driving power in life, they are at the same time the greatest danger in life...In modern life we train ourselves to think, forgetting that emotions are beyond thought and that they have supreme authority over us forcing our lives into channels we never charted.... The power of the drama to develop young minds and young emotions is not used; it seems to me, with sufficient confidence." (Ibid, Davies)

After the 1949-1950 theater season she was too tired to go on and retired to her house in Tannersville, New York. She retired to so private a life that even though she had a telephone, the only reply that a caller received was that she was unavailable except to close friends. She spent her last years writing and studying, and died in 1953 at the age of 81 of a heart attack. She came close to making a film only one more time when in 1938 David O. Selznick thought he had signed her to do a screen test for a film called "The Young in Heart." She did in fact do the screen test at 66 years of age and the results were favorable. Articles even came out in several papers claiming that she had been signed for the film, which would also star Janet Gaynor, Paulette Goddard and Douglas Fairbanks Jr. She was given dozens of film offers but never accepted any of them. Another article appeared in 1945, claiming that she had signed a contract for another film, but this never came to fruition.

Her woman companion in her later years, Louis Boynton, died in 1951 and both their names appear on the gravestone. Another mystery never really solved; all her biographers say that there was never any evidence that she was lesbian. In fact there were rumors that she did have a love affair with a young, handsome male actor when she was much younger. However, when her mother's sister burned all of Maude's journals after she died, the family story has always been that all of the secrets about her love life were in those journals. Her descendants suspect differently. They speculate that she liked men in her early life and may have or may not have had one of two men she loved. In her later life, they believe she may well have decided she liked women better. When I asked them, many of whom are close personal friends of mine, what I should write down, they said they would be upset with me if I did not write their speculations about their famous ancestor. However, biographers agree that Maude was simply celibate in her later years.

Still worshipped by many fans, even after decades, Maude Adams was brought to life again by a little novel entitled Bid Time Return by Richard Matheson. Which in turn brought about a little film called "Somewhere in Time" starring Christopher Reeves and Jane Seymour. Considered smultzy by many, there are many others who have devoted themselves to this film. There are even those who spend weekends at the Grand Hotel where it was filmed on Mackinaw Island to try and recapture the great love between the two main characters that end up being separated from each other by time itself. There are dozens of websites devoted to the movie, its stars, the hotel and Maude Adams. There are even a few ghost stories about the hotel but it is unlikely that Maude Adams ever stayed there.

It seems that Richard Matheson was in the Virginia City Opera House one day and saw a portrait of Maude Adams and became entranced by her portrait. He researched her life, discovered a missing period of time in her life, and from this got the inspiration for his story of a young man who meets a very old woman one day at a cast party of his college play. She walks up to him, places a gold pocket watch in his hand and asks him to "come back to me." The playwright begins a trail of investigation that leads him to the hotel where the beautiful "elfin" actress had performed in 1911. He figures out a way to teleport himself through time with nothing from his modern time with him that could possibly draw him back without warning. He meets her, they court, he falls in love with her, they make love, and right after this, he accidentally pulls a modern day penny, which he had forgotten about, from his suit pocket. He is pulled back through time and is unable to get back to his lover. He lies down in his hotel room, tries to go back to 1911 and dies in the hotel room unable to recreate his time travel experience a second time to get back to his paramour. At the end, her spirit comes for him and they walk off together in the mist. A romantic's dream!

With the death of Christopher Reeves and his real romance with his wife and then her early death, the tragedies Reeves endured in his horse riding fall, and his eventual emergence as another kind of real hero for spinal cord injury patients, "Somewhere in Time" has reached a widespread cult status. Many people admire not only Reeves and his wife, but also the woman actress in the film, Jane Seymour, who is involved in many charities herself and has her own worldwide fan base. Reeves became even more famous after his accident than he was as an actor, wrote a book on his life as a paraplegic and traveled all over the world to raise money for spinal cord injury research. He vowed to be walking one day. He carried out a very public and valiant struggle to keep living, and brought the subject of spinal cord injuries into the public eye in many ways. Shortly after he passed away, his wife got cancer and she also died.

Their public fight together brought admiration for both of them from around the world. Following the path of an earlier celebrity and her many charitable concerns, Maude Adams.

When one reads Richard Matheson's Bid Time Return, one is struck by the abundant borrowing from Maude Adams life. So it seems that even after death, Maude Adams's fame as an actress continues on in films like "Somewhere in Time" and "Finding Neverland," a tale about James Barrie and his lost love. Because it also seems to be true that Barrie only loved two women in his life, neither of whom was his wife Mary. One was an aristocratic woman in England named Sylvia Davies and the other was an American, Maude Adams. James Barrie scandalized England by becoming a companion and friend to Davies whose husband had died in a horrible way. She had four little boys to raise and while Barrie was a married man, he was also a rich man who could basically do whatever he wanted. He was as much in love with these boys as he was with their mother, who then died quite young herself, leaving the boy's grandmother to raise them, and Barrie to financially support them. There has always been some question as to Barrie's interest in these young boys, the widow woman and Maude Adams, who of course refused to marry anyone. (For more on James Barrie's bizarre and quirky life, the best biography is by Andrew Birkin entitled J.M. Barrie and the Lost Boys, it will haunt you!)

My favorite quotes from Miss Adams are threefold. One is about teaching, another is about her personal life and the last is about her childhood right after her father died. She used to take long walks with him where he would relate tall tales to her about winning the west. If Maude Adams ever loved a man, he would have had to be very much like her handsome and poetic father who was probably a dreamer, without a dream of his own to accomplish. She loved him most dearly as a small child and worshipped his memory all of her life.

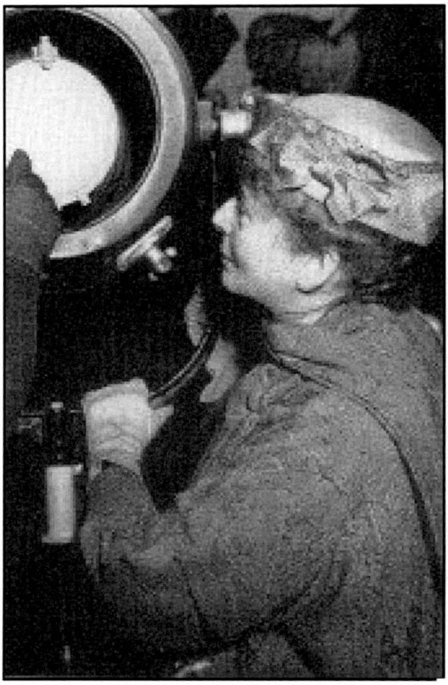

Maude at General Electric

Maude Relaxing on her Farm

"Don't let anyone persuade you that anything we do in life less than our own best is a worthy thing. You must never compromise with your life. We know when we are doing first-rate things. When we satisfy ourselves with second-rate things it is the beginning of a long, long death. We die from that minute."

"Go for first-rate things. Don't accept from yourself a second-rate sincerity, a second-rate sense of justice. Sometimes it seems that we are successful only because we have not tried hard enough for our best. If we don't compromise, we do the hard thing and we fail. We do the hard thing and we fail again. We do the hard thing, and one day we succeed, and many things are made plain to us."

"Don't be afraid of failure; be afraid of petty success. We are successful because we have not tried hard enough for our best; so that we were in danger of failing to fail. Be afraid of that long, long death which means compromise with your best, and remember that any advice that leads you away from your best is second rate." (Speech at the college)

"Maude had a shyness and modesty that prevailed through her highly successful career, a career which was her life, her love. At one time she wrote, "No man knows another, and everyman is ever another to himself. It is one of the many blessings of life in the theatre that we are always so delightfully busy being someone else that we scarcely spare a moment to know ourselves. That doubtful pleasure can always be deferred. And what a mercy! If we really knew ourselves, how could we endure it?"(On being reclusive and shy)

Maude tried to return to Utah as often as her career permitted. She loved coming home and once stated, "At Grandmother's house, there were vastly entertaining things: cows and sheep and horses and dogs and trees to climb with cherries at the top. And oh, the sweet-smelling hay in the barn and the swing tied to one of the rafters. There were fields to roam, whole fields of wild flowers-freedom." (State of Utah Commission for Women and Families. All previous quotes come from the Maude Adams website: www.bookmice.net/darkchilde/maudeadams.html)

Maude's grandfather's fields covered much of what is today a large park in Salt Lake City called Liberty Park. Among her lifelong accomplishments, she collected sixty papyrus books from the Holy Land, saw Jerusalem, France, Egypt, Switzerland, and many other countries. She loved driving cars and riding horses, owned at least a dozen big dogs connected to her many homes, met several presidents, obtained the oldest known play manuscript, played the piano, harp and cello, loved the color dark green and licorice sticks, won an automobile for being the most popular actress of her time and had a golden life-size statue of her sent to the Paris Exposition as America's most popular actress.

She was a little less than five feet tall and one of the best descriptions of her said that she was "gossamer, with a sprite-like quality, ephemeral, but radiant as the golden dust on a butterfly's wing." There was always the suggestion of something isolating on her face, a pensive, thoughtful repose, as though she were haunted by some secret sorrow even when she radiated a sweet smile. Her highly nervous temperament, always tuned to the snapping point, probably caused her frequent physical collapses.

To me, this is a perfect description of the temperament of a gifted intuitive as well. Knowing so many of Maude's descendants, many of them, intelligent, beautiful slim, ethereal, charming, and very much tiny frustrated actresses, singers and dancers: I know there must be more to genetics than I had supposed. Very intelligent, delicate, and moody, always performing, alluring and charming, hard workers and highly competitive, who focus on completing their tasks; her female descendants suffer from the same nervous system chronic ailments that most intuitives do, as well as such things as allergies, asthma and other "nervous disorders." In all the arts they are blessed with more than the rest of us, and they suffer the fates of most intuitives as well. Hiding from, or frightened by, the trials of a psychic's empathic life, they know the trials of living on the edge of one's emotions. They know, many of them, that at least one ancestor got to become what she should have been, a famous and gifted actress, an ephemeral "star."

A few summers ago I discovered a life size portrait of Maude Adams at the University of Utah Fine Arts Museum. She is dressed as a boy for her part in the play "L'aiglon." The notes on the painting I took down were taken for her descendants who had asked me to visit the portrait and intuit what I could for them. I had only recently discovered, at the time, that one could stand before a portrait and get information, not only about the painter but also about the person posing for the artist. I wanted to try my hand at this but warned them not to take to heart anything that I intuited as absolute truth. They said that they didn't care, but that it would be interesting to see what information I got, as they themselves are intuitive and find this whole field either fascinating or intimidating.

Maude Adams's descendants, Utahns and otherwise, carry her birthright. They are just riddled with brilliant, intuitive and beautiful, frustrated or successful, dancers, singers and stage performers. Many of them carry a few or many of Adams's characteristics from her amazing charisma, to her intellectual curiosity, love of people and their own stories, her great beauty and stamina, and even her amazing intuitive abilities. When I was finished, we met for lunch, a large table of mothers and daughters, Mormon and non-Mormon, some of whom resemble Maude Adams like echoes. There are whole families of what I call little sprites of children, hauntingly beautiful and yet tragically brilliant. I gave each family a copy of my notes while we discussed what happened right after Maude Adams died. Her aunt followed Annie Kiskadden's instructions in case she out survived Maude, as her mother Annie had not. This aunt destroyed all of Maude Adams's journals and diaries, which she kept copiously throughout her life. Thus destroying forever whatever private and intimate secrets Maude had as well as her actress mother's actions and thoughts as Maude saw them. This, of course, has contributed greatly to the mystic which surrounds this world famous actress to this day. Her descendants were especially curious about how Maude Adams felt about not having children and also about her living with a woman in the last years of her life. They wanted to know if she had been allowed to have, or wanted to have a personal life as well as a professional one. They also wanted to know what she was doing in those two times in her life when she disappeared for an entire year.

Before we parted company we all went over to the Fine Arts Museum at the University of Utah and I took photos of all of these women posed in front of their famous ancestor's painting as a keepsake. Three of these women have been my best friends for years, and watching them go through their own frustrations as brilliant, beautiful mothers and frustrated performers, I was pleased to write about one of the Adams who really had become world famous. And I was pleased to right some wrongs done to her in many of her biographies, but only privately and intuitively with descendants who totally accept and believe the art of intuition. So while the museum notes which I took down that day cannot be shared for lack of proof, I am including the museum notes on the John White portrait of Maude Adams which you can see today at the University of Utah Museum of Fine Arts. These notes are a fitting ending to the mysteries and allure of a very famous actress and performer, Maude Adams.

"Portrait of Maude Adams as L'Aiglon" By John White Alexander, 1905-1865 (1915)

"Alexander did portraits of women noted for their near perfect likenesses and revelation of character. He studied works of the old masters and painted Adams when she was playing the role of Napoleon's son and heir, Duke of Reichstadt L'aiglon. The Duke's name meant "eaglet" which was an affectionate name for him. He was a fragile and sickly boy who lived his entire life in exile waiting for an opportunity to claim his father's empire. He had high aspirations but did not have the strength or ambition to carry them out. He died shortly after his twenty-first birthday with no military or political success and the play was about the tragedy of unfulfilled dreams. When Alexander painted Adams, she reflected the character that she was playing, so that she appears to be introspective and melancholy with the atmosphere in the painting of foreboding as Adams feels the Duke's impending doom."

My intuitive notes rest with the family, as they should, in honor of Maude Adam's quest for privacy. In the end, I found Maude Adams and her descendants to be as fascinating as all the women in this lineage are. Having no one in my own family to share this gift of sight with, I have many friends among the Adams descendants who I feel comfortable with, because so many of them live each day as I do, outside the boundaries of what is considered the "norm." Out here, life is always a surprise, full of dreams, and visions both wonderful and tragic. Peopled with spirits and sprites and just as much light as darkness, it is a world full of endless worlds, a place one has to experience to believe in. It becomes a sensitivity beyond the realm of most people's experiences. Sad and tragic, full of light and ecstasy, I would never part with it, even though it is a complex and judged path. Just like I was once told in the teaching world, one has to live each day separately, expecting the best from one's students each moment, and stopping to hear and sense their souls whenever they come through, expected or unexpected.

Maude Adams was a child prodigy, a brilliant, gifted young woman who could have been extremely accomplished in several fields at once. She would have been an accomplished writer, speaker, inventor, researcher, teacher, musician, and even politician. She was able to blend her intellectual life with her intuitive one, and most certainly sought a "spiritual path" long before the term was in vogue. She was also a great motivator for others along the path. She was very tiny and had a beautiful "gossamer" child-like face with those sky-blue eyes that celebrities for centuries have made a living on. There was really nothing that she couldn't do and most things she chose to do, she did exceptionally well. I know that melancholy well. It was probably as simple as the isolation that one feels from others, often in knowing what is coming, or what has been. It does produce a sort of sadness that those not in touch with such things, do not understand. Genius and beauty, Maude Adams was Utah's greatest actress of all time.

SARA ALEXANDER – FROM STAGE TO SCREEN

There was a young woman named Sara Alexander whom Brigham Young personally chose to perform on stage and who transitioned from both the old Social Hall and the old Salt Lake Theatre to become a nationally known actress. Born in Wheeling, Virginia, in 1839, Sara's mother converted to Mormonism after the death of her father. She and her husband lived in the St. Louis area and little Sara was performing and writing poems even then. As she grew up, she fell in love with a young missionary who had also fallen in love with her. He began corresponding with her when he went back to Utah. Sara's family made the long trek across the plains and the young missionary named Isaiah, whom Sara loved deeply, had already married and become a schoolteacher in Parowan. As soon as Sara arrived, he proposed plural marriage to her and her negative reply showed not only her disgust for plural marriage, but also her lack of interest in marrying at all. Those who knew her felt that Isaiah was the only man that she ever loved, but she strongly refused to share him with anyone else. Between this betrayal on the missionary's part, her sister's miserable marriage, and her mother never re-marrying, this cemented Sara's decision to stay single.

Brigham Young initially employed her to teach dance to his daughters and soon she and her mother were invited to live in the Lion House. One evening, when a performer for a play being presented there did not show up, Sara took her place and read so beautifully that she was invited to join the acting troupe. She refused this invitation three separate times until Brigham Young interceded with a little commanding and entreating. In George Pyper's book he says that Brigham Young just

Young Sara Alexander
Utah State Historical Society

Sara as a Dance Instructor and Actress
Utah State Historical Society

sort of casually mentioned to her one day that she ought to join the company and Sara said, "I don't want too." "But I want you to!" said Brigham and that was that.

Soon, Sara was accompanying Brigham and other important Mormon dignitaries of the time on tours taken through little towns all over Utah where she and others would perform. She was an instant hit and because she was small she played a lot of boys' and girls' roles and many other roles "from Topsy to Ophelia." Sara started with comedies and then moved on to star in dramas. When a famous eastern actor named T.A. Lyne joined the troupe as a lead actor he invited Sara to be his leading lady. She continued to dance and was often complimented on her grace and agility. One story regarding her and Brigham is when a young actor asked Brigham's advice about attempting to ask for Sara's hand in marriage, he replied that it would be the hardest performance that he had ever attempted.

Sara continued to perform in the Salt Lake Theatre and one of her fellow actresses was none other than Annie Asenath Adams, the mother of Maude Adams, another famous Utah actress. Both women performed in Brigham Young's original Deseret Dramatic Association in the 1860s. Sara also performed with many of the leading actors and actresses in the Salt Lake Troup including the Irwins, George Pauncefort, Julia Dean Hayne, C.W. Couldock and many others. Soon however, Sara decided to leave Salt Lake City and join a troupe in San Francisco after seven years with the Salt Lake troupe.

All during this time, her two closest friends were her sister Mary Ada, who was pregnant with her fourth child, and her mother, whom Mary Ada was caring for because of her various illnesses. Their mother died and Mary Ada became desperately ill. Thus began a tug of war between Sara and Mary Ada's husband to bring her sister and her two-year old daughter Lisle to California, basically to save her sister's life. Sarah won the battle but lost the war; Mary Ada dying at the young age of 35. Sara, bitter about her sister's treatment from her husband, informed him that she would keep the child; and that is exactly what she did. She arrived in San Francisco, taking with her the 2-year-old daughter of her deceased sister, and began performing with the Barrett and McCullough Company at the California Theatre. "This infant became the charming and capable actress known as Lisle Leigh." (<u>The Romance of an Old Playhouse</u> by George Pyper, The seagull Press: Salt Lake City, Utah, 1928, pp. 164, 165 & 166).

She then moved to Chicago with Lisle and was featured with Robert McWade in "Rip Van Winkle" and in other roles there. She moved on to Broadway and performed with many of the greats of the time, including Kyrle Bellew another famous fellow Utah acquaintance character actor. This stock company also performed as far away east as Maine and as far west as Nebraska. Her last dramatic engagement on the stage was as the "Beggar Woman" in "Rust" at the Gaiety Theatre in New York City in 1924. Sara Alexander performed in the golden age of theater until her death in 1926, remaining one of the oldest performing American actresses of all time.

Her niece became Lisle Leigh and began performing with her upon occasion. Beginning in 1916, Sara had roles in six silent films and then toured with her daughter in her own company. In 1921, at the age of 83, a local newspaper interviewed her and she was still described as bright, merry and full of pep. When asked why she had never married, she said that she had just seen too much of it in Utah. Two years before her death, she moved into a retirement home and a year after her own death, her "adopted" daughter or niece, Lisle Leigh, who had made a few films of her own, died of heart disease. ("Sara Alexander: Pioneer Actress and Dancer," by Sandra Dawn Brimhall, Utah Historical Quarterly, Volume 66, Number 4, Fall 1998, pp.320-333).

Sara died in New York City on Christmas Eve, December 24, 1926. She had starred in six or seven silent films. The first one listed is "Caprice of the Mountains" in 1916 which starred June Caprice. However, I think that perhaps this was the movie entitled "Caprice," that was produced in 1913 with Mary Pickford as its star, because the synopsis fits the title. While the story is the same, perhaps there were two versions of this picture made within three years of each other? It would seem unlikely that lesser known producers had actually taken the same film and produced it again three years later with a lesser star. It is hard to guess at such things because the beginnings of the early silents were pretty chaotic and certainly many films were made without fear of copyright infringements in those days. Lisle Leigh also had a role in this picture.

Pickford starred as "Mercy Baxter," a naive mountain girl who marries a wealthy city man, who falls in love with her while hunting in the mountains. The marriage becomes a disaster and Mercy abandons her husband. In the meantime, she gets tutoring in the ways of a sophisticated lady and returns to him incognito. Naturally, it has a happy ending. What part Sara Alexander or her adoptive daughter played in this second version is lost to history, but it is more than likely that this is the first picture either of them had a role in.

The next picture that is listed is from 1916: "Little Miss Happiness" and I could find no information about this one except that it also starred June Caprice. Sara made two pictures in 1918: "The Glorious Adventure" and "The Woman the Germans Shot," where she played the role of Mrs. Clavell. This picture was directed by John G. Adolfi. She also made "The Cavel Case" with Julia Arthur and "The Passion Flower" with Norma Talmage. Her last picture was in 1919 entitled "The Jungle Trail," where she played the role of Mrs. Morgan. This film was directed by Richard Stanton.

In her article entitled "Theatrical Dancing in the Territory of Utah, 1848-1868, Debra Hickenlooper Sowell makes mention of Sara Alexander's performances, but especially what an excellent dancer she was. She really was the first excellent dance performer in the state and this is the reason Brigham Young hired her to teach some of his daughters. Young liked her a lot but also knew that in her case Sara Alexander was married to the stage and had no desire to be married to a man. She had been deeply hurt by one man, and the idea of plural marriage, while still remaining a loyal Mormon, kept her single for the rest of her life.

THE MOTHER OF THEATRE IN UTAH: MAUD MAY BABCOCK & THE OLD SOCIAL HALL

In 1991, workers dug an underground walkway from the Z.C.M.I. center which housed the Zion Mercantile for many years, then the Meier & Frank store, and now the City Creek Shopping Center. But when they broke through into the foundations of an old, rather famous pioneer building, this was a momentous occasion. All work stopped on the project and archaeologists and city planners were called in to investigate. Salt Lake City's very first theater had been unearthed, the old original social hall for which there is a replica built in This Is The Place Heritage Park up Emigration Canyon. An extensive excavation or "dig" took place right in the middle of State Street and when the archaeologists were done, it was decided to create a small Heritage Social Hall Museum just inside the east doors of the Z.C.M.I. Center. There, one could go down the stairs into a small alcove and read the historical information placed there as well as see artifacts from the dig, old photographs and a glassed in room where a section of the old Social Hall could still be seen. Presently, however, many renovations are being done with this mall, as the LDS Church owns the property. The new City Creek Center is very upscale, so the fate of the old Social Hall was left to its owners, the LDS Church. The Social Hall Museum is now located at 51 South State right next to the new Center and is a delight to visit with its much more beautiful display of the foundations of the old Social Hall.

The Social Hall opened on New Year's Day in 1853 with a dance social and the first theater performance was on January 17, 1853. Plays, bands, orchestras, dances and various other functions took place there for the entire city, including concerts by the Nauvoo Legion Military Band, created by Joseph Smith to protect his people. Mary and Ida Cook ran the first school there in the 1850s. The Social Hall had the first movable dance floor in the valley and many other such halls were then built around the state in imitation of the first one. The dance floor allowed for dance socials and then could be rolled out of the way for other types of functions in the Social Hall. When the old Salt Lake Theatre opened in 1862, the two existing theater troupes, once performing both at the Social Hall and around the state, merged together and began preparing their plays in the greenroom of this brand new theater after rehearsing in the old Social Hall. The old hall was taken over by the LDS church and became a ward social hall. One can still see what the original Social Hall was like, due to a replica of this building inside Heritage Park across from Hogle Zoo at the mouth of Emigration

Canyon, but the old foundation and information about this hall can be found in the new museum, along with the memorabilia.

The Social Hall did have one more era of revival period when Maud May Babcock opened its doors once again in 1893 to run the Utah School of Physical Culture until 1898 on the second floor. She created a special exercise costume for her ladies consisting of navy blue bloomers; sailor blouses and matching ruffled hats. For the next few years the hall was rented out upon occasion and then began to deteriorate. Maud May really loved the place though because in 1918 she had the place renovated and brought her college students in to perform as the Varsity Theater group until 1922.

"Babcock was born in East Worcester, New York. She received a B.A. degree from Wells College and a Bachelor of Elocution degree from the National School of Oratory of Philadelphia. She also studied at the Lyceum School of Acting (now the American Academy of Dramatic Arts) in New York (her mentor there was Alfred Ayres, a renowned Shakespearean scholar) She then moved on to the University of Chicago, and also spent two years in London and Paris. After beginning her career teaching at Ingleside Schools for Girls in Connecticut, she moved on to Rutgers University and New York public schools before coming to Utah at the invitation of Susa Young Gates. In 1891, Gates had attended one of 24-year-old Babcock's summer classes at Harvard and then persuaded her to come to Utah as a professor of oratory and speech at the Social Hall." ("Maud May Babcock," by Ann W. Engar, <u>The Utah History Encyclopedia</u>, University of Utah Press, 1994, p.25)

"These two 'soul mates of high purpose' said an early student at the University of Utah, Mary Johnson Webster, lobbied for women's rights and the improvement of women's health to 'improve their looks.' Susa was Brigham Young's favorite daughter and quite the feminist in her day. She was also a powerful influence in the arts in Utah in her day. Although Maud was raised Episcopalian, she joined the Mormon Church after becoming a professor at the University of Utah." ("Maud May Babcock: Speak Clearly and Carry A Big Umbrella," by David G. Pace, <u>Worth Their Salt</u>, Utah State University Press, 1996, p.149)

Maud May Babcock
Utah State Historical Society

Speech Professor
University of Utah Special Collections

A major contributing factor to this decision was a spiritual experience she had one day while she and Susa were hiking together in the Wasatch Mountains. The girls ran into an older man with a white beard and wide-brimmed straw hat who warned them not to take a certain path. Had they taken that path they would have become hopelessly lost. The old man fit the description of one of the "Three Nephites" and because of this moving spiritual experience; Maud finally decided to join the Mormon Church after resisting this for quite some time. The Three Nephites are famous in Mormon lore as three mortals that God granted the right to live on earth for eternity. They stayed to do good works and in the early pioneer days there were hundreds of stories about one of them appearing to help individuals weather their hardships. Among the Mormons they are considered the same as angels from Heaven.

But her parents were less than pleased when she joined the Mormon Church after only four months in Utah. Her mother wrote her, that "I pray daily to God, that if you open your lips to defend (that Hell Born sect) in public your tongue may be paralyzed." Possibly because of her parent's disapproval, Maud May took on the task of fitting into her new world with gusto. If when they hired her, the administration was not aware of Maud May being a force to be reckoned with, by the end of her 47 years on campus, they were! And while the students made fun of this little five foot three inch elocution teacher's pronounced diction behind her back, nearly all of them spoke of her classes as inspiring to them. While often complaining of her student's "lack of gumption," she was also known for taking her students by surprise by beaming them on the head with her umbrella when she saw them smoking a cigarette. (Ibid, Pace, p.150)

"Miss B" taught mornings at the Social Hall and afternoons at Brigham Young Academy in Provo. When she began teaching at the University of Utah on an annual salary of $500 dollars, she formed the University Dramatic Club in 1897. However, the beginnings of her student performances took place in 1893 when her first troupe of combined students from BYU Academy, the University of Utah and private classes presented an exhibition of fancy steps, attitudinizing, muscular poses, drills, steps, Swedish movements, Italian club and dumbbell performances at the old Salt Lake Theatre. And on June 6, 1895, a hundred of her female students presented "Eleusinia," which was to become the first ever university production by students in America. The play was filled with living pictures of people dressed in togas, inspired by Greek legends and was a great success.

Her first official university club plays were entitled "The Happy Pair" and "A Box of Monkeys." These two farces seemed to invite audience participation when the sophomore class decided to bombard the stage with cabbages and a few other vegetables. This deluge continued through at least one more play where a student was slightly injured in the stomach by a propelled cabbage, and Maud May sent word that this behavior was to stop immediately and it did. A few students were suspended over these incidents, which of course caused more of an incident on campus, but every year after that the club staged one major dramatic play. And by 1913 the theater club was no longer populated by only students, but also by professors and alumni, making it the first community theater in the state, as opposed to the earlier inner state traveling theater troupes.

Maud never married which allowed her the time to do other things and her influence over the growth of theater in Utah is legendary. For 47 years she was considered one of the most eccentric teachers on campus and in 1930, she finally got what she had wanted and worked so hard for, her own theater, Kingsbury Hall. She became chairman of the Speech Department just before her retirement at age 71 and four generations of speech and drama students passed through her classes. When she retired in 1938, her drama club "had the longest unbroken record of annual performances of any university drama club in North America." (Ibid, Pace, p.25)

By 1927 she was chair of her department and started her university-subsidized professional theater, the first in the nation, in the old Social Hall. This professional group ran from 1918 to 1922. She founded one college and two departments and produced and directed over 300 stage plays. She tirelessly worked towards the funding for her dream of a large theater building on the University of Utah campus, as well as for 2,500-seat outdoor amphitheater that never materialized. In the meantime she wrote several books on speech and elocution, was president of the National Association of Teachers of Speech and served for twenty years on the board of directors for the Utah School for the Deaf and Blind. She was chaplain of the Utah Senate for twelve years and was the first woman in the United States to hold that position. She worked on the planning and building of the Deseret Gymnasium, and while she died without getting the credit due her for helping to get a campus theater building, construction on Kingsbury Hall began in 1927 and the building was dedicated in May of 1930.

She also received an honorary doctorate degree and was a tireless facilitator of the regional theater movement all of her life. She was also a tireless champion for her students. She was not above paying some poor student's tuition occasionally and often invited a group of students to her Brighton cabin where she could outdo any of them hiking near the peaks there. Since she was a vegetarian, many students remembered being served her infamous fruit and nuts mush for breakfast along with her lemon water beverage. A wonderful hostess, she was also demanding and opinionated, they said. In the classroom she was ruthless and critical and yet many famous graduates of her classes credited her with giving them the confidence through drama to succeed in life. She often read every single line for the actor or actress and then made them repeat it exactly in her intonated style.

Interestingly, she often complained bitterly about the "trash of current stock companies flooding the country" and stuck to the ideals she said of the early Mormon pioneer stock companies in what was called at the time the "Little Theatre Movement." She was there when Kingsbury Hall presented the first on-stage performance by Maude Adams of "Peter Pan." "In 1936, two years before "Miss B" retired, her former students gathered for an anniversary production of "Mrs. Bumpstead Leigh," which was originally directed by Maud May in 1913. The identical cast was assembled, with only one exception; and it included famous local actress Lila Eccles and Herbert Maw, by then the governor of Utah. The gathering was a tribute to Maud May of the devotion of her students...They honored her not only with this production, but later forming a Reading Society and christening the student stage at Pioneer Memorial Theatre in her name." (Ibid, p.156)

Maud May retired when she was 71 years old. She had a duplex on 11th east and had filled it with marvelous collections from her travels around the world. She had a huge doll collection, cloisonné collection, oriental rugs, carved chests and tables, crystal dishes and lace tablecloths. It was here that many of her students still visited her, her dog Wu and her crazy parrot. Still "always" right, she died at age 87, in 1954, having used her umbrella for all those years to right wrongs by whacking people on top of the head with it. She also used to carry her little Pekingese or chow dog, Mr. Wu, around with her wherever she went. Suffice to say she became quite a fixture on campus for almost half a century and her picture is among those displayed on the second floor gallery of Kingsbury Hall. Maud May Babcock had a spirit to be reckoned with according to many accounts and ranks among the greats in the arts along with such people as Emma Lucy Gates Bowen who is the founder of opera in the far west, Virginia Tanner one of the founders of modern dance and William Christensen, who along with his brothers started more than one ballet company in the west.

She will be remembered most for the driving force of the formation of permanent theater here in Utah, although Brigham Young was its founding father and Phil Margetts was its initiator, early on. Friends with many a famous actor and actress on this side of the Atlantic, Maud May Babcock was also an excellent teacher. "Joseph F. Smith, a student and eventual successor to Maud May as chair of the speech department, wrote in a tribute to her shortly after her death...that Maud May was 'dedicated to the proposition that the only true and unfailing practicality is unswerving rectitude.'" The student theater named after her downstairs from Pioneer Memorial Theatre, the Babcock Theatre, is still in operation today on the University of Utah campus. (Ibid, p.157)

THE BARNACLE- Channing Pollock & Blanche Kendall Thomas McKey

The Barnacle

Once upon a time there was a very large family whose father owned a successful dry goods store. They built a huge three-story mansion house a couple of blocks from Temple Square in Salt Lake City, which housed a Temple and a Tabernacle for various Mormon meetings. The Thomas's owned the property in the middle of the block and right in the middle of this field was a little red barn. But the father moved this small barn to make room for a large red brick one that he planned to put a surrey, a phaeton and a couple of horses in. The huge new barn had a good roof, a solid foundation and arched windows and doorways with a very nice loft and a small double door entrance. It was built of red brick, and one of the fanciest barns in the city. The Thomas's were a very happy couple and their children were raised in a very affluent and happy home with an appreciation for the arts, especially singing and performing. Richard Kendall Thomas was a political activist and was involved in local government and Caroline Stockdale Thomas loved the arts.

When Richard and Caroline began to have children, they had a lot. The oldest child, Little Richard, only lived two months, while his twin brother Fred survived the same illness. Baby Jesse lived only seven months, but finally little Katie came along and she survived. After Fred and Katie came Artie, Rosie, and then Blanchie. Then came Maudie, and Artie and Elbert or "Petie." Elbert Thomas grew up to become a state senator. In the last batch were Henry, Ethel, and Kennie. Out of thirteen children, eleven had survived. But it was Katie, the eldest daughter, who set the tone in this fairytale family, who were all beautiful and smart, because their mother and father were. "When I grow up," said Katie, "I'll be an actress and a great prima donna and I'll write, too." Rosie and Blanchie played with their elder sister Katie, but the two of them were

The Barnacle Theater
Utah State Historical Society

Side View of The Barnacle
Utah State Historical Society

great pals on their own and loved to play house. They used the long porches around the front and sides of their house and divided them into playhouse rooms. This progressed to the winter fun of going to the theater, the Salt Lake Theatre. All the children went to both evening and matinee performances at the theater. The theater was only a few blocks away, so they could walk to it if they wanted too.

Their mother would read them fairytales and great literature by the evening fire, and Blanchie began to make her own miniature theater shadow boxes painted black, and all dressed up in homemade costumes to play the characters in the play that she created in her head. "... Blanchie's doll shows, (consisted of), a wooden box for a stage. She had several little dolls: A leading lady, dressed in a pink silk knitted dress and hat; a hero in dark blue; a villain, in black; and several others. She talked for them all, but the cute part was the way she managed to move them around the stage. It was a kind of puppet show, only instead of strings she broke branches from trees about a foot and a half or two feet long with little V-shaped flipper handles at one end that she fitted under the dolls arms. Then she held on the other end of the stick through a curtain and made them walk around." ("Four Forty Three" - a big family story by Rose Thomas Graham, no dates, family history book, provided to the author by Bonnie Quayle Thomas, p.47).

Soon, playing house and puppet shows, became "dress up." The idea that they could dress up their five brothers and four sisters in outfits fashioned from the fairy tales that they had heard appealed to Blanchie and Rosie. The first plays they performed were based on these tales and were presented in the two big rooms that they played in, with the double doors between making a perfect curtain between the stage and the audience. This is where, Blanchie said, the whole family became "lovers of the stage." They made tickets, chose a doorkeeper, and charged a penny or three pins for children, and two pennies or 6 pins for adults. They allowed "children in arms" to attend these plays because they had to come anyway. Unlike the big theaters where a sign often proclaimed that "children in arms" would not be allowed into the theater.

An hour before curtain time, the ticket man went around to the neighbors and said, "Fine show today. How many tickets would you like?" He then told the price of the tickets and said, "You can bring babies free." They also sold, taffy which they had "hand-pulled," penny candies like "Pink Pigs" or "Ears of Corn" and marshmallows or "Red Riding Hood Chewing Gum." The first performances weren't written out and consisted of a lot of singing, talking, and jumping around. What changed all this was when their Aunt Lily, who was a dressmaker, came to live with them. Suddenly, they had a costume mistress for their plays. Aunt Lily spent all her time making all their costumes and props for the neighborhood performances and she was a really particular and elegant seamstress.

In the meantime, their father had built his fancy barn, used it for his horses and carriages, but then he gradually sold off all the horses and vehicles. One day, their mother and father, who both enjoyed going to the theater and wanted to encourage their children's interest in the arts, talked about turning the barn into a theater. The prophet Brigham Young loved the theater and encouraged family entertainment among his people all over the Utah Territory. There were social halls and opera houses all over the state and hundreds of youngsters who wanted to become actors, actresses and entertainers by that time. And this was the same time that the Thomas's began to raise their children. So it was only natural, that since all of the Thomas children loved performing, that their wealthy parents build them a theater. But their father also had another purpose in mind, which was to use the theater for conventions and political rallies, which he often did. The Thomas's were in the right place, in a huge mansion that still exists today, sandwiched in between Mormon Church office buildings and quite close to Temple Square. All of the other houses along this block have long since disappeared, as has the old brick barn. But the love of acting and entertaining is a legacy in Utah, producing many superior actors and entertainers to this very day.

The Thomas's turned their fancy large barn into a theater in 1890 and the children named it "The Barnacle" like the "Tabernacle" not too far away. But before the barn could be converted to a theater, it had to be moved closer to the house, so that the children could go straight from their home and into the theater in inclement weather. Once the barn had been moved, directly behind the house's pantry area and kitchen, they began to convert it into a theater. For the Thomas's, not just plays were to be performed there, but all sorts of cultural events to broaden their children's knowledge. When the theater was built, this was when Blanchie began to write her own plays for the theater. The barn was moved and changed, and like a fairytale, they were written up in the newspaper as "the littlest theater in the world."

"The middle of the hay loft was taken out, leaving a balcony on three sides, and a row of stationary seats were put in against the walls. The front part of the balcony was wide enough for several rows of chairs with just one row in front of the side seats. A stairway led to the balcony." There were two dressing rooms, a stage with a big drop shelf that could be put down, which made the stage wider, but could also be let down for dances and parties. The children made the refreshments to be sold at intermission and the chairs were often rented out for other occasions to help support the theater's expenses. There was a big window behind the stage which was close to the kitchen door of the house. So they could also dress in the house and then step on a stool and climb through the stage window. The tiny dressing rooms were used for quick changes or applying extra makeup. The children made quite a bit of money with seat rentals, ticket sales, and refreshments to support their expenses for putting on their plays."

"The orchestra consisted of a piano and violin, played by some of the Thomas children, and the curtain was a heavy red cloth pulled back from the center by two heavy gold ropes. Neighborhood boys, who didn't want to be in the plays, soon became "curtain boys," "ticket sellers," and "intermission vendors." "Above the curtain was the cross piece called the proscenium. That is the proscenium between the stage and orchestra and often has a picture on it. We had a proscenium in front of the red curtain. The painting was of three little cupids carrying garlands of roses. There were three changes of scenery – a street scene, a forest scene, and an indoor scene. In the middle hall, besides the chairs, was a big heating stove, and the piano." There were littler stoves in each dressing room, with mirrors and tables and chairs. There were also hooks inside the entrance to "The Barnacle" for the audience's coats and hats. There were footlights along the stage, and other stage lighting above it and to each side of the stage. The Barnacle could seat 150 people, which made it one of the largest neighborhood theaters in America at the time. A New York artist named Mr. Petersen was in town to paint portraits of the children's parents, he was persuaded to design and paint the three sets as well as the proscenium arch and curtains. (Ibid, p.43)

As for who wrote the plays, Blanchie was quoted as saying, "I wrote plays long before I could spell the words I used in them." She always performed her plays in her little wooden box theater before she actually wrote them down. This was also how she rewrote her plays, by performing them first with her little dolls, and then changing the scenes on paper. One of her first plays was about a little barefooted orphan lost in the snow, finally rescued and adopted by a rich man. This play required snow, a lot of it. After cutting up lots of squares from newspaper, they "rehearsed" their snow by releasing it from bushel baskets through a hole at the back of the stage. Fortunately, it fell straight down instead of spreading out and was a success. However, the "snow" had to be cleaned up and re-deposited into the baskets for the next performance. There was another play that required a river and a bridge. They used two boards for the bridge, piled branches around it and had the "property man" splash water up from underneath the branches onto the bridge during the scene. The "prop boy" splashed his hands in a huge pan of water, and then in the climactic bad weather scene, he lifted the whole pan with another boy, and threw its entire contents onto the stage.

One time the mail clerks in their father's store put on a minstrel show and many short farces or vaudeville acts were also performed at The Barnacle. A short farce was usually presented after the play and the vaudeville acts were usually presented before the play. "People who lived near or even farther away began using The Barnacle for musicals. In one of these, another cousin was a soloist." Not just the Thomas children performed, but many of their cousins and also neighbor's children were involved in putting on these plays. But the main group of performers was smaller, because it took a lot of precociousness to do the actual performing. Blanchie's plays became such a hit that she began selling a few of them. Her first purchased play went to a book called a "Catalogue of Plays" by a man named Samuel French and this was not just a local publisher. She was upset with them though, because they changed the play's name from "When the Cat's Away" to "A Bit of Nonsense." (Ibid, Four Forty Three, p.44).

"Two brothers who lived down the block, but hadn't been there long, learned about the Barnacle and joined in. They seemed to know something about the stage, and together with Blanchie, put on some melodramas that were startling, gun play and all." These boys, especially the older one, also performed their own made-up vaudeville acts, wrote melodramas and eventually full-length plays for The Barnacle. "One of these boys became a famous New York, playwright, Channing Pollack, author of 'The Fool.' Two girls of the Barnacle days became actresses, Ruby and Millie Lindsay. But Blanchie, was the only one of the family to go on to the real stage, while some of the others have done some incredible work, notably Pete (Elbert) and Kendall (Kennie), who once had a company of their own and toured small towns. Oh yes, and Kendall got his start in the Barnacle as a baby." When Blanche came home from Broadway she joined her brothers' company for a while and of course, Pete went into politics because this was another subject fostered in the Thomas home. Most interesting is that Blanche Thomas as a child actress and playwright had her first ardent admirer in the form of Channing Pollock who showered her with bouquets of flowers and had a real puppy love or crush on his first actress long before he became an important Broadway critic and playwright. (Ibid, Four Forty Three, p.46-47).

Some of the important patrons of the Barnacle included John S. Lindsay, manager of the Salt Lake Theatre, David McKenzie actor at the Salt Lake Theatre and one of the founders of it. Horace G. Whitney, critic for The Deseret News and Ada Patterson, a local drama critic and later a famous author living in New York City. Both Lindsay and Whitney wrote histories of the Salt Lake Theatre later. Sometimes these people spotted an up and coming actor that they could recruit for the Salt Lake Theatre. Child and teen actors at The Barnacle included: Ida Drew, Irene Kelly, Gertrude and Mabel O'Malley, Rubie and Millie Lindsay, and of course the Thomas children and Channing Pollock and his brother John who later became a New York stage actor. R. Kendall Thomas, Blanche's youngest and handsomest brother, played in stock companies with Willard Mack and E. Forrest Taylor and then started his own company called the Harmon Weight Stock Company. He eventually got a Hollywood contract but never signed it and stayed home to pay attention to his other responsibilities.

In Kenneth MacGown's book, Footlights Across America (1929), the author said that the Barnacle was the first highly successful neighborhood community theater in the United States. The Barnacle produced many talented actors and actresses, and even playwrights and directors and managers of theatres. Many of these child actors went on to perform in the Salt Lake Theatre or in the other theaters around town. Some of them created their own traveling troupes and toured the west. But only Blanche (or Blanchie) Kendall Thomas McKey went to New York and broke into Broadway for a very brief period of time. You can read her story just a bit later in this section. Channing Pollock was the only one to have lived in Salt Lake City when growing up and had the privilege of performing at both barn theaters in Salt Lake City, going onto fame as a play critic in New York, as well as becoming a highly successful playwright. His "grown-up" story you will read shortly. The Barnacle became a very big success in Utah and children from all over the area came to see plays or came to perform at the Barnacle. Blanche continued writing her plays when she became a college professor and her drama students adored her. Salt Lake has the unique privilege of having had the only such child-run playhouse from which many well-known performers and others in the theater began their careers.

While The Barnacle has long since vanished, the old Thomas mansion still exists today just west of Temple Square, sandwiched between a parking lot and some huge old trees. Descendants of the Thomas family still drive by from time to time just to admire this huge mansion with its summer porches intact to the side and rear of the mansion, where once "first" imaginations blossomed, with plays growing more extravagant and moving to the front parlors. Once the parlors became too small for these productions, they were moved out to the barn and the barn was moved closer to the house so that performers could use the side kitchen as their changing room and the north kitchen window as their entrance and exit from the theatre. Theaters and politics were the most important topics in town in those days, and in some ways, still are. While the adult version of a stable turned into a theater on Main Street, The Wonderland, catered to the lower end of the theater business, The Barnacle continued to cater to children's theater, community gatherings and political rallies for quite some time. And probably like most places, the silent movies turned The Barnacle into a deserted old barn once more. But the immense size of the Thomas home can only be really understood if one is allowed to see the side or back of the home with porches galore providing even more places for plays to be performed. The influx of the movies ended this particular children's fairy tale, but introduced others!

Harold Kyrle Money Bellew – Cosmo Kyrle Bellew

Harold Kyrle Money Bellew was born in Calcutta, India on March 28, 1857. His only connection to Utah is how much he was loved there and that he caught pneumonia in Salt Lake City while performing in a play at the old Salt Lake Theatre. He was supposed to be rushed back to New York City but he didn't make it there alive and died in Salt Lake City. His stage name was Kyrle Bellew and he was a stage actor who made a few early silent films. Even though he was born in India he was of British descent and became a famous stage actor. He also liked to write songs for the stage. He trained to be a merchant marine for two years and then went to Australia where he prospected for gold and managed to acquire a large parcel of land deciding to become a rancher. An interesting fact is that there has always been some confusion as to his exact date of birth in India. It is shown as 1850, 1855, and 1857 but on his death certificate it was written as 1857. His parents were living in India when they were divorced so this may have added to this confusion. Even Bellew had stated one year before his own death that his mother had told him he was born sometime between 1845 and 1860 on a Thursday, March 28th. Obviously he liked to be vague about his age, as researchers have said that only the year 1860 has a March 28th that falls on a Thursday! (The following information is taken primarily from the Kyrle Bellew biographies on Wikipedia, the free encyclopedia.)

Kyrle's father was a high school student at St. Mary Hall and was ordained as an Anglican minister in 1848, while he was still a high school student. By 1851, Kyrle's father was the Reverend Bellew and he was assigned as assistant chaplain to the St. John's Cathedral in Calcutta, India. By 1853, Kyrle Bellew's parents were separated because his father had found love letters his wife Eva had written to a 23 year-old civil

Kyrle as a Young Actor

servant for the East India Company. By 1855, Eva had been granted a divorce and she did marry this young man who was named Ashley Eden six years later and lived with him in India until her own death in 1877. John Bellew had been her second husband after she was widowed from her first husband who was a career military officer and later died of a fever. Kyrle Bellew's father retained custody of the children because of suing Eva for "adultery" and went back to England after this, even though their mother countersued on the grounds of "ill treatment," in hopes of getting her children. In 1861, John Bellew took a new wife, Emily Louisa Wilkinson who was from Dublin, Ireland. However, Kyrle Bellew never got along with is stepmother and ran away from home trying to start a life at sea, until his father finally allowed him to try the Navy. Bellew spent two years in training for the merchant marines on the HMS Conway but he left after these two years to pursue an acting career. Typical of challenged childhoods, Bellew's three siblings had unusual lives just as Kyrle did. His older brother, Evelyn Bellew, immigrated to the United States in the late 1860s, married, had no children and died in 1900. One of his sisters, Sybil, married an engineer and lived in Bhownuggur, India until her husband's suicide in 1876. By 1891 the census that year reported Sybil as living as a nun in the Poor Clares convent in Kensington and she died in 1927. His other sister, Clare, married a soldier and had two children, but died when she was only 49 years old.

No one seems to know how Kyrle Bellew got so passionate about the theater, and with no formal training, why he decided to be an actor. With his blonde hair and handsome looks he was a shoe-in for the leading man parts in plays and it turned out, was a natural as an actor. He had a brief fling with a French actress whom he married in 1873 before he had even landed a position in an acting company. This was during the time that he was prospecting for gold and had purchased quite a large acreage of land on which to ranch while living in Australia. Eugeneie Le Grande was a French actress who had been born and raised in Paris. Le Grande had traveled with French vaudeville before performing in London and then got pregnant and headed to Melbourne giving birth to her baby on board the ship. Kyrle met her, wooed her and married her a year after meeting her, yet used the name Harold Dominick Bellew on the marriage certificate. Only a few weeks into the marriage they separated when Kyrle found out that Eugeneie had been the mistress of a famous actor named Boothroyd Fairclough who probably would not marry her when he found out about her pregnancy or she wanted to keep it secret from him and had fled. Anyway Fairclough hunted her down and discovered them on their honeymoon in Australia. Bellew was, according to accounts, not aware of this previous arrangement, although he certainly must have wondered where the baby had come from! LeGrande returned to her lover taking her child with her and for some reason Bellew waited 17 years to officially divorce LeGrande in May of 1888.

After a few years of acting under his belt he toured with the Cora-Brown-Potter stock company beginning in 1880. In 1888, Kyrle began giving acting lessons for Mrs. Leslie Carter who was a married socialite. A year later he was named as the third party in a highly public divorce between the Carters because Mrs. Carter's husband had named several men as his wife's lovers, but Bellew had the most time with her away from her home and her husband. Mrs. Carter had intended to become an actress under her maiden name, Caroline Dudley.

While on the London stage Bellew starred with many famous stage actresses such as Mabel Belton and Pattie Bella. Eventually he toured with acting troupes in the United States as well. "In the last decade of his life Bellew tended to his mining property in Australia, which required making long journeys back and forth from the United States. Finally at the turn of the century and in the US for good, he continued to be popular on Broadway premiering in such plays as 'Raffles the Amateur Cracksman.' He found time to venture into primitive motion pictures, which at the time were considered well beneath an actor of his stature." There are three film credits for H. Kyrle Bellew: "The Great Sword Combat on the Stairs" in 1902, the "Adventures of Sherlock Holmes" and the "Gentleman of France" both released in 1905. He was well known in Utah and played quite often at the old Salt Lake Theatre, where he was a beloved actor. He died on November 11th 1911 in Salt Lake City, where he had been appearing in the play "The Mollusc" at the Salt Lake Theatre. The newspapers had stated that his tour had been cancelled and he would be rushed home to be taken care of, but he didn't' make it "home" alive. He was buried in New York having no family to speak of except a son he did not ever lay claim to although to this day everyone else believes Cosmo Kyrle Bellew was his son. ("Kyrle Bellew" on Wikipedia, the free encyclopedia)

According to some accounts, Cosmo Kyrle Bellew, was born in London, England while his father was on tour, on November 23, 1885. The only indication of the truth in this matter, as to whether Cosmo Kyrle Bellew was or was not Kyrle Bellew's son is a posthumous book entitled "Short Stories" by none other than Kyle Bellew. In this book, Bellew tells the story of a protagonist "Jack" who has a sham marriage to a French actress and many of the details parallel the facts about Le Grande and Kyrle; their marriage date, the illegitimate child the French actress had accompanying her, etc. So perhaps Cosmos was born in England when Le Grande was performing there because Le Grande reportedly bore Bellew a son. The problem is that Cosmo Kyrle Bellew's birth date is often cited as 1885, when Kyrle senior was on tour. On the other hand, "Cosmo Bellew's World War I draft registration card lists a birth date of 23 November 1874, with his nearest relative listed as Marjorie Bellew. There is no mention of a son in any of Kyrle Bellew's obituaries; Bellew was estranged from Le Grande following their wedding and the fate of Le Grande's child remains unknown. Le Grande married someone else later and continued to tour in the United States, Britain and Canada. Her new or perhaps only husband left her a substantial fortune in Australia when he died in 1893.

So there are three options, either Cosmo was the illegitimate son of some other man and his mother Le Grande gave him Bellew's name anyway, or Cosmo really was Le Grande and Bellew's son born in 1874. The third option of course is that Cosmo Kyrle Bellew had absolutely no connection to Harold Kyrle Money Bellew. History demands that Cosmo be his son and yet the facts seem confusing. Anyway, Cosmo Kyrle Bellew

Eugenie Le Grande, his Wife

had quite a long career in the movies as a bit part player. He often played butlers, escorts, or an aristocrat or simply a "dignified man." His first part was in 1922's "Vanity Fair." He was in 12 movies in the "silent" twenties and about the same amount of movies in the "talkie" thirties. His most memorable one would be in 1934's "The Merry Widow," although it was an unaccredited part. His last credited part was in 1935 in the film "It Happened in Paris." After this he may have worked on the stage or continued in unaccredited parts in films. According to some he was only 63 when he died in Hollywood, California on January 25, 1948. However, if he was born in 1885 he would have been 63, but if he was born in 1874, he would have been 74. One wonders if even Cosmo new the truth about who his parents really were, unless of course Eugenie Le Grande or Kyrle Bellew had had something to do with him. The quite unusual synchronicity of a name might have been all Cosmo Bellew had to hang onto.

SUSA YOUNG GATES
& EMMA LUCY GATES BOWEN

▸•◂

THE GRAND DRAMA OF THE FIRST OPERA COMPANIES IN UTAH

Opera Comes To Utah Along With Opera Stars

The first opera company to come to Utah was a traveling one that performed at the old Salt Lake Theatre in June of 1869. The Howson Opera Burlesque and Comedy Troupe performed several operas in their repertoire as well as other lighter operettas, etc. And for the next ten years this was how audiences in Utah got to see operas and operettas. The first official opera company in Utah was formed in 1880, called the Zion's Musical Society, formed by a pioneer musical director, David O. Calder. The company rehearsed in the old Social Hall and Duncan McAllister, Henry Gardner, J.R. Morgan, John D. Spencer, W.D. Owen sang along with Libbie Sheets, Annie Midgely, Lizzie Edmonds, and Annie MacKay. The operas they tried to perform were quite an undertaking and it really was too much for this company to survive for long.

Several companies then passed through again, such as the Oates Opera Bouffe Company, Comly-Barton Opera Company and the Marie Geistinger Opera Company. However, the greatest productions of grand opera were put on by Etelka Gerster in 1884 and by the Carleton Opera Company on several return visits during the 1880s. Their leading lady was Emma Abbott she made a last visit to Salt Lake City in 1891 in December and died a month later in the Templeton Hotel in Salt Lake City of pneumonia. The whole town was in mourning after this event took place. The next local company, again short lived, was formed by a music and piano teacher, H.S. Krouse. Nettie Thatcher was the leading lady of this production of "Patience" in 1885.

Favorite local leading lady opera singers from the late eighteen hundreds to the thirties were Nettie Thatcher Andersen, Emma-Ramsey-Morris, Wanda Lyon, Leuella Ferrin-Sharp, Irene Kelly-Williams, Louise "Lennie" Savage-Riter (one of photographer C.R. Savage's daughters) who performed on the stage, but also had a beautiful singing voice, and of course, Emma Lucy Gates Bowen. These singers often sang in the local companies as well as having smaller parts in the traveling opera companies when they came to town. Some of them performed with the Mormon Tabernacle Choir and other special performances produced in Salt Lake City only.

Local promoter, John D. Spencer also formed an opera company that same year, in 1885, called the Careless Opera Company and put on some Gilbert & Sullivan operettas. All of these local companies did not leave the state, but did tour all the major towns inside the state. The Evan Stephens Grand Opera Company was created locally in 1888-89. Stephens was the director of the Tabernacle Choir and had many other

Evans Stephens Opera Company

duties so that this opera company only put on three major productions during those two years. That same year H.S. Krouse also produced an opera, so one might say that 1889 was a year of "opera fever" in Utah. The local opera singers in Stephen's company were Bessie Dean Allison, Nellie Druce Pugsley and Lizzie Thomas Edward. The leading men were Robert C. Easton, Heber C. Goddard and of course, Evan Stephens, who had a beautiful singing voice as well.

The Salt Lake Opera Company appeared in 1897 and put on a few operas as well. Some of the founders of this company have familiar Salt Lake Theatre names: Horace G. Whitney, John D. Spencer, Heber C. Goddard and Willard E. Weihe. Many of the soloists in this company went on to national fame, such as Emma Lucy Gates Bowen, Sallie Fisher, and Viola Pratt (Gillette). Three other local singers and actresses also went on to national and even international fame and these were Hazel Dawn, Margaret Romaine Browning and Ada Dwyer. Bessie Dean, Nellie Druce Pugsley and Lizzie Thomas Edward, all had the talent to have succeeded either on Broadway or in an opera company but they all chose marriage and a domestic life instead. Robert C. Easton and Heber S. Goddard also went on to national careers, but Goddard's career was short-lived because while singing for charity on a home visit, he caught pneumonia and died.

However, the biggest and most successful opera company to ever be formed in Utah, and also to tour the western states, was formed in 1915 by Lucy Gates Bowen. It was called the Lucy Gates Grand Opera Company and had a huge cast for many of the performances it gave. The leading male singers were: P. Melvin Petersen, B. Cecil Gates, Hugh M. Dougall, O.D. Romney, A.J. Southwick, Alfonzo Romero, John W. Summerhays, Herbert Gould, and Richard Hale. The leading female singers were: Margaret Anderson, Marjorie Lee Klemm, Lucy Gates, and Evangeline Thomas Beesley. Lucy also imported many guest artists from all over the country. These were the biggest operas ever produced in the state, until modern times where now there are two major opera companies based in Utah today, The Utah Festival Opera Company in Logan, started in the 1990s and still going strong. The Utah Symphony &

Utah Opera Company founded in Salt Lake City in 1978 and having merged with the symphony orchestra, is still going strong.

Emma Lucy Gates Bowen – Opera Singer, Company Founder

Born in St. George, raised in Provo, going with her family on her father's five-year mission to the Sandwich Islands, Lucy was a child prodigy where music was concerned. She played the organ, the guitar, and the ukulele and sang for church functions, all before they returned to Utah when she was 9 years old. A famous musician happened to hear her play the piano right after they returned and was quoted as saying, "Oh, nice, that child should study in Europe." Her grandmother then became determined that Emma Lucy or "Lu" as many called her, would get this chance. At thirteen, she won a prize for piano in the Salt Lake Tabernacle where all the other contestants were seventeen or older. There were three Eastern critics as the judges. Her dream then, was to go Europe to study.

GROUP OF LUCY GATES GRAND OPERA SINGERS

1. P. Melvin Petersen, as "Valentine," in "Faust." 2. B. Cecil Gates, Conductor. 3. Margaret Anderson. 4. Marjorie Lee Klemm. 5. Lucy Gates. 6. Hugh W. Dougall. 7. O. D. Romney, Jr. 8. A. J. Southwick, as "Monterone," in "Rigoletto." 9. Alfonzo Romero. 10. Evangeline Thomas Beesley. 11. John W. Summerhays. 12. Herbert Gould, as "Mephisto." 13. Richard Hale, as "Rigoletto."

Lucy Gates Bowen Grand Opera Company

Her parents saw this as a way for her to become a music teacher back in Utah and to further her musical talents. They mortgaged their house so that she could afford to go. She accompanied her older sister and her sister's new husband on their honeymoon to Germany. In 1898 they sailed for Europe and within months Lucy asked to go study in Berlin. It was very much like a scene from a Willa Cather novel, The Song of the Lark, where a young rural girl from Colorado becomes a renowned opera singer. One wonders if perhaps this particular scene is based on Emma Lucy's life story. It is the scene when she is "discovered." One day while practicing the piano, her music teacher discovered her singing and listened for quite a while, his presence unknown. He was later quoted as saying that, "He was thunderstruck at the marvelous beauty of her voice. It was so flexible and sweet; the range was so wide; the quality so pure... it was a voice of the generation." However, unlike the fictional girl from Colorado, leaving home for Emma Lucy was a little more difficult because of the long gentle arm of her religion. Over the years, various family members went over to be with her while she studied. At first, her sister went over, and then her father, then her grandmother, and finally, her mother came several times on trips that she was taking for other reasons. While they supported her, they were all gently trying to persuade her to come home to Utah. ("Emma Lucy Gates Bowen: Singer, Musician, Teacher" by Catherine M. Johnson, Utah Historical Quarterly, Volume 6, Number 4, Fall, 1966)

But Emma changed over to vocal studies and though it was a hard decision for her, she wrote her parents that, "My whole soul seems to be brought out more when I sing... I love to sing and I think one of the greatest pleasures of my future life will be in singing praises to God in his holy Temples," while noting that there was not one good Mormon teacher or singer in Utah." She had had a taste of music and singing on the international level and would not return to her home state for some time. She began studying voice at the Berlin Conservatory of Music, but upon discovering that she had to take other types of classes, she soon quit and found herself a voice teacher named Madame Correlli. However, many of the teachers had already commented on the power and charm of

Lucy Gates Bowen as a Young Singer
University of Utah Special Collections

her "sweet voice" while passing by her practice room. Many of them commented that it would really be a shame for such an amazing talent to become sequestered in Utah. She was offered her first contract and reassured her family that she only had desires on returning home afterwards to a life of motherhood and children, while teaching music and singing for her church. Even on returning home, the national tour had not been decided upon until Lucy consulted with her parents. (Ibid, UHQ, p.348)

Madame Correlli, who did not understand the Mormon ways, had her own thoughts on this blockage of her prize student's talent, "... it is lamentably wicked that she should be buried in the West, to sing only in the Mormon Temple, which was what she was expected to do, and which was the only career laid out for her by her parents, who are much opposed to her going before the public even as a concert singer, while they were overcome at the idea of her appearing in Opera. And the girl (Lucy) had no wish beyond theirs." (Ibid, UHQ, p.349)

However, Lucy eventually had total support from her family and parents in her musical pursuits and her parents finally agreed to let her tour at the very young age of 20. Her mother, who she was close to, perhaps thought of her own missed chance to study music in Europe years earlier. Every time Lucy came home, she performed all over the state for church programs and functions, as well as at the Salt Lake Theatre in full-length operas.

Eventually called "The Utah Nightingale" or "Utah's First Lady of Music," her coloratura soprano became famous in the German opera houses. But her debut performance was made in 1902 at Carnegie Hall with less than flattering reviews. Her concerts in Boston fared much better and it was there that she began to be called "The Utah Nightingale." In 1907 she continued her studies in Berlin. Her European debut took place in 1908. She was the first American girl to debut at the Royal Opera House of Berlin singing in a foreign tongue. She sang more than fifty roles in her four year run in Germany. She had a crisis with her voice where she could only sing for ten minutes at a time but Madame Correlli helped her to correct this before her debut by teaching her to sing in a different way. Five months later she had signed a five-year contract with the Royal Opera House of Berlin. Unfounded rumors from Salt Lake City caused a contract dispute with the opera house and she ended up singing with the Royal Opera House of Cassel for many years. She performed in many other European cities but the advent of World War II ended her career in Europe, and especially in Germany. This became the end of her international career.

She returned to America where she got a recording contract with Columbia Records and auditioned for the Metropolitan Opera, even though she was virtually unknown in America. The Metropolitan only

Singer and Actress
Utah State Historical Society

Lucy in Costume
University of Utah Special Collections

Opera Star
University of Utah Special Collections

offered her secondary roles so she decided to audition for the Chicago Opera where she received guest engagements with leading opera stars. She signed with them. Even as early as 1901, every time she returned home for engagements, she spoke with her brother Cecil about plans to start an opera company in Utah.

By 1915, Lucy was finally able to start her own Lucy Gates Grand Opera Company. B. Cecil Gates, besides being a musician and composer, was a graduate of the Schrwenka Conservatory of Berlin, Germany. He founded the Lucy Gates Opera Company with his sister as impresario. He was also the director of the LDS School of Music and the director of the Mormon Tabernacle Choir. The first year, Lucy performed one act of "Rigoletto," and then the following year, a whole opera: "La Traviata." Eventually, the Lucy Gates Opera Company was performing all over the Rocky Mountain West. Cecil was the musical director and conductor. Not only did she perform many operas, but she also brought in various famous opera singers from all over the nation.

Lucy continued to tour throughout the United States as a soloist and the opera company continued to flourish, but mainly in her home state. There on the Salt Lake Theatre stage they performed "Carmen," "Rigoletto," "Faust," La Boheme" and many, many others for quite a few years. With her magnetic personality, she also entertained quite a few famous performers in her living room. She probably had her share of suitors as well, although she often said that she was married to her career instead. In 1916, she met and married a Mormon, Albert E. Bowen, who was an attorney in Salt Lake City. He was a widower with twin boys to be raised. He later became an LDS Apostle and she then settled in and began to perform closer to home.

While her husband engaged domestic help so that Lucy could still perform, her mother Susa was quite outspoken about Lucy's need to be in her home state, near her family. Apparently, Lucy and her mother were as different as night and day, but they were two very outspoken women who sometimes offended those to whom they spoke. They were actually very close in temperament and had a lot in common both in interests and religiously. According to family members, they were very close all of their lives, and yet, at the same time, there were many occasions when they exchanged heated words. Susa always saw Lucy's career as a problem and they once exchanged words backstage at a performance about this.

As Lucy grew older, and her career lessened in importance to her, she was quoted as saying in her later years, "If I had to choose between home and child and a career, I'd take the home and children." While Lucy managed to bring opera to Utah, it was some forty years after her death in 1951, before a new opera company was started in Utah. In the meantime, she helped to establish the Utah Symphony Orchestra during its young and struggling years by bringing in soloists while promoting and encouraging young musicians from Utah. She became a music teacher in her later years. Apparently, she was always a prima donna, dramatic and quite a character. Critics described her voice as being abundant, lush, and lovely. Her voice seemed to emulate style, taste and elegance while having a flexible buoyancy. Her greatest talent as a singer was the uncanny ability to enunciate the words clearly whether the piece was being sung in English or another language. According to her brother, Franklin, she really had an ear for music and never wavered in her pitch or tone. She always remained true to her promise to her mother, who had also sacrificed her career, to help finance the education of some of her brothers and sisters and those of the generations to come. In the end, she became a music teacher, but was able to experience a career as an opera star as well. (Ibid, UHQ, p.354).

Besides the many traveling vocalists and the many local popular singers, there were many new vocalists who joined the Lucy Gates Grand Opera Company in 1915 for the few years that it presented operas. Here is a list of various vocalists who performed one time or consistently in her opera company both local and from other locations throughout the United States: Margaret Andersen, Nettie Thatcher-Andersen, Evangeline Thomas Beesley, Lucy Gates Bowen, Hugh M. Dougall, B, Cecil Gates, Herbert Gould, Richard Hale, Marjorie Lee Klemm, Wanda Lyon, Emma Ramsey-Morris, P. Melvin Petersen, Louise "Lennie" Savage Riter, O.D. Romney, Alfonzo Romero, Leuella Ferrin-Sharp, A.J. Southwick, John W. Summerhays, Irene Kelly-Williams.

Susa Young Gates – The Power Behind The Throne

Emma Lucy Gates was a daughter of Susa Young Gates, one of the favored daughters of Brigham Young. Born in 1856 to Brigham Young's twenty-second wife, Lucy Bigelow Young, Susa lived to be seventy-seven years old. The first child to be born in the Lion House, Susa lived up to her reputation as the "first" in many ways. While considered royalty in the Utah Territory, Susa was a fighter for women's rights, higher education for women, a great supporter of the arts and certainly, as best friends to Maud May Babcock, very active in gaining the funding and support from Brigham for stage drama in early Utah. Susa was also outspoken about issues in her church but eventually made peace with her position as a woman in her church by having a discussion with the Mormon intelligentsia. It was here that she was told that wherever there was a strong, powerful woman, there was a man a little stronger and more powerful than her leading the way. She accepted that this was the balance necessary to have happiness and spiritual wealth in the world into which she was born.

Susa often quoted what her father had told her: "Daughter, use all your gifts to build righteousness in the earth. Never use them to acquire name or fame. Never rob your home, or your children. If you were to become the greatest woman in the world, and your name should be known in every land and clime, and you would fail in your duty as wife and mother, you would wake up on the morning of the first resurrection and find you had failed in everything; but anything you can do after you have satisfied the claims of husband and family will rebound to your honor and to the glory of God." ("Susa Young Gates," by Carolyn D. Person, Mormon Sisters: Women in Early Utah edited by Claudia L. Bushman, Utah State University Press, 1976, 1997, p.202).

Besides all of her political, educational promotional and social activities, she truly was in the background, financially and supportively of both her best friend Maud May, considered to be the mother of drama in Utah, and her daughter Lucy, considered the mother of Utah Opera.

Susa Young Gates
Utah State Historical Society

Susa was a writer, teacher, administrator, public speaker, home economist, political activist, suffragist, researcher, world traveler, and held many LDS church positions over the years. "She corresponded with Tolstoy and took tea with Queen Victoria. Susan B. Anthony once offered her the post of secretary of the National Council of Women if she would give up her militant Mormonism; Susa declined." "Despite a lifelong commitment to the Church, she underwent a spiritual crisis in middle age, and as an old woman,... she lamented her inability to have the beloved daughter of her first marriage sealed to her in the temple...Still in her brilliant and independent ways she epitomized many of the tendencies of her age." (Ibid, Person, p. 199).

But most important, Susa was an accomplished musician and lover of the arts. She enjoyed success as a singer, ballerina, and actress and was an extremely prolific writer for her church. She was also an excellent teacher of piano and voice. Susa also wrote several published novels in which she spoke frankly about the intimacies of sex in marriage, something quite shocking in those days. "Teach young girls that repression is as unnatural as lewdness," she was quoted as penning in her writings. "Married people should be mated on the three planes upon which human beings meet and mingle – the physical, mental and spiritual." It was perhaps the burden of her unsuccessful early marriage that prompted her to speak and write so frankly about such things in an era when practically no one spoke of them. (Ibid, Person, p. 201).

There were five pianos in the Lion House and along with music and piano lessons; actress Sara Alexander tutored all of Brigham's daughters in drama and dancing. Susa was the most multi-talented daughter in her particular generation, both as a dancer and as a musician. One tale is told of Susa, at the age of ten, bursting from a huge rose on the stage of the Salt Lake Theatre to perform a ballet dance that brought down the house. When Karl Maeser, the founder of higher education in Utah, established the Music Department at the Brigham Young Academy, Susa was involved in organizing this department and directing two separate choral groups as well. Maeser wanted Susa to study music in Europe but she never did get a chance to do this.

She was asked instead to journey to the Sandwich Islands on a mission for her church where she met a missionary, Jacob F. Gates. They eventually married in 1880. On the one hand, she was married at sixteen and then divorced at twenty-one with two small children to raise; on the other hand, she married again, had six terrible miscarriages and bore an additional 13 children, with only five of them surviving to adulthood. She lost several of these children while on the five-year mission to the Sandwich Islands. Two of these were infants, and the others were lost to various tragedies along the way. She was by no means a stranger to tragedy, nor the fact that her first husband had been a drinker. Where she found her most luck was in marrying a man who supported her in her endeavors. She was able to found and begin publishing the Young Women's Journal for her church, once she had settled in with Jacob Gates.

In her later years, she became a vegetarian, had a nervous breakdown, experienced a crisis of faith, traveled the world as a speaker, and eventually retreated from her feminist attitudes. She was quoted as saying that, "I think a woman should respect and obey her husband in righteousness, and I think what little success I have made is because I have never disobeyed my husband or the counsel of those over me." On the other hand, those who knew her husband Jacob were quoted as saying that, "Without his willingness, you could not have done so much. So few men are willing to undergo a little personal inconvenience to let their wives do anything. The exceptions are loved so much more. A man's life is not measured alone by what he accomplishes. More than that, it is what he enables others to do." It seems that in an age of absolute control over one's family, Susa, on the second time around, found a man as advanced in her own thinking as she was. That she had the strength to do all else that she did, while spending years and years in childbirth and loss, is an amazing feat. It seems that she and Jacob were perfectly mated on all "three planes." (Ibid, Person, p.219)

All five of Susa's surviving children ended up doing something in the arts as a vocation. Her oldest daughter, Leah, became a writer and Home Economics professor. Emma became a world re-known opera singer. Harvey became a Hollywood motion picture writer, B. Cecil was a musician, composer and choral director and Franklin spent his time in broadcast radio and as a professor at BYU. All but Emma Lucy and Harvey stayed within the confines of their own state. But it was only Emma Lucy who stepped out into the world at large while still maintaining her standing in her faith. For while Susa "...frequently left her husband and many children to develop her own talents, she did not approve of such interests taking the place of home and family. Susa believed, as her father had, that a woman's first responsibilities were 'obedience to authority and reverence for the Priesthood..." And this was what she taught all her children. Emma Lucy Gates was obedient to her parents' wishes, just as they were supportive of her. ("Emma Lucy Gates Bowen: Singer, Musician, Teacher," by Catherine M. Johnson, Utah Historical Quarterly, Vol. 6, No. 4, Fall, 1996, P.344)

Susa Young Gates was not only a supporter of her daughter's opera singing, but also best friends with Maud May Babcock. She converted her to Mormonism, and helped Babcock to found a drama program at the University of Utah, as well as being instrumental in getting a theater built on the campus, Kingsbury Hall. While on the one hand Susa had been a strong supporter of polygamy and actually helped some illegal plural marriages to be performed after the Manifesto in 1890 came out making this illegal. On the other hand, she could be considered a strong supporter of the suffragette movement while at the same time advocating that women should stay home and raise their children and support their husband's endeavors. Yet on the other hand, she should certainly be considered instrumental in the founding of both music and drama programs of all kinds in Utah. She really was a "Mormon Enigma," or at least a "Woman's Enigma" in many ways. In our time today, her conflicting views on just about everything concerning women, would be baffling to say the least.

SARAH ELIZABETH CARMICHAEL- PERFORMANCE POETRY & MADNESS

A brilliant poet, Lizzie Carmichael was born in Setauket, Long Island, New York in 1838. It is possible that her parents sealed her fate although there were other factors that probably contributed to her future. It seems that her parents were double cousins and by marrying each other the chances of normal children were compromised. Out of the seven children that they had, only two survived, Lizzie and her sister Mary Ann. Mary Ann had below normal intelligence, while Lizzie on the other hand, was near genius. The Carmichaels converted to Mormonism and Lizzie's father worked on the Nauvoo Temple. In 1850, the family came west in a wagon train with many other faithful Mormons. Lizzie was twelve years old. They settled in a small home on the corner of Fifth South and State Street and Lizzie attended a little adobe school just a block away. Lizzie was very pretty and had beautiful large eyes and dark hair. She was quite shy and retiring but also described as very charming. Lizzie began writing poetry as soon as she was able to read and write and in her early teens in Salt Lake City, her father was often seen carrying his lunch pail under one arm and Lizze's latest poems under the other. As he walked to work he passed the newspaper office and dropped off her latest manuscripts for the local paper to publish.

The Deseret News had published over fifty of her poems by 1858, although her very first submission had been suspect. The young poet had to get a high church authority to vouch for its authenticity. By the age of twenty, Lizzie was a well-known local poet and yet she was the only well-known one who wasn't writing poetry with a Mormon slant to it. Eliza Snow was the premier poet at the time and Lizzie sought her guidance. Because Lizzie wrote poetry that was universal in its language and subject matter, her poems began to appeal to people outside of the Utah Territory. This worried Brigham Young a bit and so he counseled Lizzie in this manner: "Use your gifts to build up truth and righteousness in the earth and your gift will be preserved as long as you shall live. If you prostitute your powers to gain fame and gold, your light will go out in darkness." (Women Worth Their Salt: Notable But Often Unnoted Women Of Utah edited by Colleen Whitley, "Sarah Elizabeth Carmichael, Poet Genius of Pioneer Utah," by Miriam B. Murphy, Utah State University Press, 1996, pp.61-74)

Lizzie really just yearned for one thing and that was a good education. She felt that she was in a limited intellectual environment living in the early Salt Lake Valley. In the 1860s, Lizzie's fame slowly spread and she was becoming a nationally known and respected poet. One of the reasons for this, besides her obvious talent, was the fact that she was writing about the Civil War, before it, during it and afterwards. Her future husband arrived in the Salt Lake Valley with Colonel Connor's troops in 1861. Jonathan or Josiah M. Williamson was an army surgeon attached to Connor's division and actually operated on the troops who returned home from the Bear River Massacre. He and another physician traveled north fifty miles to take care of the wounded. In 1864 he was in California for a while and then served in the Civil War with the 16th Army Corps under General A.J. Smith and was in combat from 1864 to

Sarah Elizabeth Carmichael, Poet
Utah State Historical Society

Descent into Madness
Utah State Historical Society

1865 as a surgeon and soldier. In 1866 he traveled on his own back to Salt Lake City to see Lizzie.

Lizzie and Josiah probably met during the time when he was stationed at Camp Douglas in the early 1860s. Some suggest that the doctor read Lizzie's story called "The Lily of the Valley" and then he wanted to meet her and sought her acquaintance. The fact that Lizzie was in her late twenties and unmarried speaks for itself. She opposed polygamy and was already rebelling against her parent's beliefs. It is very probable that she had had marriage proposals but refused them all. This, coupled with her alliance with gentiles in town, showed her strong will and that she still had the freedom to choose on her own. Some reported that Brigham Young was perturbed with her enough to ban her poetry or shun her company, but this was never really proven. Utahns for the most part were glad to claim her, as her growing celebrity began to spread outside the territory. The poem that pushed her into national fame was the one she wrote entitled "President Lincoln's Funeral." When the San Francisco Globe Era published the poem, everyone was impressed with Sarah Elizabeth Carmichael's poetic genius. This was read all over the country as his funeral train crossed the United States.

Julia Dean Hayne, who packed the Salt Lake Theatre every day for a year, read this poem more than once as part of her performances dressed in mourning clothes. Hayne and Lizzie became fast friends in the year that Julia was performing at the Salt Lake Theatre. They became very attached to each other as artists and were both extremely complex women. Julia brought the outside world with her and Lizzie was quickly intrigued by this. Julia Dean performed this reading many times on the Salt Lake Theatre stage and elsewhere. She would appear on stage "... in appropriate mourning dress, and read the poem with a pure pathos and perfect elocution, considering the immense capacity and imperfect acoustics of the room. It requires genius to read as well as write good poetry." ("Poetic Genius of Pioneer Utah," by Miriam M. Murphy, Utah Historical Quarterly, Volume 43 Number 2, Winter 1975, p. 61)

As Lizzie's fame spread, Brigham Young, some say, tried once again to ban local publication of her poetry, but this was still conjecture.

It is more likely that individuals took it upon themselves to do the "banning." In 1866, her first volume of poetry was published and Lizzie was hoping to enter Vassar College. By age 28, she had poems in many national magazines and reviewers were raving about her poems. At the same time, her future husband, Dr. Williamson got involved in a controversial claim-jumping case in Salt Lake City. He and another man had claimed the same piece of property west of the Jordan River. They were both however, gentiles. One night while they were working their claim, they were surrounded by forty Mormon men and forced down the bank of the river. Something far worse might have happened to these two men, had not one of the forty, recognized Williamson's partner Brown, both at the time just recently mustered out of the military, as the provost guard who had treated this man kindly while in the city. The two men were then helped from the water and warned to leave the "country" as soon as possible. This incident probably contributed to Williamson's complete loss of interest in settling in the Utah Territory.

The main obstacle to Lizzie and Josiah's marriage was removed shortly after this. Lizzie's mother died suddenly at the age of 58 of a heart attack and she had been the last resistance to the marriage. The couple was married at Fort Bridger by a well-known judge, W.A. Carter and then went to live in Ohio which was the doctor's native state. The local paper The Vedette wrote favorably about this marriage because of Lizzie's growing fame and the good reputation of the doctor. The following quote shows how much most of the local people adored her: "The happy couple are both well and favorably known in this community, the gay Benedict as the late Surgeon of the Second Cavalry C.V., and the worthy bride as the sweet poetess of Utah. May their path through life be strewn with flowers, and every step a fountain of friendship gush forth to water them." (Ibid, UHQ, p.64)

Ironically, only a year after their marriage, Lizzie began to show signs of mental deterioration. However, she was still able to publish a letter in the Cincinnati Commercial in which she denounced polygamy and claiming that, "I am no Hagar wandering desolate from the tent of Mormon Abraham, but one of the few women who have grown up in the shadow of Brigham Young's despotism, and dared to defy him in the presence chamber of his power…" (Ibid, UHQ, p.65)

There are three theories on just where this mental illness might have come from, although all of them probably contributed to Lizzie's mental changes. Some historians blame this on what might have been the mental illness in her family line, others on the genetic difficulties that can arise in marrying cousins, and some, on the fact that on their honeymoon they had traveled back east and then to California. While in California, Lizzie took an accidental fall. In this fall, she struck her head on the pavement and what they called in those days "brain fever" continued to plague her for months to come. But genetics played an even bigger part because her parents had been double cousins and of the seven children born to them only two survived. Lizzie's sister was of below normal intelligence, and amazingly, Lizzie had a very superior mind. Nowadays this could have been a somewhat predictable outcome and couples who marry under these circumstances often think twice about having children. But in those days, you probably just "trusted in the Lord" and dealt with what arrived.

Unfortunately, Lizzie's poetic genius died quickly with the onset of her mental illness, caused by a combination of head injury, family inheritances and second cousins marrying. It is doubtful that Brigham Young's admonitions had much to do with it. Lizzie never fully recovered and her poetry career ended abruptly. Admirably, her husband cared for her, as well as her sister and his own mother for the next fourteen years. Although Lizzie had many rational days, she was unable to put pen to paper, and if she did, none of these poems were ever recovered. The family moved to Pinoch, Nevada and then back to Salt Lake City, while Williamson carried out a private medical practice. Friends who visited Lizzie were quoted as saying that the light of her intelligence had gone out of her eyes but that she did have long periods of lucidity. Two years after Williamson's mother passed away, Josiah Williamson also died. He had hired a housekeeper to help him, Miss Atkinson, who took over the care of the two sisters for the next 19 years. After this Lizzie became too difficult to manage and she was sent to the state mental hospital, although she had special privileges and attendants at the hospital.

In 1874, Mary Jane Mount Taylor, a childhood friend, visited Lizzie in her husband's home and reported that, "She is better now but not well enough to take her place in Society. Poor Lizzie! It made my heart ache to see her. She was so changed. The light of intelligence had gone from her eyes, and her voice had a strange sound like someone speaking in the distance, but she talked intelligently and wanted me to come again. She has a beautiful home nicely furnished. Her husband's mother and sister (live) there to take care of her. It made me feel very nervous to see her, and my health is poor I do not think I can go again." (Ibid, UHQ, p.65)

In the 1890s, another friend described her visit to see Lizzie at the state mental hospital. She said that Lizzie was a slender figure who wore close fitting black dresses with a white crepe shawl over her shoulders and was "...at Sabbath services – with them, but not of them." (Ellen J. Jakeman, An Enduring Legacy, "Pioneer Poets & Poetry" pamphlet by the Daughters of the Utah Pioneers, pp.401-404)

Some would say that Lizzie paid for her worldly fame as Brigham Young had predicted and others said that she had paid for deeply hurting both her parents and her faith by leaving it like she did. Others said that her genetic inheritance would have fallen on her anyway, regardless of where she was or what she chose to do. Still others said that it may well have had nothing to do with any of this, but was simply the result of a tragic fall and the brain damage that she received from this fall that permanently altered who she was. And certainly back in those days, time in a mental institution just meant that one would become even crazier. Historians disagree on how much time Lizzie spent there. Some say it was only in the very last years of her life, while others say that the housekeeper quit quite early and Lizzie went off to the state mental hospital to live for many, many years.

Here is a small portion of the extremely long poem that Lizzie wrote for Abraham Lincoln's eulogy, just to give you a flavor of her mid-nineteenth century writing:

"President Lincoln's Funeral"

"Toll! Toll!
Toll! Toll!
All rivers seaward wend.
Toll! Toll!
Toll! Toll!
Weep for the nation's friend.
Every home and hall was shrouded,
Every thoroughfare was still;
Every brow was darkly clouded,
Every heart was faint and chill.
Oh! The inky drop of poison
In our bitter draught of grief!
Oh! The sorrow of a nation
Mourning for its murdered chief!
Toll! Toll!
Toll! Toll!
Bound is the reaper's sheaf –
Toll! Toll!
Toll! Toll!
All mortal life is brief.
Toll! Toll!
Toll! Toll!
Weep for the nation's chief!
Bands of mourning draped the homestead,
And the sacred house of prayer:
Mourning fold lay black and heavy
On true bosoms everywhere:
Yet there were no tear-drops streaming
From the deep and solemn eye
Till the funeral train went by.
Of the hour that mutely waited

Strongest arms were closely folded,
Most impassioned lips at rest;
Tears were frozen in their sources,
Blushes burned themselves away;
Language bled through broken heart-threads,
Lips had nothing left to say.
Yet there was a marble sorrow
In each still face, chiseled deep;
Something more than words could utter,
Something more than tears could weep."

It is interesting to me that both Julia Dean Hayne and Sarah Elizabeth Carmichael "died" young. Perhaps as friends they had an intuitive sense about their futures. While Julia died in child birth only a year after her season in Salt Lake City, Sarah died in another way, her mind betraying her as the years went by. Both women were considered geniuses in their day, but those who might have enjoyed their genius, didn't get to for very long. And while Julia's grave was forgotten for a long while, Sarah lived a long life imprisoned by her mind. They were both beautiful women who had many suitors, great intelligence, and impassioned lives before they lost them at a young age. Go to the biography of the actress Julia Dean Hayne to read Sarah Carmichael's poetic tribute to Julia.

THE ACTRESS & THE POET
ADA DWYER RUSSELL & AMY LOWELL

James Dwyer was born in Tipperary, Ireland in 1831 and converted to the Mormon Church in 1860. He traveled to the Utah Territory by wagon and when he got to Salt Lake City he set up a newsstand at the corner of First South and West Temple and sold magazines, books, LDS materials, pamphlets, newspapers, etc. At the time that he started this venture he only had five dollars in his pocket. He was successful enough at this that he was soon able to open a bookstore. That little bookstore, Dwyer's Bookstore, eventually became the primary meeting place for students, teachers, professors and many other intellectuals who gathered together to have deep discussions about a myriad of topics. Soon, Dwyer was also inviting many scholars and even New York book publishers to banquets at his home. In 1886, the men who founded the education system in Utah met in the back room of Dwyer's to formulate their plans. Dwyer's reading room was considered the first library west of the Mississippi. Students from the first college in town, the University of Deseret, studied in Dwyer's back room. If Dwyer didn't have time to read a book and review it, he would give the book as a gift to someone else and in payment for it, they were to read it and review it for him.

Eventually Dwyer was personal friends with many of the New York publishers and in those days, he even converted a few others to Mormonism, including Sara Alexander, the popular actress, as he had many theatrical friends as well. His firstborn child was Mary Ada Dwyer, who was born on February 18, 1863. Dwyer also helped to haul materials to the new Salt Lake Theatre and this led to a side interest in drama. So it was no surprise that as Ada grew up, she was taught liberal thinking, surrounded by intellectual "questioners," and also learned to love the theater. "In looking back over my varied career, always back of every success is father's watchful, guiding hand. There was never any teacher of elocution, or any foreign language, that came to Utah in pioneer days, that my father did not have me take lessons from. He encouraged me to further effort and chose books for me to read, and trained my trend of thought that fitted me for what was to follow." ("Ada Dwyer: Bright Lights and Lilacs," by Chris Rigby, <u>Utah Historical Quarterly</u>, Volume 43 Number 1, Winter 1975, p.44)

Ada had all the advantages that could be given to a young woman in those days without a lot of money involved. Even at eight years of age, she was in Detroit studying elocution. She studied at the school of Mary and Ida Cook, the founders of education in Utah, and by the time she was fifteen she had learned to speak fluently in Spanish and French. She was in dozens of plays, while still studying recitation in Boston and New

Ada Dwyer Russell
Utah State Historical Society

Ada Dwyer Russell
Utah State Historical Society

York. She had leads in plays at a place called the Ellerbeck House in Salt Lake City, and also in many of her high school plays as well. When the Home Dramatic Club was established in 1880, she got to perform with them on a regular basis. She attended the Salt Lake Theatre regularly and made her debut on that stage in 1881. In 1882, when she was only 19 years old, she did a one woman evening show of recitations at the Salt Lake Theatre. That same year she went to New York and got her first part on the stage there in the play "One Error." Soon there were more roles as she toured England, Australia and all around the United States. By this time she was becoming nationally known and was definitely a celebrity whenever she visited her hometown of Salt Lake City.

In 1890, at the peak of her career, she was the leading lady with The John Drew Company, opposite Harold Russell. They began to get to know one and another and three years later they were married on February 26, 1893. Ada was 30 at the time. They had a little girl named Lorna on September 5, 1894, but Harold and Ada separated soon after the baby was born. They never divorced and yet never saw each other again. Ada let her parents do most of the raising of Lorna, although she was involved with her daughter somewhat with occasional visits to Salt Lake City when she wasn't on the road. In 1897, Ada returned for her mother's funeral, yet still Lorna stayed with relatives, although this time Ada's visit was a more extended one. Ada loved her life as an actress and by having traveled all over the world, her interest in the LDS Church had waned. Ada continued to act full time for the next 18 years but never married again. Even though she was no longer religious, her hometown still welcomed her home each time she visited with a lot of fanfare. When the old Salt Lake Theatre was torn down and a telephone company building was built in its place, it was Ada Dwyer who dedicated the large golden plaque that is still on the east side of the old telephone building today.

In 1912, everything changed for Ada Dwyer, except her last name "Russell" which she kept throughout her life. She was 49 years old. She was invited to a Boston society party of women. She met the wealthy, eccentric and newly famous poet, Amy Lowell. Lowell was just 38 years old at the time. They were an unlikely couple even though they immediately found that they had many common interests in all the arts, but especially with acting and poetry. Back in those days this sort of arrangement was nicknamed a "Boston Marriage" and it definitely was a marriage in every way. At least there is a lot of evidence that points that way even though Ada Dwyer throughout her life claimed that she and Amy were just great friends. They spent all of March together after this party, but then for the next few years they parted ways, tending to their careers and getting back together whenever they could for holidays and vacations.

Amy Lawrence Lowell was born on February 9, 1874 into the prominent Lowell family of Brookline, Massachusetts. Her grandfather, John Armory Lowell had developed the cotton industry in Massachusetts and the towns of Lowell and Lawrence in Massachusetts were named after Ada's two grandfathers, John A. Lowell and Abbott Lawrence. James Russell Lowell, the famous poet, was a cousin of John Armory. Amy was the youngest daughter of five children and they all were raised at the "Sevenels" which was a nickname they had for their house taken from "seven" and the many "L's" in "Lowells." Amy was educated by an English governess until she began private school in 1883. She went on trips with the family to Europe and also to the American west. In 1891, she had her "coming out" party or debutante ball. After this the debutante was expected to have a marriage proposal within the next year. By the end of the year Amy had not been asked and her parents did not believe in allowing girls to go to college. Amy spent her time reading. She essentially educated herself by reading all 7,000 books in her father's library and then moved on to the Boston library after this.

Thus began a lifelong passion for book collecting and reading and writing. Shortly after this she did get just one marriage proposal but the man suddenly changed his mind and married someone else. Amy had really liked the man and did have to recover from a broken heart. She did this by taking a trip to Europe and Egypt for a year to recover from this rejection. She put herself on a severe diet to lose weight and improve her health and perhaps, with the ulterior motive to make herself more

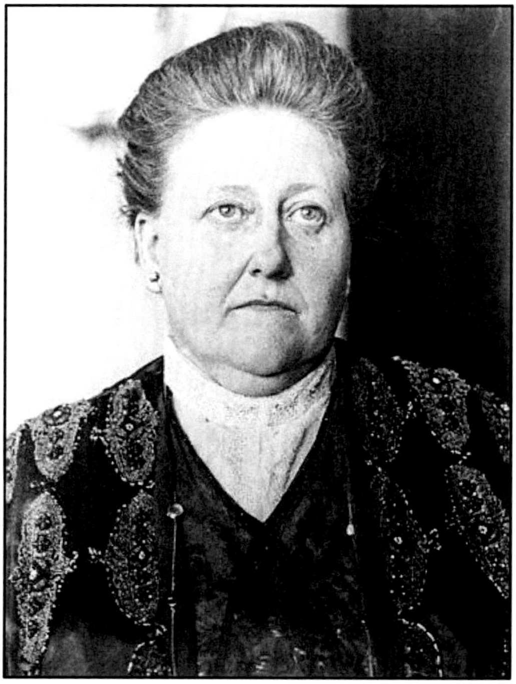

Amy Lawrence Lowell

Amy Lawrence Lowell

attractive. But this act almost ruined her health for good, as she had a glandular problem that there was no cure for and continued to gain weight throughout her life. In 1900, both her parents had died and she was already considered a wealthy socialite spinster. She bought the family home and continued her civic duties in place of her father, especially in support of education and the public libraries. Two of her brothers became famous, Lawrence became the President of Harvard University, and her brother Percival was an astronomer who founded Lowell Observatory in Flagstaff, Arizona, and discovered the "canals" of Mars.

She tried writing plays first, as she was enamored with the theater. After seeing several performances by the actress Eleanora Duse from 1863 to 1869, Lowell became inspired to try poetry and by 1902 after another Duse tour, Lowell had found her life's profession and passion, somewhat later in her life. And of course her first poems were about this famous actress, who had inspired her. Eleanora Giulia Amalia Duse had been born in Italy into a very poor family and began acting as soon as she could walk, out of necessity. She was a "genius" on the stage. She had a string of lovers of both genders, lost a child when quite young, married once later and had one daughter. She was very volatile and most of her relationships were too. She was Sara Bernhardt's rival on the stage, but unlike her, Duse was introverted, and rarely gave interviews. Even George Bernard Shaw picked Eleanor as the best actress in the world at the time.

In 1896, she gave another triumphant tour across the United States and President Grover Cleveland and his wife attended every performance. Mrs. Cleveland gave a White House tea for Duse, the first ever for an actress, and caused such a scandal that the newspapers had a heyday with it. Duse retired from acting in 1909 and then had a lesbian affair with an Italian feminist Lina Poletti. She also had an affair with Isadora Duncan, the famous dancer, and Yvette Gilbert, a famous singer. She may have had a few others but these are not provable. She spent several weeks with Isadora Duncan after the 1913 tragic drowning accident which took the lives of both of Duncan's children. With little makeup and lots of internal emoting, Eleanora Duse, introduced a new form of acting, using her body to evoke a range of emotions, sometimes so deeply passionate that she put her own health in danger. Her performances not only inspired Amy Lowell, but also the modern dance pioneer, Martha Graham.

By 1910, Amy Lowell had some poems published in The Atlantic Monthly, and by 1912, she had had her first collection of poetry published: A Dome of Many-Coloured Glass. Lowell had also established her house as a center for poetry and she became a breeder of English sheepdogs. Lowell wrote many essays, translated others' works, and wrote literary biographies. She was eventually considered an "Imagist," which Amy discovered was the name for a style of poetry which many poets in England were producing and whom the poet Ezra Pound was credited with founding or at least creating. She took it upon herself to be the first "Imagist" in America, which of course offended those in England, who were being identified with this movement. An "Imagist" was someone who used plenty of lush imagery and less verbiage, something new in poetry at the time. But she was first and foremost a businesswoman, who not only cleverly sold her own poetry, but also took over the "Imagist" movement in the United States. Ezra Pound was considered the premier English "Imagist" and of course, he was deeply offended by Amy's continued involvement in this movement and claiming to be, in his eyes, its founder. Throughout his life, Pound, continued to make scathing comments about her until he eventually removed himself from the poetry movement altogether.

Lowell was indeed an eccentric, and also could afford to be one. Perhaps this too, and the fact that she was pretty much out of the closet as far as her lifestyle was concerned, even flaunting it a little, could have added to Ezra Pound's disdain of her. Most biographies about her say that Ezra Pound was her strongest and best critic, when actually he was really pretty nasty about her. For example, Pound called the movement in America "Amyisme." He also at one time called her a "Hippopoetess" commenting on her continuous weight gains and continued to ridicule her for years even after he had left the movement. Lowell just laughed his comments off publically and continued to correspond with him; however, one would guess that privately his comments hurt her deeply.

Lowell was ridiculed for many things all her life, for being lesbian, overweight, and somewhat "Butch," even before the term was coined. She chain-smoked small cigars, wore men's shirts, was very "mannish," wore a pince nez, always had her hair done in a pompadour to add to her 5 foot height, and had a custom-made bed with exactly 16 pillows on it, and always, provided special towels for all her guests because of the dogs jumping on them. Ada had to do certain things for her when Amy wrote. She had to cover all the mirrors, remove all bright objects and stop all the clocks in the room where Amy would be writing late into the night and early morning. Lowell slept until late afternoon and Ada protected her from phone calls, unwanted visitors, and any of the other daily tasks and duties of running a household. Lowell was very outspoken for the times and never backed down from criticism, sometimes even reveling in it.

When Amy met Ada, it was love at first sight. However, there are many who say that Lowell had at least one affair after she met and was living with Ada, with the famous writer Mercedes De Acosta. The only evidence left however, is her correspondence with de Acosta over planning a memorial for Duse which never took place. Because Ada destroyed all correspondence that might be incriminating in any way after Lowell's death and upon her written request, we will never know for sure. Mercedes De Acosta's life was spread out completely in a quite hurtful and tell-all autobiography called Here Lies the Heart. And Lowell was definitely mentioned in it as one of her lovers. If true, then Amy Lowell strayed from Ada Dwyer just once in her life around 1922 to 1924, a few years before her death, something a bit hard to believe. On the other hand, Lowell would have only been between 47 and 50, and if she was not ill yet, perhaps! But knowing a bit more about Mercedes De Acosta might belay this claim, as her "tell all" autobiography named a whole slew of women she had affairs with. On the other hand, many of these affairs can be documented now. They were simply hidden to protect the careers of all these sometimes, bisexual, women.

Mercedes De Acosta lived from 1893 to 1968 and was a poet, novelist, and playwright. She was Cuban and Spanish, and was married once to a painter and socialite named Abram Poole, from 1920 to 1935. Before, during and after her marriage, she had many lesbian affairs with Hollywood's elite starting with Alla Nazimova, then Tallulah Bankhead and Isadora Duncan. After this, she lived with Eva Le Gallienne for five years and then in the next 10 years, she had various affairs with Pola Negri, an actress, Edith Wharton, a writer, Katharine Cornell, another actress, socialite Dorothy Fellowes-Gordon, and writer Amy Lowell and then came ballerina Tamara Karsavina, author Salka Viertel and actress Marlene Dietrich. Salka Viertel introduced De Acosta to Greta Garbo, De Acosta had the same heart ache as John Gilbert did, chasing Greta Garbo around trying to get her to commit to a relationship, according to De Acosta.

De Acosta, then got interested in East Indian mysticism and spent the 1950s studying Meher Baba and Ramana Maharishi, and even went to India to meet them. By 1960, Mercedes was seriously ill with a brain tumor and wrote and published her memoir for money. Of course she lost many female friends as a result of her memoir. Most of these women wanted their private life kept private, especially in those years when careers could be ruined so easily by this type of revelation. Many of these women called her a liar, both in private and publicly, and accused her of inventing her stories for fame. Most of them wiped all memory of De Acosta completely out of their lives and so it is difficult to know what the truth was. Cut off from her friends, she died in poverty and obscurity at the age of 75. However, by today's standards and even with the evidence of personal correspondence being destroyed, none of this would be that shocking. The passage of time, the change in cultural mores and the deaths of many of these famous women, makes De Acosta's memoir quite tame. Amy Lowell was not there to defend herself and neither was Ada Dwyer as by that time they had been long deceased. On the other hand, other correspondence does exist, and Hollywood insiders knowledge of these various affairs, make De Acosta's claims quite legitimate.

In the summer of 1912, Ada went with Lowell on a trip to Dublin and they spent the whole summer together. As the partnership and relationship continued, Ada then became more and more instrumental in Amy Lowell's publishing life as a poet. However, Ada continued her acting career for quite some time, and there were periods of time when they were apart and periods of time when they were together. Amy didn't like this and preferred Ada to stay with her all the time, but Ada enjoyed her theater work too much and Amy just had to accept this. But more and more, Ada began to devote herself to Amy as a secretary, critic, and eventually nurse when Amy became ill. Lowell, eventually dedicated all her books to Ada and counted on her to preserve the morning writing silence, deal with domestic squabbles among the servants, pickup library books, do research, proof manuscripts, give private critiques of Lowell's work to her, and even ask friends to leave when Amy wanted to write or was tired.

By 1914, Amy tried again to get Ada to give up her career, in fact several times. But Dwyer was enjoying her success on the stage. During this time also, Ada was needed in Salt Lake City. Her daughter got married in 1914, her father died in January 1915 and Ada spent more than a month at home. Amy really suffered while Ada was away, missing her tremendously. When Ada Dwyer Russell went back to Broadway, there were several Utahns, starring in Broadway plays as well: Maude Adams, Hazel Dawn and her sister Margaret Romaine, Viola Pratt Gillette, and Sallie Fisher, who is actually from Wyoming, but had many ties to Utah including her Mormon heritage.

Amy and Ada also became the center of a Boston social group called the "Devils." These women, some of them also in "Boston Marriages" gathered at their home for concerts, readings, book discussions and other cultural events. Amy Lowell also had a lot of quirks that Boston society gossiped about, such as writing all night and sleeping until late afternoon, her need for taunt sheets, and having an all maroon automobile with a maroon coated chauffeur. Even Ada got scrutinized by the Boston papers from time to time. And many of today's critics say that Amy Lowell's genius as a poet was overshadowed at the time by the critic's dislike of her strange eccentricities. What they especially didn't like was the rumor of lesbianism, cigar smoking, outspokenness, and the belief at the time that overweight women could not possibly be sexual beings. So nearly always, most of her poetry was severely criticized, when by today's standards, quite a bit of her poetry is lush and timely.

One of her best defenders in her day, the critic Heywood Brown, wrote in Amy Lowell's obituary that her poetry has withstood the test of time. Amy Lowell is being rediscovered today as one of America's best poets. "She was upon the surface of things a Lowell, a New Englander and a spinster. But inside, everything was molten like the core of the earth... Given one more gram of emotion, Amy Lowell would have burst into flame and been consumed to cinders." (http.www.sappho.com/a_lowell)

The breakthrough to Lowell's success came with the publication of her very successful Sword Blades and Poppy Seeds at the end of 1914. She published a new anthology of poetry every year after this in 1915, 1916, and 1917. She also began her lecture tours and usually spoke to overflowing crowds in large auditoriums. Some say all of her eccentricities helped to bring the crowds as well. By 1917, her many chronic ailments were beginning to wear her down. She was suffering from continuous weight gain, high blood pressure, and persistent hernia problems which caused her to have to go through several operations in the next few years. It is safe to say, that her constant pain probably led to many of her eccentricities, while her wealth made it possible to have them. One can also surmise that Amy Lowell perhaps escaped into her writing, as a means to disregard the chronic pain that she probably was experiencing all the time.

At the end of 1915, Ada got typhoid fever. Amy canceled her lecture tours to take care of Ada, and then Ada went to Salt Lake City to recuperate and rest. Once again, Amy, left alone, really suffered without Ada's presence in the house. Amy wrote to a friend complaining about her partner's absence: "Surely Ada's vacation is not proving exactly a joyride for me. Not that she could stop the leaks, or stanched the brook in the cellar, had she been here, but all these things are worse when our only human propinquity is a group of startled and unhappy servants." (Ibid, Bright Lights and Lilacs, p.48).

When Ada returned, the speaking tours increased and Dwyer was in charge of organizing these and arranging such things as an open window for Lowell to sit by on the train to help her high blood pressure. World War I really affected both women because Amy's purebred sheep dogs, which she loved dearly, had to be put to sleep because they could not get enough meat to feed them, due to the increased rationing. They were only able to keep one of their sheep dogs. And it was also during this time, that Lowell began to have her four separate operations and long recoveries in between each of them. In 1918, Ada's daughter Lorna caught the flu and was also pregnant with her second child. This worldwide epidemic was a frightening thing, and Ada immediately went to stay with her daughter, until she was well once again, leaving Amy alone. After each operation, Amy grew weaker, and her health began to deteriorate.

On, May 12, 1925, Amy Lowell suffered a massive stroke. She was only 51 years old. Amy's affectionate nickname for Ada was "Pete." So she asked "Pete" to call the doctor. Amy became unconscious before he got there and was dead by 5:30 that afternoon. She was cremated and buried in the family plot. Ada was given the house and a trust fund and burned all unfinished manuscripts, as well as any correspondence that might have been proof of Amy and Ada's intimate relationship or any other intimate details about Amy's life, as per Lowell's written request. Ada spearheaded the finishing of Amy Lowell's other publications after her death. The two volume biography of Keats and the poetry collections: What's O'Clock, East Wind, and Ballads for Sale were all published between 1925 and 1927. In 1926, Amy Lowell received the Pulitzer Prize for Poetry posthumously for What's O'Clock which contains a very long and descriptively rich poem entitled "Lilacs."

Just two years before this, Ada Dwyer's husband, Harold Russell had passed away as well. They had been separated for many years but Ada had kept his last name of Russell. In 1928, when the old Salt Lake Theatre closed its doors for the last time, a big celebration was planned.

Ada Dwyer Russell, was there as one of the performers to read Amy Lowell's poem "Lilacs" which was one of Ada's favorites. For all the gossip, Ada Dwyer was welcomed home with all the fanfare that her home city could muster. And Ada had a private reason for loving this poem so much because Amy Lowell had sent lilac bushes to Ada's home in 1912 as a gift of friendship and love. The lilac bushes were planted around the Dwyer home to remember Amy by. Ada was also instrumental in having the plaque placed on the telephone building that was built on the site where the old Salt Lake Theatre had been.

Ada Dwyer Russell retired from the stage after Amy's death. She did do a few guest appearances and her brother George continued to sell books like his father did in the corner of the old department store Auerbach's in Salt Lake City. Ada sold the Dwyer home in 1938, where she had been living after Amy's death, and went to live with her daughter in Chevy Chase, Maryland. She had a long illness, suffered a broken hip, and soon after died on July 5, 1952. Her funeral was in an Episcopal Church, making it clear that she was no longer LDS. Ada always maintained that she and Amy had only been friends throughout her life. However, Amy's more erotic poetry was always dedicated to Ada Dwyer Russell, and seems to say otherwise. There are several love poems addressed specifically to Ada, entitled "Venus Transiens" "Decades," "Madonna of the Evening Flowers," and many, many others. All of these poems were directed towards Ada and are full of erotic and suggestive imagery. Whatever the truth is, this truth belongs to Amy and Ada. But as for Amy Lowell's poetry, I myself found it stunningly beautiful.

"Venus Transiens"

"Tell me,
Was Venus more beautiful
Than you are,
When she topped
The crinkled waves,
Drifting shoreward

On her plaited shell?
Was Botticelli's vision
Fairer than mine;
And were the painted rosebuds
He tossed his lady
Of better worth
Than the words I blow about you
To cover your too great loveliness
As with a gauze
Of misted silver?
For me,
You stand poised
In the blue and buoyant air,
Cinctured by bright winds,
Treading the sunlight.
And the waves which precede you
Ripple and stir
The sands at my feet."

"Decade"

"When you came, you were like red wine and honey,
And the taste of you burnt my mouth with its sweetness.
Now you are like morning bread,
Smooth and pleasant.
I hardly taste you at all for I know your savour,
But I am completely nourished."

"The Garden By Moonlight"

"A black cat among roses,
Phlox, lilac-misted under a quarter moon,
The sweet smells of heliotrope and night-scented stock.
The garden is very still,

It is dazed with moonlight,
Contented with perfume,
Dreaming the opium dreams of folded poppies.
Firefly lights open and vanish
High as the tip buds of the golden glow
Low as the sweet alyssum flowers at my feet.
Moon-shimmer on leaves and trellises,
Moon-spikes shafting through the snowball bush.
Only the little faces of the ladies' delight are alert and staring,
Only the cat, padding between roses,
Shakes a branch and breaks the chequered pattern
As water is broken by the falling of a leaf.
Then you come,
And you are quiet like the garden,
And white like the alyssum flowers,
And beautiful as the silken sparks of the fireflies.
Ah, Beloved, do you see those orange lilies?
They knew my mother,
But who belonging to me will they know
When I am gone."

OSCAR ELIASON
THE GREAT DANTE – ILLUSIONIST

SALT LAKE TO SYDNEY

Note: This story is taken from Will Bagley's Sunday column entitled "History Matters: Great Dante Retains His Magic Appeal" and "Utah 'Wizard' Lies in Aussie Cemetery," The Salt Lake Tribune, October 1 and September 24, 2000, and also Kent Blackmore's The Original 'Dante The Great: His Life and Travels in Australia and New Zealand 1898-1899, 2000. Blackmore generously sent me an actual copy, hoping to promote awareness of this quite famous magician not well-known in his own hometown. (www.sydneymagic.net/eliason/oe-index.html).

Future world-renowned magician, Oscar Eliason, was born in Salt Lake City, Utah. His father, Olaf, was a clock maker for 59 years. Olaf ran a small jewelry store. He produced 35 handmade watches in his lifetime, including one for Brigham Young that had a special feature that made the watch rewind every time the cover was opened or closed. He and his wife Emma had immigrated to the United States from Malmo, Sweden when they converted to the Mormon religion. Olaf and Emma settled in Salt Lake City and Olaf opened his jewelry shop. They had nine children and two of them became "conjurors" like their father, who practiced magic tricks as a hobby in his spare time. Oscar was born in 1869 and Franklin was born in 1875. While Olaf often reproved his son Oscar for choosing magic over his watch making apprenticeship, he on the other hand, was often found helping Oscar to create new designs for various mechanisms for magic tricks that Oscar had dreamed up.

Oscar attended Rowland Hall when it was still called St. Mark's Boys School and got into magic at a very young age. In March of 1889, his first performance was for the 20th Ward Schoolhouse Young Ladies Aid Society. He was soon billed as "The Mormon Wizard" and became part of the Maltese and Hammer Minstrel show. By May of 1890, he was part of the Black Bird Minstrels and was performing at the Walker Opera House. In 1893, he saw the magician Alexander Herrmann perform. This affected his desire to become a professional magician. He especially loved sleight-of-hand card tricks and soon joined the Deseret Minstrels and did a three-month stint at the Salt Lake Theatre. He carefully developed his magic act and began performing around Utah and the surrounding western states. He also performed at Saltair as a professional magician and began traveling throughout the west, while doing another extended performance at the Grand Theatre in Salt Lake City upon his return.

About this time, he made a name for himself by exposing a fraudulent spirit medium. He got into the regular "art" of exposing fraudulent mediums, mostly because this, too, was a popular thing to do. Even the great Houdini continued this practice later on, as have many other famous magicians over the years. Spiritualism was widespread at the time and much of it was fake or trickery. A woman named Anna Eva Fay did an exhibition of spiritual phenomena at the Old Salt Lake Theatre. Eliason later duplicated each and every one of her tricks at another engagement soon after that at the Salt Lake Theatre. Harry White was another famous spiritualist that tried to perform at the theater. Eliason exposed him as well. Oscar was still performing as "Eliason" or "The Mormon Wizard" at this time, with his brother Frank, as his assistant.

In 1892, Eliason met and married an illusionary dancer from a Salt Lake Theatrical family. She was billed as Mademoiselle Edmunda, but her entire name was Julianna Edmunda Virginia Hammer. One of her greatest acts was to pedal a bicycle in midair and turn somersaults. One of the tricks that she performed with her husband was to be locked in a cage and then set on fire. It was an amazing sight for the audience to see her consumed by flames and then spring from these ashes as a "...new and more beautiful edition of Mademoiselle, corrected and amended by "Dante." Oscar had met Edmunda or "Verge" Hammer through the Maltese and Hammer Minstrels. Verge's main act at the time consisted of asking committees of men to lift her from the ground, while she used the principles of leverage to defeat them. After courting her for a short while, he married her in the Salt Lake LDS Temple on May 21, 1892. Apparently, Edmunda continued to have some ties with her religion but Oscar soon lost interest in his faith and had little to do with it even as a young man.

Oscar, Edmunda, and Frank continued to perform, including a July 1895 special performance at Saltair in conjunction with a Grand Masked Ball. Eliason was billed along with a Dr. Wilbert's "Slide for Life" performance. By 1896, their manager, William A. Brady, had them traveling through Texas, Mexico and Cuba. These were dangerous places at the time because by 1898 the Spanish-American War had broken out. They quickly returned to New York City.

By this time, Oscar had also changed his performance name to "Dante the Great." He very much liked the works of Dante Alighieri who had written "The Divine Comedy" and "Dante's Inferno." Most interesting is the fate of this name that Eliason, it was discovered, had chosen early on. "Allan Sullivan, an Australian magician and collector, has a first edition copy of Professor Hoffman's Modern Magic. On the title page is the inscription, 'Dante, Prince of Magic', written by Oscar in May 1880 when he was just eleven years old!" After Eliason's tragic early demise, the name "Dante" was used by several other magicians and in one case the use of this man's name even ended up in an Australian court. It seems that one Australian magician named Harry Jansen billed himself as Dante and sued another man named John Angus for going so far as to try and resemble his looks as well as stealing his stage name. Jansen won and Angus was ordered to quit using the name. However, only one performer had invented the name and that was Eliason, who was not there to defend his title. (Ibid, The Original Dante the Great)

Many performers over the years since have used the "Dante" name, but John Angus had gone even further in his fabrications long before Harry Jansen sued him. He had made the following claims that when reviewed were all entirely false. He said that he had also been born in Salt Lake City and had come to Australia as a boy. He said that he had toured with Oscar Eliason when he was 12 years old and had apprenticed with Eliason's mechanic, which would have been Frank Eliason. He claimed to have appeared on stage in Eliason's escape act as the boy 'who disappears inside a trunk.' He also claimed to have been present when Eliason died in Dubbo, Australia in 1899. He even claimed to have inherited props for his own show from Eliason by buying the show from Eliason's widow. Actually, Frank Eliason continued to perform in Australia until 1904 and then took his act overseas. It is most certain that he kept all of his brother's equipment and props. While Angus did adopt several of Eliason's magic tricks, these were the more common ones that many magicians of the day performed. Even when proven false, John Angus at the age of eighty-nine was still quoted in the local paper as telling his stories of having toured with Oscar Eliason and using the name, "The Original Dante."

Julianna Edmunda Hammer
Courtesy Ken Blackmore

Oscar Eliason, "The Great Dante"
Courtesy Ken Blackmore

Apparently, Eliason's stage name became even more of a legend than he did, although experts in the field agree that had he lived, he would have been one of the greatest magicians in the history of the art. A movie was released in 2007 called "The Prestige," and it is about two rival magicians in the late 1800s mixed with a bit of science fiction and Nikolas Tesla. The echoes of Oscar Eliason's life were quite evident, mixed with the fantasy of real metaphysical magic and the physical science of Nikolas Tesla. Both magicians searched for that perfect magic act that would defy illusion itself. Quite a bit of tragedy ensued when the science fiction took over. However, these characters were twin brothers who used each other as doubles, which Frank and Oscar often did as brothers. In the film one of the wives had a little girl also. This wife killed herself, in part because the twin brothers sometimes changed evenings with their wives without the wives ever knowing there were two "Great Dantons." In real life, this little girl was Oscar and Edmunda's child, Ethel, who was five years old at the time. Edmunda, after her husband died became his brother Frank's assistant and continued to perform for a while after Oscar's death. But they soon parted company and Edmunda married again while Frank went on the road for a while. In the film one of the magicians did indeed die young, under mysterious circumstances and was possibly murdered or at least assumed to have been murdered by the other twin. In the film, the magician modeled after Eliason was called

"The Great Danton" and the other magician was modeled after his brother Frank.

Interestingly, since no credit was given in the film to the story of Oscar and Frank Eliason in "The Prestige," once again parts of Oscar, Frank and Edmunda Eliason's story were "borrowed" in a strange way, long after their deaths. I was even struck by the resemblance between the actor who portrayed him and Oscar himself, although Hugh Jackman is a bit older and Christian Bale plays his partner, but is actually one of identical twins. And for me personally, seeing the film was a wakeup call. I had written the Oscar Eliason story several years before I began once again writing on these performers from Utah and as I sat in the theater watching parts of their story come to life in this film, I suddenly realized that I needed to include the Eliasons' story in one of these books. While they were not actors they were certainly performers and magicians. But I will never forget the feeling that came over me, as if Oscar Eliason had tapped me on the shoulder in the darkened theater to remind me that I had forgotten to include his story. Or perhaps he was even a little perturbed at his story being told with such close parallels and yet he was forgotten today, especially in his own home town.

By 1896, backed by Major Silva, the Great Dante's act then included such feats as "The Mahatma Miracles," "Escape from the Gallows," "The Mysterious Cycle Ride," "The Japanese Trunk Mystery," and "The Wonderful Bullet Catching Feat." In this last trick and before a live audience, he would have six soldiers from Fort Douglas load their guns and fire blanks at him. "When the smoke cleared, Eliason held the bullets in his hand. How he received them was a mystery to all but himself," said the paper. "The bullet catching feat became all the more popular when a New York magician died attempting it." Once again, foreshadowing events in the fictional movie version of revival magicians in "The Prestige," Eliason ended this national tour at the Grand Opera House in New York City. (From "History Matters" by Will Bagley, "Utah 'Wizard' Lies in Aussie Cemetery," The Salt Lake Tribune, September 24, 2000, Section 8, front page)

The three of them began touring the northeast United States and eventually they ended up in Vancouver, Canada, where they met Maurice Bertram Curtis. A well-known entrepreneur, he got them an engagement in New Zealand. They set sail for the Far East in October of 1898. They then went to Honolulu, Hawaii, where they performed for three weeks and finally, they were on their way to New Zealand. They toured with a group of 12 people, Frank and Oscar and Verge's small daughter. They made plans to visit India, China and Japan, although "The Great Dante" wished to return to Salt Lake City someday. They were very popular wherever they went. They began to earn more and more money while on tour, making more than $5,000 dollars in a single month.

Utahns followed the Eliasons tour to Australia, where the public extended their time due to popular demand. It was one of the most successful tours ever made by a magician and in Sydney; Oscar, Frank and Verge played a record 101 nights. This broke the record at The Palace for any one-man engagement. Dante performed 65 consecutive nights in Melbourne and his slight-of-hand feats astounded the people. Eliason was one of a new breed of magicians who dressed his performances in new forms and had a new and different style of presentation. He was a tall, handsome young man with gorgeous naturally curly blonde hair. He had a strong voice and his manner was smooth, pleasant and gentlemanly, unlike the vaudeville dress and bawdy joking of previous magic acts. In the late 1940s, Charles Waller wrote that "...with the exception of Chung Ling Soo, this young man was the best presenter of magic I have seen; Dante could present magic in a dramatic way. He was indeed an actor playing the part of a magician." Newspapers of the time agreed: "There is a bland and confidential air about the Professor when he is at his most mystic point, as though to say 'this is a very simple thing but I will just show it to you," and then he proceeds to be more bewildering than ever as he melts his wife into thin air'." (Ibid, Blackmore, p.3)

<u>The Sydney Mail</u> said that "In the matters of committees, Dante, unlike most conjurors, makes a point of never making anyone seem ridiculous who goes on stage, and thus he gets, and has got here, well-

known men among his audiences to go up." While Verge had the lead female role and Frank was the male assistant, Frank was an excellent magician in his own right. All three of them were quite young, charming and good looking. Wherever they went, they easily won their audiences over with their sunny personalities. Only one or two negative reviews appeared about them. In one of these, the author's only negative comment was to state that while the male part of Dante's audiences wondered how he did his illusions, the females in the audience were probably wondering whether "That nice young man's hair curls naturally or whether he puts it in papers at night." Collectors to this day would be thrilled if they could locate and collect just one of the magician's coins that were distributed free at matinees to every child in the audience, called the Medallion of Dante coin.

Oscar's nickname to his friends was "Skipper," and when he was not performing, hardly anyone recognized him in his shirtsleeves working alongside the stagehands to set up his props for the show. He did not put on any "airs" and was loyal to his fellow performers including Paul Cinquevalli, who was as skilled in his trade as Eliason was in his. Cinquevalli was a master juggler, well-known in Australia at the time. However, Eliason did have one altercation with his then manager M.B. Curtis while traveling through New Zealand. Curtis had a disagreement with the seat manager in Wellington, because he would not honor Curtis's right to get a certain number of free seats for invited guests.

More such troubles ensued, culminating in Curtis being accused of not paying for halls booked in several towns. They hired some halls and then never played in them, because Curtis was pocketing the cash. In Wanganui, Oscar was finally informed that Curtis and his wife were admitting people to the theater, accepting cash, but not issuing tickets. The cash failed to appear again when the receipts were counted and a man was set to watch Curtis to compare cash taken with what was reported. A large difference was found and Curtis ordered the season stopped until he could prove he was not a thief to Eliason. A few days later, Curtis tried to claim luggage that was due to be shipped to their next performance, but the police stopped him and locked up the luggage.

Curtis then claimed his wife was sick and wasn't seen for several days. In the meantime, he contacted Eliason just long enough to ask him to pay 510 pounds as a settlement for rescinding his contract with Curtis. But when Curtis and his wife disappeared altogether, traveling under the assumed name of the Prince of Sydney, Eliason withdrew the settlement offer and instead, sued Curtis for breach of contract.

Curtis countered with an attempt to restrain Eliason from performing, as the original contract had given him absolute control over the act. Both parties accused the other of insobriety. There was also another man suing Curtis and he supported Eliason's claims. Most reports seemed to agree that Oscar Eliason settled the whole matter out of court by paying Curtis $7,000 cash. Soon after this, Curtis left for the United States having engaged a minstrel troupe called "Hogan's Unbleached Coons." Having lost the profitable Dante act, he did do one little measure of revenge by having a character in his new show named "Black Dante," and performed a few of Oscar Eliason's more easily copied magic tricks. Eliason continued on his own, to great success, and really was headed for worldwide fame and fortune. He had a whole crop of imitators, which was in a way, a measure of his success as a magician.

"Dante now had the authority from the Governors of New Zealand, New South Wales, Tasmania, Western Australia, South Australia and Victoria to advertise his show under their official patronage. On Friday, November 17, he gave his last Melbourne show and set out northwards; he was never to return." Dante was supposed to tour India and South Africa on his way homeward to the United States; instead he went to Dubbo in New South Wales to perform in the Masonic Hall there. Sunday the 26th of November, he went hunting with his wife, his brother Frank, his stage manager, the orchestra leader and a man named Mr. Taylor at Mr. W. Samuel's place a few miles outside Dubbo. George Ernest Jones, the orchestra leader, kept having trouble with his gun misfiring. It fired accidentally several times; perhaps because he had so little experience with guns. Around 6 in the evening the hunting party was returning to their carriage when Jones' gun misfired again, only this time Eliason dropped to the ground. (Ibid, Blackmore, p.9)

A doctor removed the bullet from Eliason's abdominal cavity the next morning since Eliason had rallied somewhat the day before and they thought at the time that it was only a flesh wound. The specialist surgeon arrived that evening from Sydney because his express train had been delayed six hours. He operated on Eliason the next morning due to the fact that he had arrived so late. There were three doctors and two nurses present at this operation but a huge abscess had formed and the doctors said there was no hope. They gave him only a few hours to live. Eliason suffered great pain even though he was administered morphine quite frequently. However, septic peritonitis had set in and by Wednesday afternoon, after signing a will and saying goodbye to his wife, brother and daughter, he took a glass of champagne and passed away. Even when told he was going to die, Eliason would not believe it and kept talking about continuing his tour in a week or so. When asked if he had anything to say to his wife, he said, "No, but I think we understand each other perfectly, and that is all that is necessary."

The Eliasons had been receiving royal honors from the people in Australia and New Zealand, when a brief telegram from his widow was sent to The Deseret News announcing Eliason's untimely death on December 1, 1899. He was only 30 years old. While waiting for the details as the steamer Aorangi arrived in San Francisco, locals immediately assumed that he had died while performing his wonderful bullet catching feat. Speculation was that his manager M.B. Curtis had shot him. Curtis had been both a successful actor in Salt Lake City and an excellent manager, but he had a history with the law and had escaped prosecution when he killed a police officer in San Francisco. Curtis had also been shorting Eliason with box-office receipts, at which point Eliason had fired him. People thought that perhaps the bad blood between them ran even deeper than suspected and that Curtis was perfectly capable of trying to kill Eliason in retaliation. While Curtis was nowhere near the scene of the accident, some still thought that he had put his friend, the orchestra leader, up to making the gun mishap look like an accident. This was never proven and no one knew if Jones had any connection at all to Curtis.

The mystery in all of this is if the gun really did misfire, or if something shadier was going on to cause Oscar's sudden demise. There were several possibilities from partners, to envies, to secret loves, besides the obvious one of a simple accidental death. However, it was something far simpler when the news did arrive on the steamer and made its way to Salt Lake City via the newspapers. Eliason had gone hunting with friends, looking for wallabies and kangaroos near the small town of Dubbo. A man in the party, the pianist for the troupe, was carrying his gun when it accidentally discharged and struck Eliason in the groin. Two doctors who attended him thought that it was merely a flesh wound and would heal easily. However, Eliason lost a lot of blood, grew weaker and weaker, and was in great pain. For a while, he seemed to recover but even more complications set in and he eventually died on November 28, 1899. A statement was taken from Frank Eliason and Jones, who was in a state of collapse, and the court ruled it an accidental shooting. It was much more likely that the doctor arrived way too late to stop the spread of the infection, thereby taking away all possibility of recovery for Eliason.

His body was taken to Sydney on Thursday, a large funeral procession was held the following day to the Waverly Cemetery. Three to four hundred people attended his funeral in Sydney and many of them were theater people. His brother Frank was quoted as saying, “Oscar made so many friends in Australia, and they are falling all over themselves to render any help. We have bushel baskets full of condolences from all over Australia. It is said there never was a death so universally regretted. It was necessary for an extra carriage to carry the floral offerings to the grave.” To this day many famous and budding magicians visit the grave of Oscar Eliason where the inscription reads: “In loving memory of Oscar Eliason (Dante the Great), who died 29th Nov., 1899, aged 30 years. Deeply Regretted.” (Part II - "Great Dante Retains His Magic Appeal," History Matters by Will Bagley, <u>The Salt Lake Tribune</u>, Sunday October 1, 2000, Section B)

The magician's widow temporarily rented a cottage near where he had been buried and could not bear the thought of returning home to Salt Lake City at the time, even though most of her family was there.

Frank took over Eliason's stage name and Verge traveled with him on a New Zealand tour. After doing several shows in the goldfields, they returned to Sydney, probably because Verge was due with her second child, a son whom she named after his father, Oscar. Frank went on the road alone and traveled the area until 1904. He went to Queensland and New South Wales and then did a lengthy tour in Manila and Burma. Back in the United States, the last anyone heard of him in the theater was in 1910, in Chicago, where he was preparing to take another vaudeville show to Australia. This tour never took place.

Verge did perform in Sydney for a while as "Madame Dante." "She was seen in Brisbane at the opera house on December 12, 1900 until January 7, 1901, supported by Mdle. Rougier and a company of sixteen. She then transferred over to the Harry Richards Tivoli circuit and appeared between September 28 and October 5, 1901, performing her famous "Fuller" dances at the Sydney Tivoli. Around mid-1903, Edmunda returned with her children to the United States, and in April 1907, she married a Mr. Charles Belcher." (Ibid, Blackmore, p.10)

Interestingly, Verge's only American woman friend was another early stage star from Utah named Viola Pratt who was touring in Australia at the same time as the Eliasons. She was a constant caller right after Eliason's death and probably kept Verge going as Verge was hysterical just before her husband's death and for some time afterwards. People were on constant watch with her to keep her from joining Eliason. Viola was there for her until she was able to bear up again under the strain of this loss and join her brother-in-law on tour. Viola Pratt Gillette McFarland became a famous American actress and singer whose grandfather was the Mormon Apostle, Orson Pratt. Viola was the perfect friend for Verge at the time of her husband's death. (To learn more about Viola Gillette's story, check Viola Pratt Gillette McFarland's biography.)

There is one newspaper article from this time from The Deseret News, concerning Viola Pratt, entitled "Viola Pratt's Australian Hit," January 20, 1900, which states that she had just made a great success in a theater production of "Robin Hood" in Australia, long before her musical comedy career began. Speaking of Oscar Eliason, she was quoted, as saying that, "wasn't it sad about Oscar Eliason He was making such a big success out here, and everybody liked him so much. His brother Frank, his wife and his little 6-year-old daughter were with him; they all dined with me at Adelaide. As soon as Mrs. Eliason arrived in Sydney with the body I had her with me all the time. I was the only woman she knew, and I can't tell you how pitiful it was when her husband was buried. I held her up on one side and his brother was on the other. The cemetery at Sydney is way out by the ocean and his grave is overlooking the sea with the waves washing up against it. She has taken a little cottage near Sydney and says she can't bear to go home and leave his grave, so I suppose she will stay in Australia for some time now..."

While people in Utah probably don't even know about The Great Dante, in Australia, the people there do remember him, especially in the magician's circle of performers and entertainers. Many who visit Sydney still make pilgrimages to his grave from all over Australia. On the centennial of his tragic passing, Sydney magicians gathered at his grave to remember The Great Dante, "one hundred years on."

Oscar and "Verge" Eliason
University of Utah Special Collections

The Great Dante's Main Program of Magic Tricks:

1) Time's Flight, a borrowed watch, a glass and a handkerchief transfer from one side of the stage to a hat held by a spectator.
2) Experiments with Cards, single handed color change and tear a pack in half.
3) Dante's Buffet, organ pipes trick, supper for three laid out on a table, all produced from an empty set of metal pipes.
4) The Fate Of Madame Sans Gene, Verge is in a cabinet covered down to the waist with a curtain, cabinet suspended above the stage, pistol fired, lower half of Verge disappears, instantly appears instead in the rear of the theater.
5) Nanko (Asian Miracle), pagoda tent on stage in an eastern scene, two Asian porters dance a jig. One of them is then placed in a sack and locked in a trunk and then lowered into a second trunk, when the trick is over the two porters have changed places.
6) The Beggar's Dream, Verge enters the stage in rags and is tempted by the devil in a red cloak to a huge picnic spread out in a park. She stands on the picnic table and is briefly covered by a light canopy that falls from above. When it is lifted she is dressed in a rich gown, the devil then plucks money from the air and offers it to her. Still not tempted the devil becomes enraged and sets her on fire behind the canopy. She disappears leaving only a grinning skull behind her in the lightning and thunder that follows.
7) Karmos, Verge is blindfolded as a medium and does a number of answers written on a board to math problems, names cards, banknote amounts, etc.
8) Duck Production, three ducks appear in a wash tub covered with a cloth.
9) The Bullet Catch, Dante caught four bullets in a metal plate held to his chest fired by four gentlemen from the audience. The bullets were hot and sometimes caught in his hands.
10) Around The World In Five Minutes, large cloth map of world, flags appear from out of nowhere on the various countries and for

the finale, Verge appears in a costume that represents all the nations.

11) Flora's Manifestation Of Spring, sheet of paper twisted into a cone produces a bouquet of flowers.

12) Black Art, A scene from Faust, dancing skeleton separates into pieces as Verge dances with it, Oscar throws a cloak around her and she disappears and three doves hover where she was.

13) Creation – The Illusionary Dance, Edmunda dances using illusionary lights in a long white silk dress with wands that form billowing waves with all kinds of lighting effects and is finally consumed in a fire of red lights, etc.

14) The Sim La Séance, Frank as a medium seated in a cabinet and aided by his spirit guide Silverlight, a committee of audience members investigates all the phenomena. This one was the one that disproved mediumistic tricks with floating trumpets, ectoplasm, tambourines and harmonicas playing, etc.

15) Flight Of Birds, canaries vanish from a box and appear in a cage on stage.

16) The Inexhaustible Bottle, assorted liquids in bottles in which appear guinea pigs or rabbits that are then thrown into the air and disappear appearing in a spectator's coat.

17) Vanishing Cloak, Dante wears a top hat and cloak, and the cloak disappears.

18) The Marvelous Bicyclist, Edmunda rides a bicycle onto the stage and then up into the air where she performs various aerial feats with the bike.

19) Multiplying Billiards

20) The Miser's Dream, Restored Violin, and Burned / Restored Handkerchief

Julia Dean Hayne & Her Powerful Admirers

Julia Drake Fosdick Dean

Julia Dean was born in Pleasant Valley, New York on July 22, 1830. She had an uncle who was a famous judge and her mother was also an actress named "Julia Drake" Fosdick Dean. Her aunt was the famous actress "Frances Denny" Drake and Julia often appeared with her in various productions. Both Frances Denny and Julia Dean were independent from their husbands so it was hard to attract many theater contracts, which was a difficult thing to do as an actress in those days. Both women were free enough to terminate their marriages and by doing this they risked public censure while juggling careers and periods of being single mothers. Julia Dean Hayne had been married only once when she obtained her second divorce in Salt Lake City during the year that she lived there. She had three small children to support as well.

Julia Dean's grandfather Samuel Drake lived from 1769 to 1854. Right after he was widowed he brought his four children to New York City where he managed a theater in Albany. Soon he took his newly formed acting troupe, consisting of his four children and a few other seasoned actors to the southern states. Samuel Drake is considered one of the first in the United States to bring drama to the south and the west. Julia Drake's aunt, Frances Denny was also from Albany, New York but joined the theatrical troupe that toured the south. Samuel Drake was the manager of the troupe. In 1823, Frances met and married her comedian husband, Alexander Drake while touring with him throughout the southern states. Alexander was a comedian and never quite matched his wife's talent as an actor. In 1830, he left his wife with four children to raise, which Frances did while working full time as an actress, quite successfully for the next twenty years. Julia Dean toured with her aunt Frances early in her career.

Julia's mother was the daughter of Samuel Drake and her name was Julia Drake Fosdick Dean. Julia Drake began her serious acting career in 1821, when she was only fifteen years old. She married another actor, Thomas Fosdick and they began a joint career as actors. She then married her second husband, Edwin Dean, with whom she had two daughters, Julia and Helen. Described as having a lyrical voice with a perfectly molded Grecian face and form, Julia Drake was heading for a good career in the theater when her life was suddenly and tragically cut short in 1832. Julia Dean was only two years old at the time. Later, when the few critics who had had the opportunity to see Julia Drake perform on stage, compared her to her daughter Julia Dean, they stated that the two women's voices were exactly alike: silver-toned, clear, and joyous. They both had expressive dark eyes, dark features and beautiful, symmetrical faces. And though they stated that if you saw Julia Dean, you had then seen Julia Drake; they also stated that as beautiful as Julia Dean was, when one looked at her face, her mother's "exquisitely moulded Grecian face was not there."

Julia Dean Hayne

Julia Dean's paternal grandparents, who were Quakers, raised Julia Dean and her Quaker heritage had a very great effect on how she conducted her life, especially in refusing to perform on Sundays. As soon as Edwin Dean was able, he resumed custody of Julia and began training her for the stage. By 1843, both he and Julia were performing full-time. She was quite a sensation in her first real engagement in Mobile, Alabama, according to actor Joseph Jefferson's mention of her in his autobiography. In 1845 she had her first starring role as Lady Ellen in "The Lady of the Lake" in Louisville, Kentucky. In the same year she appeared at the Bowery Theatre in New York as "Julia" in "The Hunchback."

In 1846, only two years later and by fifteen years of age, Julia Dean was signing on in starring roles in the theater. Her confidence, stage presence, lyrical voice and dazzling beauty captivated every audience that saw her. She began in non-Shakespearean roles but eventually she did well in these roles also. By 1846 she had been engaged for an entire season in New Orleans and then became a regular star in

Julia as a Young Actress
Daughters of the Utah Pioneers Museum

Julia in Salt Lake City for the Season
University of Utah Special Collections

Southeast theaters and one southern theater was even named after her for a while. She also appeared in the Arch Street Theatre in Philadelphia. While eventually she did star in Shakespearean productions, she excelled in playing roles that involved either juvenile tragedies or high comedy. She also appeared on the stage in England at the Victoria Theatre and others, where it was said of her performances that she never overacted her parts and had a beautiful, entrancing voice.

For a few years Julia Dean became the toast of the acting stage in New York and wherever she toured. Critics said that while not the best of actresses in her early years, her beauty was the ideal for the 19th century male and she was soon being pursued by many suitors. In the meantime, she completed nine acting roles in her first year as a star. "The public had a tender affection for this young woman." Her father, Edwin Dean saw the gold mine in his daughter that he had never discovered in any other way. For the next three seasons she toured all over the United States, but especially in the southern states. While Julia acted, her father was pocketing most of her money. She earned $25,000 her first season, an exorbitant amount for that era. And her adoring fans described her as having a winning personality, a great beauty, but with a faint trace of melancholy which was both charming and perplexing. She was at her best when playing a role that allowed her to display her pathos and tenderness. With a graceful and modest manner, while not a great actress, her talent grew with the years, her beauty at long last did not supersede her talent.

Her first love was rumored to be her own cousin, another namesake for Samuel Drake. This early romance as teens was of course doomed for failure, being as they were indeed cousins. She was pursued by bachelors, fortune hunters and romantics, including a U.S. Senator, John Minor Botts, who was 52 years old. Julia was only 24 years old at the time. Senator Botts of Virginia chased her all over the south but to no avail. However, in a few years she had met and was courted by a man who would win her hand.

In 1854, she fell in love with Dr. Arthur Hayne who was from a fine South Carolina family with a senator father. Hayne was a medical doctor. He was handsome, well-born, but not very focused on a career at the time, had an uneven temperament and was prone to drinking. Julia married Dr. Arthur Hayne in Charleston in May of 1856 and all seemed well for a while. But it soon became apparent to many that Arthur was not living up to his family's expectations and in fact thought of Julia as his ticket to fame and wealth. At thirty-one years of age, Arthur Hayne had expected Julia to obtain his freedom from his family's expectations of him. His failure as a doctor and his alcoholism, and her professional success resulted in her desire to divorce him only one year later. However, the southern states stand on wives divorcing their husbands was fairly clear; no woman would ever obtain a divorce in a southern state, no matter the claims of abandonment, abuse, lack of support, etc. So for many years Julia simply lived with and supported her husband and the father of her first three children.

Julia and Arthur Hayne were married in January of 1855 and it would have been a normal expectation of the times that Hayne would ask her to leave the stage, but he never did. Speculation is that he needed her money too badly, although he presumed to take over her career in terms of changing how she was performing on the stage. While she had been acting for many years and he knew absolutely nothing about the stage, he began to advise her and her acting suffered for this for several years. In trying to please her new husband, she lost her movement forward as a trained actress and it was not until she basically separated from him while still being married to him, that her acting talent began to improve again. The Haynes toured in and eventually moved to California.

Their first company tour was in 1856. While on the steam ship headed to San Francisco, the Haynes suffered two bad experiences. One was attending the at sea burial of a young couple friend's first child and the other was a sailor on board who had been locked in the boiler room as punishment and then forgotten and left there too long. He died a few hours after they got him out, literally boiled to death. Hayne also displayed his temper to Julia for the first time when he drew a table knife on a purser who insisted that he not be allowed to sit in the Captain of the ship's seat at the dinner table. Other male passengers had to restrain him from cutting the purser badly.

In the second year of her first two-year tour in the San Francisco area, Julia Dean Hayne received $5,000 a week and performed in two plays that received good reviews: "The Hunchback," and "Camille." She first performed at the Jenny Lind Theatre, the largest theater in San Francisco and then at the Metropolitan Theatre that was the second largest theater in town. When the tour began San Francisco was at the height of the golden era of mining and gambling. But by 1860 the whole city, if not state, was in a big depression. This did not bode well for the theaters or the acting profession. This same year – 1856 – Julia was pregnant with her first child and continued to perform up until the last two months of her pregnancy. Julia and her company performed for three seasons in San Francisco. After this, the troupe went on tour throughout the mining camps of California and Nevada.

Dr. Hayne traveled with the company but had no duties to perform. In April of 1857, the Haynes arrived back in San Francisco with their seven-month-old son and bought a home. They went on a second tour of the mining towns shortly after settling in their new home in San Francisco. The second tour was seven weeks long and Julia gave 43 performances as well as one benefit performance for school children. Back in San Francisco her troupe performed at the Metropolitan Theatre, which burned down August 22, 1857 and kept the troupe idle for a month. They then did a three-month tour around California and Nevada and eventually the Metropolitan Theatre was re-built. She gave a farewell speech in San Francisco in which she stated that she would go on tour to Europe. She was three months into her second pregnancy at the time.

Having written to a Rev. F. C. Ewer for eighteen months, this was the closest Julia would ever come to being unfaithful to her husband. Julia and the reverend formed a deep friendship. The reverend often defended her in print concerning the ancient prejudice against the acting profession and it was probably no coincidence that she was confirmed into the Episcopalian Church within days of the reverend's ordination. Or that it was right after that that she announced that she was leaving

San Francisco to perform abroad. Later, when Julia did divorce her husband it came out that she had given him a huge sum of money to pay off the mortgage on their mansion in San Francisco, and he had instead squandered it on one of his own interests. The family lost their new home that would have been completely paid for. This was the final straw as far as Julia was concerned.

Still putting up with her husband at this point, the family traveled instead to Nashville, where her second son Motte was born on June 22, 1858. This son died only eighteen days later in St. Louis while Julia was visiting her father. Her son died in her father's home and nothing was ever said publicly about this tragedy. Whatever Julia's feelings were at the time, she kept them to herself. By August she was working again at the Baltimore Theatre and then the National Theatre in Chicago. In 1859 the troupe traveled to New York City and then through the south again, awaiting the birth of her third child. Julia had acted virtually uninterrupted for fifteen years. Her third child was born on September 5, 1859 and he was named Robert Y. Hayne after his paternal grandfather. Eventually the family left the east coast because of the unsettling events that were leading up to the Civil War and returned to San Francisco.

From 1859 to 1862, she performed in her best plays and had finally become an accomplished actress with numerous curtain calls wherever she performed. She performed at the Maquire Opera House in San Francisco and in the re-built Metropolitan Theatre. She became a great influence in theatrical circles all over the country. She went on some tours and got great praise for some of her new roles such as "Woman in White," "Rip Van Winkle," and "Hamlet." In November of 1861 she retired briefly from the stage because she was six months pregnant with her daughter, "Julia Dean Haynes," who came into the world on February 27, 1862. And it was in 1862 that the great Salt Lake Theatre opened its doors in Salt Lake City, but Julia was still performing near her beloved city by the bay.

For the next two years she followed what was then called the silver trail, through all the mining towns but especially the Virginia City Opera House in Virginia City, Nevada as well as Carson, Silver City and

Gold Hill. On her thirty-third birthday she gave a farewell performance with Lotta Crabtree before returning to San Francisco. Julia performed in the play and Lotta danced and sang. Julia then toured the towns along the Oregon Trail for the next three months. From 1863 to 1864, she and another actress Annette Ince were co-managers of the Metropolitan Theatre in San Francisco. Julia began playing some male roles, performed in towns where guns were going off in the streets outside the theater, and, took over as sole manager of the Metropolitan in August of 1864. Not yet thirty-five years old, Julia and her family left San Francisco for good and went to Boise, Idaho to perform. When she was in Idaho City, she made the decision to go to Salt Lake City to perform at the new theater. It was a good offer for the whole season and she and her troupe took the four-day stagecoach ride via Boise City to Virginia City, Montana and then on to Salt Lake City. This particular route was often besieged by road agents and robbers, but thankfully the troupe escaped a hold-up.

On Monday August 7, 1865, three of the Salt Lake Valley's newspapers announced the arrival of the troupe. She was engaged to perform at the Salt Lake Theatre from June 1865 to July of 1866. The newspapers of America were filled with weird tales of Mormons and the Salt Lake stronghold. The troupe really wondered if they would be allowed to perform there even though they had been engaged for one whole season. Their misfortunes of the past two years, on the other hand, seemed to be over once they saw that they played to packed crowds in Salt Lake City. However, the local newspapers began to see the weaknesses of the troupe quite quickly, as the local troupe was much more polished and experienced. The first night Julia performed she had a nasty cold and a cough that interrupted her dialogue as well. All of this was criticized, but while the female population was envious and critical of Julia, "Julia Dean Hayne kept the male population of Salt Lake City in a state of suppressed excitement." ("A Study of the Theatrical Career of Julia Dean Hayne" by Ralph Elliott Margetts, Doctor of Philosophy thesis, Department of Speech, University of Utah, August 1959. p. 289)

It was in this year that Brigham Young, night after night, watched what he thought at the time was the love of his life; perform on his own theater's stage. Young became so enamored with Julia Dean Hayne that he had her portrait painted on the side of one of his several carriages for all to see. Or at least that is the official story, while the real story behind this portrait, which was actually just a theater poster, is even more fun to hear a bit later in this brief biography of Julia Dean. Young also had a swan shaped sleigh built to carry at least fifty of his children back and forth for winter parties and holiday festivities at his farmhouse. This sleigh was called the "Julia Dean." Pulled by a team of six matching grey horses, his favorite daughter Susa Young Gates wrote about this sleigh and its passengers some years later.

"It was here (the Young farmhouse south of the city) that President Young brought on two occasions the famous actress Julia Dean Hayne as a guest. It was in her honor that the sleigh was named - the mammoth long sleigh with its high driver's seat, its green painted sides outspringing with graceful curves and holding in its capacious hay-and buffalo-robe-filled box a bevy of nearly fifty children of all ages, but all bubbling with laughter and excitement over the expected festivities of the holiday season. Drawn by spirited horses all jingling and jangling with the most musical of sleigh bells while the driver's loud whip fell skillfully and delicately on the glossy sides of the prancing teams, the brilliant stars overhead saw no merrier sight than this sleigh full of infinite happiness just behind the President's cutter-followed by the more dignified sleighs holding the mothers of these children on their way for a gala night at the farm house." (<u>The Romance of the Old Playhouse</u> by George D. Pyper, The Seagull Press: Salt Lake City, Utah, 1928, pp. 157-158)

Today one can see only the small wooden driver's seat of this huge sleigh in the first carriage house of the Daughters of the Utah Pioneer's Museum, a lasting memorial to the "Julia Dean," and another important man enamored with the actress, Julia Dean Hayne. Ardis E. Parshall, in her article "One-horse open sleigh was the real deal in early Utah," <u>The Salt Lake Tribune</u>, December 23, 2007, mentions a different take on the sleigh portrait that appeared on the side of this sleigh. She says that the sleigh was only designed to carry 24 riders but was indeed built for the 1865-1866 season when Julia Dean was performing at the Salt Lake Theatre. There were two gracefully carved swans on either side of the sleigh, with the driver right in the middle between them. The sleigh was shaped like a canoe and was pulled by a team of six horses. A Salt Lake newspaper of the times said that when the children piled into it there was likely double the number of 24 riding under buffalo robes and blankets with bells all around.

Sara Alexander, one of Brigham's favorite local actresses and tutor for his children, and Nettie Young, old enough to recall this sleigh, both said that the portrait on the side of the sleigh had come about in a different way. They claimed that one of Brigham's young sons, fifteen-year-old Ernest Young, found a theater poster of Julia Dean that had her name in large print under her portrait. And that he then pasted it on the back of the sleigh where at first no one could see it. Even though it was discovered it continued to stay there as a prank because of Brigham's interest in Julia Dean, and to the "delight of everyone...the sleigh was never known by any other name." The sleigh stayed with Brigham Young for a few years after Julia died but then was sold to Hiram B. Clawson, who even used it one time in a funeral procession because it could easily hold thirty adults. It headed the procession to the graveyard beautifully. When it became too decrepit to keep, it was sold again and became a feedbox for horses in Davis County where eventually the horses kicked it to pieces. This is why the only remaining piece is the tiny driver's seat.

One may see in the theater room at the Daughters of the Utah Pioneers Museum, a backdrop and stage curtain to the old Salt Lake Theatre, costumes and other adornments worn by the actresses, photographs, tickets, programs and posters announcing coming events. The best exhibit is the three-seat wood and red silk box where Brigham Young sat each night to enjoy his "playhouse." The three seats are so small that one can see just how much smaller people generally were then. There is also a single portrait of Julia Dean Hayne as a very young

Portrait of Julia Dean Hayne
Utah State Historical Society

Julia Dean Hayne Cooper,
Shortly Before her Death
University of Utah Special Collections

woman, and while as a drawing it enhances Dean's best features, it does not look much like her.

The best story about Brigham Young and Julia Dean Hayne concerns his favorite, most attractive, and possibly most feared wife, Amelia Folsom. This story was related by several of Young's other wives. Many of her female accoutrements and some of her fan collection and even a model of her mansion especially built for her by Brigham Young can also be seen in the DUP museum. It was Amelia Folsom, the supposed favorite and prettiest of Brigham's wives who began to worry that she was about to be deposed by this visiting gentile actress. In her book, Wife No. 19: The Story Of My Life In Bondage, Ann Eliza Webb is quoted as saying that Amelia Folsom, rather than being Brigham's favorite wife, was his most feared one as time went on. Apparently, all the other wives were afraid of her and gave her a wide berth, even when she passed them on a sidewalk, coming or going. Brigham let her have the run of the place and the other wives gossiped about how instead of having Brigham wrapped around her little finger, he was in reality a bit terrorized by her. When Brigham saw her coming he prepared himself to give into her demands before she made them. She was as beautiful as she was demanding (Information from family stories passed down from a great-grandmother who was raised in the Beehive House as a little child).

Ann Eliza told a great story about the triangle of Brigham Young, Julia Dean Hayne and Amelia Folsom. It seems that one night Brigham, Amelia and Ann went to the old Salt Lake Theatre to see Julia perform. Everyone knew Young was enamored with Julia but she refused his advances at every turn. Brigham went ahead and flirted with Julia anyway and after the performance, Amelia was steaming. They walked out on the front steps of the Salt Lake Theatre after Julia's performance, and while waiting for Brigham's coach, he and Amelia got in a heated argument. Ann Eliza was standing right by them keeping quiet in the fray! The carriage arrived and the argument continued on. Suddenly Amelia ran down the steps, leapt in the carriage and drove away, leaving Ann Eliza and Brigham to find their own way home from the theater.

Brigham tried for one whole season to get Julia to marry him but to no avail, she was not interested in him or in becoming another wife of his, and especially not interested in becoming a Mormon. She was however, surely flattered by all of the attention. In the meantime, unbeknownst to Brigham she had begun dating a tall and handsome gentile officer at Camp Douglas. James G. Cooper who was from New York State, was stationed at Camp Douglas for only a brief period of time, but it happened to coincide with Julia's tour of the west. They were keeping their courtship quiet until Julia could obtain a divorce from her first husband in the Utah courts. In fact, she divorced twice in the Utah courts, just to be certain. At the end of the second season, she and Cooper left for Montana where she was to perform and got married there. Brigham Young was devastated; having thought that he would have more time to woo her.

Trying to sever her relationship from her first husband who was squandering all of her money, this was perhaps one of the main factors that brought Julia Dean Hayne to Utah. She was touring the west and at the same time knew that the western states had relaxed divorce laws and it would be simple to file for divorce while "on tour." Julia already had three children when she filed for her divorce in Utah. The Utah court ruled in her favor on the count of a husband's neglect for her and her three children in August of 1866. She also received total control of her financial and material assets, which would have made her twice as attractive to any man who wanted wealth and a beautiful woman to boot. Her success in the western states cemented her respectability with her audiences. Perhaps watching her aunt's financial success as a single mother and actress gave her the courage to make such a bold move, banking on her popularity with her audiences. Frances had married a second husband who turned out to be an alcoholic, just as Julia's husband had been, and she had divorced him as well.

During her one season in Salt Lake City, Julia got many mixed reviews from her audiences, but by the end of the season she was once again getting curtain call after curtain call and was the toast of Salt Lake City. One of the gentile newspapers of the time, The Union Vendetta, was really thrilled when her manager announced his intentions to build a bigger and better theater than the Salt Lake Theatre, or "Brigham's Playhouse" as it was nicknamed then. Potter never actually got up the capital to build this theater but did open his Academy of Music in the city. Julia Dean finally got her divorce. Her children at the time were nine, five and three years old. She stated that her reasons for filing for divorce involved her husband's "dissolute and intemperate" habits, her unhappiness, and his brutality as a husband. He had also neglected to provide for her and her children. By September she was officially divorced for the second time but her husband had gotten sole custody of her children even though she had been their sole support. Julia fought long and hard for the custody of her children in San Francisco, traveling back and forth several times. But it was a tenant of the times that she would loose and never see them again. They grew up in San Francisco with their father and his new wife.

It was not common gossip in the city that Julia had at long last found a new love but those who knew her the best felt that this was what had spurred her on to pursue a divorce. Brigham Young still tried to pursue her, although whether he knew that he was in contest with a handsome young gentile man named James G. Cooper or not is up for question. Young probably was not fully aware of the growing attraction that this man and woman had for each other and might have thought those glances every night at the theater were for him instead. Both men attended the theater every night that they could. After 45 days in California, Julia returned to Utah to give her farewell speech on June 30, 1866. Potter's Academy of Music had to declare bankruptcy and he and Julia Dean Hayne parted ways. Sarah Elizabeth Carmichael, the famous Utah poet, often compared to Emily Dickinson, wrote a poem about her friend Julia Dean Hayne for her farewell performance entitled "Julia Dean Hayne."

"A form of sculpted beauty;
A deep magnetic face,
That draws the gazer's worship

To its intense embrace;
Her beauty presses on the heart.
Yet shines above it far.

With a strange polar luster,
Exquisite woman's star,
Her beauty hath a splendid stress
That words cannot explain,
Expression swoons in its caress---
Julia Dean Hayne.

A still repose of motion,
An animate repose;
Expressive power of silence,
No language can disclose;
Her lip, with languid motion, turns
Each leaf in feeling's book;

Her voice can picture all things, but
Her eloquence of look.
A warm pulse in the world's great heart,
She thrills its very vein;
And bids its tear-drops stay or start---
Julia Dean Hayne."

Carmichael wasn't the only one to compose poetry about Julia Dean Hayne, but many of the others go on for pages and pages, spouting her glories as a woman and an actress. Both men and women adored her, but it was the men who pursued her. Brigham Young was not the only famous man to be enamored with Julia Dean Hayne however. Mark Twain makes mention of her performances in a column he wrote for the Virginia City Territorial Enterprise, in which, even he managed to not take so cryptic a tone, as was his usual practice. He said of her performance that she basically had not overacted and had managed to out act the others in the play. There is another story of Buffalo Bill Cody who saw Miss Hayne perform the leading role in the play "Lucretia Borgia" in the play "Poisoned" in St. Louis. He fell in love too, but simply named his .50 caliber rifle "Lucretia Borgia" in honor of Julia Dean.

James G. Cooper wasn't just an officer at Camp Douglas; he was also an appointee of the United States government and had traveled west as a cavalry man but also as the Secretary of the Territory of Utah. He had southern birth and breeding and was tall and handsome. He was a great lover of the theater and also became an ardent admirer of Julia Dean Hayne. "Night after night, all season through, he sat in front nearly always in the same seat, and with eyes aglow and ears alert, he seemed to absorb every tone of her voice and catch every gleam of her eyes—her every move was to him a thrill of rapture. Out of her thousands of admirers he was the most devoted worshipper at her shrine. Up to a certain time he worshipped in silence as if she were a deity. But then mere chance had made them neighbors; the secretary's office and Mrs. Hayne's apartment were in adjoining houses, and it was not long before an acquaintanceship was formed which rapidly grew into friendship, and friendship soon ripened into love." The only known description of him is in one of three books about the history of the old Salt Lake Theatre. (The Mormons and the theatre, or, a history of theatricals in Utah; with reminiscences and comments, humorous and critical, by John S. Lindsay, Century Printing: Salt Lake City, Utah, 1905, p.325)

Very few were aware of the growing attraction they had for each other, although there was only a slight gossiping among those who knew her the best. They carried on their courting with circumspection and discretion until Julia was officially divorced. "Little did her audience suspect that often when she cast her most bewitching glances, and brightened faces with her radiant smiles, that those smiles were mounted especially for him; but he knew---how could he help but know. Cupid had drawn his bow and sped his dart." So after the close of the season, they hastily wed, bade farewell to "...the land of the Saints, and wended their way to the far East by stagecoach, the terminus of the Pacific road being yet some hundreds of miles from Salt Lake." (Ibid, Lindsay, p.51)

However, some of the facts are misrepresented by Lindsay's account of their courtship. According to state records Cooper was never secretary of the Utah Territory nor wealthy, being only a traveling agent for the firm he supposedly owned. They perhaps did not marry in Salt Lake City but in Montana or later when they arrived in New York. They soon had a brief separation or disagreement about something and Julia Dean Hayne was written about in The Salt Lake Telegraph, in an unfavorable light. Was the lady not in a hurry to divorce her first husband and marry her second? Did she have a conscience about leaving her three little children in the care of her first husband here in Salt Lake City? Separating from her second husband so quickly was not a good way to represent her character the reporter claimed. One, on the other hand, has to see that she would have been painted in a bad light due to her close association with the Prophet in the heart of Mormon Territory, spurning his attentions.

After the season ended, Julia went to Montana with her husband to perform there. She then ended her career as an actress and reunited with her new husband very quickly after in New York City. She became pregnant with her fourth child the following year, while they were still living in New York. She died in childbirth, but her daughter survived, thus ending all too soon, a brilliant and shining career in the theater. Her last appearance on the stage was in October of 1867. She was only thirty-seven years old. Julia's fourth child did not die and survived to marry into a wealthy family in Virginia some years later.

Meanwhile back in Utah, the Prophet on hearing of his beloved's death had one of his wives stand in for her and married Julia by proxy so that he could be with her in Heaven. Ann Eliza Webb, one of only two wives of Brigham Young who publicly divorced him and the only wife to travel about the country promoting her tell all book, made mention of this flirtation in one of her chapters. Later on in her book she mentions Julia Dean Hayne's passing, and speculates on just how Julia would receive the news in Heaven that she was married after her death to a Mormon while also being married to her second husband.

Julia Dean Hayne Cooper had another disappointment that may have contributed to her early death. Three days before Christmas in the last year of Julia's life, she received news that her youngest son, Robert Y. Hayne had died in San Francisco. Details of how he died and why are lost, so one has to speculate on how this affected Julia as well. Her first husband was quoted as saying that, "She would not have died had I been with her. My wife was afflicted with a chronic complaint, the nature of which I had made a study, and had held back the hand of death many times from a fatal assault. I am sorry she passed away at so early an age, comparatively. But it is fate. To this, we must all bow, sooner or later." Dr. Hayne seems to have redeemed himself in his later years. He sobered up and eventually authored two books on the treatment of alcoholism, while practicing as a doctor for alcoholic patients. The people of San Francisco felt him to be a good man and a respectable member of their community. (Bulletin, No. 18, May 23, 1896)

Apparently, Julia Dean Hayne had been frail for years and this was the real reason that she retired from the stage after marrying her second husband. She had had only one or two engagements friends said after her marriage. "She suffered from trouble in the throat---and her nervous system was a good deal shattered. She was a lady of good conversational powers, high literary culture, sparkling wit, and was greatly loved by those who knew her in private life. Her devotion to her profession was entire and religious. She loved her art, and hated everything that cheapened or degraded it." (Alta Californian, No. 14, March 28, 1868)

Ironically, Julia Dean's funeral took place in the very church where her reverend friend presided. There were many tributes to her from across the country. Lotta Crabtree gave tribute to Julia Dean Hayne on her opening night in New York. Edwin Booth, the most famous actor of the period, gave a tribute to her before his opening night in "Romeo and Juliet," and several others read some sort of tribute to her before their plays also. In reading in depth about her life, one realizes that she was a very strong woman who had faced several tragedies in her life even though she only lived to be thirty-seven years old. Looking at that lovely young face in the Daughters of the Utah Pioneers Museum, I found her features to be ethereal as well.

There is a wonderful quote about the author's friend, Julia Dean Hayne's performances while in San Francisco to begin her tour. "Our friend Mrs. Hayne played in 'The Hunchback' at the Metropolitan Theatre, and at once became a favorite in San Francisco, as she had been in New York. She had made her New York debut as Julia in 'The Hunchback' at the old Bowery Theater early in the fifties and critics predicted a brilliant future. But she married Dr. Hayne and sailed away for the gold country. I remember her lovely hair, rich golden brown and parted smoothly in the middle, drawn down over her ears. It would never stay properly sleek and flat; there was always a fluff of life about it. She died soon after the Civil War while she was still young and vividly charming, and left a little daughter, who grew up to marry one of the Langhornes of Virginia." (The Fantastic City: Memoirs of the Social and Romantic Life of Old San Francisco by Amelia Ransome Neville, 1932, Chapter II)

Modern day experts on theatrical history say that Julia Dean Hayne, although her acting career was cut short, was easily the most important and talented performer to tour the mining camps of the Northwest during the gold rush days. Opera Houses capable of seating hundreds of people were filled to capacity when Julia performed. People were charged one to two dollars per ticket, often payable in gold dust or nuggets. Theaters were even set up literally overnight just to have a place where she could perform for one night only. The only reason she is not remembered as well as say Maude Adams or Lily Langtry, is simply that she died too young to complete her legacy in the theater. Perhaps Maude Adam's manager and mother were right when they insisted on her not marrying, but instead asked her to be "married" to the theater. Women, who married, risked many things: death in childbirth, loss of their careers, and a loss of respectability if they divorced. Adams lived, succeeded and remained secretive, while Julia Dean Hayne Cooper lost her very life too soon.

An intriguing ending to the fame and remembrance of Julia Dean Hayne, appeared in a letter to the Editor of The Dramatic Mirror in New York City on August 26, 1897 entitled "The Unmarked Grave of Julia Dean Hayne:"

"Sirs: while recently walking through the beautiful Laurel Grove Cemetery at Port Jervis, New York, the aged caretaker called my attention to a good sized circular burial plot overlooking the lake in the centre of which, surrounded by mountain laurel shrubs and lilac bushes, is a sunken mound under which the venerable keeper declared rested 'as great and fine looking an actress as the country ever had,' and further stated that 'much of that time was made over her years ago in New York.' Also that 'when her body was brought on here a big crowd of theater folks came on to see 'ier buried and they cried over her open grave."

"Becoming thoroughly interested, I carefully noted the location of the actresses' lot, immediately visited the little cemetery office on the grounds, and in looking over the admirably kept records, I was astonished to find that it represented the grave of a fair member of the dramatic profession, whose tomb had been entirely lost sight of, and dramatic historians and editors have been unable for years to enlighten those of their readers, who sought to discover her grave rest. Beneath this mound rests all that is mortal of the once lovely Juliet of the American stage Julia Dean."

"The complete record of the Laurel Grove Cemetery reads: 'Name, Julia-Dean- Hayne-Cooper. Place and time that nativity, Pleasant Valley, near Poughkeepsie, N.Y., July 21, 1830. Names of parents Edwin and Julia Dean. Age thirty-five years. Place and date of death New York City, May 19, 1866. Cause of death Childbirth. Second husband's name, James G. Cooper. Buried in Lot no. 3, Section B, owned by her father-in-law, Matthew H. Cooper. Remains of deceased first placed in the Marble Cemetery General Receiving Vault, Second Street, New York City. Transfer to Laurel Grow Cemetery, Port Jervis, April 16, 1868."

"The lone cemetery official states all of Julia Dean's kindred passed away years ago, and together they are buried in the old Clove graveyard at Sussex, N. J."

"At the time of their deaths, they were in reduced circumstances and while still well-to-do, years before Julia Dean's demise. They acquired this Port Jervis burial lot that she might await the resurrection and in the place where her childhood days were so pleasantly passed."

"At the foot of the eminent actresses' grave slumbers the unnamed girl infant for whom Julia Dean surrendered her illustrious life." (This was reported without documentation, as Julia's daughter did survive)

"None of her relatives were ever able to erect a monument over her remains, and it seems a pity that this exquisite actress of another generation should forever sleep in an unrecorded sepulcher."

"Having heard and read that the noble Actors Fund of New York has caused many a granite tombstone to be erected over the graves of other worthy comrades, and as Julia Dean was so sweet and accomplished an artiste, I thought that by calling attention to this forgotten and out of the way tomb through the columns of the most powerful of America's dramatic journals, The Dramatic Mirror, it might result in placing a modest memorial stone and granite at the head of the mound under which so peacefully reposes Julia Dean, whose splendid genius Dion Boucicault compared to that of another gifted and beautiful daughter of drama, the ideal Juliet, Adelaide Neilson, who awaits the final call in distant England, beneath an imposing mortuary memorial, thanks to the influence of the loyal William Winter." (Ibid, The Mormons and the Theatre, pp. 37-39)

One would suppose that Julia Dean Hayne got her monument, and also her choice as to which husband, if any, she chose to be with, in the afterlife.

LISLE LEIGH

Lisle Leigh made only a very few films because she died on May 19, 1927. There is one reference to her stage appearances at the Brooklyn Theatre in New York City and one reference to a film that she starred in entitled "The Mountaineer" in 1908. She starred with Richard Hale and

Joel Day and the synopsis gave it a fairly poor rating even for a silent film. It seems that a movie photographer captures evidence of a crime; a robbery in which the victim was murdered and thrown over a precipice. There are moon shiners and revenuers and very bad special effects. And as one critic stated, the dummy used in the fall is the worst stuffed affair ever shown on a screen.

I am still looking for a photo of Lisle Leigh as a young adult actress, although there is a nice one of her as a middle-aged woman. Lisle Leigh had three credited major roles in the films "Caprice of the Mountains" in 1916, "The Forbidden Path" in 1918 and "The American Way" in 1919. Lisle had a part on Broadway in 1923 of the play "The Custard Cup." Lisle also starred with her aunt in "Rust" on Broadway as well as in the play "The Busybody" both produced in 1924. She was on her way to a great career in the theater, even though she had been in a few silents earlier in her life. But apparently she preferred the stage.

I did find one quote about Lisle and her aunt in an old 1911 magazine online. "In my day there (were) two leading ladies (who) were my favorites. One of them, Sara Alexander, is now living in retirement in New York, keeping house with her niece, Lisle Leigh, also a member of the profession. The other was Annie Adams." Apparently, the author of this article had lived in Salt Lake City just for two years when he was a boy and recalled visiting the brand new Salt Lake Theatre and seeing the rocking chair placed halfway up the orchestra floor where the elderly Brigham Young used to sit to watch performances. He quite admired the great actresses that Utah had produced and the author spends some time on Maude Adams as well. ("The Stage" by Matthew White Jr., Munsey's Magazine, Volume 46, 1911, pp.898-899)

In the youngest photograph of Sara Alexander, she is quite young and dressed in a brightly colored spring dress with a colorful shawl around her shoulders, bracelets, a necklace and dangling earrings. Her hair is parted at the center but she has all sorts of curls and ringlets pulled back to the nape of her neck. She seems to have dark brown hair and really is very, very beautiful. Not one thing about this photograph reflects the sort of photos one sees of the early pioneer women, dressed

Lisle Leigh, Niece of Sara Alexander

University of Utah Special Collections

in black with white collars and serious expressions. A later photograph of her seems to show that she maintained her beauty in her later years as well as being self-assured and seemly quite beautiful as well. Adopting her deceased sister's child, Sara supported Lisa's acting career as long as she lived, refusing custody by her sister's abusive husband.

One can imagine that her adopted daughter was equally as attractive and stylish when young. Sara Alexander, while not that famous outside the Utah Territory until her later years, seems to be one of the forgotten actresses of the early stage who really had talent and an independent spirit as well. She was headed for national stardom but only in her later years.

I did find mention of another suitor Sara Alexander had when she was young and performing at the Salt Lake Theatre. "After the close of this eventful season, Mr. George Waldron, who had played the leading support to Mrs. Hayne (Julia Dean Hayne) and become an established favorite, drifted away from Salt Lake, going into Montana; returning a year or so later in conjunction with Mrs. Waldron. He had found his mate and brought her to Salt Lake to make her acquainted with friends there. George tried very earnestly to get a Salt Lake wife. It looked for a while as if Miss Sara Alexander was destined to fill that place; she certainly filled George's eye. He was very much enamored of the petite and lithesome Sara, but the expected union did not materialize, and George sought pastures new, and ere long returned, bringing a beautiful wife with him. Meantime, Sara had drifted off to the east in company with a literary lady named Lisle Lester. They took with them Sara's little niece, her dead sister's baby, baby Finlayson, then just two years old. Miss. Finlayson, under her aunt's careful guidance and training, developed into a very clever and capable actress, and for many years now has been holding leading positions in prominent companies and theaters. She is known professionally as Lisle Leigh."

"The Waldrons played a short engagement and then bid a fond farewell to Salt Lake and the West. At this writing, George Waldron has been dead for 10 years, his wife, a son and a daughter survive him; all follow the stage successfully." (Ibid, Lindsay, p.56)

Lisle Leigh had a fairly long career before her death from heart disease as witnessed by the photo I so fortunately found of her. Startlingly it has a date on it showing that it was taken apparently shortly before her death in 1927 and I only found it because she signed the photo to someone she apparently was very fond of. I did find a birth date and birthplace so I hope it is accurate and this would have made her 48 when she died in New York City, if she was indeed born in 1879 in Salt Lake City, Utah.

VIOLA GILLETTE
MUSICAL OPERETTAS FROM STAGE TO SCREEN

(Most of the information in this piece is taken from Mavis Gay Gashler's thesis of May 1970, entitled "Three Mormon Actresses: Viola Gillette, Hazel Dawn, Leora Thatcher." Thesis presented to the Department of Dramatic Arts at Brigham Young University)

Viola's grandfather was Orsen Pratt who was one of the first pioneers in the Salt Lake Valley and one of the original Council of the Twelve Apostles of the L.D.S. Church. In 1841 he contested Joseph Smith's revelation on the polygamy issue when he found out that Smith had tried to seduce his only wife Sarah. He was disciplined and ex-communicated shortly after, but several months later Pratt asked to be re-baptized. Eventually Pratt had ten wives and 45 children. Viola's other grandfather was Charles C. Rich, who was an apostle and had six wives and 51 children. Perhaps some of Viola's pluck as an international star married to a non-Mormon came from her grandfather, as Viola herself remained a Mormon all of her life.

Viola was one of the first young women to leave the valley to become an internationally known stage actress and singer. Whenever Viola performed near where most of her family lived, she was always guaranteed to fill the first three rows of the theater with members of her own family. Viola was performing at the old Salt Lake Theatre as a singer when she was a child. As a young adult, she was teaching music in Salt Lake City elementary schools and performing in local opera productions.

Young Viola Pratt Gillette on the Salt Lake Theatre Stage
Utah State Historical Society

She covered ten different schools in a single day giving half-hour lessons by getting in her buggy and then driving to the next school. She also practiced daily with the director of the Tabernacle Choir, who encouraged her to study under one of the great voice teachers in New York City. Because she had fallen in love with a man of a different religion, her parents finally agreed to send her to New York for three months hoping to get her away from this man. She raffled off her horse to obtain extra funds to finance her trip east.

When she arrived in New York she immediately found a job at a local church, which had advertised for a contralto singer. She got the position over several other singers and for several years after that paid for her studying with these funds as well as giving music lessons. Then Viola began to become interested in musical comedy stage work, and wrote her parents that she intended not to marry at all. The man that was in love with her, who was a miner, immediately sold out all his mining properties and traveled to New York where he asked Viola to marry him. They were married in 1896. Soon after Viola Gillette became a famous Broadway star. Besides being a very handsome woman, her extraordinary voice promised to make her quite famous worldwide. The local papers in Salt Lake City reported that she had a wide circle of friends and admirers and was scoring several vocal triumphs in New York City. When she won a leading part in a major New York opera over 300 other contestants, the manager was quoted as saying that her voice was one of marvelous power and richness and was distinctly heard in every part of the great Metropolitan Opera building.

One critic, W.S. Lamoreux, was quoted as saying: "Utah should feel proud of the success her young artists are gaining and be ever ready to herald the triumph. The honors already won by a certain charming young woman, whose name is so well known at home, are just beginning to be showered upon her. One of the four musical aspirants lately visited New York and heard this Viola Pratt sing ' Just as I am' and other songs, says,' You can't afford to die till you have heard her wonderful rendition of that song.'

"George Sweet, her teacher, says she's the best contralto in America now and will soon be an example to the entire world. Her voice is the richest kind of a powerful mezzo soprano with wonderful compass, is extremely powerful, and her somber tones are sweet as the whisperings of angels." (Lamoreux, W.S. "A Utah Girl," clippings from the <u>Utah State Historical Society</u>, Salt Lake City, Utah, Ibid, Gashler, p.11)

In 1897, she was chosen to perform in a private concert in Washington D.C. given by President McKinley and the cabinet in honor of the Austrian Ambassador. She wrote to her parents about this evening. She told them that there had been 300 invitations and that she had performed alongside Huberman, a child prodigy violinist and Scharvenka, a famous pianist of the day. The President, his wife, many of the Senators, and all the diplomatic corps where there, she wrote, and besides receiving lots of praise from the local papers for her concert, she also received a present from the wife of the Austrian Ambassador. When she opened it, she discovered a beautiful gold bracelet with the date of the concert engraved on the inside. Besides riding in the Australian Ambassador's carriage to tour Washington D.C., she also had lunch with Mrs. McKinley, whom she described as being very sweet and lovely, but also very delicate and frail.

In 1899, Viola joined an opera company that was traveling to Australia. She performed at the Royal Opera house in Sydney, only because a good friend of hers Mrs. Fred Stone was under contract to produce a play there. Viola was in Salt Lake City at the time and Mrs. Stone was terrified of traveling by herself to Australia. She arrived at her home begging Viola to go with her and promised that she would get Viola a position in the company. Having only performed in operas and on the musical comedy stage, Viola didn't have a clue about following a director's directions and all the vocabulary was foreign to her. She says that he probably thought she was a lunatic when all the other players knew what he was talking about and she didn't. The director became extremely angry with her and wanted her fired. Finally, she had to admit to him that she hadn't a clue what he was talking about. After a few more outbursts, he calmed down and realized that it would be easier to teach her the directing cues than to find a replacement with as good a singing voice in Australia. This was her first real introduction to becoming an actress, as well as a singer.

In the production, "Robin Hood," Viola Gillette became an overnight sensation in Australia. The critics mentioned her acting specifically as being every bit as good as her singing. She played a male part, Alan-A-Dale, and stole the show with her one solo, receiving standing ovations and encore requests nightly. She performed in New Zealand in another production and the large crowd waiting outside made such a rush to the front doors that several people were knocked down and one young woman was seriously injured. There were people standing in the aisles taking flashlight photos of the proceedings and the crowd got pretty rowdy with vigorous and dramatic rounds of applause. The people of Australia fell in love with Viola Pratt Gillette and she was persuaded to stay for another season. In March of 1900 she returned to Salt Lake City.

After visiting there, she continued onto New York City to join her husband. They were traveling to Cuba where she was to perform next. However two things happened when she returned home to New York. Viola found that her husband, who had always opposed her career anyway, was becoming increasingly dependent on her income. Secondly, he was then turning around and investing that money in his various business schemes. They finally agreed to separate, but her husband would not grant her a divorce for many years. Finally in early 1906, she decided to let people know that her husband had deserted her. It was not until October of 1906 that she filed for divorce. After the divorce Gillette went to Cuba to invest what he had in sugarcane and grapefruit, living only on the money that Viola chose to give him.

In the meantime, Viola toured the United States and London. While the first few productions she was in were panned by the critics, they had nothing but praise for her acting and singing. Like many actresses of the day she tended to play as many male roles as female roles. However, being a good Mormon girl, she was a bit appalled by the costumes she had to wear. She had to wear tight fitting bodices, belts across her bosom, and men's tights with nothing under them. She was sure that she was headed straight for perdition she said, and sought the advice of her previous vocal coach. Her singing teacher told her to forget that she was wearing tights, and to keep her mind on her chest, and the audience would pay less attention to her general appearance and more to her voice. Viola, however, was still worried about whether she had done the right thing or not, having been endowed with an extraordinary figure.

By this time, Viola had become increasing popular and was receiving a myriad of fan mail from countless admirers. One columnist said that she either left them unopened, tore them up, or fed them to her dog. There was also a foreign nobleman who was totally enamored with her and had written many notes in vain to her. In the last note she received from the Baron, he said: “Adored one-- I am dying for love of you. Do not be cruel. My heart is bursting with the intensity of my passion. You are killing me by inches with your cold disdain. Lodestar of my existence, I cannot sleep at night for love of you. Noble girl!" According to the columnist, Viola's reply was to send a messenger to the Baron's apartment with a twenty-grain sulphonal powder, so the Baron could calm down. (Ibid, Gashler, p.24)

While Viola was performing in Chicago, the theater burned down on a night when she was not in the cast. There was a terrible loss of life including some people that she was close to. It took Viola some time to recover from the trauma of this incident. But by 1919, her career was in full swing again and she had met and married a young Canadian named George J. McFarlane. They were performing in the same opera company in Canada at the time. They were married on December 24th, 1906 and the handsome baritone had a great career of his own ahead of him. He had gotten his start after being a member of the Canadian Mounted Police and serving in South Africa in the Bore War. He began singing in cathedrals in Canada and Frank L. Perley happened to hear him. Perley owned an opera company in Montreal and immediately engaged the young man who rose through the ranks to be one of Canada's most excellent singers.

A typical description of Viola's physical appearance involved the words "handsome," "a picture of health and beauty," "a Grecian shaped head," "the most brilliant white neck in the world," " a blond beauty" with deep blue eyes and auburn hair, hair that waved "rich undulations over her shoulders," "a complexion as dazzling white as snow in sunshine," " her cheeks a compound of the lily and the rose," and " her lips crimson." "Her mouth might be too large for a goddess in marble, but not for a woman whose eyes were fire, whose look was love, whose voice was sweetest song, whose shape was perfect symmetry and who's every motion was dignified and graceful." She had a "beautiful soprano voice, full of force, sympathetic and of remarkable range and volume, the sense of beauty and tenderness and sweetness was such as to completely carry the audience away. Her every appearance evoked a story of applause, nor could subsistence be hoped for until the demands for an encore were complied with" ("Light Opera at the Grand Triumphant Presentation of 'The Girl and the Bandit' Last Night – Viola Gillette Scores a Success – Play Gives the Most Unqualified Satisfaction," Eau Claire, clippings from the New York Library and Museum of the Performing Arts, Ibid, Gashler, p.27).

Closer to the truth, others described her as being a large woman who was statuesque or striking and well built. Soon, Perley was billing his company as the Viola Gillette Opera Company and she and her husband were touring major cities all over the United States, including Salt Lake City. When she came to Salt Lake City, the local papers described her as a prima donna who would head the list of the comedians and comediennes surrounded by a chorus of beautiful showgirls. The opera company had seventy-nine members and would perform at least half a hundred numbers. However, Viola and her husband soon joined a different opera company and traveled even more around the United States. George McFarlane had many other interests going and was probably the one to get Viola to try the silent movies.

McFarlane had been married once before and was billed as "America's Favorite Baritone." He had a long association with the operettas of Gilbert and Sullivan. He also liked to perform as a talking comedian. He reached his peak on Broadway between the years 1914 to 1921. He also began to make 78-rpm recordings of popular songs for the Victor label in 1914. In 1917, he made a few recordings for Columbia records and also appeared in his first silent film for an obscure company called Webb Singing Pictures. In this film McFarlane, Enrico Caruso, and Viola Gillette, among others, performed behind the scenes while actors on-screen mimed their parts. McFarlane went on to produce and direct plays, as well as to perform in a few operettas. In later years, he returned to Montreal to perform for the people of his home city on several occasions. He owned his own sheet music publishing company and his name does appear in the credits of several silent films starting in 1929. He acted in 15 different feature films between 1929 and 1932, including, "Frozen Justice," and "The Famous Ferguson Case." He remained active in both Hollywood and New York City until his death in February of 1932.

One of the amusing stories that Viola tells in her interviews was about an incident that happened when she and her husband first joined this new opera company. Back in those days the zipper had not been invented yet and tightly fitting dresses were often fastened by means of strings that crossed between brass hooks at the back of the dress. One night, she had her dress tied tightly but the strings were too long. One of the men thought he could help her out by tucking the strings in as she stepped forward on stage. Instead, he accidentally pulled on the strings, which slowly untied the bow as she began to sing. She said it was an incredible feeling to know that your dress was slowly coming down in front of thousands of people. Viola had to play the entire scene with one hand tightly clutching the back of her dress, facing the audience squarely and singing her heart out.

Some of the things Viola and George did gave them a lot of press. One time, Viola got interested in driving a car and she and her mother and George were sightseeing as they approached the Grand Avenue Bridge. Viola neglected to notice the warning bell and as the bridge began to rise above them the car slowly rolled backwards but no one was injured. On another occasion, Viola was accused of sailing from Atlantic City to New York in a hot air balloon, although this never really happened. She also wagered a photograph of herself against a pair of the team members' gloves of the winning baseball team when she visited in Michigan. She won 90 pairs of gloves that day because she was to get a pair for every two points that the winning team scored over the losing team. The most outlandish and unfounded rumor that ever was published about her, concerned her being released from her contract to marry a Japanese war hero in Manila before she met her second husband, McFarlane. It was reported that while on her way to Australia, she had stopped in Manila and fallen in love with a Major Sayasha. A prince in his own land, Sayasha supposedly negotiated her released from her contract.

In 1908, the McFarlanes began performing on the Vaudeville stage. An interesting incident happened on a trip to Salt Lake City to see her relatives and perform at Christmas time that year. She made the mistake of asking a relative of hers, who was planning a huge family reunion and Christmas party; to invite them all to her hotel and also to buy presents for them and have the bill sent to her at the theater. Forgetting how many relatives she might have, she received a staggering bill from a leading department store in Salt Lake City. Not one member of her family had been forgotten. When she arrived at the hotel for the Christmas party, it looked like a convention.

Viola's most daring play was entitled: "The Beauty Spot." While the play was a great success and ran for a very long time in New York City, as well as traveling across the country, the boldness of her role gave her a lot of press attention. Apparently, the play got criticized for having too many sensational sexual nuances in the dialogue, as well as in some of the costuming. Viola wore a skin-tight surf costume with a long cloak over it. The play was compared to the Zeigfield Follies and Viola had several costumes that were described as being "exciting in their scantiness and beauty."

During her performance in "The Beauty Spot" another interesting incident took place for Viola Gillette. A young woman named Garna Gillette, claiming to be Viola Gillette's sister, was murdered. Garna was a showgirl with a striking resemblance to Viola who had told several people that she was Viola's sister to help her get ahead. She lived in Seattle and Viola Gillette had just opened at Moore's Theatre there the night before in her most risqué part. The next afternoon, Garna's current boyfriend, James Vlasos, gunned down Garna and then turned the gun on himself. He died later in the city hospital of his own self-inflicted wound. Garna had just come off of her second musical comedy company that had disbanded. She told everyone that she had remained behind to see her sister's performance and then have dinner with her after opening night. News reporters, going on this information garnished the story with a comment that Viola had noticed the empty seat reserved for her sister and became worried when she did not show up later for dinner even though Garna had talked with her sister on the phone the day before.

Viola Pratt Gillette

"Miss Gillette was seen to enter Vlasos's rooms at 4 o'clock yesterday afternoon. Four hours later three shots were heard in his rooms in rapid succession. Then followed another. When the police arrived Vlasos, with a gaping wound in his head, unlocked the door and admitted the officers. 'I shot her,' he gasped, as he lapsed into unconsciousness. The police figured that Vlasos was infatuated with the pretty chorus girl, who planned to return to New York this week, and failing to induce her to marry him, killed her and himself." ("Murders Show Girl and Kills Himself," The New York Times, February 7, 1911)

Two days later, the Times printed a small retraction entitled "Not Miss Gillette's Sister: Woman Murdered in Seattle Had Claimed Relationship to Singer." Viola Gillette contacted the papers and stated that Garna Gillette was not her sister, though the woman had made several statements "causing the publication of the misleading stories." Gillette explained that she only had one sister, Leona, who had retired from the stage when she married a Brooklyn lawyer and she was now living in Brooklyn with her husband and children. Viola Gillette, however, had been showered with condolences and presents for two whole days and continued to receive these things even after all the papers printed retractions of a sort. ("Not Miss Gillette's Sister," The New York Times, February 9, 1911)

In 1912 and 1913, George and Viola performed two seasons of Gilbert and Sullivan operettas, which then led them to tour in San Francisco. They both received excellent reviews in not only Gilbert and Sullivan operettas, but in the more serious plays that they performed in as well. Eventually, Viola made another splash in the headlines by being one of the first performers to dance that daring new dance, the tango. She was quoted as saying: "It is ridiculous to protest that the tango and the rest of the new dances are harmful, when it is bringing to American women the one thing they have never had -- beautiful feet." She went on to say that Europeans laughed at the neglected feet of American women. "With the coming of the tango, the maxie, the turkey-trot and other newer sprightlier forms of dance, it has become absolutely necessary that the feet be in perfect condition. Tight shoes are impossible. The feet must be free, must be well cared for, if a girl is to enjoy any of the so-called 'violent dances'... It won't be long before love of the new dances becomes synonymous with a graceful, easy carriage, and the comfortable, satisfied expression of the woman whose feet, one of the most important parts of her whole body, are in the condition they should be. So I say the tango is a blessing. If it does nothing else, it is teaching American women to care for their feet. It is giving them exercise that is usually badly needed, and is helping to improve their looks. If that isn't the function of a blessing, what is it?" ("Tango a Blessing Says Viola Gillette," Los Angeles Courier, December 8, 1913, Ibid, Gashler, p.46)

By 1914, the McFarlanes were in New Orleans and Viola had left her "boy" roles behind her for good. They were still traveling the country and she appeared in many plays in major cities in the country from 1916 to 1926. In 1927, she appeared as the Grande Dame of a racing stable in an Al Jolson play that toured the country. The play was entitled "Big Boy." By this time she was no longer singing and was performing as an actress only. Virginia Hall, who played a young ingénue in the play, remembered how gentle and caring she was with her, as a young beginning actress. They remained lifelong friends and Virginia Hall said the she was one of the warmest personalities she ever knew, with a sense of humor - an almost devilish sense of humor - but never mean, and always very reassuring to be with. On the closing night of the play, Jolson was preparing to sing his famous "mammy" song in blackface when he spotted Miss Gillette, in her handsome gown and stately white wig, and went up to her and rubbed his blackface makeup all over her face.

It was during this production that she lost her second husband. "When moving pictures became popular, Mr. McFarlane became a producer. He had gone to Hollywood one time to preview one of his productions, when – ironically - he was killed by an automobile while crossing the street to mail a letter to his wife. 'I was on tour with Al Jolson and his troupe when I received word of my husband's death,' she recalls. Al sent me to California immediately, paying my expenses and my salary while I was there. I can never forget his kindness and - it was one

George McFarlane

George in Costume

of the many little acts of generosity which made him a great person." "Thus that ended my career. I had no heart to go on." McFarlane was buried in Salt Lake City in February of 1932. He was only 55 years old.

Viola Pratt Gillette McFarlane returned to Salt Lake City and retired from the theater. She died on April first, Easter Sunday, in 1956. She was President of the Bountiful Art Guild and Vice-President of the University of Utah Emeritus Club. Quiet and generous until the day she died, she was well loved by both her family and her many fans from around the world. Her cousin Benjamin Rich gave her a fitting tribute at her funeral. " My father loved her and so did everybody who knew her. I don't think I ever knew a woman who had such wonderful traits of character. She was beautiful to look upon; she had a sweet musical voice. She was kind -- she was dignified. She was honorable and she had a personality that impressed itself upon everybody who knew her. She had a very remarkable career. She was one of the early glamour girls of Utah and the glamour girl of the Rich family. She helped her father and mother and their family for many years. Her career as a vocalist extended over nearly 40 years. She started her career about the time of Utah statehood. For many years, upwards of ten to twelve years, her name was on the marquises of the leading theaters of Broadway and New York. She was the toast of Broadway and she was voted the most beautiful woman on the American stage... After her husband died she wanted to come home and be with her own people and she lived in this community for over seventeen years before she died."

Miss Gillette had grace, was an aristocratic lady in every sense of the word, and had a great sense of humor. She continued to be quite lovely even in her senior years with gorgeous white hair, lovely large eyes and a beautiful smile. She was a striking beauty all of her life, both inside and out and a great ambassador for both the state of Utah and her religion. She often returned home to perform for charities and kept to her religious guidelines throughout her life.

BLANCHE KENDALL THOMAS McKEY
BEN-HUR ON BROADWAY

Blanche (Blanchie) was born on June 30, 1879 in Salt Lake City and died in 1973 at the age of 94. Her parents were Richard Kendall Thomas and Caroline Stockdale Thomas. They always had season tickets to both the Social Hall productions and the Salt Lake Theatre. Blanche, her oldest sister Kate, and Channing Pollock, all wrote plays for the family theater called The Barnacle. Kate Thomas became a well-known feminist, author, poet and world traveler and while Mormon, she was rarely in Utah and led a sort of bohemian life. Her biographical note in her Utah State History papers states: "For one reason or another she never married. Her writing is full of unrequited love for men, and later, an almost sensual passion for women." It seems that nearly all of the surviving Thomas children accomplished great things including their brother Utah State Senator Elbert Thomas, and all of them grew up loving the theater with some kind of accomplishment in the arts, but especially in drama.

Channing Pollock, the future Broadway playwright, staged the first production at the children's theater. Blanche graduated from the University of Utah in 1900, already a seasoned playwright and actress because of the many plays, her siblings and neighbor children had produced, directed and written for the children's barn theatre, "The Barnacle." She graduated with a teaching certificate, but this was not the same as earning a B.A. in college as it took a lot less time to get a teaching certificate then. She begged her parents to let her go off to take training as an actress in New York City in 1901. She was only allowed to go if she took her older sister Kate with her as a chaperone, which her sister agreed to do for her. Her parents were very much against this idea, but finally let her go as long as her sister went with her. She was only 22 at the time.

Blanche took private acting lessons in New York City from a very reputable drama teacher and she soon had a chance to audition for Klaw and Erlanger, a prestigious New York agency. Her teacher arranged the

Blanche Kendall Thomas, Actress
University of Utah Special Collections

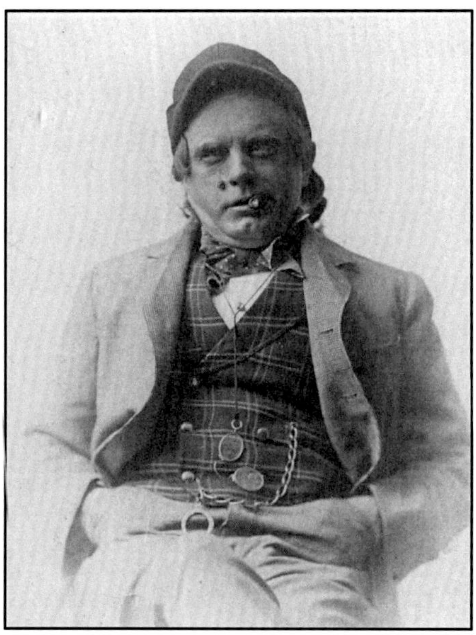

William Richard McKey, Actor
University of Utah Special Collections

audition and she did three different Shakespeare scenes as Ophelia, Juliet and Portia. The auditioner watched her through all three performances a bit bemused she thought. She didn't think she did very well but they signed her to a contract anyway. She always said that it was probably her naive charm that got her that contract and not her delivery or her looks. She was signed one week later, to her great surprise.

In 1902, she auditioned for the Richard Mansfield Company from England who was looking for three young girls for a dance number. Blanche told them that she was a dancer even though all she had ever done as a dancer was to win some prizes in waltz contests in high school. It was the famous actor Sir Richard Irving who was starring in the play "Dante." And even though she got the part the play failed both in New York and in London. However, Blanche talked about how she was so enamored with Sir Irving that she managed to sit on the other end of a bench from him and it was the highlight of this experience.

In 1904 Blanche was hired to play the part of "Hope Brower" in "Eben Holden." William Richard McKey was playing the part of "Eben" and was the star of the play. Richard was twenty years older than Blanche and their romance had begun. In 1905 and 1906, Blanche signed with the Charles B. Hanford Company and she was told that she would play leads or ingénue roles. But poor Handford could not talk his wife into giving up parts that she was too old for and Blanche ended up playing second leads that season. In 1906 and 1907 Blanche played "Annie" in "The Bonnie Briar Bush." By then, she and McKey were a steady "item."

When Lew Wallace wrote Ben-Hur: A Tale of the Christ which was also titled The First Christmas, he had spent seven years of writing and research on the book and wrote most of it under a beech tree near his residence in Crawfordsville, Indiana. He had to be convinced that such a book could be made into a play by none other than Marc Klaw and Abraham Erlanger, who had signed Blanche Thomas to her contract. When Wallace saw how they would stage the chariot race and when they agreed that Jesus Christ would be depicted as a simple beam of white light, he agreed to the producing of the book as a play. They trained eight horses that pulled the two chariots running on treadmills installed in the floor of the stage. The horses ran at full gallop while the scenery behind them ran backwards (installed on cyclorama) giving the illusion that the chariots and horses were actually moving forward at full gallop.

"Ben-Hur" opened on Broadway at the Broadway Theatre on November 29, 1899. The play was adapted for the stage by William Young, produced by Erlanger & Klaw and directed by Joseph Brooks. It was a smashing success with six acts re-divided into a dozen or so tableaus per act. With painted oriental backdrops and amazing stage sets and moving props, it was one of the most spectacular plays ever staged. The raft scene in "The World" and the chariot race in "Year One" were spectacular. The play went on the road for two weeks after opening in New York. It went overseas to Europe and Australia and the actors gave an estimated six thousand performances to over twenty million people who viewed it. The final performance of the stage version of "Ben-Hur" occurred on April of 1921. Revivals of the play on Broadway also took place in 1907 and in 1916. Edward Morgan was the first "Ben-Hur" in the first production of the play and was then succeeded by William Farnum. William S. Hart, the famous western silent star, played the first "Messala" in the play.

In 1907 there was a revival of the play from February to April of that year and Blanche Thomas was one of twenty main actors in the revival version who gave 64 performances. She was cast at "Tizah" the younger sister of Ben-Hur. Tom and Ralph Ince alternated the lead each night and both of them eventually became directors in Hollywood. The production required horses, a camel and a goat as well as a large revolving stage. There were only three such stages in the United States in New York, Chicago and San Francisco. The play boasted of five chariots, five drivers and five quadruple spans of horses. There were 400 people in the production, so to have a leading part in it was something indeed. A playbill of the performance shows Ben-Hur, his mother and Blanche Thomas as "Tizah" on the cover.

The second time the play was presented between 1899 and 1907, "The first company had closed, when, at a Sunday performance, the light portraying 'Christ' caught fire and burned the stage. 'Ben-Hur' was never again performed on Sunday." A fifteen minute silent film version came out the same year and interestingly can now be viewed on YouTube. The Kalem Moving Picture Company neglected to get permission from the Wallace estate or from the play producers, Klaw & Erlanger, and ended up in court in a law suit. The case ended up in the U.S. Supreme Court and judgment was pronounced by none other than Oliver Wendell Holmes, the Chief Justice at the time. Kalem had to pay $25,000 in damages and this was much more than it cost to make the little movie. ("Blanche Kendall Thomas McKey – Biographical Summary" by Eily McKey Pierson, August 29, 1990, p.3)

The 1925 silent movie version with Roman Navarro was the most expensive film ever made in the history of silent films costing over 4 million dollars. Once again it was Abraham Erlanger who obtained the rights for this lavish version. Those who have seen both the legendary 1959 widescreen version with Charlton Heston and the 1925 version, say that the 1925 version is the better one. One of the main reasons for this is that the chariot race was much more realistic and probably a great deal more dangerous for both the men and the horses in it. This was because the studio turned it into a real race, inviting stuntmen to enter and offering a big reward for the man who won the race. All of the Hollywood greats flocked to the set and played extras in the chariot race scene just to watch it. It received rave reviews but only turned a slight profit, although it did make the MGM Studios a major player in Hollywood.

Blanche Kendall Thomas left the New York stage after her last performance in the 1907 play, giving up what might have been a great career on Broadway and even Hollywood, had she remained. She got married. She had arrived in New York at the age of 21 and left it at the age of 28. Married in New York on Thanksgiving Day November 27, 1907, her parents opposed the marriage. "Dick" was twenty years older, an actor by trade, a gentile, and divorced with a ten year-old son. Her sister Kate was the only family member to attend the wedding. They had two children, Margaret Eily born October 5, 1909 and Richard Kendall born February 1, 1912. Eily was born in Chicago while Dick was performing in a stock company. Five weeks after the baby was born,

Blanche's mother came and got her and the baby and took them home to Salt Lake City. Eily had been named for the heroine in a play called "The Colleen Bawn."

Blanche stayed seven months with her parents and while she was at home she performed in two plays at the Salt Lake Theatre that had been written by local playwrights. These plays were "Corianton" by Orestes Bean and "Zalmona" by Ezra C. Robinson. Blanche went back to New York to her husband and to perform herself, leaving her baby with her mother. In 1911, Blanche performed with the Staten Island Stock Company but by December she had to return to Salt Lake City to give birth to her son and this time she never returned to New York City. She then traveled with a few western troupes but mainly with her brother's company, The Harmon-Kendall Players, with E. Forrest Taylor and Ralph Clonniger. As to whether she ever returned to her husband after 1912, no one seems to know or they don't want to talk about it. Perhaps he was not being faithful to her or perhaps they simply separated on grounds of incompatibility. Or perhaps she did stay with him until he died. Whatever happened, William Richard McKey died in 1918 in New York City, most probably in the influenza epidemic, but then no one says what he died of either.

Blanche then came back to Salt Lake in 1918 and became a drama teacher at Weber State College. She took her nine year-old daughter with her to Ogden but left her young son in Salt Lake City until he was able to be in full-time school. She taught there five years and then took a sabbatical and got a B.A. at the University of Utah in 1924 while living with her parents. She taught at Ricks College in Rexburg, Idaho for three years and then took another sabbatical and returned to the University of Utah to get an M.A. in English in 1928. From 1928 to 1943 she taught English and Speech at Ogden High School and then retired early due to poor health. She then lived with her daughter in Salt Lake City while her daughter's husband, George A. Pierson taught at the University of Utah.

An actress, a poet, a playwright and drama teacher, Blanche supported herself and was a great influence for many of her students. She helped to produce many plays on these college campuses, wrote and

Blanche Kendall Thomas McKey,
Poet, Playwright, Professor
University of Utah Special Collections

directed others, and also acted in many of them. She also published several anthologies of poetry. She won national poetry and playwright awards and her best anthology was entitled "House of Dreams" which was published in 1962. She wrote one-act plays, articles, short stories and several plays, for which she won many prizes. She spent the last twenty years of her life living with her daughter in New York City. But she died in Gainesville, Florida on April 8, 1973 and was buried in the Salt Lake Cemetery. It seems that life gave her a blow of some kind from which she never recovered to inspire her to keep acting. Perhaps it was disappointment in her marriage, or perhaps the reality of an actress's life was not what she had imagined. But one can suppose that she found peace living among her own people and teaching young people to act, as well as finding solace in the poetry that she wrote. And perhaps her children were another concern that made her leave the stage, where she might have had a somewhat successful stage career. She certainly had the talent and the looks and the drive to have been among them. She did continue to act throughout most of her life.

In reading about her magical and aristocratic upbringing as one of the many children of Richard Kendall Thomas and Caroline Stockdale Thomas, it is rather poignant to also read about Blanche Kendall Thomas's later years. Her life started out so free and promising as an artist, actress and playwright, performing and writing children's plays at her beloved "Barnacle." It is so obvious that she was the heart of this little theater as well as its manager and director. She very well could have ended up a famous playwright as well as actress, had things happened differently for her. Instead, whatever betrayals or devotions that came her way in terms of her husband and also his death in relation to the worldwide 1918 epidemic, caused her to "return to the fold." She effectively ended her career and possible fame as a playwright and actress in return for teaching high school and college drama classes in her home state. Beloved as a teacher and still writing plays and poetry, she gained an education and ended up in New York once again in her old age when she lived with her daughter. A strikingly beautiful woman even in her later years, Blanche Kendall Thomas lived a spiritual life even when her life took an unexpected turn or two. I hope she will be remembered for her children's theater, her children's plays and her adult life as a playwright, poet and drama teacher.

OLIVER MITCHELL MOROSCO THEATRE CRITIC, PROMOTER, MANAGER, PRODUCER & DIRECTOR

"I was born in Logan, Utah so much is conceded. A brief entry into my mother's Bible says this occurred on June 20, 1880. But another authority, Whose Who in America, maintained over a period of years that I began life in 1875. And still others, a certain musty Utah newspaper and which was unearthed while the story of my marriage to Selma was being told with headlines throughout my home state, assert I was born in 1883." Even Morosco's current information on some internet sites state that he was born in 1896 and died in 1945, which would make him only 49 when he died, is an impossibility. Perhaps the mystery of his birth date will always keep his exact age a mystery, although it is certain that he died in 1945. Other sources state that Oliver Morosco was either 49 or 69 years old when he died so tragically. (The Oracle of Broadway by Helen M. Morosco and Leonard Paul Dugger, The Caxton Printers, Ltd.: Caldwell, Idaho, 1944, page 385)

Oliver Mitchell's earliest childhood recollection was "... centered about a snow-covered hilltop in my native Logan. I have only to shut my eyes to see Mother holding me out to a window that I might watch my brother Leslie, some three years my senior, come sliding down a hill on a little red sled. And, strange to say, the one most distinct object in this memory picture is that little red sled. I have often wondered just why it should have impressed me so." (Ibid, page 385)

The second memory was of when he left Logan as a young boy, a departure shrouded in mystery. "... my second earliest childhood recollection, is the fright I got, when one night, I was awakened by the blast of a shrill whistle to find my mother, brother Leslie, and myself aboard a train headed for California." "I later learned that, for reasons she never divulged, my mother, Esmah Badoura Montrose Mitchell, that night left my father, a titled Englishman, Sir John Leslie Mitchell, never

Oliver Morosco, Theater Manager

Annie T. Morosco

Selma Morosco

Oliver Morosco, Producer, Director, Theater Owner

to see or communicate with him again. As for myself, I have never seen him since, retain practically no recollection of him, and have been able to learn little about him other than that he was a distinguished barrister and penman of Birmingham, England." Who immigrated to America after converting to Mormonism, and then came out West to the Promised Land to settle in Logan, Utah. (Ibid, page 13)

"All my life I have wondered what on earth Sir John Leslie Mitchell could have done to cause Mother to leave him, when she continued, year after year, to tolerate this man St. Mary." Esmah had remarried after settling in San Francisco and had three more children with a man named Joseph St. Mary, her second husband. Apparently St. Mary was very abusive and did not support the family at all. One can speculate, knowing Mormon history, that Sir John Mitchell probably was a very good person, but might have proposed the idea of polygamy to his first wife Esmah. And after having had two children, and having been married to her husband for several years, this may have been her response to that proposal, simply to leave in the middle of the night. It certainly was the right time in history, as it would have been in the mid to late 1880s when polygamy was still being practiced. The introduction of another wife could have caused Esmah to leave so suddenly, taking flight in the middle of the night and hiding out, in order to protect her children from something in her case, she was not willing to accept or chance losing her children over. However, the real reasons will probably remain a mystery as it did to both Oliver and his brother Leslie, although there is always the possibility of abuse of some kind as well. When his mother put up with even more abuse from his step-father, Oliver would have been quite puzzled. But in that day and age even abuse was more acceptable than polygamy and leaving the Utah Territory was much more dangerous that perhaps either Oscar or Leslie realized, especially with two sons in tow that their father might have wanted to keep. (Ibid, p.13)

What followed, explains why neither of the boys ever looked for their real father and this change in destiny was pretty dramatic. They knew that they had to earn a living for their mother since she was nearly destitute and trying to raise three younger children. They had gotten interested in acrobatics, and would practice after school. One day while they were practicing in the park, they discovered that they gathered a crowd, put their hats down and made some money. St. Mary disappeared after a while and Esmah couldn't even keep the boys in school. So every day they went down to the park and performed their acrobatics to earn money for the family. One day a man happened upon these two young performers in the park and stopped to watch them. His name was Walter Morosco and he happened to own the Royal Russian Circus at the time. Soon after, he approached their mother with an offer to raise the boys and apprenticed them to his show, which she let them do. In the meantime, they could send money home for her and the other children. It broke her heart to do it but it was the only way out at the time.

"But for all his words and arguments, there was one concession the great showman couldn't maneuver. Mother would not consent to his adopting us. She had long cherished the hope that, with the passing of childhood, I would give up show business, go to school, and become a lawyer comparable to my illustrious father. For this reason she wanted me to retain, legally at least, the name of Mitchell, the name of a noted barrister." (Ibid, page 26)

Over the next few years, Oliver was an acrobat, a clown, an elephant trainer, and an actor. Once, when Oliver and Leslie were asked to perform a very dangerous acrobatic stunt and were almost killed, then asked to do it again, Oliver quit the circus and went home to his mother leaving his brother Leslie behind because Leslie did not want to leave. However, Oliver and Leslie were never asked to perform this trick again. Eventually, Oliver went back after having a job as a messenger boy and lying about his age to get it. As luck would have it, one day he found himself delivering a message to Walter Morosco, who came around again and offered him at job more to his liking with better pay. By this time, Morosco was getting out of the circus business and into the theater management business. Oliver and Leslie would do some acrobatic tricks out front of the theater to bring in the crowd, and then Leslie would run backstage to get his makeup and costume on, while Oliver ran for the ticket booth to start selling tickets. By this time the boys were in their early teens, and they had both adopted the last name of Morosco.

Eventually, Walter Morosco owned several theaters, dated a lot of women but never married one and managed to have two "sons" to raise, that he never really adopted. He was most definitely a P. T. Barnum of his era. Oliver Morosco continued to work for Walter Morosco until he became a manager for one of his theaters at the age of 16. By 1899, at the age of 23, Oliver Morosco owned his first theater, The Burbank, in Los Angeles and was on his way as a promoter, producer, theater owner, and eventual director. By 1912, he had a hit play called "The Bird of Paradise." While this play was being performed in his theater and he was named as the producer and director of the play, he was later accused of plagiarizing the play.

Morosco's life story could easily have been an early silent film tragedy itself, about a man who reaches the top, with a wife and a son and then a mistress – one of the young actresses in one of his theaters – whose reputation and finances are ruined by a mighty clever first wife, Annie T. Morosco. He then gets on his feet again financially and marries his mistress, who eventually leaves him when he runs out of money a second time. Then he finds a little unsettled peace with his third wife, who writes his autobiography that isn't published until several years after their divorce. He then loses everything again, begins drinking a little and is living in a boardinghouse where he marries the manager of the boardinghouse. Soon after, he walks in front of a street car and dies the same year that his third wife also dies. His autobiography comes out a year before they both died. Yet in the end, Morosco's story is about perseverance, hard work, and never giving up on the American dream. The autobiography came out in 1944 when Oliver was 68 years old, his most likely age. A year later, he was struck and killed by a red line streetcar in Hollywood at the age of 69 and legend has it that he had eight cents in his pocket when it happened.

He had managed theaters in San Jose, San Francisco, and Los Angeles, while also producing over 40 plays on Broadway, starting in 1909. Raised in San Francisco, he had leased The Burbank as a young man and gone on to own and manage six theaters in the Los Angeles area alone. After The Burbank, Morosco opened The Casino Theater, which was later called the Empress Theater and operated it for only a few months in 1905. In 1908 he opened The Majestic in San Francisco, and by 1913 he had opened another theater in Los Angeles. The Morosco Theatre then opened in New York and was producing plays that were changed weekly, which was a new concept at the time. He had many hit plays on Broadway, and even sponsored an Oliver Morosco Writing Award for a young up-and-coming playwright and by this time he had begun moving into Hollywood hoping to write and produce films. He had used his apprenticeship with his adopted father Walter Morosco quite well.

One interesting piece of trivia about Oliver Morosco, the promoter and producer, is that he produced a very successful version of L. Frank Baum's eighth book, The Tik-Tok Man of Oz on the west coast. Baum's combined production of The Wizard of Oz and The Road to Oz in 1902 on the east coast had been a smash hit with the popular comedy team of Montgomery and Stone playing the tin man and the scarecrow. So Morosco signed a deal with Baum and brought this comedy team out to his Majestic Theatre in Los Angeles and in this stage production the comedy team played the Clockwork Man and the Shaggy Man. The play premiered in March of 1914 but the times had changed a bit and while the play was a hit in Los Angeles, with a summer run in Chicago, it never made it to Broadway. Morosco closed the show while it was still showing a profit.

But while Morosco was very good at raising money and promoting his various businesses, Oliver Morosco did not do so well, where women were concerned. While his substitute father, Walter Morosco, thought very little of women, and knew many of them, he never married. Oliver, on the other hand, was married four times. It was his first wife, who took his money, and then ruined both his and his second wife's reputation in a legendary publicity blitz that rivals any such "War of the Roses" of today, in Hollywood. Not only was it a national and then international topic in just about every newspaper, the length of time that it was drawn out made Annie T. Morosco a very wealthy and "wronged" woman, while Oliver and Selma Paley Morosco had to start again with nothing. One cannot blame either party as one can always see two sides to any story.

Annie raised their one son, Walter Morosco Junior, and he became a Hollywood producer. Selma had a stillborn daughter and then another daughter with Oliver named Helen. Just as Oliver was getting back on his feet and recovering from financial ruin, he was planning to open a place called "Morosco Town." Instead, because of several poorly invested land deals, he had to file for bankruptcy in 1926. Selma left him with her baby girl. He lost everything again and then the Great Depression gave him a double blow in 1929. He then became very ill, and a little, very strong and aggressive actress that he knew, nicknamed "the Arizonian" stepped in to nurse him back to health. Helen Dugger Morosco helped Oliver get back on his feet and proposed writing the autobiography. She was both an actress and screenwriter and besides thinking it would be good therapy for Oliver, she also thought that they could make some money that way. However they divorced in 1933 and the book did not come out until 1944. The book gives one the impression that Oliver Morosco was on top of the world at that time, and perhaps he was.

The last time he saw his mother before she died, she reminded Oliver that he had disappointed her by his lack of adherence to his ancestral roots. "Son, I saw your ancestral home in Birmingham. In ruin, covered with weeds and falling into decay. I think the sight broke my heart. Your father, Sir John, was the one love of my life. You're the image of your father, so remember what I am saying to you. There is no permanent happiness to be derived from extravagance, drinking and gay living. That was the nearest she ever came to confiding in me the sorrow she had known with Sir John, my father." (Ibid, page 319)

According to Oliver, Annie, his first wife was maliciously after him all the time, overweight, cold, a recluse, and always sure to know how much he earned and how much was hers. Selma, his second wife, was tender, sweet, brokenhearted over the loss of her first child and always supportive, and when she left him, told him to find another woman to love. Helen, his third wife, was a hero worshipper, who could manage his affairs better than he could. She married Oliver on Valentine's Day in 1929 at the height of the depression. But Helen McRrueer, sued Oliver for divorce in 1933 on the grounds of desertion. Oliver married his fourth wife, Dorothy Morosco, in the same year. She was a former Colorado socialite, who was running an apartment and boardinghouse at the time. But his theatrical days were definitely over by the late 30s, and even though he was in a few early silent films probably as an extra, his own movie company never produced a film. By the beginning of the 40s, Morosco was really down on his luck, drinking, and with little of his fortune left. His third wife, Helen, married an actor, Sterling Lawson, but died unexpectedly herself in 1945.

Oliver's brother Leslie continued acting on the stage, but his son Walter Morosco Junior was more successful eventually becoming a producer in Hollywood. He married a famous silent star in 1922, Corinne Griffith, although some other data bases say that they got married in 1924 and were married until 1934. Corinne Griffith was one of the most beautiful stars in Hollywood at the time and also one of the shrewdest financially. She had four husbands, kept her private life just that, and had a long and fruitful career. Walter Jr. worked for 20th Century Fox and a couple of other studios and produced some very good movies. My favorites of his are "Sentimental Journey" with John Payne and Maureen O'Hara and his most famous one which is called "Wing and a Prayer" about a World War II fighter pilot starring Don Ameche. Another favorite of mine is "Mother Is a Freshman" with Loretta Young, which was his last film in 1949. His first film starred his then wife, Corinne Griffith and she was nominated for an Academy Award for this film made in 1929. He produced 37 films between 1921 and 1949 and wrote four more in the early twenties. But, unfortunately, after a career as a producer starting in the 20s, Walter Morosco Junior, died of a stroke at age 49 in the late forties, cutting short a promising career.

When third wife Helen wrote Oliver's autobiography, she answered Oliver Morosco's question about his memory of watching his brother Leslie slowly sledding down the long, slightly inclined hills of

Logan, Utah. Morosco wanted to know why that particular vision stood out in his memory so clearly. His wife's take on this was really a foreshadowing of events to come as well as a clear statement about Oliver Mitchell Morosco's journey through life. Helen replied to Oliver that a red sled shiny against the white snow represented something just out of reach but very enticing. It was just like an animal or small child, she said who could not resist a bright gleaming object, even if it turned out to be a fiery flame. The animal or child would move towards it even though it might be hurtful or dangerous, or even very destructive. And that was why Oliver couldn't forget the intense emotions he felt about the shiny red sled in the snow, he was always reaching for absolute success and never really getting it.

But I have my own theory on the red sled, provided for me from a friend whose grandfather used to recite this Christmas poem to his grandchildren. One evening we were talking about her recent divorce and she suddenly recited the one poem that stood out in her memory from her childhood. "Dear Santa, bring me a wagon that's red. If the wagon won't fit in my stocking, put the stocking in the wagon instead," a comment on Oliver Morosco's persistence in life, which brought him fame, fortune, and heartbreak.

CHANNING POLLOCK

Channing Pollock wasn't born into a fairytale world of wealth, wonderful parents and an idyllic upbringing, but the Thomas's provided this for the time he and his brother were in Salt Lake City. He was born March 4, 1880 in Washington, D. C. He spent three years abroad with his mother and brother and then grew up bouncing back and forth between Omaha, Nebraska and Salt Lake City, Utah. When he was ten and living once again in Salt Lake City, he fell in love with an Auerbach girl and assumed she was Jewish. Auerbach was a large department store in downtown Salt Lake City, which her father owned. But it wasn't until Channing was 30 that he found out he was also Jewish. His father, Alexander L. Pollock, was from an area in Austria – Hungry, which was 40 miles from Prague. He never really knew his father, even though, all told, he had lived on and off with him for 14 years. His father took his family abroad when Channing was a toddler and left them there, twice.

His mother was a pretty Christian woman from Virginia named Verona Larkin. His father was a short, swarthy man with black, kinky hair and was at the time serving in the weather bureau when he married Channing's mother. When Channing was an infant his father moved the family to Omaha, where he had been transferred. His father then began editing an evening newspaper, in-between dark broodings and sudden eruptions of temper, which the family had to experience. They were not necessarily poor, having a garden, an orchard, a stable, carriages, horses, a sleigh, and one servant. But while others in the neighborhood paid for these things, his father painted his own house, his mother did her own housework, and their maid was a neighborhood "hired girl," thus putting them at the lower end of the scale in a wealthier late eighteen hundred's neighborhood. With two girls and three boys, his mother had her hands full and their father wanted nothing to do with them. Channing became an indifferent student in school because he found it so boring.

His father then became editor of the Omaha Herald and later The Watchmen, newspapers that for a while prospered. Then suddenly, his father sent the whole family to live with relatives in Austria. When, in a few months, his father joined them, he was arrested only two hours later for evading service in the Austrian army. He had been a citizen of the United States for 10 years and was quickly released. But afterward, his father locked himself up in his room for a week and wouldn't speak to anyone. He quickly returned to Omaha, but did not send for his family until 11 months later. Channing had written his first play in Prague when he was eight years old, entitled, "How to Win a Girl – In Four Acts."

In 1888, in Omaha again, his father bought a drug store, which did not prosper, his mother complained of no money, and the whole family, minus their father, was sent back to Austria once again. With no money to get them home, they waited, while his father wandered to Salt Lake City to become a real estate salesman. Instead, his father got a job as the editor of The Salt Lake Herald and then sent for his family.

Channing Pollock,
Journalist, Critic, Press Agent

Channing Pollock,
Travel Author and Lecturer

Channing Pollock, Playwright

Channing called Salt Lake a "mud hole" at the time, but, he also called Omaha a "mud hole" too. Once he had been there a little while, he described Salt Lake City as "...an attractive town, whose crystal-clear mountain water ran down both sides of these tree-lined streets." He says that looking at the buildings where Brigham Young had lived, "... one could guess the number of wives by the number of windows and doors." His family's first brush with polygamy was when they hired a cook, who turned out to be the fourth wife of a prosperous merchant in town. He found the Mormons to be, rather than strange or "evil creatures," "... a simple, self-reliant and scrupulously honest people." And the Thomas children described Channing as "different." No young boys in those days used a cane and wore white gloves even in the summer. (<u>Harvest of My Years – An Autobiography</u> by Channing Pollock, the Bobbs – Merrill Company: Indianapolis and New York, 1943, p.38)

While <u>The Deseret News</u> was Church-owned and <u>The Salt Lake Tribune</u> was considered the gentile newspaper at the time, <u>The Herald</u> remained middle-of-the-road on issues of the day. His father eventually started his own paper, <u>The Evening Times</u>, so he could more freely express his own opinions, along with his silent partners. Channing's own savings for a bike went into the founding of this paper. "I must have been a maddening youngster. For no reason I can perceive now, I began to be sure I was a genius, and did my best to live up to the part... I also put wet towels in cold water and tied them around my head. Somewhere I had heard of another genius who did that, and the idea appealed to me." Channing's sense of humor as a writer is very evident when he tells about a second incident which happened while they were living in Salt Lake City. His Uncle Fred, who was living with them at the time, once made fun of him so much that Channing decided to kill himself. Channing prepared a noose, threw it over a rafter in the attic, put the noose around his neck and stood on a packing box. He stood there for a quarter of an hour before his family found him, his mother was hysterical and Fred responded by turning him over his knee." (Ibid, Pollock, p.40)

"It followed 'as the night the day' that I should organize a company of actors. A dozen of us children had bungled through plays of my composition on an improvised stage in the garden of the hotel that sheltered us in Salt Lake. Now, however, Heaven had revealed itself. The family of Elbert Thomas, currently United States Senator from Utah, was well-to-do, and they turned their unused stable into a really charming tiny theater, which we called the Barnacle. There we youngsters presented several plays under my direction, and so badly that after witnessing a performance my father made me refund the admission fee, which was $.10 – my first clash with dramatic criticism! However, we progressed, and in time did 'The Noble Outcast,' with the balcony scene from 'Romeo and Juliet,' in the Salt Lake Theatre, for the benefit of the Unitarian Church. My brother John was the Outcast, and I was the black-mustached and silk-hatted villain, James Blackburn. Also, I played Romeo – feeling very immodest in my lavender silk tights."

"Neither my Shakespeare nor my scholarship seems to have won much acclaim, but I was not without ambition, industry and self-reliance. I enjoyed bathing in the Great Salt Lake; it never occurred to me to beg an increase in my allowance, but I got a job as cash boy at two dollars a week in a department store. One of my duties was sweeping the aisle, in which I operated; the first morning, I swept up and spoiled an expensive bolt of ribbon, to pay for which I had to work seven weeks without wages. By then the summer was over, and, bathless, I went back to school. On several occasions, I earned 'two bits' by acting as supernumerary with professional companies in the Salt Lake Theater. This was one of the oldest playhouses in the United States. It was owned by the Mormon Church, and, therefore, probably was the only theater that for a considerable period began each of its performances with prayer."

"In spite of these histrionic experiences, I decided to be a dramatist rather than an actor. However, the first of my works to be given professionally was a song. Another stable in town had been turned into a theater. This was a larger barn, on a main street, when it emerged, white – painted, as Wonderland. To the end, though, a wooden horses head over the entrance was never removed. There were two floors; paying a dime, one climbed to the upper, where one saw human skeletons, bearded ladies and a short minstrel show. Than one paid another dime, descended another flight of stairs, and witnessed a forty – minute version of 'East Lynne' or 'The Romany Rye.' There was some question whether the bearded ladies or the members of the other stock company were the greater 'curios.' I recall a 'heavy man' named George Caine, noted for death scenes – shot through the heart, he had been known to devote 10 minutes to expiring and his really charming daughter, Georgia Caine, afterwards a popular star of musical comedy. Either Georgia's legs, which were lovely, or my interest in drama may explain the fact that for me attendance at Wonderland became practically perpetual motion. With my annual pass – because of the Evening Times – I spent most of every Saturday climbing to the 'curio hall,' descending to the theater, or emerging, re-entering and repeating the procedure."

"I don't remember a word of the lyric I finally wrote for that minstrel show, but it was fitted to a popular air and mailed anonymously. After that, my ascents and descents were not limited to Saturdays; I went every day after school and every night after dinner. Halfway up the stairs one evening I heard a comedian singing my song. That was the thrill that comes once-in-a-lifetime! After the performance, I waited in the street to present myself to the comedian. I don't know which was more astonished – he that finding that the author of his lyric was a small boy, or I at discovering that even without his burnt cork mouthpiece he was one of the blackest Negroes I have ever seen."

"In quest of literary experience, I spent many hours hanging around the Evening Times, and was occasionally rewarded with a minor assignment. The Emma Abbott Opera Company opened a brief engagement at the Salt Lake Theatre, and I was sent to report on the notables present. Unfortunately, the same evening had been appointed for rehearsal in the Barnacle, so I got my list of distinguished patrons from the management early that afternoon, attended the rehearsal, wrote my story, and turned it in. A few minutes later, my father sent for me. 'Did you enjoy the theatre?" he asked. Unwarned, I answered in the affirmative."

"'That proves you have considerable powers of imagination,' my father remarked, 'because Miss Abbott is ill and there was no opera.'

Then he wheeled his chair, not angry, but in deadly earnest. "I hate a liar,' he said, 'but, of all the liars, the one who lies to the public is the worst. To inform people is a great trust. I should like to think this small betrayal might be the only one in your life; that, if you're going to be a writer, you will learn that good writing must be honest writing, and it comes not from a man's mind, but from his heart, his soul and his deepest convictions.' That may have been blowing up an ant hill with dynamite, but I have remembered it nearly 50 years."

"About this time the family was overtaken by its first real misfortunes. John's head was crushed under a streetcar, and he survived only after a very long illness. Then I came down with typhus, and when I recovered I was to learn that my other brother, Lee, had died of diphtheria several weeks before. He was just over four years old, a grave, quiet child, he had been very close to me. Together we had dug and planted a small vegetable garden behind our house, and arranged to sell our produce to a neighboring grocer. Every week, we carried our lettuce and radishes to this customer, and even now one of my poignant recollections is of a day when, on our way home, I thought it fun to evade the little fellow leading him to think himself lost. Half an hour later I found him sitting on the curb where I left him, his pennies in hand, not in tears, but waiting in serene confidence of my return. On my first morning out of bed, my grandmother took me for a drive and broke the news to me as gently as she could."

"Lee, I think, had been the favorite child; neither my mother nor my grandmother ever got over his death. Father forgot his sorrow in a fine poem, and then locked himself in his room, emerging to find no distraction in work. The 'gentiles' had won the last previous elections; statehood had become a matter of months and, for the moment, one writer was without deepest convictions. Utah's current executive, our friend, Governor Thomas, had gone to Washington, enthusiastically vocal as to my father's part in the victory, and soon afterward, as related, the head of our house was appointed United States Consul at San Salvador. In the circumstances he was glad to go. The death of my baby sister Lillie had followed Lee's, also of diphtheria, and the expense of these illnesses had left us financially distressed. Moreover, for all these reasons, father had lost interest in the Times. He had run that newspaper three years, and that was a long time for father to run anything."

"Vague and brief as were our relations, my father remains, with a single exception, the strongest influence in my life. His discipline was sporadic and prompted by moods, and his precepts were confined to rare and rather ponderous homilies, but I should think it's difficult for anyone to escape the forces of his example. He was as honest a man as I had ever met, and the most passionate and selfless for what he regarded as evil or injustice. The milk of human kindness was in my mother's blood, but whatever I have of unrest, of industry and idealism and enthusiasm, I attribute to my father and to the fact that he was a Jew." (Ibid, pp.41-44).

Channing's father died in San Salvador of an illness he had contracted while they were there. Of the five children that his mother had had Channing and his brother John were the only ones left. At the time of his father's death, he had been deeply in debt, and the family ended up stranded in South America with no way to get home. Channing, at the age of 14, was sent home to earn their passage. That same year his favorite grandmother passed away. It was 1895, and Channing decided not to return to Salt Lake. Because he was now the breadwinner of the family and his father had always said, the place for an author was in New York City. Besides, he had an aunt on the way there, his mother's sister, Ella, who was a government clerk in Washington D.C. Washington D.C. was his birthplace, and it was on the way to New York, so he stopped there to earn a little money and live with his aunt. He went back to school and in his spare time wrote 100 short stories and kept applying for a newspaper job. In the meantime, Congress had awarded his mother $5000 in recognition of his father's" heroic death at his post of duty," which made his mother comfortable financially, and that was why he was able to attend high school.

He finally won a short story contest and earned his first money as a writer, $250. His mother was now able to send him to college and he went to Bethel Military Academy in Warrenton, Virginia, in his mother's home state. He attended there, once again having lots of trouble with authority figures and formal schooling, until one night a Colonel he was having trouble with, destroyed the furniture in his cabin in retaliation for not obeying his rules and regulations. In response, he "smashed" the Colonel, catching him red-handed in the dirty deed. When the Major said he would do nothing about it and simply said, "You were warned," Channing quit school. Since there was no train out of Warrenton until the next day, he walked five miles, waited six hours at the train station and never returned. Suffice to say he never graduated college because of this incident.

He went back to Washington D.C., wrote a freelance article on an incident that happened there and got a job at The Washington Post as a reporter. All the time he worked as a journalist he was writing plays and stories. At 16 years of age, he had written and acted in his first play, and by the time he was 18, he had two plays produced at the Grand Opera House. His favorite quote from a famous playwright was "Plays are not written, but rewritten. The best built drama is like a house of cards; disturb one card, and the whole structure falls," by Dion Bouicault. In 1897, he got a job at the New York Dramatic Mirror and finally reached New York City. He was still writing plays and they were being produced at little or off-Broadway theaters around town. His mother married a Senator, William N. Roach, at the same time as his first big production became quite a costly failure. "Children of the Ghetto" did not do well at all, but Channing Pollock was soon the resident critic for the paper, for all the plays on Broadway.

Becoming a journalist, critic, press agent, and playwright, Channing Pollock finally got what he had wanted, except for his own very successful play on Broadway. During his press agent days, Pollock also acted as a promoter for various plays. In those days promoters came up with outlandish schemes to garner audiences for their plays. Nowadays these stunts would have brought about all sorts of liable suits against the producers of these plays. But in those days everyone got away with these stunts, the more outlandish, the better. The newspaper folk really enjoyed reporting them too! A 1905 play called "Fantana" needed a stunt to catch the public's attention and Pollock was hired to fill the bill. Pollock told everyone a chorus girl in the play had a dog that wore diamond earrings. They put cheap fakes on the dog using bubble gum, but the reporter covering the story knew they were fake and refused to print the photo. Caught red-handed, Pollock had to make the stunt real by getting the dog's ears pierced and renting a pair of diamond earrings from Tiffany's just to get the photo in the paper.

Pollock also announced a matinee for a 1906 play entitled "Happyland" for women only and then arranged for a man to crash the matinee dressed as a woman. Fortunately he had another man try to attend the matinee with his wife and when he couldn't go in, he made his wife leave with him. This "real" stunt garnered even more good publicity for the show. Another stunt was for a play called "Pretty Peggy" which starred Margaret Mayo. He had Mayo make the claim to the newspapers that she could write a play in a day. She bet playwright Theodore Burt Sayre that she could write a good play in 24 hours if he gave her the synopsis. Sayre gave her the synopsis and she and Pollock where locked up in an apartment while Pollock's stenographer typed the four-act play that Mayo supposedly dictated to her. Newsmen guarded the suit while they wrote, so no one could cheat. But a pre-written play had been hidden in the room some time before and Mayo and Pollock spent the day eating and chatting while the stenographer typed away on whatever she felt like. At six o'clock Mayo and Pollock emerged from their den with the play "The Mart" in hand, triumphant. Interestingly, Margaret Mayo actually was a good playwright, besides being a good actress. Later on she wrote several successful plays on her own and the two most successful were named "Baby Mine" and "Polly of the Circus."

Other stunts Channing Pollock came up with included a chorus girl in the play "The Royal Chef" being kidnapped just after this play opened in 1904. Nena Blake was kidnapped in costume from the theater itself on opening night. She was actually sent halfway across the country while the police searched for her in New York City. Her sister was also a chorus girl in the same play and every night, Bertha Blake, would kiss a man from the audience who claimed to have never been kissed. In another stunt, actor Adele Ritchie's niece changed her name to Adele Ritchie Junior and then was publically "wooed" by a "Siamese Millionaire," just to promote the play that Adele Ritchie was appearing in at the time. (Broadway: An Encyclopedia by Ken Bloom, Routledge, November 11, 2003, p.512)

"To each of the new plays I devoted a couple of columns, written in the two hours between curtain fall and going to press, and then rewritten for the evening edition." During the time that he was a resident newspaper critic, he got to attend quite a few plays, starring either Ellen Terry or Maude Adams. And by 1906 he was married to his wife and was beginning to have many successful plays on Broadway. He says in his autobiography, that on his way to his many successes on Broadway, his biggest success being a play called "The Fool," he had fallen in love with three women. "Maude Adams was a moonbeam. Ellen Terry was a flame... My worship of Ellen Terry, with minute, inglorious idolatry of Maude Adams, became a spiritual bigamy. So notorious that, when I married, seven years later, a wit declared that I had committed 'trigonometry.'" (Ibid, Harvest, p.80 & 96).

The plays that Channing Pollock presented on Broadway were either written by him, or he had written the dialogue, or he had written a book, which was made into a play, but they were all his plays. From 1904 to 1931, Pollock had 22 successful plays on Broadway. In 1953, his last, unexpected play was a tribute to Ethel Waters, which he wrote the English lyrics for. His first play on Broadway was called "The Pit" which ran for several months in 1904. He had two plays on Broadway in 1906 and one every year after that until 1911. In 1912 he had two plays on Broadway, one play in 1913, and two in 1914. In 1915 he had one play on Broadway, one in 1918, two plays in 1919, one play in 1920 and his biggest play in 1923, "The Fool." In 1926, 1928, and 1931, he had his last plays on Broadway: "The Enemy," "Mr. Moneypenny," and "The House Beautiful." As he says in his autobiography, by 1932, he had seen the theater shot from under him and he was able "to see the writing on the wall." He began to consider changing his profession at the age of 52. So he began writing articles for magazines, traveling, and going on the lecture circuit.

In 1938, his mother died of the same illness, his stepfather had died of years before, and their only child Helen was all grown-up and living her own life. Channing and his wife took to traveling for the next 20 years and in this way he could also write articles for magazines about his travels and other issues he chose to write about. When World War II arrived, he and his wife settled down to wait for the duration of the war. And he did see the war end, but just barely, because he passed away in 1946 at the age of 66. I read a lot of autobiographies in my research for these many stories, but Channing Pollock's autobiography was one of the standouts. Not only because of his writing style, but because of the interesting life that he led, especially before he settled into writing and producing his Broadway plays.

One of the best things he had to say in his book was about all the deaths he had had to suffer in his family and it is a very poignant way to end this brief telling of his life. "My dear dead are more with me now than while they lived, and they are with me unchanged, forever painless and carefree and young." The young players of the Barnacle, play on. (Ibid, Pollock, p.47)

THE RISE OF BURLESQUE & THE FALL OF POLYGAMY:

Actresses & Their Painters, Photographers, Politicians & Prophets

In exploring this particular time period, there were certain key figures involved in the massive changes that took place in societal morays between 1890 and 1915, all over the nation, as well as in Utah. These changing times, were made even more interesting locally, because they coincided in Utah with the Manifesto to end polygamy in 1890 under the Presidency of Wilford Woodruff, making Utah available to become a state in the union by 1896. At the same time the nature of the theater was changing all across the United States due to what they called "combinations." Combinations were traveling troupes, along with various short features, which rotated in and out of the theaters in all the major cities, taking the place of local theater troupes. The local theater troupes had to take to traveling to smaller towns within individual states in order to survive. Along with these "combinations" came the outside world, something that the old Utah Territory, because of its isolation could control, but the coming state of Utah could not. Most theaters began to have many more rowdy burlesque and vaudeville acts, fewer quality plays, and more and more pretty girls with less and less on. The end of polygamy was certainly not a tidy affair, nor was the end of wholesome theater entertainment in Utah. The rise of this kind of entertainment brought in the crowds. At the same time that new marriages into polygamy went underground, especially from 1890 to 1915, theaters and acting troupes were becoming more and more visible, and more and more raunchy. Highly successful at attracting larger audiences, these "lower" forms of entertainment were what audiences wanted, while what were considered "uplifting" plays had half full theaters. There is an interesting parallel between all of these changes in Utah and the world of entertainment's changes from stage to screen. So I decided to show these changes through a few of the key "players" of this period who contributed to this as one reads their biographies. It is one way to catch the flavor of the times.

The "players" on this stage of changing times both nationally and locally, involve two prophets of the LDS Church, Brigham Young and Wilford Woodruff, one painter, George M. Ottinger, two photographers Charles Roscoe Savage and Charles Ellis Johnson, one United States Senator, Senator Arthur Brown, and a host of actresses from those pursued to wed, become additional wives, become mistresses, or were simply related to these men in some fashion, as daughters, wives, nieces and other in-laws. Brigham Young pursued actress Annie Adams when she was young but she chose from two tall, dark and handsome gentile suitors and left the LDS Church instead. Many of Brigham Young's daughters and even a few sons, as well as some grandchildren also acted on the old Salt Lake Theatre stage. Actress/singer Mary Jane Abbott McAllister, married the painter George M. Ottinger and their brief time together is also quite interesting. Ida May Savage, Lennie Louise Savage Riter, and Marianne Sharpe were all related to the famous photographer, Charles Roscoe Savage, who had four wives, none of whom acted on the stage, although C.R. upon occasion did. All of these daughters acted on the Salt Lake Theatre stage and one of them became a locally and nationally famous opera star. Photographer Charles Ellis Johnson, fell in love with acting and theatre as a young man and while he had many other interests and businesses, this was his first love.

Johnson was also linked with Lydia Mary Olive Mamreoff Von Finkelstein Mountford, the actress of religious tableaus, who was linked to the LDS President at the time, Wilford Woodruff. Woodruff is famous for signing the Manifesto and writing his interesting diaries. The mystery of whether he ever married Madam Mamreoff or not still exists today. Woodruff also had a famous granddaughter in Hollywood named Josephine Woodruff, although her Hollywood name was Edwina Booth. Senator Arthur Brown, known as the "gentile polygamist" in Utah, seemed to have no qualms about how many women he romanced, or how publically he did this. His subsequent murder by one of these women and the trial that followed caused a media sensation in Utah, as well as in Washington, D.C. His late in life association with Annie Adams Kiskkaden and his subsequent murder trial might have contributed to Annie on her own deathbed begging her sister to destroy all of Maude Adam's diaries if she outlasted her niece, to protect Maude from any scandal or publicity, as Annie had had to go through a scandal late in life herself.

Like any play, all the characters are entangled with other characters from families, friendships, to relationships; while the storyline brings them all together by the end of the play. All of these connections are by blood, by profession, by love without law, and by the resistance to change or the embracing of it; but in the end they eventually find their way to some sort of connection to the theater and acting. Along the way these true life tales form a mighty interesting "play." The stories are unbelievable and the cast of characters is endless during this era of great change in the world and particularly with the stage to screen transitions of the times. However, the various "acts" of this play form one large melodrama whose plot is quite convoluted in the biographies you are about to read. It is a "play" which certainly would have brought in the crowds.

George Martin Ottinger

George Ottinger was born in 1833 in Springfield Township, Pennsylvania. His parents separated in 1846 and George then had no home, so he lived with relations and friends until he was 17. At 17 he decided to take to the high seas for adventure and went to sea on a whaler, the "Morea" with another young man from the area. They went to a port in Peru and then decided to desert. The captain sent some sailors after them and when they caught them they spent some time in jail. The two of them had walked 39 miles without any water and they were almost dead by the time they were happily captured. He and his companion then went to the gold fields in California by getting a job on another ship in Panama, at which point they deserted again. It took 58 days and going through a lot of storms, to get to San Francisco, because they walked across the isthmus to the east coast and then walked back again when they heard about the gold to be found in California. He quickly became disappointed with the gold fields and he and his shipmate bought passage to China. A mutiny aboard ship midway there stopped them from ever reaching China. The ship put in at Honolulu and Ottinger then visited Shanghai, Sumatra, Java, Madagascar and the Cape of Good Hope with his friend. Finally George decided he had had enough and decided to return to the east coast of America to study painting and drawing, which was his first love, anyway. He arrived at his mother's house in New York in 1853 and was only twenty years old when he began his first formal art studies. While working as a clerk at a sugar plant, he

George M. Ottinger in Costume
Utah State Historical Society

studied at the Pennsylvania Academy of Fine Arts in Philadelphia and then moved to Lanchester, Pennsylvania where he painted miniature portraits to earn a living.

At 22 years of age, he joined the militia and served his full tour of duty, then went back east again, although a little closer to the South, and worked as a clerk in a fruit store in Louisville, Kentucky and also as a photograph tinter. During the time that he was formally studying art, his mentor was Robert W. Weir. Weir had two sons, John Ferguson Weir and J. Alden Weir, who were also painters. Even his daughter Dorothy Weir became a famous painter, and also married a descendant of Brigham Young, the sculptor Mahroni Young, who finished the "This Is the Place" sculpture at the mouth of Emigration Canyon in 1947. (Taken from "George Ottinger was jack-and master-of all trades" by Kristen Rogers-Iversen, The Salt Lake Tribune, June 19, 2011 and Utah Art, Utah Artists by Swanson, Olpin, Poulton & Rogers, Gibbs Smith Publishers, 2002, p.33)

Ottinger & the McAllister Musical/Acting Family

Ottinger's mother, who had been a Quaker, had joined the Mormon Faith in the 1850s. She had always wanted to go to Utah, and she begged her son to return home and take her to the promise land. Ottinger eventually agreed to take her, although he was planning on going to the California gold fields to try one more time to strike it rich. They left for the Utah Territory in 1861 from Winter Quarters where they met by chance with my third great grandmother, Eliza Thompson McAllister who had been good friends with George's mother where they had lived previously. Each wagon had to have two families sharing it, so George and his mother who had all this equipment, joined with Mrs. McAllister, her 16 year-old grandson William James Frazier McAllister, my great grandfather, and Will's divorced aunt Mary Jane Abbott McAllister Cullen and her little daughter, Mary Elizabeth Cullen. Eliza bought a half interest in everything they had to caravan west. Will's mother and father and sisters and brothers came a few months later in a different wagon train, but Will had been given the task to help his not so healthy grandmother get to the Salt Lake Valley. Will and his grandmother were very, very close. So close that on the day she died, Will sat up in bed in the middle of the night and told his wife that his grandmother had just died halfway across the valley.

Having a lot in common, the two young men, Will and George, became friends. George was 28 and Mary Jane McAllister was 32 years old. She had had a very short marriage to Edward Cullen and had a young daughter from this union. She was also very attractive and had all the makings of a great stage actress, singer and musician, so it is not any wonder that George fell in love with her. As the family story is told, George, being an artistic type, spent most of his time courting Mary Jane on the over thousand mile trek, while poor Will, who knew absolutely nothing about herding stock, had to do most of the work. When they got to Wyoming the teamsters they had hired deserted the train for better wages at Fort Laramie and Will had to show George how to herd the cattle, although he still ended up doing most of it according to his memoir. But this did not ruin the friendship between them, both of them being artistic, George with a brush and Will with instruments and singing. The family worried about Will being able to accomplish this trek successfully because he had been a sickly child. They would have been amazed to know that Will outlasted everyone, including his two wives, and died at the age of 98. When the company arrived in the valley, the Ottingers were invited to stay with Will's uncle, John Daniel Thompson McAllister who had only two wives at that time.

George Ottinger married Mary Jane Abbott McAllister after they arrived in the Salt Lake Valley on January 9, 1862. Mary Jane, as well as being beautiful was a gifted musician and music teacher. She was immediately popular as a vocal coach and instrumental music teacher. She gave private lessons, taught music in the schools, and sang and acted at the Salt Lake Theatre, as did her brother, John D.T. McAllister, singing at the request of Brigham Young. John D.T. McAllister, along with his other duties as a Salt Lake Marshall, and a fire marshal for the fire department, also acted in various roles in plays performed at the old Salt

Lake Theatre. Eventually, George Ottinger also became the fire chief to earn money while he taught art classes at Deseret Academy. Will's aunt was immediately taken into the acting troupe, and was just beginning to do leading roles in musical comedies on the stage. A month after she had her little son with George in November of 1862, Mary Jane was rehearsing for her latest leading lady performance at the Salt Lake Theatre for a coming holiday program. "She took a heavy cold that turned to pneumonia and died from that fever before the first Thanksgiving Day Program was prepared. Her baby son was taken to his grandmother Ottinger." In 1864 he married his second wife Phoebe Neslen and she raised his son with their other children. ("The McAllister Family Reach Utah" by Eleanor H. Hall, a family history, June 15, 1995 and "George M. Ottinger, 1833-1917, from Wikipedia, the free encyclopedia)

During the year that Mary Jane and George were happily married, George painted his mother-in-law, Eliza Thompson McAllister. This painting was passed down through the family, and now hangs in the Springville Art Museum in Springville, Utah. It was the first portrait painted of a woman in the entire Utah Territory and when George later became a famous western painter, this woman's sour face became slightly famous. As a descendant I often wondered why she looked the way she did, until I heard how her life had gone. She had married, had four children, and then tragedy struck. While they were still living back east, her husband, William James Frazier McAllister Senior, went down to the local pub occasionally for a drink. One day he went to the pub and when he got there, there was a young man very drunk whose mother had come to beg him to come home. He began abusing his mother and Eliza's husband got in-between them to help the young man's mother. The younger man got William Senior caught between a heavy stool and the counter with his arms pinned behind his back and just kept twisting him until he had broken both of William's legs and both of his hips. From that day on his was an invalid and Liza had to figure out how to support her children.

For the next nine years, John Daniel Thompson McAllister, the oldest son, traveled from his home every morning and carried his father downstairs. He then came back each evening to carry his father back upstairs. He was the only one who knew how to carry his father a certain way, because any other way, caused William Senior extreme pain. That "pain" was translated onto the face of my third great grandmother as she stares out at you from the museum wall, along with her occluded jaw which gave her a permanent frown. John D. T. McAllister, Richard Wesley McAllister and Mary Jane McAllister, all joined the Mormon Church with their mother after their father passed away. John D.T. went west first and soon had four wives and many important jobs in Salt Lake City. He greeted the rest of the families or relatives when they arrived in the Salt Lake Valley. J.D. T. and Richard W. performed on the Salt Lake Theatre stage along with their sister, Mary Ann and her husband George Ottinger. All of the McAllister children were handsome and tall, blessed with beautiful singing voices and could also play several instruments. They also were found to be talented actors and actresses, although only Mary Jane chose acting and singing as her main profession for the brief year that she had as a lead actress at the old Salt Lake Theatre. My great grandfather was sent to southern Utah where he continued to sing, direct the choir and travel about to play for the various dances in the small towns nearby. He and my particular great grandmother also formed a drama troupe and performed plays besides the many other jobs they had such as running a boardinghouse, bee keeping and several town businesses, etc.

As for George, obviously he did not ever leave the Salt Lake Valley to live anywhere else again. Two major supporters of the brand new Salt Lake Theatre, John T. Caine and Hyrum B. Clawson waylaid the first real painter to come to Utah and offered him a good paying job painting all of the scenery for the theater's plays. He did this for the next four years and also found a new wife to raise his son and the other children they would eventually have. Besides designing and painting scenery, he was also the make-up artist for the company's actors and actresses when a more complicated make-up design was needed. He worked with Henry Maiben who was the set decorator and another actor on the stage, and even performed in some of the plays. George Ottinger married Miss Phoebe

Neslen on December 3, 1864. He remained married to her for 53 years and she died in 1927, ten years after George. Ottinger continued to paint and his works are well known in artistic circles both locally and to some degree nationally. One can find his paintings in local art books, on line or displayed in various galleries which exhibit local historical art works, such as the University of Utah Fine Arts Museum or the Springville Museum of Art, etc.

George Martin Ottinger's interests were divided between painting and photography until 1872. During Ottinger's four years with the theater, he began a second job with R. C. Savage. He then broke off from the partnership that had been quite successful and made a studio in his home so he could paint full-time. But he had to take a series of part-time jobs to keep his family afloat. He was an assistant engineer or fire chief for the fire station from 1876 - 1890, an art professor at the Deseret Academy of Art, Deseret University, from 1882 to 1892. He was also the president of the Deseret Academy for a short term. He founded the Deseret Artist's Union, as painting was what he really loved. He painted landscapes, seascapes, biblical or historical scenes and portraits.

He was the Salt Lake City water works Superintendent from 1883 to 1890, and adjutant General for the Utah National Guard from 1894 to 1897. He had been a member of Nauvoo Legion and so had experience to help in the formation of the first Utah National Guard in Utah. He was also the Salt Lake fire chief for a number of years and even painted himself posing at a fire. This painting can also be seen at the Springville Museum of Art. Many of his paintings were from his travels as a young man in Mexico and Europe, although he also painted Utah landscapes and portraits. He especially liked to paint historical paintings about the history of the Aztecs and called this series, the conquest of the Americas. He also acted on the stage and in some of the Shakespearian plays, which he had a particular fondness for, at the old Salt Lake Theatre.

George Martin Ottinger died in 1917. There is a large stone in the Salt Lake City Cemetery which has George Ottinger and his two wives names engraved on it: "Ottinger, George Martin Ottinger 1833-1917, Mary McAllister Ottinger 1829-1862 and Phoebe Neslen 1835-1927.

Apparently Phoebe had several children but among them was Mary Jane's boy William McAllister Ottinger who was born in November of 1862 and was only two and a half weeks old when his mother passed away. He was raised by George and Phoebe along with their many other children and died in July of 1906, so he was only 44 years old when he died. Mary's five year old daughter, Mary Elizabeth Cullen, was raised by someone in the McAllister family.

John Daniel Thompson McAllister

John D.T. McAllister sang and acted at the old Salt Lake Theatre along with his many other jobs for the city. While up at the special collections library doing research for my actor books, the librarian pulled up a random photograph to use while she explained how to look for the boxes of photos I was going through for these theater books. When the librarian turned the computer screen around for me to look at it, there was a very old but quite familiar looking face staring back at me. The librarian stated that his photo was in one of the boxes but there was no information about him except his name, J.D.T. McAllister. This sent me on a journey to find out more. Since there are dozens and dozens of full boxes of photos just on this subject alone, I was mystified. Was the librarian that intuitive? Was it one of those waking dreams or synchronicities that just come to you in the day time? Or, was there nothing random about it at all? Storytellers are often summoned by those who are eager to tell their story whether they are here or deceased, so I will always wonder about this particular synchronicity. That out of the thousands of boxes full of photographs this was the one the librarian happened to pull up to explain to me how to use the computer to find particular photos I was looking for. I ended up writing up a note on his life to place with the photograph and the librarian hopefully added it to his computer information. Perhaps, John D. T. chose that particular photo for me to find, out of gratitude for being remembered by an ancestral researcher, but then, I am a believer in such things while many others are not. And then there is my long departed mother who used to talk about this person all the time. She was a researcher too.

Charles Roscoe Savage

C. R. Savage was an even more handsome man with curly hair, a mustache and a beard. The ladies must have adored him as he took up the practice of polygamy and had four wives. He was born in South Hampton, England in 1832. He was only 14 when he joined the Mormon Church. He served two missions in the 1850s in Switzerland and in England, and then immigrated to the United States. When he got to New York, he became interested in photography. He had a photography studio in Council Bluffs, Iowa, and he and his first wife took their children across the plains in 1860. When he got to Salt Lake City, he worked with Marsena Cannon, another early Utah photographer who moved to Southern Utah a year later in 1861. George Ottinger arrived a year after Savage, but they did not form a partnership until about three years later. During Ottinger's four years with the theater, he began a second job with

Charles Roscoe Savage and George Martin Ottinger
Utah State Historical Society

R. C. Savage. The two men went into business together with Savage doing the photography and Ottinger doing the tinting and painting over the photographs to make them colorful. They opened the Savage & Ottinger Art Gallery and besides painting over Savage's tints, Ottinger also displayed his paintings for sale. They advertised as "Savage and Ottinger, Ambeotypists photographers on glass." (Painters of the Wasatch Mountains by Robert O. Olpin, Ann W. Orton, and Thomas F. Rugh, Museum of Art and History, Gibbs-Smith Publishing, 2005, pp. 39-41)

Savage began having some of his photographs published in Harper's Weekly. His photos were soon sold all over the United States, Canada and Mexico. Some of his more famous photos were of the joining of the two railroads at the Golden Spike ceremony at Promontory Point and other railroad pictures, Zion National Park and Yellowstone National Park. He had signed a contract with the Union Pacific Railroad and took photographs for them for the next 40 years. Unfortunately he had two studio fires, the first one in 1883, which he had to witness. The second occurred two years after his death in 1911, and this fire destroyed many of his glass plate negatives, burning the entire building to the ground. Much of his photography work was lost, but there are many photos to be found in special collections at the various Utah universities.

Actresses All: Ida May Savage - Maude Adams
Nan Savage - Lennie Louise Savage Riter - Marianne Sharpe

Not much is known about Ida May Savage, except that she was a daughter of Charles Roscoe Savage. She was best friends with Maude Adams when they were teens in Salt Lake City together. Both of them had the desire to be a famous actress. They acted together in school, sometimes on the Salt Lake Theatre stage, as well as in Westminster College productions, where Maude went to school with Ida May. C. R. Savage had four wives and 13 children. He died in 1909 at the age of 77, and while most of his work was lost, he was a great deal more successful in his life time than George Ottinger, perhaps due to his forty years with the railroad and advancements in photography at the time. Ida May and

Maude Adams continued their friendship through the years, especially when Maude Adams made her brief visits to her hometown of Salt Lake City.

Lennie Louise Savage and Nan Savage were other actress daughters of C. R. Savage and there is also another daughter named Marianne Sharpe, listed on the roster of actresses at the old Salt Lake Theatre. There is a photo of Marianne Sharpe and the only evidence of her ties to C.R. Savage, is that it is written on the back of the photograph that she is a daughter of Charles Roscoe Savage, and with four wives Savage probably had a lot of daughters. Lennie Louise Savage is the most famous of the four. She was in the chorus at the old Salt Lake Theatre and was quickly singled out as having a great operatic singing voice. She was soon playing leading acting parts in operettas and operas performed on the old Salt Lake Theatre stage. She was also the best looking of the three and apparently had a very enchanting personality that won audiences over as well. She is mentioned the most in the old theater books about Utah as well as having many photos in color of her in costume, which were quite expensive in those days as the colors had to be painted in. But her father, being a photographer, probably helped to defray the cost. Lennie Savage Riter went on to sing with the Tabernacle choir and then joined intermountain opera companies playing leading roles and traveling the west. (See page 56 for photos.)

Charles Ellis Johnson & Ruth Young

Charles "Charlie" Ellis Johnson was born in St. Louis, Missouri, on March 21, 1857. Born into a Mormon family, his mother was a third wife of Joseph Ellis Johnson. He and his mother came to Utah in 1862 to join his father's other two wives and children. The entire clan lived in Spring Lake Villa, which is near Payson, for a few years and then moved to St. George. Charles Ellis Johnson was eventually one of twenty sons of Joseph Ellis Johnson. Charlie's father Joseph came from a Presbyterian family in New York and had 16 siblings. Everyone in his family converted to the Mormon Church except Joseph's father. Joseph's first wife,

Charles Ellis Johnson in the Holyland

Charles Johnson, Photographer

A Johnson Risqué Picture

Lennie Louise Savage

Harriet Snider, traveled with her husband through all the places that the Mormon converts emigrated to, from Kirkland, Ohio to Springfield, Illinois were Charlie's father became a schoolteacher. In 1846, Joseph and Harriet moved to Montrose, Iowa and opened a store, then they moved to Council Bluffs and opened another store, and Joseph also became a postmaster, farmed, and edited a newspaper in Council Bluffs. He married his second wife, Hannah Maria Goddard in 1854 and then moved both wives to Omaha, Nebraska where he founded another newspaper.

He married Charlie's mother in 1856, but kept this marriage secret because of her family's disapproval of plural marriage and the rising dangers of being prosecuted in Nebraska for practicing polygamy. When he began to have a lot of legal problems, business difficulties, and at the same time having political aspirations, it was soon apparent that he had no choice but to immigrate to the Utah Territory. Joseph did not travel with any of his wives. Eliza and three-old Charlie went first, the other two wives traveled together, and Joseph followed. By 1865, Joseph was running a printing press, nursery, a store, and continued to manufacture his medical remedies. The year after they got to Salt Lake City, they moved to St. George in the southern end of the Territory.

Charlie grew up in St. George in a family with a lot of intellectual strengths in literature and the arts. So he was quite a bit more cultured than the other boys he knew even though he had to go to work very early on and had very little formal schooling. Besides his interest in writing for his father's newspaper, he also loved botany and anthropology. But his biggest love was the theater: "During my growing-up I took the usual interest in amusements, but more especially in theatricals. In our local entertainments, I frequently played humorous and other parts, and for a number of years was manager of our local theater. Owing to the large family, which my father had to support, it was necessary for all who could, to earn or help to do so. For this reason, I did not get much chance to attend school and what I did get was scattering. There were no schools at that time in our section that were higher than the junior high of a later [sic.] date." Charles junior learned all of these businesses as well, pharmaceutical, herbal remedies, printing and photography while having available to him the largest library of books in town which his father owned. He also got interested in anthropology through a doctor from the Smithsonian Institute who spent a long while in St. George investigating Indian burial mounds and he learned to speak several local tribal languages as well. ("Salt Lake City Re/Visioned: Charles Ellis Johnson Images Then & Now," at http://www.cejohnson.us/cej.html).

Serious and hard working at the time, he looked up to his father, who was himself a "borderline" or "cultural" Mormon, always questioning his faith, avoiding church positions and usually wanting to live as far away from the center of his religion as possible. To that end he moved his family in 1878 to central Arizona, but Charlie stayed in St. George, and for good reason. He had met Ruth Young, one of the daughters of Brigham Young at the Winter House in St. George. His family lived next door to the Winter House. This was where Young brought members of his many families to stay in the winter months in the warm sunny weather in southern Utah. Ruth was introduced to Charles through Susa Young a favored daughter of Brigham who was also an outspoken, independent woman who all her life became quite well-known in her own right. At this particular time she and her sister Mabel had been banished to the Winter House for having helped their older sister Dora, who at 17 had eloped with a man considered a drunkard by their parents. Susa and Mabel joined the local Home Dramatic Troupe for something to do and Charles junior was also a member of this acting troupe. Susa married her first husband who was a 21 year old dentist whom she met in St. George when she was only sixteen years old. This became a great mistake and did not last very long. She pretended throughout her life that this marriage had never happened or at least never talked about it to anyone. Her half-sister Ruth was only sixteen or seventeen herself when introduced to twenty one year old Charles Ellis Johnson. Susa set up the date because she had met Charlie in the acting troupe and two months after they married she was divorced from dentist Marley Dunford.

Charles and Ruth were married in 1878 and continued living in the Winter House until they could get a place of their own as Brigham

Young had passed away five months earlier and left Ruth the winter home. They had three children, two sons, Ellis and Jay Elliot, and a daughter, Adelia, who died at one years-old. Charlie's brother wrote of Charlie's marriage much later that "His marriage to Ruth Young was an impermanent union, and the couple separated when their two sons were still quite young. He never remarried. The boys lived alternately with each [parent] until they reached adulthood." Johnson's sister-in-law elaborated further: "Ruth told me she was used to having a good time, going to parties and so forth. Charlie had his pharmacy and didn't have time for that sort of thing. Eventually Ruth went to California with another man and took the two boys with her. Later she sent the boys back to Charlie." Ruth Young Johnson lived in California for a while but in her later years came back and lived in Salt Lake City by herself until she passed away in old age. Since she never divorced she was probably not married to this other man and probably returned home alone. ("Charles Ellis Johnson-Every Point of Interest," Chapter VII, The Signature Books Library on line, Set in Stone, Fixed in Glass by Nelson R. Wadsworth, p.4, at http://signaturebookslibrary.com)

The couple moved back to Salt Lake City in 1892, where Charlie worked as a druggist for ZCMI. He partnered with Parley P. Pratt Jr. for the Johnson-Pratt Drug Company. In 1893, he also partnered with another photographer Hyrum Salisbury for the Sainsbury-Johnson Photo Gallery. But by the end of that year both the photography business and the druggist businesses were suffering. By buying out Salisbury's half of the photography business and selling the drug store to Parley Pratt, Charlie had enough to establish The Johnson Company Photography Studio. This slowly got him the money to rent the old Deseret News building and also to eventually open a Kodak and Souvenir Shop next to his photography studio not far from the Salt Lake Temple. By 1895, however, Charles and Ruth had separated, and though they never divorced, they never lived together again.

Charles Ellis Johnson & Minnie B. Ridley

It was after this that Charles Johnson was free to explore all facets of his profession and also recall his love of the theater. He loved the freedoms that people in the theater seemed to enjoy and was active in not only photographing actors and actresses, but occasionally acted himself on the stage. He balanced his professional photography life with his theater life and took hundreds and hundreds of photo portraits of actors and actresses as the old Salt Lake Theatre. They often wore their costumes for the production they were in and he became proficient at what he called "female glamour poses" which could be a single portrait, a tableaux or even scantily-clad posing. Johnson went to the theater often, photographed lots of actors and actresses, took a lot of pictures of the old Salt Lake Theatre, and advertised to photograph pretty young actresses between the ages of 18 and 30. He loved to photograph burlesque and vaudeville acts, as these were coming into vogue more and more after the turn-of-the-century. Interestingly, Charles Johnson took all his own photographs of these young women. While most other photography studios that even did this sort of thing to make extra money, usually farmed these photos out to their apprentices considering it simply an extra way to make money, Johnson enjoyed taking the photos himself, a true artist.

Charlie Johnson took images of Utah and the West for tourists, photographed news events, did portraits of prominent LDS officials and wealthy patrons, photographed many of the important buildings in town, and did many famous views of the bathing beaches and resorts along the Great Salt Lake. He sold his father's "Johnson's Oil of Science" remedy for just about any ailment and printed the labels and did all the advertising himself in his print shop. But he eventually turned most of his interest to the photography studio and shop and did very, very well. The largest collection of his photographs is housed at Utah State University and some of his other subjects in larger quantities are: Ute Indian studio portraits, cabinet cards of performers, one of his brothers in portraits and performances, glass lantern slides of actors, singers and celebrities, portraits of women, the Mormon Tabernacle Choir on tour, souvenir album photos of Salt Lake City, various Salt Lake Pioneer and Jubilee parades, wild and domestic animals and flowers posed with children or women, the Chicago World's Fair, Brigham Young and of course the largest collection is entitled "Burlesque, Risqué and Artistic Stereo Views" which graduates from a neck or shoulder shown or reclining women dressed in exotic costumes in the late 1890s, to strange poses such as actresses dressed as men or two women together, to two women undressing each other or men taking garters off of women, and finally in the 1910s, semi-nude women altogether.

Madam Olive Mary Mameroff Von Finkelstein Mountford

Madame Lydia Mountford came to town in 1897 and took the LDS Church leaders by storm. Charles' photography studio stood right under the shadow of the Mormon Temple. His sister-in-law was named Minnie B. Ridley and she ran all of his business interests quite well, helping him to make even more money. She was considered his business manager, and he met her, right after he returned from his two-year stint to the Holy Land with Madame Mountford. He had gone with the older and quite famous actress who had her own traveling troupe to perform biblical scenes from the Bible while she lectured on the subject. Madam Mountford had convinced him to go with her as her photographer because she had made an agreement with the directors of the 1904 St. Louis World's Fair where they would present an exhibition of photographs, dramatic readings and Biblical tableaux. He took over 2,000 photos while there and Utah State University and Brigham Young University have these archives.

Madam Olive Mary Mameroff Von Finkelstein Mountford, arrived in Salt Lake City and charmed the entire city with her imagined and performed scenes or tableauxs from the Bible, accompanied with her dramatic lectures. Known all over the world as the "Diva of Fantasy Bibles and Other Victorian Entertainments," Madam Mountford was almost 6 feet tall (5'9") with blond hair, handsome features, and an "Amazonian" figure to the envy of many an actress, at least while she was young. She traveled and lectured for 25 years, giving over 200 lectures and theater presentations in over 5,000 appearances all over the world. Her reputation for presenting the "living Bible" as events, and her charisma as a performer and preacher was impeccable. Her Jewish background gave way to more of a Spiritualist-Christian take on religion as she traveled about as a "religious" actress, writer and charismatic lecturer.

During her year in Salt Lake, she had many admirers, among them, Charles Ellis Johnson, and the then Prophet of the Mormon Church, Wilford Woodruff. She asked Charlie to go with her on her trip to the Holy Land to take pictures. They traveled together in 1903 and 1904, hoping to stage an exhibit at the 1904 St. Louis World's Fair after they returned home. Asking a woman to unveil her face for a photograph in the Holyland, said Charlie, was like asking a woman in the United States to show her ankles, shoulders, or neck. But when the pair returned to the United States, the fair had been put under new management, and the new management would not honor the previous contract that they had signed in 1903. So they never got their exhibit at the World's Fair. Madame Mountford left St. Louis in a huff and Charlie tried in vain to peddle his spectacular pictures of street life in Jerusalem in 1903. While he was gone Johnson's sister-in-law was hired to oversee the store and the studio, although this is thought to have been the best way to "title" Charlie's eventual relationship with "Miss Ridley." Of course a sister-in-law could not also be a "Miss," but this seemed to satisfy people, but no one was ever sure just what their relationship was.

Charles Ellis Johnson & His Risqué Photography

After this, Charlie continued his photography business in Salt Lake City, with Minnie for the next ten years. He had left the business to his younger brothers, who almost went under while he was away, but it was Minnie who picked up the pieces and put them all in order again. She straightened out the drugstore, studio, souvenir store, and everything else in no time. But by 1914, Minnie had suddenly passed away and immediately after this Charlie sold his business as soon as he could and interestingly, moved to live with the Ridley family in San Jose, California in 1916. He hardly knew Minne's family and yet chose to go live with them, leaving everything behind him, including his thirty-year photography business, his two sons, brothers and sisters, associates and friends. He lived with the gentile Ridley's for the next nine years. There are many who say that while Charlie never married Minnie, he considered her his true wife. Although the history books refer to her as either his sister-in-law or Miss Ridley, it was much more likely that she was his girlfriend in a day when this was most certainly frowned upon. And since Charlie was never divorced from his wife, this was probably the only way things could be handled living within the era and culture that they did. But this will always simply be speculation.

There is also speculation that besides being dissatisfied with living in the heartland of Mormonism, Charles Johnson, after Minnie's death had nothing to keep him there and his interest in taking risqué photographs might have begun to get him in trouble or least affected his business with others in town. This interest, however, coincided with the entire country's interests, especially in the theater world. Nowadays, Charles Ellis Johnson would have been called either a "Social or Cultural Mormon," as he was at first socializing with his own people and appeared to also be a believer. Later on, he quit believing and apparently saw himself as simply coming from this particular culture. Johnson died in 1926, but was always quite the "Renaissance" man. His taste for attractive women and his connections with gentile theater troupes moved right along with the emergence of more and more risqué and bawdy material in the show houses. Madame Mountford continued to correspond with Johnson until her own death.

"Johnson did, however, have a connection with Burlesque and Vaudeville Theater and photographed hundreds of actors and actresses from the Walpole Salt Lake Theater as well as national tour groups. One of those women, Ella Wheeler Wilcox, wrote to him in 1903 from the

Brown Palace Hotel in Denver, Colorado. Johnson's recent photographs of Wilcox revealed her bare neck, shoulders and upper bosom, which was fairly typical for many of his portraits. In response to one man over the impropriety of her photographs, Wilcox wrote: 'Tell the gentleman... that I am sorry. He should object to a little bit of neck. He probably had a surfeit of neck in his plural wives, and it gave him a sort of physical indigestion. You see, what a terrible thing polygamy is sometimes, when it unfit some men for appreciating a pretty shoulder." ("Appreciating a Pretty Shoulder: The Risqué Photographs of Charles Ellis Johnson," by Daniel Davis, Merrill – Cazer Library, Library Faculty and Staff Publications: Utah State University, Utah Historical Quarterly, 74, p.133)

Changing Times – Theaters - Movie Houses - Relationships

Beginning in 1890, Johnson began his risqué female photography around the same time that burlesque and vaudeville were really coming into vogue. It was also the year that the Manifesto ending polygamy came out and President Wilford Woodruff had been the one to pass down this Manifesto for LDS members. While women were showing more and more skin on stage even at the LDS Church owned Salt Lake Theatre, it was becoming increasingly impossible to keep the outside world from seeping into the theaters. Also, because of the end of polygamy, families all over the state were trying to disentangle themselves from each other: husbands, wives, sister wives, and children, while many others simply went underground and continued to not only practice polygamy but secretly marry additional wives clear into the 1910s. Women were in many cases suddenly left with no way to support themselves or their children and had to go underground, as they were still married to husbands who were not legally married to them. Many husbands chose a certain wife and left the rest high and dry. Other men continued to support their many wives at the risk of discovery and losing everything. A very few women took everything and would not let their husbands or the other wives, come home. It really was every man and every woman for themselves and continued to be so into the 1940s when the last of the original polygamists began to grow older and pass away. Heber J. Grant was the last Prophet to have had plural wives and he died in 1945. Grant was the last living member of the Council of Fifty and had three wives, but two wives had passed on by the time he became prophet.

The world and life as it had been, everywhere in America, was turned topsy-turvy at the same time that the theater was preparing to give way to silent cinema. With the advent of film, stage theaters were desperately trying just about anything to keep their audiences, while other theaters began to convert their stages to movie screens. The entertainments got bawdier and raunchier because that was what sold and that was what brought in the money. So while theaters either joined in or failed, bringing this into a wide open and very public world stage, polygamy, what was left of it, went deep underground and the idea of "spiritual wives" became the practice after this. "Spiritual wives" were taken in name only, not consummated but guaranteed a place in heaven with their husband. If you did marry in a civil ceremony, then you also had to be married by "proxy" in a Mormon Temple by having a man and a woman stand in for you until the couple could meet each other again in Heaven. The practice of polygamy also continued in most cases, so some brides were still "sealed" to their husbands during Wilford Woodruff's presidency. The practice of "proxy marriage sealings" continues today and some believe the practice of taking "spiritual wives" does as well.

The old Salt Lake Theatre could no longer afford "... high class of amusement that would be intelligible and entertaining... but when we get really high-class performances in that theater. The benches are practically empty, while vaudeville theaters, where exhibitions of naked dress, obscenity, of vulgarity, and everything else that does not tend to elevate the thought and mind of man, would be packed from the pit to the Dome." Apostle Rudger Clawson's comment actually instigated the movement to sell the theater, but it was not until 1928 that this took place. The first all – female chorus appeared in Salt Lake City in 1907 and by 1912 musical comedies and vaudeville regularly had all-female reviews and they were wearing less and less. By the 20s, the silent movies and photographs reflected this worldwide change. Men went to watch these revues, and at the same time, there were men in the Mormon Church who continued to marry more wives. Charles Johnson's photographs were merely a record of the changing times and certainly innocent in comparison to what came after that. By the 1920s, the fantasies of Hollywoodland, had overtaken the whole country, and nothing had been established as yet, to monitor or even censor what one saw on the stage or on the screen. (Ibid, p.140)

Madam Lydia Mamreoff Von Finkelstein Mountford & President Wilford Woodruff

In 1890, the pressure from the United States government and the desire for statehood produced a Manifesto to end polygamy in the Mormon Church. Wilford Woodruff was the Prophet of the LDS Church, and it was he who released this Manifesto. Woodruff had five known wives depending on what history you read and took a 6th wife later in his life. Not all of his wives were concurrent however: Phoebe Whittemore Carter, Mary Ann Jackson (Mary Ann divorced him), Emma Smoot Smith, Sarah Brown and Sarah Delight Stocking are the five identified as being officially married to Woodruff. He had 33 children, but 13 of them died before he did. The sixth and seventh wives are speculated on, but not totally proven. He was church historian for 33 years and during this time, "He was baptized for the dead in behalf of the signers of the Declaration of Independence, and other founding fathers, after he claimed to receive a vision, visitation or manifestation of the departed spirits of these men." He loved to go fly fishing and the people's nickname for him was "God's Fisherman" in reference to his fishing and his missionary work. He was said to have taken a 6th wife, just before the Manifesto was issued. He was also famous for helping the church with many financial difficulties due to the various polygamy trials and other legal issues because of polygamy. But his most important contribution to the office of President of the LDS Church, were his many journals and diaries that have helped historians understand this period in LDS Church history. Upon the death of President John Taylor in 1887, Wilford

Madam Mary Olive Mameroff
Von Finkelstein Mountford

President Wilford Woodruff

Woodruff was sustained as the Church President in 1889, at the age of 82 years.

When Madam Lydia Mountford came to town in 1897, Wilford Woodruff had been President of the Mormon Church for eight years, which means he was 90 years old. Lydia Mountford was 49 years old. It is well known in Mormon Church history, that Wilford Woodruff greatly admired Mountford and definitely had fallen in love with her. On the other hand, there is some disagreement, as to what took place after this. The records are not clear enough to state emphatically that President Wilford Woodruff married Lydia Mountford, however, records indicate that Woodruff took a vacation trip to Oregon in February of 1897 and would not allow the wife he had chosen legally or her daughter to accompany them, even though they both wanted to go. He only allowed his male secretary, L. John Nuttall, to accompany him, and both men went under assumed names. While in Oregon, Woodruff and his secretary took a side trip to San Francisco for two days and then went back to Oregon to finish their vacation. Lydia Mountford was appearing in San Francisco at the same time, with her theater troupe. It is alleged that Woodruff got on a steamship, and with his male secretary, as witness, married Lydia Mountford on board ship. This marriage took place seven years after the Manifesto but was given "plausible deniability" by the fact that they were not married in the United States but on the ocean.

Supposedly at the time, one of Woodruff's sons stood in for him, and Susa Young Gates, Brigham Young's most dynamic daughter, who was a sister-in-law of Wilford Woodruff, stood in for Lydia Mountford when the Temple marriage took place by proxy sometime soon after this according to some historians who have researched these events. To this day Susa Young Gates's papers are being scrutinized by some to find out if she ever makes mention of this event in them as of course Woodruff says nothing of this particular event in his diaries. "Thomas Alexander, Woodruff's biographer, after examining the evidence, concludes that the relationship was one of friendship and mutual admiration.

But, she (Madam Mountford) was invited to speak at general conference, and it is a matter of record that in 1920, three years after her death, she was vicariously sealed to Wilford Woodruff." This event somewhat solves the mystery of this incident, because what other reason would there be to do this some twenty two years after this event, except a binding companionship and mutual admiration between the two? And the very thing that Woodruff is remembered for, his prolific diaries, offer the rest of the story, as they are full of his great admiration and abiding love for Madame Mountford. He only wrote of his health issues in them more often than Madame Mountford. He referred to her as "M" and even mentions getting massage treatments from her that benefited his health immensely. ("Two Views of Palestine in 1897: What a Difference a Century Makes," by Davis Bitton, Meridian Magazine, 2002, http://www.meridianmagazine.com/history bits/02808century.html).

Madam Mountford with her Family
Author's Collection

Mountford was a Jewish Russian who had lived in Jerusalem, who had arrived in Salt Lake City on February 1897 and had immediately talked to the leaders of the Mormon Church about performing on the church's stage, the Salt Lake Theatre. Many of the leaders were suspicious of her, but Woodruff was soon entranced by her. Woodruff attended all of her lectures in the Mormon Tabernacle and mentions her repeatedly in his diaries and journals. While Woodruff and Mountford never intended to live together or even really be together, they were joined at least "spiritually" as a couple and the rest is pure speculation with Woodruff being 90 years old. Those who study post-manifesto marriages, also say that Woodruff approved quite a few other marriages that took place either on steamships, in Mexico, or in Canada in the next years after the Manifesto. Even without these new marriages, there were hundreds of families still living in polygamy but doing it in hiding.

Woodruff died just a little over a year from this when he was barely 92 and interestingly, he died in San Francisco. Lydia Mountford continued to travel and lecture and act. Von Finkelstein was her maiden name and the Mountford came from an English civil servant whom she had married in India, where he continued to live and work. It is never made clear if she had divorced her first husband, but she likely had and just kept his name. On finding a photo of her, one becomes aware of the fact that she also had two children with her first husband. She was an imposing woman of great intellect and wit, with a lot of talent as an actress and speaker. She was five feet nine inches tall with the girth to match this. Charismatic and used to getting her way, Lydia Mountford could enthrall many. Susa Young Gates, while not tall, was also a great lecturer, an intellectual and interested in the arts and women having the vote, etc. She was also a world traveler and had had an audience with the Queen of England. She was also used to getting her way, a strong advocate for plural marriage and is said to have been the sister of the sixth wife of Wilford Woodruff whom he had also secretly married with Susa Young Gates assistance to do so. This marriage soon ended in divorce before the Manifesto came out. Gates also encouraged marriages after the Manifesto was issued, encouraging one of her own daughters to marry into polygamy. Leah Dunsford was her daughter's name and she married Abraham Cannon, a polygamist, but he died a year after this and then her daughter married a single man, John A. Widstoe.

President Wilford Woodruff

Wilford Woodruff had come into the Salt Lake Valley with the first advanced party in 1947. He had joined the Mormon Church in 1832 and completed two missions in England before traveling west with the caravan to the Utah Territory. In 1875 he was appointed church historian and did this for the next thirty years. In 1880 he became one of the members of the Council of the Twelve and then President of the LDS Church in 1889. He had been born on March 1, 1807 in Farmington, Connecticut where his father was a miller. He grew up in a very religious environment and over time learned to be a miller himself, as well as an avid outdoorsman, farmer and stockman. Besides releasing the Manifesto, writing his diaries, guiding all of the financial woes that the various trials were costing the church because of polygamy, and leading a fast growing church, he is known for one other important production. Her story comes along somewhat later, but Josephine Woodruff is the last puzzle piece in this story about actresses and their men during this time of great change nationwide.

Senator Arthur Brown

Born in 1843 on a farm in Schoolcraft, Michigan, his family soon moved to Kalamazoo, Michigan. Brown graduated from Antioch College in 1862. He got his law degree from the University of Michigan in 1864 and began practicing law in Kalamazoo. He moved to Salt Lake City in the Utah Territory in 1879 due to a scandal he had caused in his home town involving his wife and a mistress. His Wife, Mrs. L.C. Brown and his daughter Alice were left in the dust when he took up with Isabel Cameron who was the daughter of a Michigan Senator. He set Isabel up in a fine home with her own carriages and horses and deserted his wife.

Eventually his wife separated from him, keeping custody of their daughter, all his friends condemned him, and his wife tried to shoot Isabel when she found her in his law office one night. Leaving all of the scandal behind him he arrived in Salt Lake City hoping to get the appointment as U.S. District Attorney of Utah however this job did not materialize. In the meantime, Isabel Cameron followed him out there, his first wife divorced him and he was then able to marry Isabel, with whom he had a son named Max. By 1894 he was prospering in a law firm and became one of two freshmen senators appointed from Utah for the U.S. Senate. He only served one year and in the summer of 1896 attended the Republican National Convention in St. Louis, where he met the secretary of the Republican State Committee, Anne Maddison Bradley.

Anne Bradley was married to Clarence A. Bradley but had many interests outside her home in clubs, committees and various other organizations. She began an affair with Sen. Arthur Brown in 1898 and was soon separated from her husband who retained the care of her two children. By 1899 she was living with Brown on and off and in 1900 she had had a son by Brown named Arthur Brown Bradley. Her husband Clarence left their children with his wife Anne to finish raising them and then began drinking. His heart broken, he then had several arrests for drunkenness before he went to Nevada to work for the railroad. He built up gambling debts, embezzled from the railroad and ended up spending two years in jail. After this he disappeared into history and no one knows what happened to him. Anne Bradley now had three children to raise with her reputation in ruins and her only support being Arthur Brown.

While still married to Isabel, Arthur Brown and Anne Bradley eventually ended up living together in Grand Junction, Colorado while awaiting Brown's divorce from Isabel Cameron Brown. Then Brown separated from Isabel and was living in rooms at a hotel in Salt Lake City while awaiting his divorce from Isabel. In 1902, Isabel was living in the family home on South Temple and Anne Bradley, who was patiently waiting for the divorce also, was living in rooms at the hotel, the Independence, quite close to where Isabel was residing. Rather than even considering a divorce, Brown's wife Isabel hired a private detective to get evidence so that she could charge the two with adultery. She also had them charged more than once with adultery which made everything public and ripe for the newspapers, as well as threatening to make over 300 letters from Anne to Arthur public. The second complaint put forth by Isabel was followed through by local police and Anne Bradley was dragged by both arms through the streets by two policemen with Arthur Brown screaming at the police all the while. By the fourth complaint, Brown had struck an officer, called his arresters "an aggregation of cowards" and was followed ranting and raving down the streets by a cluster of reporters and photographers.

Brown attempted to get his wife to divorce him, offered her $100 a month and ownership of their home on South Temple, but Isabel turned it all down saying that "she wanted nothing but the senator." However, there was another reason that Isabel did not want the divorce at the time and that was that she was to be presented in court the next year in front of the Queen of England and unmarried ladies were restricted from the Queen's court at that time. Brown had his home in Salt Lake City, a large ranch in Idaho, owned a number of smaller farms and had a number of mining claims, so he was quite well off and able to pay off those who offended him. "The illicit affair continued with all parties involved (ending) in a dramatic confrontation in a Pocatello, Idaho hotel where Isabel Brown,... threatened to kill Anne Bradley and intimidated Arthur by ordering him to open the door to his hotel room or she could mash it in. The former senator did." Brown asked the witness present, a lawyer friend of Brown's, Soren X. Christensen, to stay with him as he faced the two women "The combatants spent the night accusing each other of all sorts of indiscretions, and Brown, according to Christensen, gave Bradley a revolver as protection against his wife." ("The Shooting of Arthur Brown, Ex-Senator From Utah," by Linda Thatcher, History Blazer, November 1995, p.2 at http://historytogo.utah.gov)

Believing everything settled after this, Brown went forward with his attempts to gain the divorce while Anne Bradley was three months pregnant with their second child. This particular matter was apparently settled by God, because in August of 1905, Isabel Cameron Brown died of

Young Entrepreneur Arthur Brown

An Older Senator Brown

cancer, thus paving the way for Anne Bradley to marry Arthur Brown at last. Bradley quickly obtained her divorce from her first husband but suddenly, Arthur Brown was in no hurry to marry her and kept putting it off. After setting a date to marry in June of 1906 wherein Arthur became ill and did not show up, Anne realized that Arthur might not honor his promise to marry her, so by August and a last date set for the wedding, she decided to make other plans. She was now 33 years old and a divorced woman with four children to support. After literally begging Brown to marry her, she finally formulated a different plan. She asked Brown to give her $2,000 to set her up in a business by which she could support her children and herself alone and he agreed to do this. She began buying stock for a stationary store she intended to set up in Goldfield, Nevada and then suddenly found out that Brown had never intended to finance her business.

Brown left for Washington D.C. a few days later to represent a mining company which had filed a suit before the Supreme Court. He left the city and left no money for Anne Bradley. "That evening she visited his law office and found that he had left a train ticket for her to Los

Angeles. On December 3, 1906, she supposedly left for Los Angeles, but her sister (who was watching her children) received a telephone call from her saying that she had decided to go to Washington instead, as she believed if she went to Washington that Senator Brown would be willing to provide her with a stock of goods for her store; that he was there on some big, some important case, and that she knew he would rather buy her a stock for her store than to have her there bothering him." ("The 'Gentile Polygamist:' Arthur Brown, Ex-Senator from Utah," by Linda Thatcher, Utah Historical Quarterly, Volume 52, Number 3, Summer 1984, p.239)

Arriving December 8th in Washington, she went to his hotel, the Raleigh, and registered as Mrs. A. Brown but insisted on staying in a separate room. However she found Arthur Brown's room and searched through his belongings, finding a bundle of letters from Annie Adams Kiskadden. Annie Adams, now 58 years old, had met the lawyer Arthur Brown when he helped to settle her father's estate in the 1880s. They had continued a friendship but no one knew about the letters or that according to Annie Kiskadden's own testimony later, she and 63-year-old ex-senator Arthur Brown were intending to marry. Apparently Anne Bradley read all the letters and reached the same conclusion, that they intended to marry, and then tore all the letters up and went out and wandered the streets, returning several times to see if Arthur Brown had returned. She came back and laid down in her own room until she heard his walk in the corridor down the hall and then went and knocked on his door. According to her testimony she told him she had come to get him to keep his promise to her and then after that she could not remember anything but the shot that was fired. Apparently Brown had rushed towards her and tried to grab her but she could not remember if the shot went off before this, she had aimed and fired, or it had gone off in the struggle. It was the revolver Brown had given her to protect herself from his former wife and she claimed to have never fired a revolver in her life. The bullet was tightly lodged in his pelvic bone so they could not remove it when they operated. It took Arthur Brown six days to die of kidney failure and to the end he claimed that he had done nothing wrong and that he had never wronged anyone and was innocent of all said against him.

Alice Brown and Max Brown arrived in Washington but refused to have Annie Kiskadden accompany the body when they went to Salt Lake City where their father would be buried in Mt. Olivet Cemetery, stating that "We know nothing about her, or dad's relations with her." Annie Adams Kiskadden arrived in Washington on her own and announced to everyone that she had been the cause of the shooting, as she and Arthur Brown had intended to be married. She also stated that she might have been Anne Bradley's best friend in a sense because she had asked Arthur Brown to make things right with Anne, several times, before she would be ready to marry ex-senator Brown. Annie Adams Kiskadden was still very active in theater, but after this scandal she went immediately to New York City and devoted the rest of her life to her only remaining child, the internationally famous actress, Maude Adams. She never returned to Utah to live. She made a statement in public that: "When the Senator first proposed marriage to me, I plainly told him that it was his duty to marry Mrs. Bradley. But he gave me every assurance that marriage with Mrs. Bradley was impossible. He refused positively to marry her and told me, he would not marry any one. Under these circumstances I consented to be his wife if he could arrange matters satisfactorily for Mrs. Bradley. He told me that he would do this, and I understand that he had communicated with her and had asked how much money she would need." (Ibid, UHQ, p.242)

Arthur Brown, described by his many friends to "hold grudges" and being a "good hater," could be quite public about his actions. He had written a will in August of 1906, cutting Anne Bradley out of his will entirely and denying that their two sons were his. He also stated that he never married Anne Bradley and never intended to and told his executor to contest any claims she would make for her or her children on his estate. He left everything to his two children, one from each wife, and even stated that whether these two boys were her children or not didn't matter, because he disowned them anyway. As Anne Bradley awaited her trial, quite a few things came out not known to the public, such as the fact that she had had several miscarriages and three abortions, one of which was allegedly performed on her by Arthur Brown. The last abortion was performed only weeks before she shot Arthur Brown. In July of 1907 she was transferred to a hospital where she was operated on for a badly lacerated cervix.

In November of 1907 her trial finally began. The prosecution had a main witness that had heard Anne state that unless Brown acknowledged her second son, she would shoot him. He claimed that she had already made two attempts with the revolver to shoot Brown. The defense went with temporary insanity with accusations of several criminal operations performed on Bradley, one by Brown. And that she had several relatives with mental illness and that she had been hit on her head with a hoe when she was a child causing her to have severe headaches and sometimes strange behavior. They also played on the jury's sympathies with all of the trauma inflicted on her both mentally and physically in her association with Brown.

On December 2, 1907, the jury acquitted her of the crime with a verdict of not guilty. After she was freed she rejected a fund that had been taken up for her and said she planned to earn her own way from Washington to Salt Lake City. She was found insane but was allowed to keep her children which the newspapers had a heyday with. The boy's grandmother brought a suit against the estate of Arthur Brown on behalf of the two boys but they never received a settlement. Anne Bradley worked at several jobs in Salt Lake City and then moved to Price, Utah. Bradley had one more tragedy strike her when on a trip to Nevada; she left her oldest children in charge. One of her sons from her first marriage, Matthew, and one of her sons from Senator Brown got in a fight over who would do the dishes and who would cook. Arthur, the son of the senator, stabbed Matthew several times and Matthew died of his wounds. No legal action was taken because the coroner ruled it "accidental wounds." Anne Bradley returned to Salt Lake City in 1921 and operated an antique store until her death from a heart ailment in 1950 at age 77.

One wonders just how many lives Arthur Brown might have continued to ruin had he lived. Would he have really stopped with Annie Kiskadden? Even if Anne Bradley's life involved other men, Arthur Brown was definitely a part of hers, no matter how nutty she might have been or become, because of his inconsistencies and cruelties. Wherever the truth lies, and in this case, the thread always seems to wind its way back to Arthur Brown, this was a man with very little conscience. But most interesting to me is why a woman like Annie Adams Kiskadden, actress and mother of Maude Adams, would succumb to such a man with such a history? A strong, financially independent and still quite attractive woman who had lived on her own since the death of her twins and her husband for many, many years, she was devoted to her one remaining daughter and everyone said so. Perhaps it was loneliness when her daughter was on tour, or perhaps it was living in Salt Lake City and only spending some of her time in New York City with her daughter, Maude, who never married at all. Or perhaps she had really loved this man for many years as a companion and friend and figured and really believed that at long last Brown was finished with his philandering?

But one mystery has been answered for me, and that is why Annie made a request of her sister to destroy all of Maude Adam's journals if she outlived her and her daughter. Maude Adams had several mysterious absences in her life never accounted for, and this was how Richard Matheson was able to write his novel, Bid Time Return. Adams also lived with another woman for many years later in her life and they are buried side by side. The party line is that her agent forbade her to marry although she had many suitors, which then allowed her to become a renowned and highly charismatic actress who would not be in danger through marriage or childbirth. Speculations about these missing periods in her life are that she took around the world trips, or met a young man and had a brief "fling." The other mystery about her life is why later in her life she chose a woman as a companion. None of these mysteries can be solved, as all of Maude's journals were burned by her aunt according to family history, under orders from her own mother, Annie Adams. So therefore the mysteries remain. But did her mother Annie Adams

Kiskadden have an even stronger reason for having them destroyed? Was it based on her own experience in the spotlight with letters of evidence to Arthur Brown, either having been destroyed or kept or disposed of later? With them gone, it was only her word that mattered. Perhaps Annie wanted to protect her only daughter from the same sorts of things when biographers got a hold of Maude's life. Annie may even have feared what her own daughter might write about her and Brown.

This convoluted story about the changes in the theater world and the end of polygamy, begins with Annie Adams who had many suitors including Brigham Young when she was a young woman, and it ends with Annie Adams Kiskadden when she was dragged into an unwanted scandal when she was 58 years old, probably because of a friendship that turned into something else. So one might say that she is symbolic of the times when young pretty women, actresses or no, powerful or not, were pursued by men of power, fueled by their own whims. After Brown's murder and the scandal associated with the trial that followed, Annie Adams Kiskadden immediately returned to New York City to be near her daughter, never lived in Utah again, never acted again, and never married again. She devoted the rest of her life to her one remaining child, the internationally famous actress, Maude Adams.

II — EARLY SCREEN TO FIRST SILENT CINEMA

"Brigham Young" Movie Poster

Victim of the Mormons – Clara & Brother Larson

ANTI-MORMON & PRO-MORMON SILENT & TALKIE FILMS – 1911-1950

There were more than thirty films made during the silent film era to cash in on the wave of anti-Mormon sentiment at the time, especially in Europe. Riding the crest of this wave, theater managers and film producers could see the dollar signs as the public eagerly attended the controversial films; mainly exploiting Mormon polygamy tales that seemed very exotic to the movie going public. Almost none of these films survived, as did the other 80 percent of silent features, a sad loss whatever the subject of the films. Some of these titles included Denmark's Nordisk Films' "Victim of the Mormons" and "An Episode of Early Mormon Days" whose theme was "The Mountain Meadows Massacre," which was re-released in 1912 by the French film company Pathe Frere, both made in 1911. "The Mormon," "Marriage or Death" and "The Danites" were all made in 1912. Others were entitled "Deadwood Dick Spoils Brigham Young," "A Study in Scarlet" in 1914, "A Mormon Maid" in 1917, "Riders of the Purple Sage" in 1918, "Married To A Mormon" and "Trapped by the Mormons," both made in 1922.

The 1911 Danish "Victims of the Mormons" was released in Britain a year later. In 1922, a new film, "Trapped by the Mormons," was certainly the most damaging to the image of the LDS Church at the time. It was extremely inaccurate and yet exotically exciting to audiences who knew nothing of the faith or any of its accurate history except "polygamy." It was also a high quality production, which attracted larger audiences and unlike the rest of these films, it was much longer. In this Danish version, a Mormon missionary named Reverend Larson goes to Copenhagen and charms a young woman named Clara. He takes her to Utah to add her to his stable of wives – which appears more like a harem in the film. Then she is rescued by her father and her brother and the reverend accidentally shoots himself. "Trapped by the Mormons" added to this simpler story, with attempts to mesmerize and kidnap three British girls. Elder Isoldi Keene looks like Bela Lugosi with his long black cap and wide hypnotic eyes. He gets Nora Prescott to run away with him against her father's wishes and her boyfriend Jim is a detective and tracks her down in London. Isoldi's first wife tells the truth to Nora and she rejects Mormonism immediately but the Mormons decide that both women must die to atone for their sins. Jim bursts in on the scene and saves the women, and the Mormons go to jail. By modern standards it is wildly humorous for both Mormons and gentiles alike.

There was a huge anti-Mormon feeling that had started in 1911 and continued into the early twenties, especially in Great Britain. At first, the Mormon Church ignored these films but then they realized that these films were really harming their image throughout the world. The then Governor of Utah, who was not a Mormon, was upset too. He attempted to censor the 1911 film by demanding that the film be altered for Utah audiences but his demands were ignored and the film was shown in Utah in February of 1912. "Victim of the Mormons" was released the same year that an anti-Mormon play was traveling the country called "Through Death Valley" or "The Mormon Peril." Foreign mission presidents realized the misrepresentation was going to hurt them and quickly let their church leaders know about the situation. There were even attempts to pass out literature in front of theaters, with a cash reward to anyone with knowledge of actual kidnappings of English women, to be shipped off to Utah and then made into polygamous wives.

As the anti-Mormon films began to mount up in 1911 and 1912, local concern also mounted. "The Mormon" was about LDS Saints attacking a wagon train in order to obtain more wives. "The Danites" was about the run down and murder of the Williams family. In the first reel, the Mormons disguised as Indians attack the William's wagon train. A young sister and her younger brother escape and join another wagon train headed west but they are witnesses to the massacre of their family and the Danites need to hunt them down and kill them too. Joining the second wagon train in disguise, they gun down "Nancy William's" little brother "George." Nancy disguises herself as a boy and takes the name "Billy Piper." In the second reel, she goes to a western camp where the leader of the second wagon train had settled. Billy is in love with the wagon train leader, Sandy, but he has fallen for a beautiful new school marm who has just arrived in the camp. Sandy marries the schoolteacher and Billy becomes friends with her even though her heart is broken. The schoolteacher discovers Billy's true gender, as do the disguised Danites in the camp still tracking Nancy down. Sandy holds off the Danites in a gun battle while Nancy/Billy escapes, only to die of a heart attack, as the Danites appear to be closing in on them.

"Marriage or Death" was about women being forced into polygamy against their will and all of these films were produced in 1911 and 1912. The two films on the Mountain Meadows Massacre were of course bringing attention to a dark spot in LDS Church history. The Massacre at Haun's Mill of Mormons by gentiles and subsequent persecutions did not have the same sensationalism that these anti-Mormon films could garner. In San Francisco, there was a riot at the opening of "An Episode of Early Mormon Days" on the Mountain Meadows Massacre, when several local Mormons stood up and protested the film right in the audience, and then the fight was on. When it was discovered that the same film company, Pathe, that had cooperated with the National Film Board concerning "Victim of the Mormons," had then turned right around and released the Mountain Meadows film without review in the same year, the film company had to prove that they were in

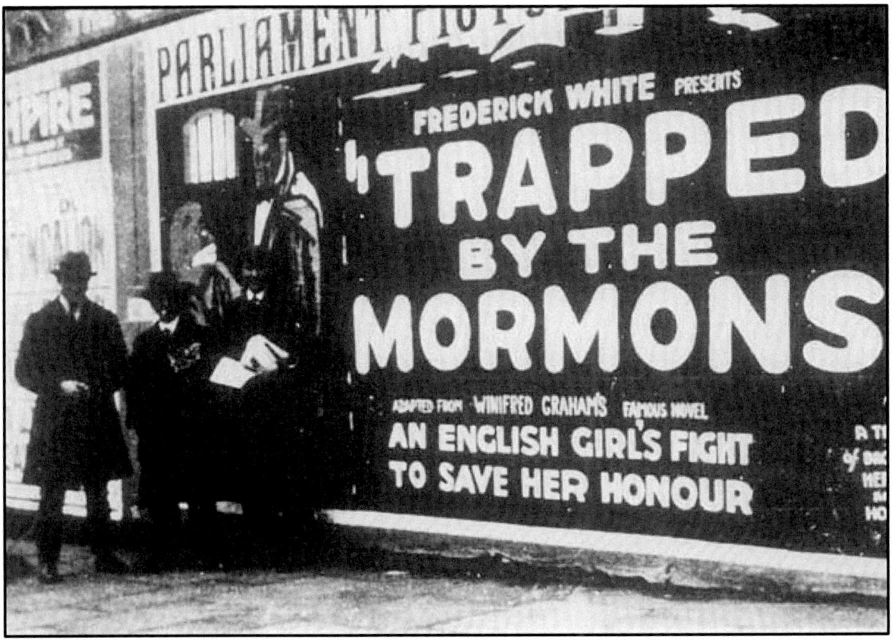

Billboard for "Trapped by the Mormons" in Britain

"Elder Isoldi" – Louis Willoughby

Isoldi Indoctrinates Nora Prescott

Evelyn Brent, the Star of the Picture

their rights to put this film out uncensored, unlike "Victim of the Mormons."

They responded by saying that "To prove they were not singling out Mormons for persecution, an official told the Mission President that the company was also filming "The Hunchback of Notre Dame," which portrayed the Catholic clergy unfavorably and that Pathe expected Catholics to 'make a rumpus when it comes out.' Pathe had invested thousands of dollars in each film, and they could not justify withdrawing expensive films from circulation 'simply because some one's feelings might get hurt.'" ("Scandalous Film: The Campaign to Suppress Anti-Mormon Motion Pictures, 1911-1912", by Brian Q. Cannon and Jacob W. Olmstead, Journal of Mormon Thought, Volume 29, No.2, Fall 2003, pp.41-78, p.68)

Slowly realizing that they might have to combat the entire and ever more powerful film industry, the Mormon Presidency first decided to fight for censorship joining with their non-Mormon neighbors in Utah, who were appalled at the misrepresentation, and when that was not very successful, they then decided to make their own film. "One Hundred Years of Mormonism" was only successful in Utah so this too failed. However, the LDS Church learned from this experience and by 1918 when "Riders of the Purple Sage" came out, this same community cooperation helped the Mormons and gentiles in Utah counteract the bad publicity that this film generated. "A Mormon Maid" which can be viewed along with "Trapped By The Mormons" today, is an interesting mix of anti and non-anti elements and Frank Borzage, who was born and raised in Salt Lake City as a Catholic and eventually became an Academy Award winning director in Hollywood, was the male lead in the movie. He was always on the edge and very artistic as a director and was no stranger to controversy during his life. Mae Murray was said to have later regretted being in the film and was uncomfortable making it at the time.

According to Mormon film scholars, because it was a prestigious film from a notable studio, it was the most potent and important anti-Mormon film in the history of silent films. Directed by Cecile B. DeMille and produced by the (Lasky) Famous Players, it was the most advertised film to date in the history of cinema. It played all over the world and for months, film audiences flocked to it, especially since Frank Borzage was by that time a very popular film idol. Once again, LDS leaders attempted to suppress it but were unsuccessful. There were scenes in the film that especially offended them because they depicted sacred temple rituals and robes that were not only sacred but entirely inaccurate. Today Mormon and non-Mormon scholars alike would like to see this film get more attention because of its pivotal role in silent film history, both in general and specifically in Mormon Church history. They compare "A Mormon Maid" to "The Birth of a Nation," which misrepresented many subjects and brought to light many other ugly subjects as well.

In the film, settlers are rescued from Indians by a group of Mormons and are forced to go live in Salt Lake City. Hogue, their father, is forced to take a second wife by Brigham Young and his first wife kills herself when she hears about it. Another man, Burr, who wants her as one of his wives, takes their beautiful daughter Dora prisoner. She attempts to escape and her father is killed in the gun battle. She is forced into a marriage ceremony where she lies about her maidenhood in order to avoid the marriage. She escapes again with her Mormon scout boyfriend Tom, and a renegade Danite aids the two. Burr catches up to them and Dora is forced to shoot him. The Danites that pursue them have hooded outfits on like the KKK, which is totally ridiculous to modern audiences but not so to those who research the early Mormon history. While there were no hoods, the Danites did disguise themselves and often struck under the cover of darkness. When Dora unhoods one of the Danites, she discovers that her father had not died and had disguised himself as well, and the three of them escape Mormon country forever. Perhaps another reason "A Mormon Maid" was popular is that it was a quality film with a hometown leading man in it who was also very popular at the time, and it was, after all, a good romance with lots of adventure and controversy in it.

The LDS Church learned one important thing from these earlier experiences in the silent era. They learned that censorship wasn't very workable when fighting such a powerful industry and that one had to

The Mormon Film, "The Life of Nephi"
Colored Plates, 1919.

fight fire with fire. In 1929, the LDS Church established their own production company and from 1929 to 1953, they put out a series of educational (nearly all local films) shorts and documentaries on such subjects as "The Message of the Ages" of the centennial pageant staged at the Salt Lake Tabernacle in 1930, and "Corianton: A Story of Unholy Love" which was a large scale production of the story of The Book of Mormon in 1931. Other titles say what they were specifically about: "Where the Saints Have Trod" in 1947, "Latter-Day Saint Leaders: Past and Present" in 1948, "Church Welfare Action" in 1948, "The Lord's Way" also on LDS Church welfare in the same year, "Temple Square" in 1949, and "The Temple Endowment" in 1955.

Other than this, two film shorts, a 1898 short entitled "Salt Lake City Company of Rocky Mountain Riders" and "A Trip to Salt Lake City" made in 1905, were the only other commercially made silents that were neutral about Utah and the Mormons. The first short was a documentary footage film of LDS people in an early newsreel about the Spanish-American War. The other was simply a comedy of a man traveling on a train with more than one wife and his many children and some sleeping car slapstick. It is only about 3 minutes long, and therefore, hardly enough time to show anything realistic. The Mormon Church made some silents for educational purposes during this time and the Clawson brothers, Shirl and Chet, made nearly all of them. The two brothers produced all these lost films between 1916 and 1929 and many of the subjects were about Book of Mormon tales such as "The Life of Nephi" and were sponsored by the LDS Church. Tragically the films were lost when a fire destroyed their library and laboratory in 1929. "The Life of Nephi" was released in 1915 using local non-professionals in the film. While the film is lost, 40 hand-painted color slides remain, which were recently discovered in the LDS archives.

Two commercial films made during the silent era to combat the anti-Mormon sentiment, and with the cooperation of the LDS Church authorities, were "One Hundred Years of Mormonism" in 1913 and "All Faces West" in 1929. The 1913 film was made specifically in response to the bad press that the Mormons were receiving. The LDS Church was very upset about the poor image that was being shown to the rest of the world after so much anti-Mormon literature in texts, pamphlets, dime novels, popular magazines, plays and traveling lectures, etc. So their first response was to make a film produced by Harry Y. Kelly, directed by Norval McGregor, with a screenplay by none other than Nell Shipman, one of the first women film makers and scriptwriters in Hollywood who spent a great deal of time in the west filming her own action adventures. The consultant on the film was Levi Edgar Young. Made on three reels and 90 minutes long, this was indeed a Hollywood style spectacular. The only film sanctioned by the Mormons during this era, it drew on authentic experiences of still living Mormon pioneers who had made the trek across the continent and featured many of the memorabilia and relics of this trek. The script came from an LDS writer's novel, John Henry Evans that was published in 1905. The film ran in Salt Lake City and took three tours throughout the west, but negotiations to screen the film in London and the East Coast were not successful.

"All Faces West" premiered in Salt Lake City on March 2, 1929 and was directed by George Pyper, with Levi Edgar Young as the consultant on this film as well. The film was also known as "The Exodus" or "The Exodus of the New World." The film used Hollywood stars Ben Lyon and Marie Prevost. The new film company was so excited about the success of this film, that they began building a studio in Sugarhouse and announced the pre-production of a second local film called "The Malamute Kid," which was supposed to be an adventure tale that took place in Alaska. Unfortunately, in 1928, the talkies started to arrive and the Pioneer Film Company could not raise enough money to make sound productions. A composer named Roland Barry had however, already put together the film score for this second movie and it was used in the play version that was a success because the composer had already recorded it. The film "All Faces West" premiered at the Victory Theatre but was not financially successful and the film is lost today.

What the LDS Church learned from the experience was the realization that the power of films and media, which could be used to help rather than hinder them, was something they needed to use for their own image. Thus the Utah film industry, both commercial and religious today has been and is being explored in all of its various facets. In 1939, when the exploitative "B" movie, "Illegal Wives" came out starring Ann Marin, Charles Maurice and Slim Simms, directed by Patrick Carlyle, it was eclipsed by the 1939 release of a major motion picture done with full cooperation of the LDS Church, "Brigham Young." This film starred Vincent Price, Dean Jagger, Mary Astor, Tyrone Power, Linda Darnell and John Carradine as Orrin Porter Rockwell. It was released by Twentieth Century Fox, filmed in Nevada, Utah and California, and produced by Darryl F. Zanuck. It so moved some of its actors that Vincent Price, who played Joseph Smith, wrote to the then

"Wagon Master" – Johnson and Dru

Ben Johnson, Harry Carey, Jr., and Ward Bond

LDS President to obtain more books to study Smith's life. Dean Jagger, who played Brigham Young, ended up becoming a Mormon some 32 years later.

The leaders of the LDS Church were allowed to review the script at least three times and Academy Award winning composer, Alfred Newman, integrated several Mormon hymns into the movie's musical score. The First Presidency of the Mormon Church put on a special screening before the film premiered in Salt Lake City, simultaneously at seven theaters downtown. All of the stars were in attendance and after the huge parade they valiantly tried to make a personal appearance at all seven theaters but didn't quite make it. About 215,000 Utahns came to Salt Lake City to see the parade and 8,000 of those people saw the film, which was a world record even to this day. Special excursion trains from the Union Pacific Railroad took passengers to and from town all day long. A gala dinner hosted by President Heber J. Grant was held at the Lion House that evening. The miracle of the seagulls was shot on the shores of Utah Lake and the Mormons felt vindicated at last. They had for the first time been properly represented by a major motion picture. (When Hollywood Came to Town: A History of Moviemaking in Utah, by James V, D'Arc, Gibbs-Smith Press, 2010, pp. 50-53 & 224-228)

The only other motion picture to represent the Mormons appropriately was a 1950s western entitled "Wagon Master" directed by John Ford. This film was backed by none other than Mormon friendly Howard Hughes. "Wagon Master" starred Ward Bond, Ben Johnson, Harry Carey Jr., and Joanne Dru. The story is about two horse traders called Sandy and Travis who are hired by a Mormon wagon train to lead them to the San Juan River Valley where they have been directed to settle. They are first joined by a stranded "hootchy kootchy" show and later by a family of outlaws hiding from a posse. The outlaws eventually take over the wagon train and Sandy (Harry Carey Jr) and Travis (Ben Johnson) are able to kill all the outlaws and lead the Mormons, including their leader Elder Wiggs (Ward Bond), to their valley. The writers affiliated with the LDS Church had read The Book of Mormon, while Ford knew what he wanted without this, and Hughes insisted on silly puritanical costumes in order to back the film. A spin off from this movie was the television series "Wagon Train" starring Ward Bond. One of the actors in the film, Russell Simpson, had played a Mormon pioneer three times, the last one being "Brigham Young and Bad Bascomb," released in 1946.

Many films have been made since, much more respectful of the dominant culture here and the LDS film industry is blossoming today. A few commercial films addressing Mormon subjects fictionally or even autobiographically, have hit the main stream and a steady stream of LDS Documentary films have been somewhat successful locally. LDS and non-LDS films that are being produced now have a wide range of subjects such as the comedy "Napoleon Dynamite" or they are historical memoirs with touching themes. There are now different themed films both pro and con such as "Angels in America" and there has even been a recent Broadway musical and major motion pictures such as "Saints and Sinners" which is about World War II. But my favorite is the less well-known "Pride and Prejudice" movie based on four BYU co-eds. This film is really well done. All of these various views of the LDS experience have put before the public a much more favorable picture, especially those with their universal themes and literate scripts, thus helping people outside of Utah to be better informed about the Latter Day Saints. Because, unfortunately, most people in the United States still view the Mormons as a cult. The Mormon Church leaders were right about the film industry being quite powerful in changing minds and hearts. The media can work for them in many positive ways. On the other hand, with the advent of the internet, the truth and even the rumors about early LDS Church history has become available to everyone, so that the LDS Church will have to find ways to respond to this new development. They must find new ways to represent themselves in a more positive way historically. Simply trying to omit the facts or smooth them over will not work in today's information highway world. Some say the best thing to do is just own up to the past, honor what you can, and apologize for the rest, while moving on into the modern church that everyone can be quite proud of, if people, in general, can become better informed.

ORA (Whytock) CAREW & EDITH BOSTWICK SILENT ENTERTAINERS

Ora Whytock Carew

Ora Carew, actress, was born on April 19, 1893 in Salt Lake City and died in Los Angeles, California on October 26, 1955. She was educated at Rowland Hall, an Episcopalian Seminary school in the Avenues of Salt Lake City. She had many engagements in musical comedy, stock companies, and vaudeville. Goldwyn discovered her and the best movies that she was in were "Go West, Young Man," and "Too Many Millions," for Metro Goldwyn. Then for Universal studios, she did "Love's Protégé," "Loot," and "Under Suspicion." She was described as being five feet three inches tall, 120 pounds with brown hair and brown eyes. She loved outdoor sports and loved motoring around in her "raceabout."

Carew played luckless but dignified victims in her earliest films such as Mrs. Dickinson in D. W. Griffith's 1915 "Martyrs of the Alamo." But she was soon a Mack Sennett Bathing Beauty making 14 dollars a week. By 1919, she had gotten a supporting role with fellow Utahn Betty Compson in a western serial entitled "The Terror of the Range." Her first official screen credit in a full length film was in 1921's "After Your Own Heart." She was also in Bert Lytell's "Sherlock Holmes" serial and in a melodrama called "Three Days to Live" both made in 1922. Some of her short-lived career highlights were "Big Town Round-Up" and "Smiles are Trumps."

Carew starred in some films with Mary Miles Minter and was a real dark-haired beauty. Her real name was Ora Whytock and she began acting in films when she was twenty-two years old. Her first film was "Saved by the Wireless" in 1915. She landed sporadic roles in Hollywood but worked hard to get the ones she wanted. Often, however, the better roles went to more experienced actresses. She never quite got the best roles but kept trying. In 1925, after appearing in "Cold Fury," she finally decided to retire from the film industry. She was 62 years old when she died.

Ora Carew is best known for her early roles in the Keystone comedies and sometimes had a small part in a Fatty Arbuckle film. One person reviewing her 1916 comedy "Dollars and Sense," with Joseph Belmont pretty much summed up how the audience viewed Carew's career in Hollywood, although one has to wonder if she just never got a chance to star in a quality film where she could "shine." "Ora Carew was a blonde actress in silent films who was pretty but not especially talented." He claimed that she had more success as a screenwriter, although I never heard that she did this. If she did, then great news for anyone brave enough to tackle this biography, as it was difficult to find out much about her.

Carew kept trying for bigger roles throughout her short career but kept losing to bigger stars in Hollywood. She did continue to live in Los Angeles after she retired and did have one husband named John C. Howard. I was unable to find out any more about her and don't know if she had any children or what she did after she quit the movies.

Edith Bostwick

Edith Bostwick was a cousin of Ora's and she was also a silent film actress who did bit parts in the movies. I could find little about her except that she was born in Golden, Colorado in 1882 and died in Hollywood, California in 1943. She seemed to have been hooked up with her neighboring Utahn, Mack Swain, and made some comedies with him and later with Chaplin such as the silent movie "The Pilgrim." She starred in approximately 16 silent films from 1912 to 1914. She also performed on the stage quite a bit during the early twenties but finished all of her performing by 1925. Most of her films were shorts or she had uncredited roles in these silent films. She then married J. Farrell MacDonald and gave up acting altogether.

Ora Carew

Ora Carew in Costume for Film

Ora Carew Portrait
Silents are Golden

Ora Carew as an Older Actress

J. Farrell MacDonald was a lifelong actor, singer and film director. He was born in 1875 in Waterbury, Connecticut and his career lasted 41 years. He started out acting in minstrel shows and then got small parts in silent films and was soon directing some of them. He was in L. Frank Baum's 1914 film version of The Patchwork Girl of Oz and he was in 44 silent films altogether from 1911 to 1918, as well as directing another 35 silents. And while he decided to start directing films for the better part of his later career he continued to act in character roles, mainly in westerns and Irish comedies. MacDonald transitioned to the talkies with ease and he acted in many more films from 1930 to 1951. He had even begun directing television shows until his sudden death in 1952 at the age of 77. He outlasted his wife by nine years, did not marry again and performed in 325 movies throughout his entire career.

MARGUERITE CLAYTON & BRONCO BILLY ANDERSON ACTION ADVENTURE STAR & WESTERNS COWGIRL

Marguerite Clayton, actress, was born on Apri1 12, 1891 in Ogden, Utah and died December 20, 1968 in Los Angeles, California. Not much is known about her early years but she was discovered by Bronco Billy Anderson and was his regular leading lady for many years before World War I began. Her real name was Margaret Fitzgerald and she attended St. Mary's Academy in Salt Lake City when she was older. Her parents were Irish and Welch and she was the third of four children and while she claimed to enter show business without any stage training as all, this was later disputed. Her father was a mining engineer and she sang at the Tabernacle as a young girl. The family moved from Salt Lake to San Francisco in 1910 when Margaret was 19 years old. Her father ran a bar there and Margaret answered an ad that the Essany company had put in the paper for hiring actresses in their new western based company.

She only had bit roles for about a year and a half when she was handpicked to star opposite a cowboy leading man named "Bronco Billy" Anderson because she could ride and shoot. Not having much experience with acting she looked to Anderson and her various directors for guidance in learning the art of acting. Clayton also acted on the stage during this time and also acted for the Liberty studio. She made over 60 films with Anderson starting in 1909. But by 1915 she was playing other kinds of parts with leading actor Richard Travers, doing dramas and light comedies. By 1917 she was one of 12 players acting in Black Cat features which were two reel comedy dramas based on Black Cat Magazine. While she was no longer held down to westerns and was happy about this, her career was beginning to peak. Marguerite Clayton made at least 176 known action films from 1909 to 1928. Her first film was entitled "A Mexican's Gratitude" and her very last film was entitled "Inspiration." Clayton had however, become co-owner of the film company called Essanay, where she also eventually starred in some melodramas on her own.

Essanay didn't last long, however, and Clayton went on to star in films at Liberty in other melodramas as her career began to fade. One of these films is still available for viewing, "Wolf Blood," which even today is timely because it was one of the first (1925) films made about werewolves. Another of her well-known films was as a supporting role with Norma Talmadge and Pedro de Cordoba in the film entitled "The New Moon." Her best-known movie at this studio was called "Bride 13." In 1917, she began freelancing with Paralta and Artcraft, Paramount and Paragon. And in 1918 she had her last hit movie entitled "Hit-The-Trail Holliday" which was from a prohibition play written by George M. Cohan. In 1922 she sued Pathe for $50,000 when she was accidentally struck by a pipe on set which left a permanent facial scar for which she possibly received some kind of settlement. While she continued to work in film in the U.S. and Europe, by the end of the silent era her career was over.

There is however, an interesting story about the filming of "Bride 13." Just imagine a naive small town girl running off to Hollywood and starring in one of the big budget serials with a whopping true adventure

Marguerite Clayton as a Young Woman

Marguerite Clayton as an Older Woman

Marguerite Clayton in Street Clothes

Marguerite Clayton Playing Card

story behind it. "Bride 13" was a fifteen-part silent serial filmed in the fall of 1919 mostly near Gloucester near Cape Ann. The film was produced by Fox Films and starred Jack O'Brien and Marguerite Clayton who were accompanied by a film crew of fifty-five people. Part of the story was shot near New Port, Rhode Island where an amazing castle was built just for the film. The story involved the abduction of 12 beautiful daughters from 12 very rich fathers who all lived in New York City. Rotten Moroccan pirates whisked them off to a submarine where they were then taken to this far off island where the impregnable castle was located. Clayton was the thirteenth abduction who was the heroine scheming to free her 12 "sisters."

One of the first things that happened during the filming, besides trying to meet a tight schedule with a million dollar budget, was when an eighty five mile-an-hour tornado struck Cape Ann and particularly Salt Island where the castle had just been completed. The newly built movie castle was entirely flattened and washed out to sea and the crew was ordered to build another one with only a month to do it. The hundred foot towers went up once more just for this part of the filming. Then the company moved on to Gloucester to a place called Harbor View on Wonson's Cove where old timers recall the various embarrassing antics of the film crew. They got the Navy to loan them an old submarine, the R-1, and they also bought an ancient schooner called the Mineola, which had been built in 1860. They fixed the schooner up with floats, sails and anchors and put four experienced sailors on her, along with all the actors who were playing pirates and towed her around to Brace Cove. A bloody fight on deck was filmed as the pirates took over the schooner, while two of the experienced men performed a death-defying stunt by scrambling sixty feet up and then diving down into the sea.

As the two men struggled for their lives in the sea, the Mineola sailed on towards shore headed for mass destruction. One man jumped into the water to help the other two who were in trouble and four others leapt overboard to save these three men. Soon everyone is trying to save everyone else and all the crew finally got on board, with at least two stunt men badly injured and rendered unconscious. Seconds later, the Mineola crashed into the shoreline, as well as a gigantic yacht, and historians will always wonder if someone was filming all of this, as it is not in the film but should be! After this first exciting week of filming, word spread and thousands flocked to Brier Neck where the second week was about to be filmed. They came by bike, auto, motorcycle, horse, trolley, on foot and even in small boats to watch the excitement and local law enforcement had a tremendous time containing them all. The third week the tide turned foul near Salt Island, and the chief cameraman was swept out to sea, his lifeline snapping. He was rescued by two of his assistants who dove in to save him.

In the fourth week, a 450-pound cannon being used on the parapet of the castle during the fight scene, got stuffed with too much powder and when it went off it ruptured its moorings, took the two men operating it with it and crashed through the tower floor landing precariously on a ledge. One of the men dropped thirty feet through a hole followed by the debris and the other was knocked out for about five minutes. Neither of them was hurt and they went back to work. In the same week, they had also brought in a huge old hot-air balloon with a wicker basket underneath which was going to be fired up when the hero slashed through the pirates and leapt into the basket with the heroine, flying up into the sky.

On November 10th, another huge crowd gathered to watch the filming of this scene. The Chief Gunner's Mate on the R-1 submarine volunteered to play this scene as the stuntman for the film star Jack O'Brien. Three thousand people were at Good Harbor while this man cut his way through the pirates, a stuntman at his side as the "bride," leapt into the hot-air balloon but the air had cooled and the balloon would not go anywhere. On the second filming, the bag ripped and they had to repair it. On the third filming, as the two men staggered up to leap into it, the balloon got away from its handlers and sped out to sea with no one on board. Some of the crew got into cabs and chased the balloon down the beach, finding it limp and lifeless several miles away.

Before the dramatic ending of the film where they were to blow up the castle on Salt Island with six cameras readied to film, the brides, wearing very little, and the pirates, wearing too much, had to swim in the cold November water to the waiting submarine. One of the pirates ended up stranded on a buoy. Twenty cans of gunpowder and a whole lot of dynamite were also readied for the final scene of the serial. Warning bombs went off and everyone watched as a mere two charges sputtered off and the castle remained intact. Faulty wiring made them re-shoot the scene, but not before the pirates were captured by an Arabian gang and dragged off over the rocks of Eastern Point. The Mineola was then finally blown up and the castle was readied for one more attempt at its demise as well. Everyone cleared out of the area once more and the first warning bomb went off and then the second. At long last a huge explosion blasted into the sky, a rain of debris showered into the ocean and the spectators oohed and awed. Within a day or two, Salt Island was back to normal and the movie crew was gone.

Marguerite Clayton's life story seems to be lost after about 1928 when she left her movie career and married her U.S. Air Force husband, Victor Bertrandias. But I do know that she starred in at least one picture with Art Acord, another Utah grown western star from Glenwood, Utah. They performed together in the "Skyhigh Corral" in 1926. She also starred in several pictures with Harry Carey. In 1928 she retired from the movies and began her private life in Los Angeles with her husband. He died seven years before she did in 1961. In 1968, when she was 77 years old, she died of her injuries in a road accident. She was buried next to her husband, Major General Victor Bertrandias in the Arlington National Cemetery. But her long and quite illustrious career in the movies ranks her up with the greats of the era when it comes to performing many of her own stunts, saving her money rather than losing all of it, and making dozens of entertaining movies in Hollywoodland.

MICKEY DANIELS – "OUR GANG"

Mickey Daniels was one of the little boys in the "Our Gang" movies in the early twenties. He was born October 11, 1914 in Utah as Richard Daniels Jr. according to several sources including The Ultimate

Dictionary of the Silent Screen Performers by Billy H. Doyle and several other sources connected to the original "Our Gang" series as well as LDS famous personality lists. However, 21 years after his death, when he died in a transient hotel in San Diego, California in 1970, someone researched further and found out that he had actually been born in Rock Springs, Wyoming and that he had lived in Utah after this. I have no problem including him on this list of Utah personalities, however because he did have connections to Utah, lived there for a while, and Rock Springs is just across the eastern border. Utahns are always traveling back and forth to Rock Springs and vice versa. But it is interesting to note that since I am a Utahn I know that Rock Springs is a pretty redneck town whose history is connected to the railroad, the mines and the oil industry. You have to check your guns in before going into most restaurants or hotels there.

Mickey's father was an American actor who had been born one of ten children in Gwubach, Wales in January of 1864. The senior Daniels broke into the movies a bit late in life at the age of 42. He appeared in 27 silent films between 1922 and 1926. Perhaps after this he was behind the camera in some capacity because he continued to star together in some of the "Our Gang" productions with his son Mickey. They also starred together in several Harold Lloyd features while Mickey's brother Leonard worked at the Roach Studios in the transportation department for the next twenty years. But Mickey not only had his father's help in securing his position as one of the original "Our Gang" series, he also had a very famous child star aunt named Bebe Daniels, who was the most instrumental in getting Mickey into the movies.

Bebe Daniels was born Phyllis Daniels in Dallas, Texas in 1901 and began her acting career as a very young child. She had her first starring roles at age 7 and at 9, she had the lead as Dorothy in the 1910 version of "The Wizard of Oz." By 1919, she was at the peak of her career both as a child and teenage star. Having become an adult she signed with Cecil B. DeMille, hoping to leave light comedy parts behind her and gain more serious attention as an actress. Unfortunately DeMille gave her secondary roles instead. But by 1924, she had signed with other studios and began to gain attention as a more serious leading actress with such

Child Actors

Collage of Mickey Daniels and Mary Kornman

Child to Adult Stars, Daniels and Kornman

As Clowning Teens

Mickey in Teen Movie

movies as “”Madame Beaucaire” with Rudolph Valentino. But she found that she had to return to light comedies in order to maintain her star status and by 1929 she was at the top again in Hollywood. In the thirties she made quite a few musicals and a few pre-code film noir movies but she had also decided to retire from film in 1935.

By this time she was in her second marriage to the comedian/actor Ben Lyons and he had taken their family to London where he was performing in a play. As a couple they did radio shows together for the BBC. Living in London all through World War II, they broadcast for the allies as well and after the war she received the Medal of Freedom from President Harry S. Truman when they returned to the United States. By 1948, however, the whole family had returned to England where Bebe stayed for the rest of her life. The whole family, including Richard, Barbara, and their children, were on a radio sitcom together from 1951 to 1961 entitled “Life with the Lyons.” Bebe Daniels died of a stroke at the age of 70, was cremated in London, but was buried in the Hollywood Forever Cemetery in Los Angeles. Her husband and children remained in England.

Mickey had even more help getting his first role in the movies. Still photographer, Gene Kornman worked for the Hal Roach studios and his daughter, Mary Kornman was the first female child star in the series. Gene Kornman was a good friend of Richard Daniels and got his son Mickey a screen test, although screen tests in those days were quite casual. Mickey made $37.50 a week at first, but within three years he was making $175 a week as a member of the “Our Gang” series. He made over 60 “Our Gang” shorts and features in the twenties, then graduated to a set of adolescent serials called “The Boy Friends” and made about 20 of those shorts and features in the early thirties. From 1933 to 1946 he had small roles or uncredited bit parts in approximately 26 films, some of them in the UK. His last known bit part went uncredited in the film “The Mask of Dijou” made in 1946.

Mickey Daniels had one of those strange and different faces that audiences seemed to love in those days on children. One type of child star face was of course beautiful while the other type would be considered quite strange by today's standards. There was always one little boy in "Our Gang" or even "The Little Rascals," which came a bit later, who didn't have to use a gimmick to make himself odd. For example, "Alfalfa" had his cowlick that stood straight up in the air and "Spanky" had his little beanie hat. But they were still cute and didn't grow up to look really odd. In "Our Gang" Mickey Daniels was the "odd faced" boy and in the later talkie version, "The Little Rascals," it was "Froggie" who held the distinction of being the odd man out.

With sandy red hair and lots of freckles, crooked teeth and a wide smile, he was the "character" in the group. The first set of children, six in all, consisted of a toddler, one girl, a fat kid, a little black boy and a couple of tough looking white boys. Daniels only enjoyed a film life as a young boy and in a few things as a teenager, while he became a quite strange looking adult. At the time though, he was a very popular child star with his trademark toothy grin, which could quickly turn to a scowl. After he left the movies not much is known about him except that he did marry and had one child. Mickey Daniels quit films in 1946 and became either a construction worker or a taxi driver, depending on which source you check. He died in complete obscurity from cirrhosis of the liver in a San Diego hotel room in January of 1970, probably a victim of alcoholism. Maybe he was unable to transform his strange face into a comedian as a few others have done, although it is more likely that he was an early and less publically known casualty of the child star syndrome which many others have succumb to over the years.

In a paper on "Our Gang" by Neil Anthony from Pathe films, entitled "Those Jolly Rascals Known As "Our Gang," a sort of publicity article for director Hal Roach and Pathecomedies, the first set of Our Gang actors are presented to the public as happy, healthy children well taken care of by the studio. The article mentions that 54 "Our Gang" comedies had been made in just four years' time and that all the children were easy to direct and work with. They had their own private classroom on the studio lot and their teacher is quoted as saying: "Put children in a school room day after day and they want to look out of the window – put them outside the window where things are going on and they'll pay closer attention to their text books." The article also mentions how Roach would set up a scene as something fun and then just film the kids playing ball, to get natural dialogue. It also mentions how popular the children were and how they had to keep the crowds away in droves when they were filming. (From the official "Our Gang" web site)

Knowing Mickey Daniel's face I have seen him in bit parts in movies in the late thirties and early forties as a young man. It almost seems as if they didn't know quite how to cast him. He wasn't a comedian who could get away with an odd face, but he wasn't handsome enough to play even the side kick of someone handsomer. He was only 55 when he died. He must have had a sad life after he left the movies and he must have been divorced when he died, since he was living alone.

And then to have that face which was oddly cute as a child and very strange as an adult, must have been a burden few of us can fully understand, no matter how tough our high school years were. What kind of a childhood did he have I wondered? What did he do as an adult? In the end I gave up on finding more information about him. Yet as I wrote about all these actors and actresses I found myself being haunted by a few of them, and Mickey Daniels is one of them.

One hears about all the trials and tribulations of today's child stars, but Mickey Daniels was a forerunner for all of them, and the other side of the mirror, for even someone as tortured as Judy Garland, who managed to succeed anyway. So many child stars were exploited by studio heads in those early days, especially if they did not have parents to stand up for them, or even had parents who also exploited them as well. Some of these studio heads and their henchmen were not above introducing addictions into the mix, especially in the form of over the counter prescription drugs to keep their young stars "peppy" and ready to work. Others, starting so young in life found fame a difficult thing to deal with, especially if they happen not to have a good foundation of self-esteem and self-worth. Their "night terrors" became "day terrors" and they had to find ways of coping with all these things. Even today, one reads again and again about the struggles of young television sitcom stars once their fame lessens and adulthood has arrived. In Mickey

Daniels case you also had a quirky but charming kid who grew up and became a not so attractive adult. Looking at the photos of Mickey and Mary together it is evident that he really liked her, but it was an impossible situation for all of her kindness and caring as a person.

DONNA DREW – WOMEN DIRECTORS & LOST STARDOM

A sad and quite tragic fate awaited Donna Drew, an up and coming movie starlet in early silent Hollywood. Drew had black ringlets down her back and a captivating charisma of "the girl next door" variety. She would have had a chance at bigger and better romantic comedy parts as well as westerns, or even the type of parts that made Janet Gaynor and Mary Pickford's audiences swoon. She was born in Salt Lake City, Utah in 1896. She went to Hollywood to become a star and was one of the few fortunate ones who was on her way in just a few films made in 1917 and 1918 when she was just 21 years old. She was a bit taller than the average 5 foot to 5 foot two height of most of the young women stars then, but still short enough to be a bit littler than her male leads. Her best feature was her bright, infectious and captivating smile.

Drew starred in "The Flame of Youth," "The Lair of the Wolf," and "49-71" in 1917. She starred in her last film in 1918 "Madame Spy." Ruth Ann Baldwin was a new director in the earliest days of Hollywood and one of very few women directors at the time. She joined Universal Studios in 1913 as a screenwriter and was soon editing films as well. Her first screen-written movie was "The Black Box" made in 1915. Very soon the studio asked her to direct a movie. She picked a great screenplay, a suspenseful western parody that had a great plot entitled "49-71." A millionaire from the east sends his male secretary out west to engage a hard up acting troupe to populate the deserted ghost town of Nugget Notch, so that he can relive his early days in the gold rush. Every generic character in a typical western is parodied and slightly surprising from what one would expect. The lawman, the hero, the gambler, the saloon keeper and villain, the heroine and even the saloon girl, don't quite do

Donna Drew in "49-71"

Donna in a Different Light

Western Girl!

That Smile!

what they are supposed to in the story. There are a few surprises in the underlying subplot as well. Donna Drew got a great part in this film and it was a real treat to see this Salt Lake girl before her death in this little restored film. Drew died in the flu epidemic in 1918 in Helena, Montana.

A newly released DVD has two silent films on it by two early women directors. The other film is called "The Ocean Waif" and had to be restored with damaged sections and a few missing parts but the Donna Drew film is crystal clear and fun to watch. While Ruth Ann Baldwin was just starting her short three year career as a director, Alice Guy-Blanche was at the end of her career when she made "The Ocean Waif." Blanche was French and was born in 1873 in Paris. She had directed pictures for Gaumont of Paris from 1896 to 1907. She then moved to the United States and opened her own studio in Fort Lee, New Jersey called the Solax Company. She was only able to run her own studio for four years from 1910 to 1914. She then went to work for The International Film Service as a director. This studio was owned by William Randolph Hearst. She retired when the silent film era came to a close. She directed pictures for Hearst that had a similar theme and plot. The pictures had to have a romantic story, a romance with Pygmalion aspects, but with no brutality, plenty of pathos and a somewhat dramatic ending that was also "happy." Donna Drew's picture had all of these elements in it but also had some delightful twists in the plot as well.

When I first wrote about Drew I had very little information, and while I still have very little about her early years in Utah, I was delighted to get to see her on the screen. There weren't even any stills that I could find at the time. Perhaps now with the release of this little film, there will be some. But the best surprise was to see not just an acting job but a real personality to a person one is writing about who has long since passed away. The miracle of film some might say, but I think it is the way in which Donna Drew's personality shines out on the screen from decades ago, as though one had just met her yesterday. Some performers just have this quality and Donna Drew, tragically, had one of "those" gifts. It is possible that had she lived she may have been a very accomplished comedic actress.

ARTHUR GUY EMPEY – W.W. I HERO & CELEBRITY DAUGHTER

Arthur Guy Empey & "Over The Top"

Arthur Guy Empey was born in Ogden, Utah, in December of 1883 and died in Wadsworth, Kansas on February 22, 1963. He was a World War I hero who wrote his own biography of his war experiences and as a result was able to act in several silent films in Hollywood: "Over The Top" in 1918, "The Undercurrent" in 1919, "Oil" or "Millionaire for a Day" in 1921. Empey was considered the Audie Murphy of his generation. Later, he formed his own company called the Arthur Guy Empey Pictures Corporation and produced some films. He was also the screenwriter for several films including "Troopers Three" in 1930 that he also produced. This movie was about three failing actors: Rex Lease, Roscoe Karns and Slim Summerville who join the army for food and lodging. Empey produced "Into No Man's Land" in 1928, which he also directed. He wrote the scripts for approximately eight films. Empey married the beautiful Marguerite Andrus and they had one child together named Diane Marguerite Empey.

Empey's book, Over the Top, was an international best seller and is one of the best written, firsthand accounts of war. Better than All Quiet on the Western Front, Empey uses a Hemingway style narrative that is often powerful and straight to the point. The story of his being a recruiting sergeant in New York and after the sinking of the Lusitania, subsequently enlisted with the Royal Fusillers in England, is a powerful one. The book was a huge hit selling over a million copies and fueling the effort to get the United States to support the war effort in Europe. Empey was mustered out of the Fusillers when he was injured in combat. After his time in Hollywood he continued to write popular fiction. He passed away at the Veterans Administration Hospital in Wadsworth, Kansas and gave most of his medals to patients in his ward.

Arthur Guy Empey, World War I Hero, Author and Filmmaker

Two of the best chapters in the book concern a matter-of-fact description of why a wounded soldier is so much more expensive for the government than a dead one. He is relentless in his chronological details following a wounded soldier through the system and this description is as timely today as it was right after World War I. In another incident he is woken up along with a few other young men in the middle of the night, blindfolded and led to a place where these young men will be lined up behind a blind to execute one of their own, a hooded deserter. Empey, however, doesn't let the story stay just that, but finds out the young man's name and the details of his story leading up to his execution, wherein the reader finds out how it was all a series of mistakes and tragedies that led to this young man's so-called desertion. But what was popular with the public was his addition of "Tommy's Dictionary of the Trenches" that he included at the end of the book. It was a dictionary of words of British soldier's slang making the book intelligible to both Americans and Brits. This was something that many have now copied in other war memoirs since, just to explain the jargon used in whatever war they are writing about.

Eventually Empey, besides appearing in a few films, writing a few books and producing a few movies, wrote the words for a few songs. His most popular song as a lyricist was entitled "Your Lips Are No Man's Land But Mine." It was termed a "romantic war ballad" at the time and was quite popular. There is one interesting mystery about Empey after he came back from Britain as a hero. When he first came back he wrote his book and gave lectures across the land for the National Geographic Society. Then he also made appeals for Liberty Loans, the Red Cross and the Tobacco Fund to help out in the war effort. All during this time he was trying to get back in active duty in the United States Army. Even though he had physical disabilities due to his war wounds while in the service in Britain, he was finally given a commission as a Captain in the National Army. However, three days after receiving his commission, the War Department rescinded this order and discharged him from the Army with an honorable discharge. No explanation was ever given as to why this happened, but the controversy over this went all the way to President Wilson and all the way back down to Empey. The reasons for Empey's discharge were kept confidential and never revealed to Empey or anyone else.

Two movies that Empey directed were "Into No Man's Land" and "Little Mickey Grogan." His 1918 film, in which he starred, basically, told his experiences from his book, except that in the film his name was Sgt. James Garrison Owen. And while in the book - which is an excellent read by the way - he barely mentions that the sinking of the Lusitania is what inspired him to join the British military. In the movie version, they had a spectacular recreation of the sinking the Lusitania, which was very unique and expensive for a silent film in 1918. In "Little Mickey Grogan," child actor Frankie Darro helps out the hero and heroine through some difficult times. The hero is an architect who is going blind and afraid of losing his girl because of this. The girl is spending time with a bully prizefighter. Little Mickey saves the day for this couple and reunites them, after going through some quite difficult times to do this.

In the other film, "Into No Man's Land," the heroine is a young woman whose father is the head of a ring of thieves, only she doesn't know it. The father hires an attorney to help him out with some trouble he is in, but when the attorney finds out that the man is a crook, he quits. However, during the time that he is employed by the father, he falls in love with the man's daughter. The father flees the country to escape a hit man on his trail and ends up joining the Army to hide out from the hit man. The young attorney gets drafted. These two men meet in the trenches, during the First World War and while the father knows that the attorney knows who he is and is basically after him, he does not know that the young man is in love with his daughter. It is only when the young attorney is wounded, and in his delirium, he calls out the daughter's name several times that the father realizes this young man is deeply in love with his daughter. The father disappears at the front and the young attorney thinks that he has been killed. After the war, the lawyer and the young woman marry, thinking her father is dead. Years later, a "tattered stranger," who is dying, comes to their door to see his daughter one last time. This was quite an inventive story for the times and certainly able to carry quite a bit of action and suspense, so Empey had another hit on his hands.

As to what happened to Empey, in his later life, I don't know, but I do know he lived in Los Angeles and went to the Veterans Hospital in Wadsworth, Kansas where he died. He was 80 years old. I do know that he and his wife had a daughter named Marguerite Empey on July 29, 1932 and that the Empeys did get divorced at some point according to what I could find. This daughter became an international celebrity in her own right, having inherited her mother's looks and body, and her father's entrepreneurial skills and talents of fearlessness and business sense. She definitely paved new roads in a very unusual way.

Diane Marguerite Empey or Diane Webber

Diane Marguerite was probably one of the most beautiful women in the world, akin to a young Liz Taylor in looks, and built like Marilyn Monroe. Everything about Marguerite was really her and all natural. Born and raised in LA, she first studied ballet with the Russian Ballet mistress and ballerina, Maria Befeti. She was planning to be a dancer and actress. Soon, however, she was in the chorus line at Bimbo's in San

Marguerite Empey as a Young Girl

The Name Change, Diane Webber

Diane in the Movies

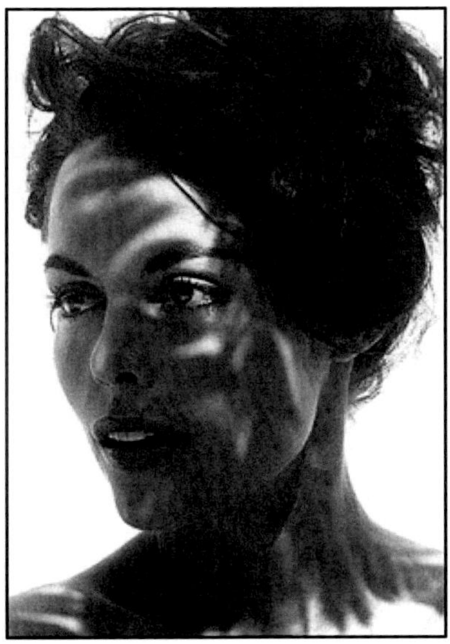

Naturalist, Nudist, Author and Pin-up, 1955

Francisco. By 1955, when she was just 23 years old, she was on the cover of Playboy Magazine as May's Playmate of the Month. She also married Joe Webber and took the name of Diane Webber. She was once again on the cover of Playboy in February of 1956. After this, she became interested in being a Naturalist, which then led to being interested in nudism and she began appearing on the cover of various nudist magazines. In finding dozens of photos on the web, I had a difficult time finding some where she was adequately covered, as she was quite proud of her body and one can find photos of her almost anywhere to this day.

She wrote a book about nudism and her own family called Those Wonderful Webbers and also posed for many famous photographers as a model. She was on the cover of several albums, including Less Baxter's "Jewels of the Sea," Nelson Riddle's "Sea of Dreams," and Xavier Cugat's "Chile Con Cugie." She also appeared in a few soft porn films such as "Mermaids of Tiburon" in 1962 as the Mermaid Queen, and in "This Is My Body" starring as herself. She also had small roles in "The Trial of Billy Jack" from 1974, "The Witchmaker" in 1969, "Sinthia, the Devil's Doll" and in 1968; she appeared in "The Swinger." She was also on a few television shows: "Peter Gun," "Alfred Hitchcock Presents" and "Voyage to the Bottom of the Sea."

Diane Webber kept her name after she divorced her husband. And in 1975 she was found guilty in a postal obscenity case, but eventually the case was overturned. She was 5'2" tall, which should have given her a disadvantage as a model, but her measurements made up for it: bust 39C, waist 23"and hips, 37." She started out with brown hair and then she became an exotic looking black haired beauty and was the fantasy pin-up for men all over the world in the 50s and even for a while in the early 60s. She was also an expert belly dancer and started her own belly dancing troupe called the "Perfume of Araby." She even played a belly dancing instructor in one of her parts in a movie. She passed away August 19, 2008 from complications following surgery for cancer in Los Angeles. She was 76 years old.

MARY KORNMAN

Mickey Daniels had a good friend in the "Our Gang" series named Mary Kornman. And in fact, Mary's father, Eugene Kornman, who was a photographer and Hal Roach's still – photo cameraman, was instrumental in getting Mickey his job, as well as movie work for both of his own daughters. Mary's mother, Verna Kornman, had been in a few silent movies herself when she was younger. Mary was born in Idaho Falls, Idaho on December 27, 1915. Her sister, Mildred was born 10 years later, on July 10, 1925 in Beverly Hills, California. This age difference accounts for why Mary and Mickey were such good friends, because Mildred was so much younger. Gene Kornman was also the still photographer for Harold Lloyd, as well as a good friend of his. And this also accounts for how it was that Mickey Daniels ended up in some Harold Lloyd movies as well. Both Mary and Mickey had some ties to Utah and a common heritage, and a background from the West. However, Mary was quite a beautiful little girl and was acting by the time she was eight years old. Her parents had guided her through the silents as the female star of "Our Gang," but by the time the talkies came in, Mary was too old to continue playing in the series. She and Mickey Daniels went on to play in the adolescent series "The Boy Friends," and made quite a few films this way.

There is a telling detail in one of the photos of Mary Kornman, where she's wearing those wide leg slacks that women wore in the 30s and on the thigh of the right leg, is a black-and-white portrait of Mickey Daniel's face. They were obviously the best of friends, although Mary Kornman was one of the few child stars from "Our Gang" to successfully move into adult film roles. She went on to star with such greats as John Wayne and Bobby Steele, who were at the time famous cowboy stars. She also starred with Fred Astaire, Bing Crosby, and Jack Oakie in some teenage and young adult films. In nearly all of these films, she was either the heroine in a western or the college-aged, petite and blonde, girl next door. She made several films in the 30s and the only time she got to play

"Our Gang" Child Star

Teens Mary Kornman and Mickey Daniels

Mary and First Husband

Mary and Horse Trainer/Second Husband

something entirely different was in a cliffhanger serial called "Queen of the Jungle," released in 1935. While Mary was quite good in this serial, the producers of this film had used quite old jungle footage that was poorly spliced into the episodes and easy to spot, making it a pretty shoddy affair for audiences.

Mary Kornman made "Desert Trail" with Wayne in 1935, and "A Calling of Dan Matthews" whose subject was about teen drinking, which was made in 1936. In 1937, she made a Bob Steele Western "Smoky Smith," and had also been married to cameraman Russell Tover since 1934. She divorced him five years later, in 1939. She then married Ralph B. McCutcheon, who was a horse trainer. She actually looked him up to help her ride better and teach her horse some stunts for the movies. This marriage lasted. They settled on a ranch in a place called Sand Canyon and Mary left the movies at the end of the 30s to be with her husband. Had she remained in the movies, she probably would have had a long and successful career. McCutcheon's claim to fame was that his horse "Fury," starred in a lot of movies like "Black Beauty" and "My Friend Flicka" in the forties and on television in episodes of "Bonanza," "Rin Tin Tin" and "The Monkees."

Mary, although very shy, always found good parts in Hollywood until her early retirement. However, one of her primary objectives was to put her younger sister through school with all the money that she earned. Had she stayed in the movies, she probably would have had a good career and a solid one. Her sister Mildred says she was the levelheaded one and her own "Rock" in life. But instead, Mary Kornman spent her life quite happily married, never had children, and spent her time with the horses that both she and her husband championed. But she was also a loyal friend and kept in contact with all of her Hollywood friends, throughout her life. Described as a kind and genuine person, one wonders if she maintained her close friendship with Mickey Daniels as well. Or , if he was the one to not maintain this friendship, as he died three years before Mary did in 1970. One can only speculate on this, because Mary Kornman, "sadly passed away at the young age of 57 of cancer on June 1, 1973, after a long illness, Mildred by her side. Ralph would follow in 1975. They were both buried at the Linn Grove Cemetery in Greeley, Weld County, Colorado." ("Mary Kornman," by John Frank, Official Mary Kornman Website, at http://marykornman.com)

In an interview in 1960, Mary Kornman, was asked what it was like to be leading lady of the still popular silent series "Our Gang." She replied that being in "Our Gang," was a lot of fun because for a young child it was like playing. "I have no regrets... We didn't have to be talented – which is natural for kids... I think we had a privileged childhood working in those films." ("Mary Kornman," Wikipedia, the free encyclopedia, http://en.wikipedia.org/wiki/Mary_Kornman)

MILDRED KORNMAN – RICKI VAN DUSEN

Mildred appeared in over twenty "Our Gang" films in both the silents and into the talkies. She never had a speaking part; she was just added in whenever they needed more children to fill in the scene like in a school classroom. She was rarely in a scene with her sister Mary, because by the time she was in the series, Mary and Mickey Daniels had gone on to "The Boy Friends." Just as beautiful as her sister, she had a more elegant look, as opposed to Mary Kornman's more cute sort of "Debbie Reynolds" style. Chubbier when young, she has always been proud of the fact that she was born in the front room of their house in Beverly Hills. Her name was given to her in honor of Harold Lloyd's wife Mildred, because the Lloyds we're good friends with her parents. Mildred actually started acting at the age of one when placed in a little wagon on the "Our Gang" series. Just before Mary left the series, Mildred joined it. Her career with "Our Gang" lasted from 1926 to 1935.

Millie attended grammar school in Beverly Hills, and then went to Hollywood High School. By this time, she was already established as a model and was elegantly beautiful. She had begun professional modeling at the age of 16, but she had been modeling all through and even after the Depression years to help her family's finances out. At age 18, she got married and began a career in films in the 40s, which is when she changed her name to Ricki Van Dusen. She appeared in several films in

Millie Kornman, Child Actor "Our Gang"

"Our Gang" and Ricki Van Dusen, Model

Ricki Van Dusen, Actress

Ricki Today, Designer

the 40s, many of them starring Betty Grable and June Haver. In 1944, she was in "Up In Arms," in 1945, she was in "The Dolly Sisters" and "Diamond Horseshoe," and in 1946, she was in "Cinderella Jones." What steered her career away from Hollywood, was that her husband went to war, and she moved to New York City with their young son Stephen, to make better money as a model, while her husband was away at war. She had a highly successful modeling career in the late 40s, 50s and 60s, and was one of the first models to be called a "Supermodel."

As Ricki Van Dusen, she was on the cover of many famous elegant magazines such as Vogue, Glamour, Charm, and Vogue Pattern. And she was, and still is, one of the most beautiful women in the world. She also did photo advertisements for Revlon, Cutex, Helena Rubinstein and Elizabeth Arden. All of the famous New York photographers photographed her. And like her sister before her, she sent home some of her money to help support the family. She gave birth to her daughter Darragh and right after this returned to California and began commuting to New York to continue her modeling career. Later she opened a boutique in Encino, California called "Van Dusen Green," which was highly successful. She also began to study photography. For the last few years, she has enjoyed her family and has done a lot of traveling. She also worked for some charities and occasionally spoke about the "Our Gang" series or her modeling career. Today she would be 88 years old and is still quite stunning. She has her own official website.

MARION MACK
BUSTER KEATON & "THE GENERAL"

Joey Marion McCleery Lewyn – Joanne McGuire

Nicknamed "Joey Mack" and then using her real name for her first acting jobs, Joey McCleery later was given the studio name of Joanne McGuire and ended up with her final acting name as Marion Mack, which she chose on her own. She was born on April 9, 1902 and was raised in the mining town of Mammoth, Utah where her grandfather had been a miner. Her mother continued to live in Mammoth after she divorced her husband when Joey was only three years old. In 1870, an outcropping of stone was discovered at a place called the Mammoth Mine and three cowboy brothers herding cattle from Texas went in together and bought the mine. They settled there and soon discovered a rich ore body of gold, silver, lead, copper and bismuth. By 1890, there were several mills, smelters and even an upper town or Mammoth that was the mining district and a lower town or Robinson, which was the business district. From 1900 to 1910, there were over 3,000 people living in these two towns. Families were crammed into the same living quarters all together or lived in places without roofs while the building went on to accommodate them. Eventually, the business district had four huge hotels, a railroad station, markets, liveries, stables, laundries, saloons, lumber yards, all sorts of shops, dentists, lawyers' offices, barbers, a newspaper office and several churches and schools.

Later one of the hotels was remodeled into the Tintic District Hospital, and several doctors lived in the town. Middletown was established in 1910 and Marion Mack witnessed some exciting events while she was growing up there. She witnessed a town fire, which started in a Chinese laundry and destroyed ten businesses, and she was in town when a woman gave birth to the first quadruplets ever in Utah, back before such things could be helped along medically. Spanish artifacts were constantly being found, both authentic and fabricated. One time, two boys soaped up the train tracks and the first train that arrived careened down a very steep grade at full speed and was totally out of control. It then just stopped by itself at the bottom as if the whole thing had never happened. Perhaps her father, like her grandfather, was one of the miners who hid pieces of ore on their persons because even just one little piece was worth a whole week's wages. Or perhaps her father was one of the businessmen there or one of the miners who left town after her parent's divorce. Mammoth produced for 75 years before the town became completely deserted. (<u>Utah Ghost Towns</u> by Stephen L. Carr, Western Epics: Salt Lake City, Utah, 1995, pp.91-92)

In high school, Joey dreamed of becoming a movie star and at the age of 18 after graduating from Mammoth High School, she did something about it. She wrote to Sennett and enclosed some photos of herself. "I was a hillbilly, but I wanted to be in the movies. Mr. Sennett's manager wrote back to me and said they would be happy to interview me if I ever came to Hollywood. He was very polite. But I had to be properly chaperoned." At eighteen years of age, Joey was allowed to go to Hollywood. She went with her father and his new 24 year old bride, Louise, as chaperones. In another version of these events, her father was not on a honeymoon but on a business trip with his new wife and without his knowledge, Joey slipped away and went right to the Mack Sennett studios. McCleery set the record straight when she told what really happened. "My father didn't want me to be in the movies. But my stepmother helped me and when we came to California, we got into Sennett's office without him knowing it. And he was furious when he found out." ("Marion Mack, Buster Keaton Co-Star, Is Back," by Lynn Symross, The Los Angeles Times, p.4 – http://www.silentcomedians.com /forum.viewtopic)

"Sennett had bathing beauties, girls frolicking in the surf, but not in bathing suits like you see now. We had bloomers and were completely covered. But Sennett, as far as father was concerned was a no-no. Everybody else loved Sennett pictures, but not my father. I got a job there right away for $25 a week. I figured I wasn't too bad. That's all he paid Chaplin when he started. But my father wouldn't speak to me. He stayed mad for a long time. I guess he spoke to me once or twice." For all intents and purposes, Joey had been disowned by her father. On the other hand, how many young girls have the moxie to not only write such a letter to Hollywood, but follow through on it regardless of the consequences which she surely knew, in her case, would follow? (Ibid, p.4)

She signed an eight-year contract which would pay her $25 dollars a week. She entered a beauty contest for the Ince Studios and as winner of the contest, that studio wanted her also. She agreed to pose for some publicity shots at The Billion Dollar Theater and one of Ince's employees made the comment that she was quite a lemon, and why had Ince picked her? Ince was quite upset when he learned that she had signed with Mack Sennett, even though Sennett was the biggest name in Hollywood at the time. For Sennett, Joey became Joanne or Joey McGuire, but she got tired of just standing around posing in bathing suits and took the first offer that came her way.

Joey went on to other studios and made Sunshine Comedies for Fox Films and Mermaid Comedies for Educational Pictures. "But later, when I started playing leads...they wanted me to have another name so, I dropped Joey and made Mack out of McCleery." She was also Art Acord's leading lady in several of his westerns. Art Acord was from Prattsville, later Glenwood, Utah and at the time they found a little common ground. She spent a year at Universal making these westerns. She then was engaged with the Cohn Bros. for a series called the "Hallroom Boys"- two-reelers that got her into feature films when CBC evolved into Columbia Pictures. Marion Mack married Louie Lewyn in 1923 and they stayed married for the next 50 years until Louis Lewyn's death in 1971.

A funny story about her husband is that he was the same employee who several years before had pronounced her a "lemon" at the Ince Studios. He didn't realize this until after he had spotted her among the bathing beauties on the lot, asked her to pose for him separately and then asked her out, although she was not allowed to date as yet. Finally, he gave her a ride home, asked her how she had gotten started in the movies, and heard all about the Ince Beauty Contest. Lewyn was from Houston, Texas and was in Hollywood freelancing snapshot images of the stars for studios until he got a permanent position at the Max Sennett studios where he met Joey.

Mack's most famous role was starring in "The General" with Buster Keaton as Annabelle Lee in 1927. They needed a girl with long curly ringlets and Marion had the right look. One version says that Norma Talmadge mentioned Mack's "right look" to the director's wife and the other version says that it was her hairdresser, Perc Westmore, who suggested her to the director. Anyway, she got called in to read for the part of a "dumb" southern belle, as she called it, primarily because of

Young Starlet

Marion and Clara Bow

Marion and Buster Keaton

"The General"

her long hair and ringlets. Unfortunately, she had just bobbed her hair, so Westmore made her a lovely ringlet wig to wear for the screen test and she got the part. She wore this long dark wig to film the movie in Oregon for the next five months. She and her husband agreed that they did not ever want to be separated for that long again, and so Marion Mack, alias Joey McCreery, alias Joanne McGuire, alias Joey Marion McCreery, retired from the movies.

Marion became her husband's production partner and made a few final appearances in such productions as 1927's "Alice in Movieland," which was a film short that she and her husband produced. She was also the star in "Carnival Girl" where she was allowed to write her own scenarios for the film and another film called "One of the Bravest." Mack achieved star status in a feature she had scripted herself entitled "Marion of the Movies." Lewyn produced all of the few features they did together after this including the series "Voice of Hollywood." Marion was the writer and coordinator for this venture as well as starring in all of them herself, but 1927's "The General" was her last feature film.

They then went to Paramount and made the series "Hollywood On Parade." They made musical shorts at Warner Brothers for the servicemen during World War II. One of their film shorts called "Fiesta in Santa Barbara," made in 1935, had her old friend Buster Keaton in it and a new rising star named Frances Gumm or Judy Garland. It was Louie Lewyn who showed his film short to MGM and launched Judy Garland's amazing career. In 1960, they sold their mansion and matching Rolls Royces and moved to Costa Rica to retire. Marion's husband died in 1969 and she moved back to Costa Mesa where she only kept in touch with two famous stars over the years, Clara Bow, until her death, and Rudy Vallee, until he passed away as well.

In the late 1920s, Lu and Joey invested $100,000 in a real estate venture in Whitley Heights with Harold Lloyd. They were doing really well and had John Barrymore, Mary Pickford and even Rudolph Valentino as their neighbors. "He (Valentino) had some great danes and walked around the hill every night. Lou used to walk with him sometimes." She also said that Howard Hughes used to come up and visit

Ralph Graves who was one of their neighbors. They would sit on the porch and talk to Lou. She says that she wasn't so sure about Hughes even though everyone said he was a millionaire. She thought he was a four-flusher! This investment had a lot to do with Joey choosing to become a real estate agent later on. But it was not until 1949 that she ventured into the business. She said she didn't want to end up sleeping on a park bench in New York. "It was wide-open spaces when we came down here. Matter of fact, when I came to Hollywood it was a small place too. You could look down Vine Street and see nothing but farms. Then how it grew with the movies." (Ibid, "...Co-star is Back," p.5)

When Joey Lewyn got her phone call at the age of 77, she thought it was a joke. "All these years ago no one knew about me. I guess everyone thought I was dead. But I can assure them I'm not. I had two heart attacks last year and had only a 10 percent chance to make it, but here I am." It was seven years ago that a man contacted her from of all places, Paris, France. This man was New Yorker, Raymond Rohauer, a film collector and historian who usually hunted for lost films. She finally admitted to Mr. Rohauer that she was indeed Marion Mack. He eventually convinced her to come out of seclusion and go on tour with him to promote Buster Keaton film festivals. Since their first meeting they had toured all over the United States, Canada, Japan, the Middle East and Europe.

On December 18, 1972, Marion Mack made a personal appearance at a Toronto screening of the 1926 "The General." After the screening of the film, she was also interviewed on-stage by Raymond Rohauer. It turned out to be the first time she had made an appearance concerning this film since it came out in 1926. She said that in 1927, no one connected with the picture thought much of it, including Buster Keaton, and the producers. She also said that she was practically out of the picture business when it came out and there were no personal appearances for this film. She said that this interview would officially be the first personal appearance she had ever made for this film and that she had even had to buy her own ticket to see "The General" in 1926. She and her husband attended the opening and were just as surprised as everyone else who had worked on the film when the audience responded so favorably. Audiences after this kept the money rolling in on this film and it became a smash hit in the twenties.

Once in a while she would attend a revival of the film but hardly anyone believed her when she claimed to have co-starred with Buster Keaton. When asked how she got the part, Mack replied that Keaton was looking for an old-fashioned girl to play Annabelle Lee. "Well Percy Westmore who was making up Norma Talmadge for some picture, heard from her, and of course she knew it because her sister Natalie, was married to Keaton. And Percy mentioned that he knew a girl with just the right hair, because he had been my make-up man on 'Carnival Girl.' And Norma said to Percy he should try and find out if I was available and he called me and first thing he said was: 'Well, Raymond, this was the year everyone was bobbing their hair and so only about a couple of days before I cut my hair short, too, and I told it to Percy and he said 'Don't worry, we'll give you a fall or something.'" ("an interview with marion mack" by Raymond Rohauer, 1972 screening of "The General," December 18, Bits & Pieces #6 – Marion Mack@Buster Keaton: From Butcher Boy To Scribe)

Mack wore a fall attached to her real hair to the interview with Keaton, Clyde Buckman and Lou Anger, the studio manager. She was hired on the spot and mentions that Keaton was pretty much a private person who hung out with his own pals and didn't do much with the Hollywood scene. It took six months to film the movie in the studio and then on location in Oregon. "First in the spring, around April, we stayed (in Oregon) for about four months. Then we went back to Hollywood in September to do the studio scenes, and in October we went back to Cottage Grove for some more outdoor shooting." They stayed in the only hotel in town and every morning they rode on the little train for an hour each way. It is the same train that is seen in the film. Buster had his own chef and he prepared a lunch meal for everyone so they could stay there all day. (Ibid, p.3)

Clyde Bruckman was a Keaton associate and could see the comic potential in a book called "The Great Locomotive Chase" based on an actual Civil War incident. Keaton took a bare outline of the story and made the book into a comedic film masterpiece. The elaborate vignettes, stunts and attention to historical detail, made "The General" equal to other comic epics of the time like "The Gold Rush" with Charlie Chaplin. In the film, Keaton plays Johnnie Gray, a railroad engineer in love with trains and a young woman named Annabelle Lee. His train, "The General" is stolen with Annabelle Lee on board. Keaton has to take another locomotive and go after the stolen train behind enemy lines. The long chase from south to north and back again climaxes in a dramatic battle scene – the single most expensive shot in silent film history. There is even a real locomotive which plunges through a burning bridge into the river below. With six months to film and hundreds of Oregon National Guardsmen as extras on the film, there were many difficult shots that had to be taken. ("Marion Mack-the girl in Buster Keaton's epic," by Rick Vanderknyff, Calendar: Entertainment Desk, The Los Angeles Times, November 15, 1987)

"The picture was shot without a real script. There was only an outline that they had to follow. You were told the scene but then you had to make up your own dialogue and if anyone had an idea they tried it and if they liked it they kept it in the movie. "Like when I have the scene when I'm getting on the train Buster is driving, and I'm still supposed to be mad at him for not enlisting, I made a big business out of admiring the medal my brother was wearing, and polishing his uniform buttons just to show how much I admired him, because of course I know Buster is looking at me. And this was not in any script, but they said it looked cute and so it stayed in." (Ibid, "an interview with Marion Mack," p.3)

In other incidents where they improvised, Mack mentions the scene where she is supposed to be feeding the fire for the train engine but she was totally ignorant of what to do. She saw a very small piece of wood and picked it up and threw it in. Keaton liked this and built his own comedy routine into it. He picked up an even smaller piece of wood, not more than a splinter, and threw it in, just to see what I would do. I threw it in and then he jumped on me like he was going to choke me. At the last moment he kissed me on the cheek instead. "I think I got that kiss more for thinking of the gag than for anything else."

Apparently, Keaton was a very shy person although some people mistook it for aloofness. Off screen, he often played baseball with his friends and even during the shooting of the film they would stop the train and play ball for a couple of hours delaying the shooting schedule. Natalie, his wife, traveled with him. Mack says that she had always worked with outgoing leading men and was quite comfortable with them, but with Keaton, he stuck to the business at hand. At first it was quite uncomfortable, she said, but later on he warmed up a bit and she found him to be a nice and warm person who was actually very humble. At the same time he started playing jokes on her and one of the first gags he pulled on her was to have a couple of guys grab her from behind and hang her upside down over a cake of ice. They left her there for an hour and it ruined her make-up. She got really mad and found Keaton and punched him in the eye. He had a shiner that delayed filming for a week. Later she realized he would go to any lengths for a laugh, but wasn't being mean about it at all.

So the practical jokes did not stop. "So he kept it up even after you hit him in the eye?" "Oh boy, he sure did. Like the time he found out that sometimes I used to like to take my bike and go up about three miles from Cottage Grove to a spot on the river that was nice and secluded, and there I would swim. So he and a couple of his buddies sneaked up after me one day, and found where I left my clothes and tied them up in such knots that I couldn't unravel them. And so I had to pedal back to Cottage Grove in my bathing suit, and this was quite a shocking thing to do in 1926, you simply didn't ride a bike in your bathing suit in those days, and a wet one at that!" (Ibid, "an interview with Marion Mack," p.4)

He also played tricks on her in front of the camera. She was supposed to have a double do all of her stunts and the girl was hired and there every day, so she relaxed about this. They ended up never using her stunt double once. In the scene where she was in a sack and Keaton was to step all over her, they were supposed to cut the scene, let her out, and put the stunt double in the sack in place of her. But before she knew it they were filming and Keaton was stepping all over her. She however, did not get hurt and she always supposed that it was Keaton's vaudeville training that had saved her. Another incident with the sack was when Buster was supposed to pick her up but with the stunt double inside it. Instead, he left her in the sack and she was ten pounds heavier than her extra so she got her revenge. In the same scene, when he emptied the sack, it was full of old army boots. Accidentally, his own shoes came off and he played the scene for all it was worth letting his own shoes fall into the other shoes and comically trying to find them. When Mack was back in the sack, Keaton had to carry her again and he did.

Another time Mack was told that all she had to do was be there to set up the scene and then they would cut to her extra and the extra would get drenched from the water tank by the train. This was when Buster grabbed the big spout and it came off accidentally the wrong way and they all got wet. He immediately realized it was funny, and so he turned around and put the spout in the right way but also pulled the wire that releases the water at the same time and Mack got soaked twice. Both times she was taken by surprise and it would never have looked that good if it had been pre-planned and if the crew had not kept the cameras running. Keaton always told the camera operators to keep the cameras rolling in case something unexpected happened, and they had another comedic scene take them by surprise.

Some of the scenes that were done in the studio were also quite difficult. There was a night scene where Buster and Mack were running away from the cottage. "We had to film on the back lot at night with rain and wind machines. We came in every night at about 7, and stayed until maybe 1 a.m., and this went on for three weeks, and each night we got soaked to the skin, it's a wonder we didn't catch pneumonia. But as I said we just never thought much about it. It had to be done, so we did it." There were a few indoor scenes that were actually done outside in Cottage Grove with fake walls but no ceiling. Most of the scenes were approved after one or two takes. The special gag scenes sometimes took five or six takes. The whole movie was tightly edited and Keaton took out all the scenes, which would have dragged the movie out too much." ("an interview with Marion Mack," Ibid, p.6)

"When "The General" premiered in New York, Lewyn said, it played next door to "The Jazz Singer," the first successful talkie. "The General" was moderately successful, but because it was so expensive to make it lost money. The studio began tightening up on Keaton, and his career began to decline. He died in 1966, not long after he was rediscovered by a new generation of film fans." (Ibid, "Marion Mack-the Girl in Keaton's Epic," p.1)

When asked at this time why she never made another full-length picture after making this one, Mack replied that she was really an old-fashioned girl at heart anyway. Her husband didn't want her to be away that long on location and she knew there would be friction if she stayed in the business. He also needed her to help him write the short films he was going to produce for Paramount and she said that she really enjoyed that work more than she did acting. She just began refusing all the offers she got and the calls soon stopped. She said that this probably worked since Lou and Marian stayed married, unlike so many divorces in Hollywood at the time. She said that she and her husband would have been about to celebrate their golden anniversary, but that he passed away two years before this happened.

When asked if she and Keaton remained friends after the filming, she replied that yes they did and that she saw him on and off over the years. On New Year's Eve the very next year, she and her husband attended a party in the nightclub where Buster Keaton put on one of his best tricks; the famous "slide." She always believed that he did this on purpose to embarrass one of the glamour girls of Hollywood named Peggy Joyce. He slid on his stomach right across the whole dance floor. Sitting there across the floor was Peggy Joyce in all her finery with her amazing and very expensive jewelry collection adorning her. Keaton slid right into her and pretended to get all mixed up with her and she ended up on the floor because Keaton had tipped her chair over. Mack always believed that he just wanted to take her down a peg or two.

Finally, Mack commented on Buster Keaton's excessive drinking. She said that when she knew him he never drank while working and he was still at the top of his profession. But later with his marriage on the rocks, there were not many of the kinds of films he wanted to make and he did begin drinking. Once Keaton and a bunch of his Hollywood friends paid a visit to the Lewyns but when they got to the house the Lewyns had gone off on a trip. Keaton and his friends stayed in their house anyway for three days straight. They ran the servants ragged, raided the liquor cabinet and put their house in a mess before they left. But by then, however, Joey and Lu seldom saw him. She said that she preferred to remember him when he was at his best. "When we were playing little jokes on each other up in Cottage Grove on our little train. That was the real Buster. Funny as hell on the screen and a true friend off the screen. They just don't make them like that anymore. He was the best of them all."

At this appearance and in this interview, Marion Mack's husband was still alive and Mack was not free to talk about what really happened to end her rise to stardom as an actress in 1927. Marion Mack probably would have been one of the greats had she continued in the business. Although she went on to be a successful screenwriter with her producer husband into the late 1940s, living only 40 miles from Hollywood, she never went back. Ten years after her husband's death she whimsically told the real events that had caused her to retire so early from films. Her husband, during the filming of "The General" had been so jealous that she had realized it would be either him or the movies. She chose her husband because he didn't want her to be away from home so much and always stuck to this story that it had been the better choice for her. All that acting and writing had become a chore for her, she said at the time, and she wanted a change, so she went into real estate and became quite successful at it. She and her husband owned several big houses and three Rolls-Royces, but she did miss her friends in Hollywood and everything changed about her lifestyle quite quickly. She had had to change her whole mode of living.

When she got all of these opportunities to travel and began getting book interviews and television show offers, Joey Lewyn began to admit that perhaps she had made the wrong choice in her life. She had had a good life but she began to see what she might have missed had she stayed in acting. She was getting seven fan letters a week from all over the world just since she had begun to tell her story to others and was happy to be promoting the old films without all the explicit sex and violence in so many of today's films. She also commented that comedies were the "international language" of film even today.

In 1989, Marion Mack was 87 years old. When asked if she missed acting at all, she simply said, "No." When asked if it ever bothered her that she never received any film credits for her work on all these shorts film series, she replied that eventually she did receive film credits for the "Mary and Sally in Hollywood" film short series that she did for MGM only after she insisted upon it. "The studios were always reluctant to acknowledge women who were behind the camera. They claimed a man's name on the screen is always more impressive to the public." After her husband passed away, Mack began sculpting and painting and eventually traveled the world. Her son, Lanny Lewyn, did bit parts in the movies in the thirties and then decided to become an electrical engineer. He had several patents for stereo-disc sound reproduction and lived with his family in a nearby town. He and his mother were quite close and his mother was still painting portraits of her close friends. (Whatever Happened To...? (Eleventh Series) "Marion Mack" by Richard Lamparski, Crown Publishers, Inc.: New York, 1989, pp.110-111)

Joey Marion McCleery Lewyn died on May 1, 1989, the same year that Lamparski's book came out when she was 87 years old. The best quote about her and her personality would be what she had to say about making movies. "Talk about movies, I heard movies were tough. They were, but I was lucky, like something out of a script itself. I walked right in and got a job. I don't think you could do that today. But I learned from the movies. They didn't stop me, nothing stops me." Still beautiful in her eighties, I think Marion Mack secretly enjoyed being rediscovered decades after her stint in the movies. As any one approaches old age, nothing is as satisfactory as being able to tell one's story and having an audience interested in that story. But one has to have lived a story worth telling, and Marion Mack did. (Ibid, "Marion Mack, Buster Keaton Co-Star, Is Back," p.5)

MORONI OLSEN

Chautauquas, the Voice in the Magic Mirror & Buffalo Bill

Moroni Olsen was one of those "bridge" actors who went from stage to silents to talkies to television with ease. He was nearly always the lead in his younger days on stage. Later, he was a character actor who played distinguished parts because of his classically trained voice and lofty appearance. Born in 1889 in Ogden, Utah, he was educated in the public schools and then went on to be educated at Weber State Academy, which was later renamed Weber State University. He never appeared in a high school play because there was no drama coach available. But in college he joined the extracurricular Weber Alumni Dramatic Association under the guidance of Ms. Cleghorn, a new English teacher there. He then went on to attend the University of Utah during the years that Maud May Babcock was bringing drama to the University setting. While Babcock was the founder of the speech and physical education departments at the University, her first love was the theater. She spent years not only developing a theater department but also championing the building of a theater on campus. Her work with elocution and voice training, graduated many a student ready to act on the stage. Moroni Olsen achieved great success as a stage actor using this voice training. And while Olsen went on to national and international fame both as a stage actor and in Hollywood, he returned many times to put on performance benefits for both Weber State University and the University of Utah.

Chautauqua was a word for traveling performances that spread across the country in the late 1800's, before traveling theatre troupes replaced these events. These became a permanent feature each summer

Moroni Olsen, Young Stage Actor
University of Utah Special Collections

In the Movies

in Utah beginning in 1911 through 1914, where players would perform at Glenwood Park each July. The Chautauqua movement itself had begun in 1874 as a weeklong Methodist Bible study retreat in New York State. The name itself came from the place where it had been held: Chautauqua Lake. These performances provided a wide variety of cultural and educational events that were considered self-improvement activities. Circuit entertainers brought seven-day programs with them bringing a variety of entertainments to these Chautauquas. By 1907, even preachers and bishops were encouraging the locals to embrace the idea. Ogden City organized Utah's first Chautauqua in 1911, but instead of engaging one of the traveling troupes, they created their own local and more permanent one that lasted for ten days. Besides lectures and speeches, several forms of amusement and entertainment were presented. Lectures, round table discussions, and a Junior Chautauqua for children offered presentations and classes. These Chautauquas also provided musical interludes, pageants, devotional services, and dramatic presentations. Various LDS choirs participated, as well as various other choirs. There was even a sign language presentation by the students from the State School for the Deaf and Blind. Local brass bands, soloists, quartets and ensembles performed. There were dramatic readings and at least three separate pageants. Over 200 school children marched into the park to perform drills, games and folk dances. Pipe and drum drillers from the Thistle and Caledonian Societies performed, and rousing patriotic speeches were given on the Fourth of July.

Olsen started out as a Chautauqua Utah tent-show performer in about 1913 when he was just out of school or perhaps still in it. In 1913, this Chautauqua began with a huge parade under the direction of David O. McKay on July 24th. That was the last year that Pioneer Day was included in the events. Maud May Babcock, the mother of theater in Utah, was the first to bring stage performances to Utah audiences in this manner in 1913. Her Dramatic Club put on several performances. By 1915, the local Chautauquas were abandoned for contracting with the various more professional circuits available across the country. Circuits were seven-day affairs complete with bell ringers, Swiss yodelers, small orchestras, instrumentals, vocal quartets, soloists, music from other countries, classical overtures and highlights from operas, World War I patriotic music, and selected dramatic presentations. Since theater in those days was still considered suspect, especially in rural America, the productions were always of a high moral character. This traveling theater movement eventually broke this reputation and cleared the way for more creative dramatic productions later on. But it also became a less wholesome affair, especially for Utah communities, so if the booked circuit Chautauqua failed to appear, small towns would pull together their local talent and put one on anyway. Because these Chautauquas became so popular all across the nation, many performers got a chance to expand their professional talents into a wider arena, performing on the stage. Several Utah performers also got this chance, including promoters who got to create their own Chautauquas in foreign countries such as New Zealand and Australia.

The peak year for Chautauquas was in 1924 when "an estimated 30,000,000 Americans sat in brown tents pitched near some 12,000 Main Streets and enjoyed lectures, music, drama, and other cultural items." After this, the third phase consisted of various attempts to revive the idea both nationally and locally, centered on a silent film showing. They became motion picture Chautauquas, with ice cream socials, bands and musical groups, all centered on a film to be shown. Vaudeville numbers were still performed and so were various other variety shows along with the film and various plays and dramatic presentations. Such cities as Parowan, Cedar City, St. George, Richfield and even Beaver, managed to have successful Chautuaquas for a while. This makes me wonder if Betty Compson was still living in Beaver and got her start there before moving to Salt Lake and playing her violin on stage. Beaver had one of the most successful Chautauquas in the state for many years in the 1930s, too late for Betty though, as she was a famous Hollywood star by then. By 1932, however, the Chautauqua circuit came to a rousing halt all across the nation. The Great Depression had a lot to do with this, as well as the emergence of more stage theaters available to the paying public and then later, movie theaters and other forms of entertainment, cheaper and better done. ("Chautauqua and the Utah Performing Arts" by Janice P. Dawson, Utah Historical Quarterly, Spring 1990, Volume 58, Number 2, pp. 140 and 141)

After World War I, Ogden native Moroni Olsen had become a well-known Chautauqua circuit actor performing in Canada and the United States. He then turned his attention to performing on the stage circuit in such plays as “Carson of the North Woods,” “Turn to the Right,” “The Taming of the Shrew,” and “Their Honor the Mayor.” He offered dramatic readings such as “The Terrible Meek.” Along the way, Moroni Olsen managed to get a lot of classical training as an actor. He studied in one of the leading dramatic schools back east and then spent some years in stock companies and was also a “platform” reader of plays. He worked with Maurice Browne and Ellen Van Volkensburg in their “Little Theatre” ventures in Salt Lake City and Seattle. He went to New York in 1920 to perform at the Carrick Theatre until 1921 and then performed at the Manhattan Opera House and the Provincetown Playhouse, returning home in the spring of 1922 to gather players together and form his own company.

From Chautauquas to circuit acting and then forming his own traveling company of actors, Moroni Olsen had a highly successful eight years of traveling the west and Canada when he formed a popular repertory company. The Moroni Olsen Players of the Circuit Repertory Company was formed in 1923 with Janet Young and Byron Foulger. Janet Young was always the leading lady for the plays and played opposite Moroni Olsen as the lead in most of the plays. Byron Foulger, known for his character parts in the movies and on television when he was older, got his start with these players and met fellow performer and future wife, Dorothy Adams there. They married and performed on the stage and the radio, but Foulger went on into films and television later. Janet Young was a gorgeous brunette and while I could find plenty of pictures of her, I was unable to find more of a biography. Dorothy Adams, on the other hand, had bit parts in several movies, her biggest known part being Gene Tierney's maid in "Laura."

This traveling company, The Moroni Olsen Repertory Company, had some daring and original ideas for the times. Their basic premise was that large and small towns in the west never got to see Broadway plays performed. They saw traveling vaudeville, road shows, local productions and picture shows, but never a Broadway show. They wanted to bring these productions to the people. Not many stock companies were in the west at the time and most of them were not very good. Olsen wanted to bring quality ensemble plays to the west, and that is exactly what he did. The company also refused to discuss individual performances, as there were no "stars" or "prima donnas" in the Olsen Company. So they were really the model for future playhouses where many film actors and actresses got their start especially in Southern California, such as the famous Pasadena Playhouse.

A Boise, Idaho paper put it the best way: "Moroni Olsen seems to have solved the big problem of the legitimate stage. The really good actors of yesterday were developed in the stock companies; but the movies put an end to stock success. A group of players cannot survive night after night at the same theater in the same city, changing from play to play and setting to setting—not in competition with the movies. It is not that actors are unwilling, but the public will not go. It prefers the finished fake of the cinema...Moroni Olsen, who is more than something of a genius as a dramatic director, has found it possible to make good actors, actors destined for big success, in circuit repertory. It is, in a way of speaking, the stock company on wheels. His players run around a circuit with one play, then run around the same circuit with another, then a third, and maybe a fourth and fifth. Good houses are thus assured. The company's welcome is never worn out. And financial success assures histrionic ability." ("The Moroni Olsen Company" – Chapter XXV and "On Tour with the Olsen Players" – Chapter XXVI from "Three Mormon Actresses: Viola Gillette, Hazel Dawn, Leora Thatcher," by Mavis Gay Gashler, thesis for the Department of Dramatic Arts, Brigham Young University, 1970, pp.128-147, p.129-130)

The company played where someone would sponsor them and members of the cast never signed contracts, their word of honor was considered one. They wanted nothing to do with unions because they nearly always caused them trouble and back in those days they were not required to join one. Another critic, George O'Neal of the Oregon Journal, said of this troupe, "Over a grocery store in Ogden, Utah, there is a loft heated by two coal stoves. In this obscure retreat was developed an idea that had commanded admiration through all the Northwest and supplied many play-hungry people with substantial dramatic fare. Commercial theatres, for reasons of one sort or another, had not been able to furnish this same intriguing drama. This loft is the home of the Moroni Olsen Players' Circuit Repertory theatre, an original experiment in play production that has in its conception the elements of a sound, vital, and permanent institution. With just $2,000 in capital, a wealth of intelligent enthusiasm, the loft and two coal stoves already mentioned, a buoyant spirit of adventure, a devotion to fundamental truth in drama and unfaltering courage, they have started the career of their unique theatre, the first circuit repertory theatre." (Ibid, "Three Mormon Actresses," pp.131-132)

O'Neal goes on to tell how they practiced in this tiny home in Ogden, produced five plays a year for both Ogden's Orpheum Theatre during their first season and then took those five plays on the road for 15 towns and cities in Utah and other western states. They produced one play per month in the winter while doing preliminary rehearsals for the next play to come. The communities contracted out to them and the actors received regular salaries, all equal with no "star" pay among them. In every place they performed, the audiences increased during the season. By the second year alone they were performing 25 plays instead of 15. Each member of the cast had additional duties to perform besides their roles in the plays and they had come from as far away as Maine and as far north as Vancouver. They did a lot with the barest of props and scenery and the cast members openly welcomed criticism as a healthy way to improve their performances. Members included many who went on to film and television careers besides Moroni Olsen himself: Leora Thatcher, Byron Foulger, Frank Rasmussen, Dorothy Adams, and Joseph Williams. Others that acted in this ensemble were: Ethel Baker Callis, Stanley Farnsworth, Stanley Russon, Edmund Greenwell, Alonzo Mosley, W.O. Robinson, Thatcher Allred, Sumner Cobb, Harry R. Allen, Clarence Talbot and William Kilby, and occasionally, Lila Eccles Brimhall.

Another reviewer from Twin Falls, Idaho commented on how every part of every character had a performer equal to the task. He also said that the intensity of the dramatic features made the company way above average in their performances. Their attention to detail in every performance showed the company's true appreciation of the dramatic arts. The words they spoke were clearly and loudly annunciated and yet delivered in a conversational tone for realism. He felt that the company presented their plays artistically and intelligently because of their director and also commented on how Mr. Olsen himself was an excellent actor with considerable background in classical training as an actor. In short, all of their reviews during the eight years they toured were highly complementary and even visitors from the east who saw their plays commented on their superiority to actors on the New York stage. The Moroni Olsen Players had proven to everyone that acting in America was not a lost art. Wherever they went in the west, they were treated with critical praise, many curtain calls, and much spontaneous applause.

When the last play was presented in 1930, "The Ship," many critics hailed this company's departure from the scene. But it seemed that the movie houses had finally won out and audiences were falling off to go and see a silent movie, which was cheaper and easier to do. In their last hurrah, one critic from Santa Barbara, Paul Whitney, said, "The Moroni Olsen Players have been eight years in the weaving of last night's magnificent performance. They think, react and respond in the same beautiful pitch. They are like a glorious constellation combining their light into one brilliant radiance. They have been called the Theatre Guild of the West. Certainly they have brought to the hinterland of the broad western states plays of unquestionable worth and beauty. In communities where dramatic appetites have been satiated with movies, they have developed a taste for something better. Certainly the Moroni Olsen Players have made a wonderful contribution toward the cultural advancement of many small cities...which have spoken drama only through having been subjected to it in High School auditoriums..." (Ibid, pp.140-141).

Moroni Olsen then headed for New York City after eight years with his own traveling troupe. After several successful seasons on Broadway and of course years and years of touring with one of the most prestigious stock companies that he himself had created, Moroni Olsen moved to Los Angeles where he directed the Pilgrimage Play, which was a very popular passion play which was staged every year before the arrival of motion pictures in Los Angeles. He really is the ideal representative of every facet in the history of the acting profession, because he even headed for Los Angeles before the town was known as "Hollywoodland" and acted on the stage there. When the silents arrived he was still a stage actor, but by 1934, he had begun his long run as a character actor. Olsen played Porthos in the 1935 version of "The Three Musketeers," and this performance has always been considered one of his best roles in the movies. It is said that while many of his roles were as a supporting character in less than star quality pictures, Moroni Olsen always managed to transcend the material handed him in films. He played in a Wheeler and Woolsey comedy in 1936, called "Mummy's Boys," which didn't offer him much in the way of a part. However, because he often played a madman or lunatic, he managed to ignite the screen even though it was a simple comedy. Eventually Olsen was on the New York stage in such productions as “Man of Wax” with Lenore Ulric, “Mary of Scotland” with Helen Hayes, “Romeo and Juliet,” and “The Barretts of Wimpole Street” with Katherine Cornell. He worked in Hollywood as well, appearing in over one hundred films, including “Brigham Young,” “Madame Curie,” “My Favorite Spy,” “Mildred Pierce,” and many others.

His aristocratic bearing and classically trained voice soon got him better parts. He played Buffalo Bill in “Annie Oakley,” in 1935 with Barbara Stanwyck, Robert E. Lee in “Santa Fe Trail” in 1940 with Errol Flynn and Sam Houston in 1952's “Lone Star” with Clark Gable. While he received an Oscar nomination for Best Supporting Actor for his role as Congressman Stone in 1949’s “Command Decision,” ironically, he is best known for being the voice of the Magic Mirror in Walt Disney's Academy Award winning full-length cartoon, “Snow White.” Here is a partial list of some of his films, although they seem endless, as more keep surfacing all the time. Some of them have not been seen for years and years, while others have been located and are being restored. Others are quite popular and shown all the time, although in every film, he plays either a secondary role or a minor role.

Olsen starred in “Annie Oakley” and “The Three Musketeers” in 1935, and all of the following movies were made just in 1936: “Mummy’s Boys,” “The Witness Chair,” “Two In Revolt,” “Yellow Dust,” “Grand Jury,” “The Farmer In The Dell,” “M’liss,” and John Ford's “Mary Queen Of Scotland” as John Knox with Helen Hayes as his co-star. In 1937, he made, (besides “Snow White and the Seven Dwarfs,”), “Adventure’s End,” and “Manhattan Merry-Go-Round.” In 1938, he was in “Kentucky” with Loretta Young and “Marie Antoinette” with Tyrone Power. In 1939, he performed in “Rose Of Washington Square,” “Susannah Of The Mounties” with Shirley Temple, “Allegheny Uprising” with John Wayne, “Invisible Stripes,” “Code Of The Secret Service,” and “Madame Curie” with Greer Garson. In 1940, he was in “If I Had My Way” with Bing Crosby and “Santa Fe Trail.” In 1941, he was in “Dive Bombers.” In 1942, his films were "Dangerously They Live," "Ship Ahoy," "Reunion in France," and "The Glass Key" with Alan Ladd and Veronica Lake.

In 1943, he played in a Howard Hawks production called "Air Force" and "Ali Baba and the Forty Thieves." In 1944 he did "Buffalo Bill" with Joel McCrea and Maureen O'Hara that was filmed in Paria, Utah; and another sort of "B" picture called "Cobra Woman," which has become a cult classic. In 1945 he performed in the Academy Award winning film "Mildred Pierce" with Joan Crawford, and in another movie entitled "Don't Fence Me In." In 1946, he did "A Night in Paradise" with Merle Oberon and Alfred Hitchcock's "Notorious." In 1947, he was in "Black Gold," "Possessed," "Life With Father," and a little known but newly discovered fifties detective forerunner, called "The Long Night," with Henry Fonda, where he played Buck Henry, the chief of police. Lovers of this genre were very excited to find this film and there are even web sites about it! In 1948, he was in "Calling Northside 777," and in 1949 I could find only one film called "Task Force," although I am sure he made more. In 1950, he was in "Father of the Bride" with Spencer Tracy and Elizabeth Taylor, "Life with Father," and "The Life of Emila Zola." In 1951, he made "Father's Little Dividend," and in 1952, he made "Lone Star."

In 1954, he starred with Lucille Ball and Desi Arnez in "The Long, Long Trailer," and probably would have had many more years in television through his association with them, perhaps in comedy had he not passed away that year. In 1952, which probably got him the part in the 1954 movie with the Arnezes, he played a scene stealing part as a judge in one of the "I Love Lucy" episodes. He was 65 years old and the episode was called, "The Courtroom." Olsen was always a devout Mormon and while in Hollywood, he taught Bible studies to young people in the Beverly Hills Ward for the Latter Day Saints Church. He was a lifelong bachelor and had only one nephew surviving him, Edward Olsen. "Olsen's last visit to Utah occurred in July 1954, when he spent several days in Ogden updating staging for the Pioneer musical "All Faces West," in which Igor Gorin, world-renowned operatic baritone, reprised his role of Brigham Young. He also narrated a pageant in the Salt Lake Tabernacle, featuring the Mormon Tabernacle Choir and San Francisco

Moroni Olsen as Buffalo Bill

Opera Soloist Carl Palangi. Olsen Died before Thanksgiving that year in Hollywood." He was buried in Ogden. ("Voice behind 'Snow White' Mirror, Ogden actor never forgot roots," Living History by Ardis E. Parshall, The Salt Lake Tribune, Sunday, September 28, 2008)

As I watched Moroni Olsen in these various parts, I was amazed at how hard he worked and how obsessive he was with his work. When one realizes all of the stage performances, often as the lead; plus running an entire company; along with all of the films in Hollywood somewhat later in his life, it is astounding! On top of this, he was one of the original founders of the famous Pasadena Playhouse and performed there in the evening. He also trained younger "up and coming" performers in plays and workshops there in the forties and fifties. They called themselves Eighteen Actors and among these were such stars as Dana Andrews, Victor Jory, Morris Ankum and of course, Moroni Olsen. As an independent theater, they produced over sixteen different plays. Moroni was active as both a performer and director in these productions and was the guiding force behind Hollywood's annual Pilgrimage Play each year.

It is impossible to speculate about how many more things he might have done had he lived any longer. On the other hand, perhaps all this hard work was what contributed to his early death. Although I was unable to find out very much about his private life - like so many Hollywood secrets it will remain so - his public life is an amazing tribute to acting in general. When you think about it, he saw it all: small town play productions, Chautauquas, vaudeville, burlesque, traveling troupes, stage acting in New York, radio, the silent screen years, the talkies and movie making in Hollywood in its peak years. He even witnessed, and took part in, the advent of television in its golden years! Moroni Olsen has to be considered one of Utah's long lasting acting and directing pioneers, more so than even the five decades of Loretta Young's career, considering that he began his career on the stage in 1910 or even earlier. He also spent more time in the west than any of his contemporaries, acting or performing or directing and running an acting company, as well as returning to his home state for so many benefit performances.

My favorite of all his roles demonstrates how handsomely striking and commanding an actor he was and that would be when he starred as Buffalo Bill Cody in Barbara Stanwyck's version of "Annie Oakley." He had an outfit to die for and a screen presence that didn't often show up in his later years when he was asked to perform mundane supporting roles as a doctor or lawyer or judge, etc. Had I been a teenager in the thirties, I definitely would have been a "groupie!" His amazing stage presence and his Shakespearean trained deep and commanding voice were all that it would take. I would have loved to have seen him on the stage in his younger days, and I think he was one of Utah's finest actors besides John Gilbert of Logan.

THE MORONI OLSEN CIRCUIT REPERTORY COMPANY PERFORMERS:

Dorothy Adams

Dorothy Adams married Byron Foulger and they both got their start with The Moroni Olsen Players. The rest of their story is told later. Most of the couple's major work was done on radio, film and television. They both had long careers as character actors, especially Byron Foulger, for which he is most famous, while Dorothy Adams is more famous for her stage work, especially with the Pasadena Playhouse. However, she also worked in radio and did do small roles in major Hollywood films. Her biggest part was as Gene Tierney's maid in the film "Laura." Byron and Dorothy Foulger are featured in Away from the Fold, Volume II.

Lila Eccles Brimhall

Lila Eccles Brimhall had a very long career on the stage but she also got her start with The Moroni Olsen Players. She remained mostly in Utah but did travel throughout the west with other acting troupes as well as teaching drama at universities. Her entire story is featured in Volume II.

Ethel Baker Callis

Ethel Baker Callis was born in Mercur, Utah, a little mining town in the west desert, on December 14, 1902. She was born to Alexander Steel and Margaret Owena Morgan Baker and raised partially in this little town. Callis got her start with The Moroni Olsen Players in Utah. She also trained under Maud May Babcock in the early 1920s. Callis toured with many other stock companies after the Olsen Players: the Ralph Cloninger Stock Company, the Henry Duffy Players, the Fulton Theater

Players, the Wilbur Dramatic Players, and the Wilkes Theater Players. Besides traveling with all of these stock companies, she also performed for entire seasons in various places in California and in Honolulu, Hawaii.

Eventually she settled in El Paso, Texas, where she had met her husband, David Marion Callis, who was also an actor. They were married on July 10, 1928 in Los Angeles, California. In 1929, the Callis's formed their own stock company, the Baker – Callis Players, so that they could settle down in one place for a while. But her husband died in the 1930s, and after his death in 1934, she found a job working for the Central Casting Welfare Department in Hollywood. She worked in this capacity at Warner Brothers Studio for the Central Casting Agency. Her job was to try to find work for the hundreds of actors and actresses that had converged on Hollywood during the Depression. Both she and her husband, being LDS, needed to have their marriage "solemnized" in an LDS Temple so that they could be married for time and all eternity. This ceremony was completed many years after David Callis's death in the Salt Lake Temple on September 6, 1955. Another man, usually a relation, stands in for the bridegroom and the couple is married again by "proxy."

Ethel Baker Callis
University of Utah Special Collections

Callis returned to Utah in December of 1941 and brought her two daughters with her. She acted in several University of Utah theater productions. In the early 50s, she got her Master's degree and worked on a thesis concerning the life of Maud May Babcock. This thesis was never completed, but some of the chapters are contained in the theater collection at the University of Utah. For the rest of her life she appeared in theater productions throughout the Salt Lake and Park city area and completed many LDS church "callings" or responsibilities as well. She was with The Silver Wheel Players in Park City and performed at the Silver Wheel Theatre there. She also performed on the University of Utah campus at The Pioneer Memorial Theater, the Babcock Theatre and in Kingsbury Hall. One of the old Orpheum Theaters downtown was converted into an LDS Theatre called The Promised Valley Playhouse and she also performed there.

Ethel Baker Callis also had her own radio program on KSL, as well as performing on local television programs throughout her career in Salt Lake City. She is best remembered for her many performances at the Silver Wheel Theatre in Park City. She had two daughters, eight grandchildren and 18 great-grandchildren. She passed away on April 21, 1995 at the age of 92 and was buried in the Wasatch Lawn Cemetery in Salt Lake City.

Women Actresses of the Moroni Olsen Players and One Admiring Actor
University of Utah Special Collections

Stanley Farnsworth

Stanley Farnsworth was born in 1906 in Circleville, Utah. He graduated from Bear River High School in Garland, Utah, a small town close to the Bingham Copper Mine just outside Salt Lake City proper. He not only performed with the Moroni Olsen Players early on, but he also performed with the O. L. Farnsworth Imperial players and later the Taylor Players. These stock companies traveled throughout Utah and the Intermountain West. He then moved to California where he lived for several years doing freelance radio work and writing and narrating children's stories. He became somewhat involved with the film industry and did appear in one Walt Disney production and in several other movies produced by the LDS Church. He earned his living in the agricultural business for many years.

Moroni Olsen Players
University of Utah Special Collections

When he returned to Utah, he produced over 20 commercials in Salt Lake City and was a lifetime member of the Salt Lake Advertising Club. He was on the Board of Directors for the Salt Lake County Fair and was involved in the media field for Utah farming for many years. He also wrote a column for the Salt Lake Tribune for 15 years and was the farm service director for both the Tribune and KSL radio. He also was an advertising representative for the owners of the Salt Lake Tribune. He was always a performer, either as an auctioneer in the stock and farming business, or as an actor in the theater. He was deeply involved in the Silver Wheel Theater in Park City with two of the other actors he performed with in The Moroni Olsen Players. He died after a long illness on August 27, 1976, at the age of 70.

Frank Rasmussen

Frank Rasmussen probably has the longest and most famous career after The Moroni Olsen Players. He was born on a farm in Millard County, Utah on January 21, 1886. His parents were Mormon pioneers, Hans Rasmussen and Sina Sorenson. His education was scattered, because he needed to help his father on the farm. He was able to finally get a high school diploma from Brigham Young University when he was 21 years old. He taught school for a while and then attended the University of Utah, where he got involved with the Maud May Babcock Varsity Players. He ended up alternating between farming, teaching, and acting throughout his life, and also ended up making some movies in Hollywood as well. He performed locally, while at the same time, teaching at such schools as Box Elder High School, Millard High School, and even the University of Utah.

His first job, he was hired as stage manager and actor at the Social Hall Theater in Salt Lake City in 1919. In 1920 he became a founding member of The Moroni Olsen Players and toured with them throughout the west, while at the same time, leaving it to tour with two other companies internationally. He toured with the Ellison-White Chautauqua Company to Australia and New Zealand, and the Swarthmore

Chautauqua on the East Coast. In the late 1920s, Rasmussen began working with the Weber College Little Theatre in Ogden, Utah locally. But by 1929 he was in California, working with the Major School of Acting at the Figueroa Playhouse. And by the 1930s, he was acting at the Pasadena Community Playhouse and the Hollywood British School of the Theater. It was during this time that he appeared in several motion pictures, while also working as an actor, director, dramatic director, and manager at these local theaters in California.

He appeared in three major motion pictures, the first two were in 1937, "The Toast of New York" and "They Won't Forget." He played a clerk in "The Toast of New York." In 1938, he played a spy chief named Beckstrom in the film "The Marines Go Forth." He was also able to have some other uncredited parts in movies in the 30s. He then went on a mission for the LDS Church, and when he returned he spent the rest of his life in Fillmore, Utah, teaching and farming. His involvement in the theater after this was sporadic. He taught for several years in Fillmore and then eventually returned to farming. Any involvement in the theater after this was working with productions for the LDS Church as a director and playwright in Fillmore. He died August 8, 1975 in Fillmore, at the age of 89.

Stanley Russon

Stanley Russon was born on February 4, 1905 in Utah. He graduated from the Latter Day Saints University and got involved with the Maud May Babcock players in the 1920s that often performed in the old Social Hall or on the University of Utah campus. He then performed with the Moroni Olsen Players. Eventually, over the next fifty years, he performed in many community theaters and University theaters such as the Babcock Varsity Theater, Salt Lake Theatre, the University Theater, the PlayBox theater, Pioneer Memorial Theatre, and the Lagoon Opera House. In the 1960s, along with Stanley Farnsworth and Ethel Baker Callis, he was on the executive board of the Silver Wheel players in Park

City. He was an actor, a director, and a playwright for local theater. He also did drama productions for his LDS Church.

Along with all his theater work, he earned his living as a jeweler in Salt Lake City for 49 years. He married Eileen Russon, who he met in the theater, and one of his daughters, Shirley Russon Ririe, was the co-founder of the Ririe-Woodbury Dance Company, which is a modern dance company. Stanley Russon won several awards throughout his career as an actor: the Best Actor Award from the Play Box Theater, the University of Utah Emeritus Honor Award in 1971, and the Robert Freed Memorial Award. He was a member of the Pioneer State Theater's Hall of Fame. He died on January 25, 1988 at the age of 83.

Leora Thatcher

Leora Thatcher went on to national fame as a leading lady who performed amazing character parts on the stage and on the radio. The rest of her story is told in Away From the Fold, Volume III.

Joseph Williams

Joseph Williams was born March 23, 1882 on a farm in Pleasant View, Utah. His family moved to Ogden and it was in that city that he received most of his education. He earned his living in many ways, in order to be an actor, but most of these ways were actually associated with the theater. He managed a music store, ran a costume shop, taught school, and served as musical director of the Utah State Industrial School. He performed in both community and LDS Church productions and often worked as a stage manager in many local theaters. He toured with The Moroni Olsen Players extensively in the early years, and then later performed with them intermittently until 1931. When the company disbanded in 1931, he gave up his acting, and became the stage manager for Kingsbury Hall on the campus of the University of Utah. He spent the next 53 years building scenery and stage sets for theater productions, until his retirement in 1953. He died in 1957 at the age of 74.

Janet Young

Janet Young was Moroni Olsen's leading lady in all of his plays. There are quite a few photos of them together and the sparks do fly, but no one knows if this is acting or a real romance. Since Olsen was a lifelong bachelor one does wonder if perhaps he had an alternative life style and perhaps had a partner, or if he simply never found someone to marry or was married to his career. Back in those days such things were rarely spoken of, so one can only speculate that he might have liked Janet Young more than we can suppose, or that they were very close friends, or that they really respected each other as actor and actress. For all of my searching I never was able to find more on Janet Young's life, who she married or if she had children, etc.

Harry R. Allen - Thatcher Allred
Sumner Cobb - Edmund & Virginia Greenwell
William Kilby - Alonzo Mosely
Gordon Nelson - W.O. Robinson – Clarence Talbot

Listed as other members of the eventually entitled Moroni Olsen Circuit Repertory Company which operated in the 1920s, I could find no information about these other actors, but did locate a few photographs of some of them. Perhaps their descendants have researched these actors and could tell us more.

Moroni Olsen & Janet Young
University of Utah Special Collections

VERA SISSON

Vera Sisson was born in Salt Lake City, Utah, on July 31, 1891 and died in Carmel, California, August 6, 1953. Her grandparents came from Blackhawk, Colorado and her parents Charles W. and Carrie L. Frehan moved to Utah just before or just after she was born. This probably explains the varied reports on her birth place being either Utah or Colorado. She started in films as an extra but landed a bigger part in the 1908 film "The Helping Hand," when she was only sixteen years old. Later she landed the starring role opposite J. Warren Kerrigan who was a matinee idol of the times. The chemistry was unmistakable and she skyrocketed to fame making several films with Kerrigan. She made a series of outdoor melodramas in 1915 and 1916 with Kerrigan. However, after this, she was once again playing supporting roles. She continued as a character actress and never again had starring roles in the movies. She was an incredibly beautiful and dainty young woman who managed to pose nude a few times probably to pay the bills but in very artistic and modest poses for some modeling jobs when she first came to Hollywood.

Vera as a Young Starlet

A Playing Card Portrait

10 THE UNIVERSAL WEEKLY

"THERE IS A DESTINY"

Victor Drama, with J. Warren Kerrigan, George Periolat and Vera Sisson.

JACK, THE YOUNG DOCTOR, SUDDENLY REALIZES THAT HE LOVES THE LITTLE FISHER MAID.

Jack, a young doctor, is spending his vacation with friends at the seaside. Jeanne de Jean lives on a lonely island with her grandfather. Under guise of a boatman, Jack meets the girl and wins her love. A jealous friend turns the grandfather against him. Then Jack makes a heroic swim across the channel during a storm and saves the sick grandfather. All ends well.

Western "There Is A Destiny"

Vera Sisson's first films were made in 1913: "Helen's Strategy" and "The House in the Tree." She is mentioned in 1914 as being seen with many of the early Hollywood legends at a charity affair in New York City where hundreds of men brought flowers, candy and programmes just to get to see or even speak to the many young starlets and Hollywood legends of the times. Mabel Norman, the Gish sisters, Wallace Reid, J. Warren Kerrigan, Tom Mix, D. W. Griffith and a host of others were present as well. She also made seventeen films in 1914 and as mentioned before, films then were shot in two or three days, which accounts for so many.

In 1915 she made ten films, and in 1916 she made five films, and in 1917 she only made two films. She only made one film in 1918 called "The Married Virgin" but this was her big break-through part because she starred opposite Kathleen Kirkham and Rudolph Valentino. Valentino played a suave gigolo trying to woo an unhappily married wife of a well-to-do businessman. But he also had an ulterior motive in mind, trying to finagle a large sum of money from the family. The film also came to be billed under the title "Frivolous Wives." There are some great photo stills of Valentino sitting in a car while romancing the actress Kathleen Kirkham, a married woman in the film, with whom he is having an affair. This particular photo is sometimes mistakenly identified as being actress Vera Sisson because she played second lead to Kirkham. When the couple's plot to blackmail the woman's rich husband falls through, Valentino turns to Vera Sisson, who is his lover's daughter. He tells her that in return for her hand in marriage, he will save her father from a life in prison, because her father has suddenly lost his fortune. But the count's second plot is foiled by his former lover, who is also Vera Sisson's protective and scorned mother.

In 1919, Sisson made four films: "Experimental Marriage," "The Veiled Adventure," "The Heart of Youth," and "His Official Fiancé." The only other important film project she participated in during the years after this was a 15 episode serial called "The Avenging Arrow" in 1921 and this film is presumed lost. Her last film was in 1926 called "Love 'Em And Leave 'Em," by this time she had made eighteen films altogether.

"Love "Em and Leave "Em" starred Evelyn Brett, Louise Brooks and Lawrence Gray. Vera played Mrs. Whinfer in this romantic comedy.

In her early years, Vera also managed to star opposite Lon Chaney Senior in "For Cash" in 1914 and another film only a year later, "The Trust." The synopsis of this film "The Trust" and another one she was in, entitled appropriately "Paradise Garden," are quite interesting and show how this was an era of total freedom in filming before quite a few subjects in film became forbidden for many years due to the Hays Office. In "Paradise Garden" there was a lot of brief nudity, partying and "adult situations." It was even termed a "debauchery amongst the rich and famous." Virginia Rappe and Harold Lockwood starred in this film with nude female dancers and water nymphs. The hero gives a series of wild parties at his Long Island estate and tries to seduce Rappe several times. And of course, Virginia Rappe is infamous now as the young actress that Fatty Arbuckle supposedly raped and then left for dead, when she suffered a ruptured bladder at a drunken party in 1921 and no one helped her. After her death, the subsequent trial and publicity ruined his career. This film is the only surviving one of Virginia Rappe's career in Hollywood and Vera Sisson was the only other female lead in the film, an eerie foreshadowing of events, although now many believe Arbunkle was innocent of this crime.

In "For Cash," Lon Chaney Senior billed as Mr. Brown, is Sisson's father. He refuses his daughter's request to marry the young man she loves because he is an artist and it is Chaney's dying wish as well. Vera is put in the custody of his attorney and the hero falls into a disreputable lifestyle because he is heartbroken. The hero is painting pictures for another man who cannot paint but wants the notoriety and is a "cad" to boot. The movie ends with an assault scene where the villain is attacking Vera and the hero is able to rescue her upon hearing her screams. They finally wed each other, but the assault scene is quite graphic. Vera Sisson retired from films in 1926 and was already married to actor/producer Richard Rosson. They remained married until 1953 when Rosson committed suicide. It is true that Rosson committed suicide because he was despondent over his health problems and could no longer deal with the emotional and physical pain that these problems were causing him.

Richard Marquez Rosson was born in 1893 and began his career as an actor, while later becoming an assistant director for "A" movies and a director for quite a few "B" movies. He was in over 100 films as a silent actor and began his acting career under the name Dick Rosson. Some of his more famous early silents include "The Patchwork Girl of Oz" in 1914, "Number Please?" in 1916, "The Secret Garden" in 1919 and "Polly of the Storm Country" in 1920. He and Vera had parts in many of these early movies together and eventually fell in love and married in 1921. Russon had done little directing except for one 1917 film, but by 1926 he had gotten his big break in directing when Gloria Swanson had a big fight with her director at the time, Lewis Milestone, on the set of "Fine Manners." He was called in to direct in Milestone's place and the picture was successful enough to win Russon a long-term contract with Famous Players-Lasky. He also directed several other famous silent stars in films such as Louise Brooks.

Vera Sisson, "The Married Virgin"

Richard Rosson, Director,
Husband of Vera Sisson

But in 1929, Russon directed his first talkie film and it flopped. This set his career back as it did for many actors and those behind the scenes while they tried to transition to sound films. Director Howard Hawks came to his rescue when he asked Russon to be assistant director for the 1932 film "Scarface" which has become a cult film today. Russon continued to work for Hawks in many capacities besides assistant directing for the next few years, while at the same time directing many "B" films himself. An interesting bit of trivia about Richard and Vera Sisson Russon is that in 1939 while they were in Vienna, Austria filming a movie, they and two British Nationals were arrested by the Gestapo for supposedly filming a military hardware warehouse. They were detained as spies and held in jail for 34 days before they were officially released.

Russon's last movie as a director came out in 1943. It was a World War II movie entitled "Corvette K-225" and while the credits said that Howard Hawks was only the producer of the film, most people knew that he had helped Russon direct it as well, even though Richard Russon was given full credit as the director. Apparently Vera retired from acting in 1927 and Richard retired from directing in 1944. I don't know what either of them did after this and there are no reports of them having any children, although they could have living out of the limelight as they did. After a difficult illness, Richard Russon apparently figured out a way to kill himself as he died of carbon monoxide poisoning in May of 1953 only a month or so after his sixtieth birthday. Just one year later Vera took an overdose of barbiturates and was only 62 when she died. Perhaps she missed her husband so much that she couldn't live without him. Or perhaps they both had drug addiction problems? Whatever the reasons for Vera, loneliness may have been a huge factor in her decision to take her own life.

There are a few striking similarities between two Utah born starlets, Ora Carew and Vera Sisson, which are intriguing. They both retired from films around the same time, they both died at 62, they were both born in Salt Lake City, and although Sisson started earlier in her career, they both had about the same amount of success in Hollywood. They possibly each had only one husband and both were petite with light brown hair. Perhaps they had even more in common than this, or perhaps Carew had a more sedate life after Hollywood than obviously Sisson did. Did they know each other in Hollywood? Perhaps so, because it has been my experience in doing all this research that Utahns quite often did gravitate to each other over their years there. It is possible they made one picture together, but I could not verify this.

MACK (MORONI) SWAIN & CHARLIE CHAPLIN

Mack Swain was born in Salt Lake City on February 16, 1876 and died in August of 1935. His parents were Robert Henry Swain and Mary Ingeborg Swain and he was born into a Mormon household with his real first name being Moroni. He began his career in vaudeville as a stage actor and managed his own troupe for twenty-two years before trying his hand at Hollywood. He toured with stock companies, vaudeville troupes and minstrel shows where he began developing his persona of a giant, jovial clown. He was six feet two inches tall and weighed 280 pounds. He was married to Cora Claire King for a short while but no one seems to know when he married or how long he was married, except that she was probably four years younger than him as she was born in 1880.

He broke into silent comedy films when he signed with the Mack Sennett's Keystone Kops Studio in 1913 and became one of their regulars. In 1914, he starred in his own comedy series entitled "Ambrose." This is where he really developed his wide-eyed character wearing a top hat and a huge mustache to play off his fellow comedian Chester Conklin, who played "Mr. Walrus" in the series. Their best film together in the series was a one-reeler entitled "Lose, Speed & Thrills." Swain also did several films with Roscoe "Fatty" Arbuckle such as "Fatty's New Role" in 1915. He used his Ambrose character in Arbuckle's films as well. He then played at least one comparatively straight role in the movie "Tillie's Punctured Romance." He did one role with Syd Chaplin in 1916 called "Gussie the Golfer" and another one with Gloria Swanson in the same year called "The Pullman Bride." Many famous silent actors got their start with Keystone including Charlie Chaplin, Roscoe "Fatty" Arbuckle and Mabel Normand.

After leaving Keystone in 1917 and having made 26 films with Chester Conklin, he worked with Chaplin imitator Billy West at Bull's Eye studios in a few films and then made the minor series "Poppy Comedies" for Charles A. Frohman's "Frohman Amusement Corporation." Two shorts of this series survive "Heroic Ambrose" and "Innocent Ambrose" both from 1920. Swain directed "Innocent Ambrose" himself. The 1917-1918 flu epidemic pretty much ended Frohman's company due to the dropping off of audience attendance. Billy West made more than 20 silents from 1917-1918, imitating Charlie Chaplin's "The Tramp" exactly.

After this, Swain worked for several minor studios in silents and had a disagreement with one of the studio's producers and was blacklisted. He had taken his "Ambrose" character to the L-KO Kompany but it soon went under. Chaplin was a good friend of his and rescued Swain and his career. It eventually turned out that he had his greatest success in several of Chaplin's silents. Officially, his typecasting had put him in this rut, but unofficially, the studio boss had so much power in Hollywood that many studios were afraid to hire him. Fortunately, Chaplin at that time had more power than any studio boss, so in 1921, Swain began working at First National studios with Charlie Chaplin. Soon, he was playing supporting roles for Charlie Chaplin and used his own created character again, "Ambrose." Ambrose had now become a huge man with a giant bushy mustache, bowler hat and a modeled spit curl in the middle of his forehead.

However, while Charlie Chaplin's "Little Tramp" character made him a super star, Mack Swain's Ambrose character began to work against him, giving him too many typecast parts over and over again. Chaplin helped him out of this rut by casting him as the villain in the 1925 film, "The Gold Rush" where he could play a different type of role. After all, Mack Swain had contributed to Chaplin's world famous comedic character. Chaplin collected his spontaneous garb as he states, in trying to create a vagrant with refined manners but with many opposites in his clothing, large pants, small hat and vest, large shoes, etc. The only thing

Mack Swain without Make-up

Mack and Charlie Chaplin

Keystone Kops

"The Gold Rush"

Chaplin owned in what he created was the whangee cane. Arbuckle gave him his father-in-law's bowler hat, Chester Conklin gave him the little cutaway tailcoat, Ford Sterling gave him the size fourteen shoes, and Mack Swain gave him some crepe hair that he fashioned into a mustache. While Chaplin is considered the genius behind silent film, but especially comedy, all of these comedians knew each other in those times and many of them were close friends starting out.

In the early twenties, Mack Swain played character parts in many Chaplin films such as "The Idle Class," "Pay Day," and "The Pilgrim." But he is most remembered for one of Chaplin's most famous films "The Gold Rush" released in 1925, where he played "Big Jim McKay" and managed to steal a scene or two. In the later twenties he was in such films as Al Christie's "The Nervous Wreck" in 1926, "Mockery" with Lon Chaney in 1927 and "The Last Warning" with John Boles in 1929. He also starred with Mary Pickford in "My Best Girl" and John Barrymore in "The Beloved Rogue." Swain then got other offers for different parts as the talkies were coming in. He appeared in "Stout Hearts and Willing Hands," a picture that was nominated for an Academy Award in the Best Short Film category. This film has many of the early comedians in it such as Bobby Vernon, Hank Mann, Harold Lloyd, Chester Conklin and Ben Turpin.

Mack Swain appeared in "Gentlemen Prefer Blondes" in 1927 and "The Sea Bats" in 1930. He also starred in some Mack Sennett sound shorts in the early thirties. He made his last films, "Midnight Patrol" in 1932 and "Bad Boy" in 1935. Up until then he was a favorite of audiences everywhere but somehow the talkies became the death of his film career. Here are a few titles of some of his other films: "Hands Up!" "Whispering Pines," "The Lizzies of Mack Sennett," "The Immigrant," "The Rink," "His Prehistoric Past," "The Bank," and "The Shamrock and the Rogue." He also starred in one of John Wayne's early cowboy movies and someone either with the same name, a relative, or with film clips of the real Mack Swain's earlier work, used his name in a movie called "The Funniest Man in the World," made in 1967. Maybe this movie was fashioned after his life; someone will have to enlighten me as to this strange twist of events.

Mack Swain was a very mysterious man and not much is known about his private life. He died at the age of 69, right after making a film. He was married once to a woman named Cora King, but the information states that they had no children. In real life, without his make-up on, Mack Swain was actually a fairly handsome man, although a bit portly. He died of heart failure in Tacoma, Washington on August 25, 1935. He was only 59 years old. In his career he appeared in 107 films from 1913 to 1932, making an average of five short films during his peak years from 1914 to 1920. In 1914 he made a record 70 of these films.

But it was Chaplin who came to Swain's rescue when his career seemed to be going nowhere. It is hard to imagine what these two had in common besides silent film and comedy, but they did indeed like to work together and had a unique chemistry as comedians. Charlie Chaplin came from a very terrible background starting out with his parents in England in the music halls and stage plays. His mother was a singer/actress who struggled with mental illness and his father was also a singer/actor, but his parents separated when he was 3 years old. He and his half-brother lived with his mother when she was not in an asylum and then they were sent to live with his alcoholic father and his mistress. Charlie was then sent to a boy's school and then his father died when he was 12. By 1901 he was living with and performing with a troupe of young male dancers and soon got his big break with a role in a stage production. The rest of his tale is fascinating history, especially his perchance for romancing and marrying many young girls, probably looking for a mother or sister, or just love itself. He, of course, is a legend now.

GRANT WHYTOCK

Grant Whytock was Ora Carew's brother. He was also a fellow actor in the early days of his career. He was born June 18, 1894 in Salt Lake City, Utah. He and his sister were both educated at Rowland Hall Episcopalian School in Salt Lake City. In the early days of his career, he was on the "miscellaneous crews" for many films. By 1910, he had gotten a few bit parts as an actor but eventually made his way into the film editing department of a studio. He became a film editor, producer, and worked in the editorial department on many, many films. By the twenties he was editing films for several editorial departments in various film companies. He also tried his hand at film production as an assistant producer in the forties, as well as a few films in the fifties and sixties. He tried freelance editing from time to time as well. He had a long and very prolific career in Hollywood as a film editor from 1917 to 1970. His first film was made in the United Kingdom under the title "Darlings of the Gods" and also released in the United States under the title "Sirens of the Sea."

He edited several very important films in the twenties such as "The Four Horsemen of the Apocalypse" in 1921, "The Prisoner of Zenda" in 1922, "Scaramouche" in 1923 and helped edit the 18-reeler, "Greed" in 1924, for which his work was not credited. He is credited with editing three films in the silent teens and thirteen films in the silent twenties. In the thirties he edited another thirteen films including "The Unholy Garden" in 1931, "I Cover the Waterfront" in 1933, "The Emperor Jones," "The Count of Monte Cristo" in 1934 and "The Man in the Iron Mask" in 1939. In the 1940s he edited five films but turned his attention

Actor, Film Editor, Brother of Ora Carew

Lifetime Achievement in Film

to assistant production for another seven films including "Kit Carson" in 1940, "Cheers for Miss Bishop" in 1941, and "Brewster's Millions" in 1945. In the late forties, fifties and early sixties he produced some films under the title associate producer, including "The Return of Monte Cristo" and "The Black Arrow" in the late forties; "Lorna Doone" and "The Steel Lady" in the fifties and five films in the sixties, the most well-known was a western, "40 Guns To Apache Pass."

At the same time he was still editing many other films, nineteen films from 1934 to 1968, most of them "B" movies. The most interesting to me after the forties are the movies "The Mad Magician" in 1954, "It, the Terror From Beyond Space" in 1958, and "Invisible Invaders" in 1959. He seems to have edited a lot of "B" westerns, a few Sci-Fi thrillers and some film noir detective stories. Besides these three genres he did a miscellaneous mixture of other subjects such as a few romantic comedies. His last editing job was on a television film, "The Christine Jorgensen Story" in 1970. He made two appearances in Hollywood documentary films that had been filmed before his death in 1972. "The Man You Loved to Hate" and "Hollywood: A Celebration of the American Silent Film" which were both released in 1980. He was married to Leotta Whytock who was also a film editor for many years. He died on October 17, 1972 in Los Angeles, California at the age of 78.

STANTON WILLIAMS - SILENTS CHILD STAR

▸•◂

ESTHER WILLIAMS – SISTER SUPER STAR TECHNICOLOR FIFTIES

Stanton Williams

In the beginning, Esther and Stanton's family had very close ties to Utah. However, Esther's mother never even knew her three oldest siblings because they died before she was born. Her mother, Bula Myrtile Gilpin came from a family of twelve children with nine surviving siblings.

Portrait of Stanton Williams

Her father had suffered a war injury in the Civil War, which necessitated the family moving out on the dry prairies where his rheumatism was not so painful. The family moved to Fort Dodge, Kansas. A boy not much older than Bula had spoken for her from a neighboring farm when she was only thirteen years old. His name was Louis Stanton Williams. They carried on a faithful courtship for the next nine years. Both sets of parents were upset about this. Louis's parents wanted him to stay and run the farm and Bula's parents did not want their daughter to marry a farmer. Bula's mother said she would rather die than let this marriage take place.

So, Bula and Louis had to elope to be married. They ran away together and were married on June 1, 1908 and then set out for California. It was by chance that they ended up settling in Salt Lake City, Utah. It was simple; they had run out of money. And they ended up living in Salt Lake until Stanton was discovered as a stage and then movie star. So this means that from 1908 to probably 1917 or 18, they continued to live and work in Utah while having three more of their children. Stanton was six when he was discovered at the Wilkes Theatre in Salt Lake, so the family probably did not move until around 1918 at the latest, to Los Angeles. The movie version of the stage play "Eyes of Youth" was released in 1919 and though Stanton's part was small, it was his first full feature film. Stanton had a natural talent for mime and drama and stole every scene he was in.

Stanton Williams was the oldest brother of Esther Williams. He was born on September 4, 1912 in Salt Lake City, Utah. Their father was a sign painter and their mother was a housewife. Esther was the youngest child of five, but it was her brother Stanton that started the whole family interest in the movies. The family was Christian Science, or at least their mother Bula was and this was most definitely their downfall concerning Stanton. Stanton was "discovered" when he was six years old. Esther Williams says in her book: "Stanton had a charisma, a personal magic that from his earliest years charmed everyone from stage luminaries to Hollywood producers. The beginning of his career was classic, the stuff legends are made of." (Million Dollar Mermaid by Esther Williams, New York: Simon & Schuster, 1999, p. 18).

Marjorie Rambeau & Stanton

In 1919, Marjorie Rambeau was appearing in the play "Eyes of Youth" at the Wilkes Theatre in Salt Lake City with a touring stock company. It was she who discovered Stanton and helped him begin his career in the theater. Ms. Rambeau was not happy with the company's chosen child. They were rehearsing a scene where Rambeau was to tell the tragic story of the lost princess and the child actor was supposed to cry a lot. She looked down and not a single tear was in the little boy's eyes. She told the director that she could not work with a child who could not cry on cue. They had been rehearsing for hours and still no tears were streaming down his face, while Ms. Rambeau was crying like crazy.

Stanton was in the theater at the rehearsal because his father, Lou, had gotten a job sign painting. He had a small studio next to the theater where he steadily painted the theater's lobby cards and posters as each new production came to town. "My brother Stanton, fascinated with the theater, would sneak through the stage door, hide in the wings, or curl [up] behind the plush velvet seats to watch the rehearsals." (Ibid, p.19).

Ms. Rambeau, in desperation, spotted Stanton hiding in the theater seats and pointing at him shouted at the director that she thought this kid could probably do better than what she had to work with. The director responded by asking Stanton to come up and sit by Ms. Rambeau while she told the story of the fairy princess to him. "Stanton's big, beautiful eyes—he was a glorious angelic child—opened wide, the tears came streaming down, and soon he was sobbing and Rambeau was sobbing. She turned to the director and said through her tears, "Oh, my god, this child is so wonderful; I have to have him." (Ibid, p.20).

Marjorie Rambeau, Actress who Discovered Stanton

The director quickly called their father from the lobby and signed Stanton on the spot. Stanton cried on cue for every performance. In the story Stanton played a not very bright boy who meets a fairy princess and gets carried away to a magical kingdom and night by night Marjorie Rambeau fell more and more in love with this little boy. She simply adored him. She worked on Stanton's parents all during the time the production was in town to get them to allow him to join their stock company. Finally Stanton's parents agreed to allow him to go on tour with the stock company and they certainly needed the money. Bula accompanied Stanton on tour.

They went to Seattle, Denver, San Francisco and Los Angeles after they left Salt Lake City. He appeared on the stage with another child actress, Mary McAllister in "The Little Princess" and received rave reviews such as '...a wee bit of a youngster who hails from the state of Utah and now making his first traveling tour...a bright future for this little fellow.' In the "Eyes of Youth" play, however, Rambeau had more lines written for Stanton's part and when a movie studio wanted to make a film version of the play she insisted that Stanton continue to play his part in that version. But while Stanton did get to play the part in the movie, Clara Kimball Young unfortunately replaced Marjorie Rambeau.

Marjorie Rambeau actually wanted to adopt Stanton, because she was so in love with this little boy. And that was what – among many other things – made Esther's mother go on tour with her own boy. Rambeau would not have been the best of mothers anyway. Her mother, Lillian Bernette, was one of the first female doctors in the west, who also divorced in the day when this was a very difficult thing to do. In 1898, Lillian took her two daughters to Nome, Alaska. There she tried to start a hospital, but the people there would just not accept a female doctor. With her mother unable to make money, little Marjorie Rambeau dressed as a boy and performed in the local saloons to bring in money for the family so they could earn their way back to the states.

Finally, when she was discovered to be a girl, she was signed to a vaudeville tour of Alaska. She became, just as Esther Williams did, the breadwinner for the family. She was soon being called the "Bernhardt of the Klondike," and performed in plays, as well as giving dance and drama lessons in a little hall, which the family rented out. By then the family had enough money to return to the states. And while no one knew she was only 12 years old at the time, the miners gave her a silver-tipped ermine coat as a farewell present. Unfortunately, little Marjorie had also been introduced to alcohol, while working in the saloons. She joined a theatrical troupe in 1910 in Los Angeles, and by 1913 she was on Broadway. However, by 1923, she had become an alcoholic and was losing many theater offers. To her credit, she did fight to overcome her addiction and did for many years remain sober, but the toll on one so young and with so fast a growing up period, must have been very heavy.

Rambeau went from child star to Broadway leading lady soon after, and then went on to star in some silent films. She continued to work in Hollywood, but more as a supporting character by the time the talkies arrived. She was nominated for a Best Supporting Actress role in a film called "Primrose Path." She got some Tugboat Annie films and other character films and in 1953 she was nominated again for an Oscar in "Torch Song." She was married three times, first to actor, director, producer and writer Willard Mack from 1913 to 1917, then to actor Hugh Dillman from 1919 to 1923, and finally to her childhood sweetheart in 1930. This man had proposed to her many years ago, when they were both too poor to get married. She remained married to him for the rest of his life. By the time they married they were both well off. In 1945, her sister and she were in an automobile accident. Her sister was killed and she barely survived. She made only a very few films after this and moved to Palm Springs in 1957, with her ailing husband. She never had any children and died on July 15, 1970.

By this time Stanton had signed a contract with Harry Garson who was the production manager of Equity Pictures and Stanton was now headed for silent movie stardom as a child actor. Garson Studios helped the family to move to Los Angeles and their father found a small piece of land surrounded by truck farms for one hundred dollars. For an additional hundred dollars he got the shell of a small house constructed on the property. Esther's mother went to California carrying her new baby David. A short while later June and Maurine, the older sisters followed. Pretty soon the whole family was there together, all of them placing their dreams and financial success on the rising stardom of Stanton, the chubby, cherubic youngster. All the Hollywood Studios wanted him and he was acting at several of them.

And in August of 1922, Esther Williams was born in the living room of this small house where the whole family was sleeping until they had enough money to add on bedrooms around it. By the time Esther was born her mother had had enough of childbearing and rearing. She handed over the raising of Esther to her fourteen year old daughter Maurine. Bula became Esther's grandmother instead. And Stanton, as he grew up, began turning into a frail and sensitive young man of sixteen.

"The day he died…My mother came out of the house and said, 'Be quiet. Stanton is ill.' We'd all had a late Sunday lunch and eaten heartily, but he had complained of feeling funny. Mother suggested that he take a warm bath and get into bed. Later that evening, he told us that his stomach was numb. My father called the doctor. Bula called the Christian Science practitioner. In the process of normal digestion his intestine had developed a kink, and his colon had burst. The doctor never arrived; he got lost in a Los Angeles fog; the practitioner was out of town; and even the fire department couldn't find our house. By 9:30 that night, Stanton, alive and happy hours before, was dead." (Ibid, p.22).

When Stanton signed a contract at six years of age, Bula was carrying Esther's older brother David, but it didn't matter, Stanton was the family ticket to California. Esther, the fifth and last child, wasn't wanted according to her autobiographical account. Her mother took hot mustard gas, went horseback riding and even jumped off a chest of drawers, but Esther was born happy, healthy and laughing. In the meantime, Bula traveled with Stanton. But by the time Stanton was 16 he was frail, sensitive and contemplative, although he still had a lot of plans for the future. Eight-year-old Esther absolutely worshiped her older brother.

Esther's parents were never the same after that evening. "Stanton had been our pride, our hope, our golden prince. His talent, his good looks, his ambition had been our only chance to break out of poverty; yet given us courage and kept us altogether. Now he was gone, somebody had to take his place or we would all be lost. My brother David was frail and asthmatic. My sister Maureen suffered from emotional problems that I couldn't understand at my age, but which made her sadly overweight from compulsive eating; my other sister June was a malcontent. My mother took refuge in her spirituality. While my poor father was barely able to bring home enough money to keep food on the table. So I looked about me and realized that none of them could replace Stanton as the rock on which the family stood, then I would have to be that rock myself. My mission in life was as clear and simple as that... suddenly this little girl was in a race against time to be an adult." (Ibid, p.15.)

Esther Williams "The Million Dollar Mermaid"

The great hope of the family was gone and so was their brother Stanton. Esther Jane Williams, born into a family that would now grow poorer during the Depression, became interested in swimming. Not because she could swim at the time but because her mother asked the city council to put in a swimming pool at the local city park. On opening day, Bula was asked if she knew any little children that could swim to inaugurate the pool and give the new city park and recreation center some publicity. She volunteered her daughter. Esther was cute enough, outgoing enough, precocious enough to do it, that is, if she could swim. Maurine took Esther to the ocean, got her in the water and Esther discovered that she loved it. It only took a few days for her to learn to swim and on opening day she flung herself into the pool, got her first swimming medal and heard her first applause. The large audience fell in love with Esther and Esther fell in love with all the attention. Just like Stanton, Esther was a "natural."

Then when Esther was just 13, something came along in the Williams household that changed her position in the family. She was still becoming the breadwinner but her mother and father still missed their

Esther Williams Pin-up

Swimming Champion

Swim Queen Movie Star

Million Dollar Mermaid

golden boy, Stanton. Unbelievably, a neighborhood boy, Buddy, who was clever and who was also 16, had just lost his mother. He had no father and was surviving alone in little shack down the street. Bula liked Buddy, he was kind, sympathetic, understanding and seemingly gentle. And he wasn't any ordinary young man; he was Captain of the football team, an excellent student, and even Student Body President at the local high school. Bula soon invited Buddy to come live with them and she and Esther's father had a new "Stanton." Popular, funny and charming, he was dark and stocky; the opposite of Stanton in looks, but like him in every other way. The whole family took Buddy on as a replacement for Stanton. Esther's parents came to life again, and Buddy could do no wrong.

Unfortunately, just a few weeks after moving in with the Williams, Buddy announced to Esther that he fantasized about her all the time and after weeks of fending off his advances, one night, he simply entered her bedroom, put his hand over her mouth, overpowered her and raped her. Esther had no idea what to do. But he told her if she told anyone they would not believe her anyway and then he would find out. It was the 1930s, her parents were in love with Buddy, she was now just barely 14 years old and so she remained silent for months. Who would believe her? Her brother, David found out about it and tried to keep Buddy away from her, but Buddy beat David up over and over again. David was smaller than Buddy but he tried to protect his sister anyway. In the end, Esther couldn't stand this either so she told her mother. By this time she had turned 15, her parents confronted Buddy and he promised never to do it again. Esther realized in listening to the conversation that her parents "were trying to find a way to be both my parents and his parents. They couldn't help themselves. They couldn't bear to lose Buddy, who had taken Stanton's place in their hearts. They couldn't face another loss like that, and they fiercely wanted to believe that Buddy would stay and Esther would be safe." (Ibid, p.28.)

She says that it was a moment of truth for her. She was on her own. No one was going to help her. She had to handle this herself, and so she did. She got Buddy alone and when he tried to apologize she said to him that he would never touch her again, and that he would leave their house for good. She told him that from now on, she would, kick, scream, and claw, leaving all the evidence she could. And being tall, strong and pretty athletic, she knew she could do this. By the end of this confrontation, six-foot Buddy was on his knees pleading with her to let him stay, but she was adamant. Two days later, Buddy joined the Coast Guard and disappeared from the Williams lives for good.

As soon as Esther was old enough she was invited to compete on the team from the Los Angeles Athletic Club. She set new swimming records and acquired many medals. She was the National AAU champion in the 100 meters freestyle. As a United States competitive swimmer, the American appetite for pin-up photos of beautiful women in swimming suits was growing and Esther Williams fit this bill. Even as a teenager she was constantly being photographed at her various swimming meets and soon her picture was everywhere. And it did not take Esther long to realize that she had taken Stanton into her life so completely that he had become a part of her soul. Strength and giving became not only major themes in her life, but also conflicts that would shape her adult life. The strength to be born when she wasn't wanted, the strength to pull her whole family together and the strength to be a competitive athlete, stuntwoman, Hollywood performer, and wife and mother.

Esther went on to win many more swimming medals and competitions and was preparing for the next Olympics when producer Billy Rose was the first to approach her to star in a traveling show he called "Aquacade." Her family needed the money and so she gave up the dream for the Olympics and took his offer and in some ways it was a worthy sacrifice. But her experience with performing in "Aquacade" was terrible she says in her autobiography. There were major problems with sexual harassment, a huge abuse of power, and all kinds of dishonesty with the various agents. However, it did give her experiences on how to deal with all of these issues when she tackled Hollywood a little later.

It was so bad that Esther decided to quit show business right off the bat and go home and become a housewife. Esther went to work in a department store. However, the Hollywood Studios had Sonja Henie, the

Olympic ice skating champion, who had had some success with several of her films in the late thirties and pin-ups were becoming more and more popular. MGM Studios wanted to find a beautiful woman athlete, preferably a swimmer, and Esther Williams was at the top of the list. The plan was to present a series of films with a modest, moral young woman who had that healthy out door look, had romances with nothing going on in the bedroom, yet at the same time ran around in swimming suits along with a lot of other young women doing synchronized swimming with her. Esther by this time was married, had a steady job, and a disdain for Hollywood. The siege by MGM lasted a whole year before Esther signed a contract when she was only nineteen years old.

Esther was tall for the movies, five feet eight inches, but she had a great body and long athletic legs. MGM put her to work immediately taking deportment, elocution, acting, dancing and singing lessons. All the while they were capitalizing on her many, many pin-up photos distributed all over the world. However, Esther had an independent mind, lots of self-confidence and was a good businesswoman. Her picture was now on the front of many popular magazines. She was also fast becoming the third most popular pinup girl after Betty Grable and Rita Hayworth, for the men in uniform. She visited hospitals and cheered up the soldiers during the Second World War

Her first film was entitled "Bathing Beauty" and she starred opposite Red Skelton. It was a huge financial success. She did not win acting awards and the critics fried her movies, but the public adored her and every film was a financial success, rather like the formula Elvis Presley films in the sixties. One of her Hollywood friends said at one time that Esther Williams had never had a theatrical career and that she had gotten into the business by mistake. She was quite upset at not getting the studio to raise the standards in her films and allow her to do more than just smile, swim and walk around. Esther, on the other hand, after her huge financial losses from her second husband, used her good business sense to go into business partnerships marketing swimming pools and sportswear and she also advertised for these products. She had a very good income from these various ventures.

By the sixties a bathing beauty pin-up had become obsolete with people like Hugh Hefner and his Playboy bunny magazines coming into vogue. And at only thirty years old Esther was looking older to male audiences. Also the big studios could not make those light, happy, colorful entertainment films any longer. Audiences and studios alike were looking for more drab serious dramas and it was becoming easier and easier to show a lot more of women's bodies on the screen than it had been in the fifties. Esther left MGM and did a couple of pictures for Universal and then left the movies to perform in her own stage show.

Esther Williams's autobiography with Digby Diehl published in 1999, Million Dollar Mermaid, is considered one of the best auto-biographies written by a Hollywood star to date. The book is full of tell all stories about other famous stars and is quite frank about Esther's life both as a movie star, athlete, stunt woman, business woman, wife and mother. It is full of humor, irony, soul searching and most of all "strength and giving." Well-written, poignant and compelling, it is above all else, a story about a woman's life who survived all sorts of things while keeping her dignity and hope. She never just let others hand her things, defended herself when she needed to, worked very hard and went after what she needed, although it did take her a while to get it. I can see why it was on the New York Times bestseller list for a while, not for its juicy Hollywood gossip – although this is fun to read - but for the way in which any woman reading it can relate to various parts of Esther Williams life story. She never let herself get hard edged, superior, or even angry, she kept her femininity and her sense of humor through it all. She stood up for herself when she needed to, while in other times in her life, wondered just why she was there.

What many people do not know is that behind that beautiful body and face was a very intelligent, superior athlete who performed dozens of stunts never attempted before, just so movie audiences could be entertained. And that during that time, Esther survived many injuries and several near death accidents because there were so few people in those days who understood how making these films underwater could be quite dangerous or that Esther Williams was performing original stunts which no one had ever done before. At one point in her biography she states this by talking about Christopher Reeves' accident which left him a quadriplegic. In more than one of her stunts she nearly drowned and in another she snapped her neck, and she attempted things she hadn't the first clue about, quickly and quietly, so as she says, but for the grace of God...

Esther Williams was active as a film actress from 1942 to 1963. She had five husbands: Artie Shaw, whom she was only married to for 4 months, Leonard Kovner from 1940 to 1944, Ben Gage from 1945 to 1949, Fernando Lamas from 1969 to 1982 when he passed away, and her fifth husband Edward Bell until her death. Her older brother Stanton died on March 3, 1929 at sixteen years of age. By the age of sixteen herself, Esther had won three U.S. National Championships in breast stroke and freestyle. She was unable to compete in the 1940 Summer Olympics due to many obligations and the outbreak of World War II in Europe. President of her high school class she had started college and was working in a department store just before her offer for the Aquacade came along.

Her rise to stardom began with World War II when she became as popular a pin-up as Betty Grable and Rita Hayworth, especially among the younger soldiers. Making "Bathing Beauty" with Red Skelton cemented her popularity and she went on to star with many of the famous leading men of the time such as Van Johnson, William Powell, Howard Keel, Victor Mature, Ricardo Montalban, Fernando Lamas and Jeff Chandler. According to her book she had affairs with Victor Mature and Jeff Chandler while on set and for a while afterwards when she was single again and before she married Fernando Lamas. Her tell all book was quite the sensation and some of the things she said about her fellow stars stirred up quite a bit of controversy. She had three of her children with Ben Gage whom she left because of his alcoholism and extravagant spending of most of the money that she had made.

While making these often dangerous films because of the stunts she thought up herself to do or others thought up for her to do, she had four children. She performed water skiing stunts while she was pregnant

"Eyes of Youth" - 1919

Stanton Eats the Banana in Class

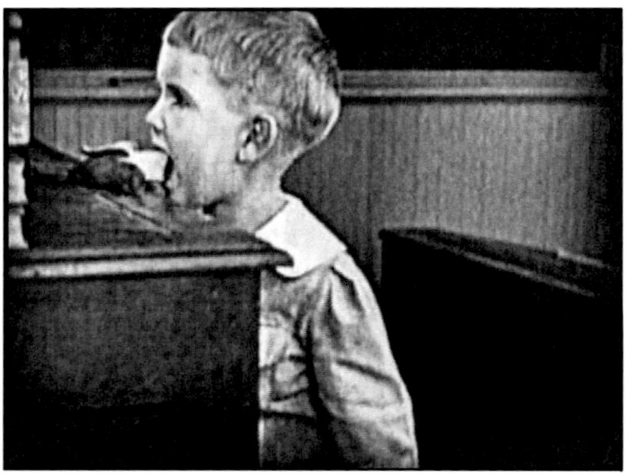

Discovered, Stanton Eats the Banana off the Teacher's Desk

Stanton is in Trouble Again

Stanton Sticks his Tongue Out at the Class

Teacher, Clara Kimball Young, Puts Dunce Cap on Stanton

and was constantly inventing new and different stunts for the camera. She escaped death several times. In one incident she was wearing a flannel suit which dragged her to the bottom of the pool and she had to unzip it and swim nude to the surface in order not to drown. In another she took a 115 foot dive off a tower and ended up in a body cast for seven months. In still another, she nearly drown again when swimming in a painted black tank because the trap door was also painted black and she could not find the latch. A crew member noticed that the door wasn't opening and pulled her out just in time. Over the years she had ruptured her ear drums several times from so many hours under water.

She left MGM in 1956, driving off the lot and breaking her contract, tired of meaningless roles. She did one dramatic role for Universal International that same year and then quit making films altogether. Married to Fernando Lamas at the time she stayed home and finished raising her children. However, she did continue to do television work but put most of her time into building up her swimming suit business and working with another namesake company that sold pool and swim suit accessories. She worked as a commentator for the Summer Olympics and wrote her autobiography. In 2007 she had a stroke, from which she never fully recovered. In 2010 she appeared at the Turner Classic Movies Film Festival in Los Angeles. Esther Williams died in her sleep on June 6, 2013. She had made around 30 films in Hollywood although the film "Million Dollar Mermaid" – her nickname on the lot and what she named her book – was one of the highest grossing movies of all time.

The Legacy of Stanton Williams & His Sister Esther

When Esther Williams went through her LSD therapy, as Cary Grant had done before her, and before the drug became a 60s icon, she found it useful. There were therapists experimenting with this drug in their practices in the 50s, and finding it helpful in treating some patients. Cary Grant felt it really helped him to come to grips with many things in his own life. She talked with her close friend Cary Grant, before deciding to try this type of therapy. Esther Williams writes about the session with this drug that made her realize her closeness to her deceased brother, and the symbolism of her own path in life. "The first thing I saw was my father's face the day my brother Stanton died... I saw my father's face as a ceramic plate. Almost instantly it splintered into a million pieces, like a windshield when a rock goes through it. The shards fell to the floor. He was left faceless. Then I looked at my mother. All the emotion had drained out of her, and her soft, kindly features had hardened... Why did my mother take me, the youngest, with her on the night of the viewing at the mortuary? Why did she take eight-year-old Esther instead of sisters, Maureen and June, or my brother David? Why did she take me to watch her absolute nervous collapse as she threw herself across Stanton's coffin, sobbing, 'Why did you leave me?' 'Let me go with you!'" (Ibid, p.15.)

Later, she would have another such vision, which showed her what happened to her, what her life's path would be. She saw herself as a man morphing into a woman and back to a man and then back to a woman and on and on. Finally, she split in half, right down the middle and became a woman on one side and a man on the other. She finally understood that she had literally taken a part of Stanton into her own soul to keep her family afloat. She also knew that throughout her life, she would have to be both the man and the woman in her life, in order to survive. Strength and giving – an eternal conflict, and one that Esther Williams never showed the world until her autobiography came out.

However, Stanton Williams is really the Utah connection in this story and it is a tragic story as well. His rise to stardom however short was still what had placed Esther Williams in the position to be "discovered." I have found at least two films that Stanton performed in, but I am still on a search to find at least one studio portrait or movie still of Stanton the child actor. Having tried family and archives with no success, I only know of two films Stanton Williams performed in entitled "Eyes of Youth" released in 1919 and "The Forbidden Woman" released in 1920 in which Stanton played the part of "Jimmy" and Clara Kimball Young played "Diana Sorell." Both films starred Clara Kimball Young. She was the star who took Marjorie Rambeau's role in the film version of the stage play where Stanton had been discovered. Apparently "The Forbidden Woman" is considered a "semi-lost" silent film as there is only one print that survived and it is not available for public viewing. Perhaps someday they will restore this film, or at least make copies of this film so we silent movie lovers can see it.

Fortunately the "Eyes of Youth" survived and because of a renewed interest in Clara Kimball Young's movies and silent films in general, as well as the continuing fan base for Rudolph Valentino, one can view the entire movie on YouTube in nine segment increments. Apparently it was the bit part as a scoundrel that got Valentino his starring role in "The Four Horsemen of the Apocalypse." In the film version they "modernized" the scene with Stanton and Clara Kimball Young from a fantasy scene in which Marjorie Rambeau read a story book to the little child star on stage while he sobbed, to a school teacher scolding a little boy who is caught eating a banana in class. Stanton stole the entire scene when told to stand with his arms behind his back right in front of the teacher's desk as punishment. The peeled banana is right in front of him and the teacher's back is turned as she writes on the blackboard. He spontaneously ate the rest of the banana using only his mouth, while the entire class watched laughing and giggling. He gets caught and then is made to sit on the high stool in the corner while the teacher puts a dunce hat on him. At which point, when her back is turned again, he continues to make faces and stick out his tongue at the class. And even though it is 1919, it is a timeless incident that we can all relate to with our own school day memories.

One can see the resemblance to Esther, as I imagine all of the children in the Williams family must have been quite physically beautiful, but it is more than that. The spunkiness, natural talent in front of the camera, the charisma to hold an audience's attention, a sense of humor about life, and the intuition to be in the right place at the right moment, it was all there. No matter how poor, at least the two children from this family that I have now at last seen on film, shared a creativeness, spontaneity and liveliness, that made both of them a natural for the stage or screen. No matter who directed them, they both added a spark to the scene that most of us would not think of or could muster up in front of either a live audience or a camera lens. It helped me understand more deeply the close psychological and intuitive connection between Esther Williams and her brother Stanton. A little bit of Esther must have died the day that Stanton died to, even though she was made to feel second best to her brother according to her autobiography. The love between siblings was there anyway.

In William's book she states that the "Eyes of Youth" on stage was "...the story of a young 'dunce' boy who meets his fairy princess and is carried away on an iron steed to a fabled land of turreted castles, glittering tinsel and bright lights." I suppose that this stage version, in a way, better represents the story of Stanton and Esther Williams, with Stanton gone to another land and his sister Esther becoming the "fairy princess" for the family. Perhaps such tales can become indicative of many siblings, with a sister's "earthly" hardships masked by wealth and fame and amazing fortune, an older brother's untimely demise, and an entire family damaged by this loss. On the other hand, spiritually, it was the oldest child who could watch over his siblings much as a guardian angel would from atop his "iron steed" while living in a "fabled" land. The strength to live a life well can come not only from within, but also with the help of those who have passed before us. (Ibid, p.19.)

IV — INDEX

AWAY FROM THE FOLD INDEX

Volume I – Stage to Early Silents

A

B

C

D

E

F

G

H

I

J

K

L

M

N

O

P

R

S

T

U-V

W

Y

stage with tragedies. It is built exclusively for ourselves and our own holy fun." Although within only months, tragedies were being performed there and eventually the performers received a salary. (Ibid, Wife No. 19, p. 378.)

Z

IV — BIBLIOGRAPHY:

BIBLIOGRAPHY:

AWAY FROM THE FOLD: VOLUME I - STAGE THROUGH EARLY SILENTS 1850 – 1920 VOLUME 1

Acosta, Mercedes De Acosta. Here Lies the Heart, Ayer Publishing Company, 1975.

Affron, Charles. Star Acting, Gish, Garbo, Davis, E.P. Dutton: New York, 1977.

Alexander, Thomas. Things In Heaven & Earth: The Life and Times of Wilford Woodruff, a Mormon Prophet, Signature Books, January 15, 1993.

Allen, Julie K. "The White Slave Trade Gets In 'A Victim of the Mormons,'" Kosmorama, May 31, 2013 at http://www.kosmora.org.

Amende, Coral. Hollywood Confidential, A-Plume Book, 1997.

Bccjohnh. "Madame Lydia Mary Olive Mamreov von Finkelstein Mountford and Interpreting the Past," Common Consent, a Mormon Blog, November 5, 2004, at http://bycommonconsent.com.

Bagley, Pat. "Maude Adams: Utah's 'most illustrious daughter'," the Salt Lake Tribune, Sunday, July 2, 2006.

Bagley, Will. "Early Utah's most famous actor adored his leading lady," the Salt Lake Tribune, Sunday, July 11, 2004.

Bagley, Will. "Utah Wizard" and "Great Dante Retains His Magic Appeal," the Salt Lake Tribune, September 24 and October 1, 2000.

Baker, Cella R. "Pioneering Escape Act," the Salt Lake Tribune, Sunday, May 23, 2004.

Birchard, Roberts. "On January 8, 1919, a group of 15 cameramen founded the American Society of Cinematographers." Here are their stories: American Cinematographers, August, 2004, pp.1-4.

Blackmore, Kent. Oscar Eliason, The Original 'Dante The Great': His Life and Travels in Australia and New Zealand. 1898-1899, revised edition, 1987, published by Kent Blackmore, 8/33-35 Muriel St., Hornsby NSW 2077.

Blackwell, Earl. Celebrity Register 1990, Gale Research, Inc., 1990.

Blum, Daniel. A Pictorial History of the American Theatre 1900-1956, Ambassador Books, LTD: Toronto, Canada, 1956.

Blum, Daniel. A Pictorial History of the Silent Screen 1890 to 1929, Gossett & Dunlap: New York, 1953.

Bohn, Thomas W. and Stromgren, Richard L. Light and Shadows: A History of Motion Pictures, Mayfield Publishing Co.: Mountain View, California, 1987.

Bowers, David. "Thanhauser Company Film Preservation, 1988-1993 at tco@thanhouser.org.

Bowser, Eileen. The Transformation of Cinema 1907-1915, University of California Press, 1990.

Bradley, Martha Sonntag. A History of Kane County, Utah State Historical Society, 1999.

Bradshow, Melissa and Adriene Munich. Selected Poems of Amy Lowell, Rutgers University Press, 2002.

Brimhall, Sandra Dawn. "Sara Alexander: Pioneer Actress and Dancer," Utah Historical Quarterly, Vol. 66, No. 4, Fall 1998, pp.320-333.

Bushman, Claudia, et. al. "Susa Young Gates" by Carolyn Person, Mormon Sisters, Women in Early Utah, Utah State University Press, 1976, 1997.

Cannon, Brian Q. and Olmstead, Jacob W. "Scandalous Film: the Campaign to Suppress Anti-Mormon Pictures, 1911-1922," The Journal of Mormon Thought, Fall, Vol. 29, No, 2, 2003.

Carr, Stephen L. Utah Ghost Towns, Western Epics: Salt Lake City, Utah, 1995.

Carter, Kate B., editor. "History of Drama in the West," Daughters of the Utah Pioneers, historical pamphlet, November 1941, pp.77-116.

Castor, Rachelle Pace. "Maude Adams: No Other Actress Can Take Her Place," Women Worth Their Salt: Notable But Often Unnoted Women of Utah, edited by Colleen Whitley, Utah State University Press: Logan, Utah, 1996, pp.189-201.

Claire, Eau. "Viola Gillette Scores a Success – Play Give the Most Unqualified Satisfaction," New York Library-Museum of Performing Arts (Gashler.)

Clayton, Marguerite. "Wolf Blood – 1925," www.silentsaregolden.com; "Gilbert 'Bronco Billy' Anderson: World's First Movie Star", http://users.aristotle.net/russell/art/bronco and "Bronco Billy Anderson Interview,"www.wildwestweb.net/bronco.html.

Coe, Brian, consultant. One Hundred Years Of Cinema, Kingfisher Kaleidoscopes – A Living Encyclopedia, no date given.

Comden, Betty. Off Stage, Simon and Schuster, Inc.: New York, 1995.

D'Arc, James V. When Hollywood Came to Town: A History of Moviemaking in Utah, Gibbs-Smith Publishing, 2010.

Dark Child On The Web. "Maude Adams Main Page," and "Maude Adams Photos," (An excellent and thorough website with complete manuscripts of out-of-print books.) http://www.bookmice.com/darkchilde/maude/adams87,html.

Daughters of the Utah Pioneers. History of Kane County, Kane County Commission, Utah Printing Company, 1970.

Davies, Action. Maude Adams, 1901.

Davis, Daniel. "'Appreciating a Pretty Shoulder:' The Risqué Photographs of Charles Ellis Johnson," Utah Historical Quarterly, Volume 74 Number 2, Winter 2006, pp. 131-146.

Dawson, Janice P. "Chautauqua and the Utah Performing Arts," Utah Historical Quarterly, Volume 58 Number 2, Spring, 1990.

Dizikes, John. Opera In America: A Cultural History, Yale University Press: New Haven and London, 1993.

Doyle, Billy H. The Ultimate Directory of The Silent Screen Performers: A Necrology

Of Births and Deaths and Essays on 50 Lost Players, The Scarecrow Press, Inc.:Metuchan, New Jersey and London, 1995.

Drew, William M. Speaking of Silents: First Ladies of the Screen, The Vestal Press, Limited: Vestal, New York, 1989.

Kornman, Mildred (Ricki Van Dusen) Official Website.

Koszarski, Richard. An Evening's Entertainment: The Age of Silent Feature Picture, 1915-1928, University of California Press, 1990.

Eliason, Oscar. www.users.bigpond.com or www.illusionata.com and www.sydneymagic.net/eliason/oe-index.html.

Empey, Arthur Guy. Over The Top, published in May of 1917 but available at Page By Page Books.com, his experiences as a World War I soldier and hero before putting this and others on the silent screen.

Engar, Ann W. "Theater in Utah." Utah History Encyclopedia, edited by Allan Kent Powell, University of Utah Press: Salt Lake City, Utah, 1994, pp.551-554.

Everson, William K. American Silent Film, Oxford University Press, 1978.

Fantin, Linda. "Final Bow: Promised Valley Playhouse: Only ghosts remain," the Salt Lake Tribune, Sunday, August 11, 2002.

Frank, John. "Mary Kornman," Official Mary Kornman Website at http://www.marykorman.com.

Gallagher, Dan. "One of the first woman 'indies' shot films in Idaho in the 1920s," the Salt Lake Tribune, Saturday, December 20, 2003.

Gashler, Mavis Gay. "Three Mormon Actresses: Viola Gillette, Hazel Dawn and Leora Thatcher," Master of Arts Thesis, Department of Dramatic Arts, Brigham Young University: Provo, Utah, May 1970.

Goodman, Jack. As You Pass By: Architectural Musings on Salt Lake City, A Collection of Columns and Sketches from the Salt Lake Tribune, Kearns-Tribune Corporation, 1995.

Goodman Jack. "Capitol Theatre Once Called The Orpheum," the Salt Lake Tribune, December 25, 1994.

Goodman, Jack. "Cityview: Broadway Centre Awaits glass finish," the Salt Lake Tribune, April 21, 1991.

Graham, Rose Kendall Thomas. "443," A family history of the Thomas children and the Barnacle theatre, no date, 137 North West Temple, Salt Lake City, 16, Utah, courtesy of Bonnie Quayle Thomas.

Greenberg, Martin H.; McSherry, Jr. Frank D.; Waugh, Charles D. Hollywood Ghosts, Rutledge Hill Press: Nashville, Tennessee, 1991.

Hall, Eleanor M. "The McAllister Family Reach Utah," Family History, June 15, 1995.

Hall, Ella. Websites: www.picturegoer.net/EllaHallApril17.htm - www.silentmovies.org - www.gono.com/adart/movies.

Hayes, Helen and Dody, Sanford. On Reflection: An Autobiography, M. Evans and Company: New York, 1968.

Hayne, Julia Dean. Comments and reviews from the press: Alta Californian, No.14, March 28, 1868; Bulletin, No. 18, May 23, 1896 and Dramatic Mirror "The Unmarked Grave of Julia Dean Hayne," New York City, August 26, 1897.

Hayne, Julia Dean.: Historic Speakers Bureau or http://www.historicspeakersbureau.com/speakers/Julia Dean Hayne.html.

Hayne, Julia Dean. "Julia Dean Hayne – Virtual American Biographies" or http://www.famousamericans.ne/juliadean/

Heights of Some Silent Screen Actresses. http://www.chariot.net.au/`dk.ks/BettyBronson/heightsofactresses.html.

International Broadway Database or IBDB or www.ibdb.com. Biographies on: Hazel Dawn, Viola Pratt Gillette McFarland, Oliver Morosco, Channing Pollock and Margaret Romaine.

International Movie Data Base or IMDB or www.imdb.com. Biographies on : Cosmo Kyrle Bellew, H. Kyrle Bellew, Ora Carew, Marguerite Clayton, Ella Hall, May Hall, Mack Swain.

Iversen, Kristen Rogers. "George Ottinger was jack-of-all-trades," the Salt Lake Tribune, June 19, 2011.

Jakeman, Ellen J. "An Enduring Legacy," "Pioneer Poets & Poetry," Daughters of the Utah Pioneers, pp.401-404.

Johnson, Catherine M. "Emma Lucy Gates Bowen: Singer, Musician, Teacher," Utah State Historical Quarterly, Volume 6, Number 4, Fall, 1996.

Johnson, G. Allen. "Looking Back at an American Master," S.F.Gate.com, Sunday, July 22, 2006.

Keystone Films – Fatty Arbuckle at http://www.sunrisesilents.com.

Lamoreux, W. S. "A Utah Girl," clippings from the Utah State Historical Society, 1950s.

Lamparski, Richard. "Marion Mack," Whatever Became Of...? Volume 3, ACEBKS: New York, 1970; Volume 4, Crown Publishers, 1973; Volume 5, Bantam Books: New York, 1974; Volume 8 – 1982, 9-1985, 10-1986, 11-1989, all from Crown Publishers, Inc.: New York.

Latter Day Saint Characters In The Movies. "Somewhere In Time" 1980 at http://www.ldsfilm.com/movies/somewhereintime.html.

Leonard, William T. & Parish, James Robert. The Funsters, Arlington House Publications: New Rochelle, New York, 1979.

Lindsay, John S. The Mormons and the Theatre, or, The History of Theatricals in Utah: with reminiscences and comments, humorous and critical, Century Printing: Salt Lake City, Utah, 1905.

Lisa's Silent Movie Page. Lisa's Nostalgic Café: "A Brief History" at http://www.angelfire.com/retro2/lisa/silents.html.

Los Angeles Courier. "Tango a Blessing Says Viola Gillette," December 8. 1913.

Lowe, Denise. An Encyclopedic Dictionary of Women in Early American Films 1895 – 1930. The Haworth Press: New York and London, 2005.

Matheson, Richard. Bid Time Return, Buccaneer Books, 1995.

Margetts, Philip. "The First Mormon Actor," Philip Margetts Archive, Antiques Roadshow/2006/Tour/SLC, Utah at http://www.pbs.com.

Margetts, Ralph Elliot. "A Study of the Theatrical Career of Julia Dean Hayne," Doctor of Philosophy thesis, Department of Speech, University of Utah, August 1959.

Masek, Mark J. Hollywood: Remains to Be Seen, Cumberland House: Nashville, Tennessee, 2001.

Mitchell, Glenn. A-Z Of Silent Film Comedy, B.T. Batsford Ltd. : London, 1998.

Morosco, Helen M. and Dugger, Leonard Paul. The Oracle of Broadway, The Caxton Printers, LTD: Caldwell, Idaho, 1944.

Murphy, Miriam B. "Sarah Elizabeth Carmichael (1838-1901): Poetic Genius of Pioneer Utah" Women Worth Their Salt, Utah State University Press: Logan: Utah, 1996, pp.61-74.

Murray, John A. Cinema Southwest: An Illustrated Guide To The Movies And Their Locations, Northland Publishing, Inc., 2000.

Musser, Charles. The Emergence of Cinema: The American Screen to 1907, University of California Press, 1990.

Nelson, Richard. "Utah Filmmakers of the Silent Screen," Utah State Historical Quarterly, Volume 43, 1975.

New York Times. "Not Miss Gillette's Sister," February 9, 1911 and "Murders Show Girl and Kills Himself," February 11, 1911.

New York Times, 2006 c All Media Guide at nytimes.com/movies – Biographies:
Ora Carew, Arthur Guy Empey, Moroni Olsen.

Neville, Amelia Ransome. The Fantastic City, Houghton, Mifflin Co.: Cambridge, Massachusetts, 1932. (San Francisco and Julia Dean Hayne)

Olmstead, Jacob W. and Cannon, Brian Q. "Scandalist Film: The Campaign to Suppress Anti-Mormon Pictures," Journal of Mormon Thought, Volume 29, Number 2, Fall, 2003.

Olpin, Robert O., Ann W. Olpin and Thomas F. Rugh, editors. Painters of the Wasatch Mountains, Museum of Art and History, Gibbs-Smith Publishers, 2005.

Olpin, Swanson, Poulton, Rogers, editors. Utah Art, Utah Artists, Gibbs-Smith Publishers, 2002.

Pace, David G. "Maud May Babcock," Worth Their Salt: Notable But Often Unnoted Women of Utah, edited by Colleen Whitley, Utah State University Press: Logan, Utah, 1996, pp. 148-157.

Parrish, James Robert. The Hollywood Book of Death: The Bizarre, Often Sordid Passing of More than 125 American Movie and TV Idols, Contemporary Books, McGraw-Hill, 2002.

Parshall, Ardis E. "One-Horse Sleigh was the real deal in early Utah," the Salt Lake Tribune, December 23, 2007.

Patterson, Ada. Maude Adams A Biography, 1907.

Person, Carolyn D. "Susa Young Gates," Mormon Sisters: Women in Early Utah, editor Claudia L. Bushman, Utah State University: Logan, Utah, 1977,

Pollack, Channing. Harvest of My Years – An Autobiography, Bobbs-Merrill: Indianapolis / New York, 194-.

Powell, Allan Kent, editor. Utah History Encyclopedia, University of Utah Press, 1994.

Pyper, George Dollinger. The Romance of the Old Playhouse, The Seagull Press: Salt Lake City, Utah, 1928.

Rasmussen, Kenneth, editor. Adams Family History Book, courtesy of Joyce Quayle Phil, descendant of Annie Adam's sister.

Rhoades, Richard. A Hole in the World: An American Boyhood, Simon & Schuster: New York, 1990.

Rhoades, Richard. "Don't Be a Bystander," Parade Magazine, October 14, 1990.

Rigby, Chris. "Ada Dwyer: Bright lights and lilacs," Utah Historical Quarterly; volume 43, page 45.

Rigdon, Walter, editor. The Biographical Encyclopedia and Who's Who of the American Theatre, James H. Hineman, Inc.: New York, 1966.

Robbins, Phyllis. The Young Maude Adams, G.P. Putnam and Sons: New York, 1956.

Roberts, Patrick. Movie facts and feats: a Guinness Record Book, Sterling Publishing Company: New York , 1980.

Robinson, David. From Peep Show to Palace The Birth of American Film, Columbia University Press, 1996.

Rohauer, Raymond. "an interview with marion mack," parts of this interview are taken from The General by Richard Anobile, pages 1-8. Interview of Marion Mack taken from: Bits and Pieces #6 – Marion Mack @ Buster Keaton: From Butcher Boy to Scribe.

Schindler, Hal. "Utah's Scandalous Senator: Utah's 1st Legislator Left Sorry Legacy," Utah History To Go, @http://www.sltrib.com, March 5, 1995.

Scott, Patricia Lynn. "Sarah Ann Sutton Cooke" Women Worth Their Salt Too: Utah State University Press: Logan, Utah, 1998, pp.1-27.

Shipman, Nell. The Silent Screen and My Talking Heart, Hemingway Western Studies Series: Boise, Idaho, 1987.

Siegel, Scott & Siegel, Barbara. The Encyclopedia of Hollywood: An A-Z of the Heroes, Heroines, and History of American Film, Facts on File: New York, Oxford & Sydney, 1990.

Silent Films On Video. http://www.silentsaregolden.com/silentvideolistA-Z.html.

Sisson, Vera, articles on her life and career:
http://members.aol.com/Chaneyfan/54.htm.,
http://homepages.rootsweb.com/~scismfam/verasission/ pages 1 – 15, and at
http://us.imbd.com/Bio?sisson,%20vera.

Slide, Anthony. Silent Players: A Biographical and Autobiographical Study of 100 Silent Film Actors and Actresses, The University Press of Kentucky, 2002.

Sowell, Debra Hickenlooper. "Theatrical Dancing in the Territory of Utah, 1848-1868," Dance Chronicle, Volume 1 Number 2, 1977, pp. 96-126.

Stenhouse, Fanny. Tell It All: A Woman's Life in Polygamy, Kessinger Legacy Reprints, Kessinger Publishing, date not given but released during Brigham Young's later years.

Swain, Mack at www.goldensilents.com/comedy.

Symross, Lynn. "Marion Mack, Buster Keaton Co-Star, Is Back," The Los Angeles Times, p.4 at http://www.silent comedians.com/forum.viewtopic).

Tapia, John E. Circuit Chautauqua, McFarland & Co., Inc.: Jefferson, North Carolina, 1997.

Thatcher, Linda. "The Gentile Polygamist: Arthur Brown, Ex-Senator from Utah," Utah Historical Quarterly, Volume 52, Number 3, Summer 1984, pp.231-245.

Thatcher, Linda. "The Shooting of Arthur Brown, Ex-Senator From Utah," Utah Blazer, November 1995.

Vanderknyff, Rick. "Marion Mack – the girl in Buster Keaton's Epic," Calendar: Entertainment Desk, The Los Angeles Times, November 15, 1987.

Vreeland, Janelle. "Marguerite Clayton: The Bronco Girl of the Essnay Company," Curtains: keeping early and silent film alive, July 27, 2013 at earlysilentfilm.blogspot.com.

Wadsworth, Nelson B. "Chapter VII: Charles Ellis Johnson – Every Point of Interest," The Signature Books Library on line at http://signaturebookslibrary.com.

Wallace, Irving. The Twenty- Seventh Wife, 1961.

Walker, Robert M. and Starr, Alexander M. "Shattering the Vase: The Razing of the old Salt Lake Theatre," Utah Historical Quarterly, Volume 57, Number 1, Winter, 1989, pp.64-88.

Walsh, Rebecca. "Theater May Succumb to Parking Plan," the Salt Lake Tribune, Tuesday, October 15, 2002.

Warren, Robin O. "They Were Always Doing Shakespeare," Borrowers and Lenders: The Journal of Shakespeare and Appropriation, University of Georgia publication on the web at: http://atropos.english.uga.edu/cocoon/borrowers/request.

Webb, Eliza Ann Dee (Young). Wife No. 19: The Story of My Life in Bondage, Dustin Gilman & Co., 1875.

Webber, Diane and Lange, June. Those Wonderful Webbers: Naked and Together, Elysium, Inc., 1967.

Weight, F, Harmon at AFI Catalogue of Silent Films, http://www.afi.com.

White Jr. Matthew. "The Stage," Munsey's Magazine, Vol. 46, 1911.

Whitney, Horace G. The Drama in Utah: The Story of the Salt Lake Theatre, The Deseret News: Salt Lake City, Utah, 1915.

Whytock, Grant. Ora Carew's brother and fellow actor at http://www.silentsaregolden.com.

Williams, Esther & Diehl, Digby. The Million Dollar Mermaid, Simon & Schuster: New York, 1999.

Williams, Esther at http://www.lovegoddess.info./Esther.htm.

Wikipedia – The Free Encyclopedia, The Wikipedia Foundation, Inc., a non-profit charity, Wikipedia.org. Listed biographies from this source: Bronco Billy Anderson, Ada Dwyer, Arthur Guy Empey, Buster Keaton, Mary and Millie Kornman, Amy Lowell, Oliver Morosco, Moroni Olsen, Channing Pollock, C.R. Savage, Nell Shipman, and Esther Williams.